The First Chinese Embassy
to the West

The First Chinese Embassy to the West

THE JOURNALS OF
KUO SUNG-T'AO, LIU HSI-HUNG
AND CHANG TE-YI

TRANSLATED AND ANNOTATED
BY
J. D. FRODSHAM

CLARENDON PRESS · OXFORD
1974

Oxford University Press, Ely House, London W.1

GLASGOW NEW YORK TORONTO MELBOURNE WELLINGTON
CAPE TOWN IBADAN NAIROBI DAR ES SALAAM LUSAKA ADDIS ABABA
DELHI BOMBAY CALCUTTA MADRAS KARACHI LAHORE DACCA
KUALA LUMPUR SINGAPORE HONG KONG TOKYO

© OXFORD UNIVERSITY PRESS 1974

PRINTED IN GREAT BRITAIN
BY WILLIAM CLOWES & SONS, LIMITED
LONDON, BECCLES AND COLCHESTER

TO
PROFESSOR LIU TS'UN-YAN
This book is affectionately dedicated

WORKS BY THE SAME AUTHOR

The Murmuring Stream: the Life and Works of the Chinese Nature Poet, Hsieh Ling-yün (385-433). 2 vols.

An Anthology of Chinese Verse: Han, Wei, Chin and the Northern and Southern Dynasties.

The Poems of Li Ho (791-817).

New Perspectives in Chinese Literature.

PREFACE

My interest in Kuo Sung-t'ao goes back to the time, several years ago now, when I was first giving courses on the history of nineteenth-century China. It was brought home to me then that the history of China's discovery of Europe—and indeed of the rest of the modern world too—was a comparatively neglected province of historiography. This book is an attempt to map out some hitherto uncharted territory. I hope it will encourage others to do the same.

Since this volume is essentially a study of Kuo Sung-t'ao, I have translated his journal in full, while confining myself to rendering into English only the most pertinent sections of the journals of his two companions on the mission. Ideally, I should have liked to translate both Liu's journal and Chang's in full. But this would have added greatly to the length of this work while supplying the reader with little extra information, since many of the entries in these two journals more or less duplicate those in Kuo's.

These journals themselves present considerable difficulties to the translator, who finds himself forced to identify a bewildering number of people and places veiled in the obscurity of nineteenth-century Classical Chinese. To the problem of tracing Chinese officials—who often only appear under their styles (*tzu*) or their personal names—one must add that of identifying Westerners. Thus Mai Hua-t'o and Chin Teng-han are not Chinese, though they bear good Chinese names, but Westerners, being respectively W. H. Medhurst and J. D. Campbell. Generally, however, the Westerners whom Kuo encountered did not possess formal Chinese names and hence must be identified through those sinicized versions of their own names which Kuo himself invented. This is always difficult and sometimes impossible. We can only identify, for example, A-k'e-na-heng and Ssu-mei-erh-ssu as Captain Cornelius O'Callaghan and Sir John Smale, respectively, with the help of English-language sources. Where such sources are lacking, as in the case of Kuo's fellow-passengers, the translator is generally helpless. So certain minor personages who appear briefly upon our stage must inevitably suffer the fate of Achilles when he hid himself among women; we shall never know their names.

The problem is further complicated by the fact that Kuo wrote in Classical Chinese, a language which though habituated to the problem of transcribing barbarian names had still not succeeded at that time in evolving a standard transcription for the names of persons, places and things outside the ambit of the traditional Chinese tribute-system. So Kuo refers to Egypt as *Mai-hsi* (Arabic *Miṣr*) and not as *Ai-chi*, the term now in regular use. Similarly, Cairo (modern *K'ai-lo*), is by Kuo called *Chia-yi-lo*. Such non-standard forms abound confusingly throughout the text. In short, Kuo either availed himself of the old classical place-names, if he could find them in his geographical *vade mecum*, the *Ying-huan chih-lüeh* of Hsü Chi-yü, or else invented his own transcriptions, using such characters as occurred to him. Unfortunately for the translator, Kuo was rather hard of hearing and spoke Mandarin with such a thick Hunanese accent as to render himself scarcely intelligible to the Peking court, as Prince Kung complained. Hence it is hardly surprising that his renderings of foreign names—half-heard at best and then further distorted by his Hunanese dialect—should be phonetically erratic. The reader must not be unduly surprised to find Caesar (modern *K'ai-sa*) transcribed as *Chia-fei-sa-erh* or his rival Pompey (modern *P'ang-p'ei*) transcribed as *Pen-p'iao*. In any case, I have made a point of giving Kuo's renderings in full, so that the reader may see them with all their imperfections on their heads and judge for himself as to whether or not they correspond to the Western names I have placed after them.

The above comments also apply to the diaries of Liu and Chang, though here, on the whole, the task of identification was less difficult than with Kuo, since their Mandarin was better and their hearing much less impaired.

At the moment China is once more engaged in establishing relations with a world from which she has more or less been cut off for a quarter of a century. I hope that this record of the Chinese discovery of Europe, with its account of insights and misunderstandings, prejudices and sympathies, will help Westerners to understand the type of problem which the Chinese find themselves facing even today, as they once more take their place in the consort of nations.

J. D. FRODSHAM

Canberra—Dar es Salaam
May 1972

ACKNOWLEDGEMENTS

I OWE a special debt of gratitude to three of my friends, all members of the Faculty of Asian Studies, Australian National University, Canberra, without whose aid and encouragement this book would have been much the poorer.

Professor Liu Ts'un-yan, ever generous with his time and energy in spite of heavy administrative commitments as Dean of the Faculty, was kind enough to give me the benefit of his encyclopaedic and meticulous scholarship. I have profited enormously from his careful reading of the entire manuscript. The dedication of this volume to him is but a small acknowledgement of a scholarly debt I can scarcely hope to repay.

Sister Julia Ching, whose talents and erudition are comparable to those of her ancestor, the poet Ch'in Kuan (1049–1101), rendered me invaluable help in the elucidation of the diaries of both Liu and Chang.

Miss Ludmilla Panskaya, a dedicated research assistant, found and returned scores of books for me, checked the typescript, and spurred me on to finish the work. Had it not been for her, this book would doubtless still be in manuscript. The index was largely compiled and wholly typed by Mrs Thelma Richardson.

To all of these, and to others not mentioned here, go my sincere thanks.

Finally, I must record my gratitude to my wife, Tan Beng-choo Frodsham, whose forbearance and good advice made this work possible.

CONTENTS

LIST OF PLATES	xiii
INTRODUCTION	xv
1. *Shih-hsi chi-ch'eng* (*The Record of an Envoy's Journey to the West*) of Kuo Sung-t'ao	1
2. Kuo's Memorial *re* Ts'en Yü-ying, Governor of Kweichow	85
3. Kuo's Memorial on Foreign Affairs	88
4. Kuo's London Letter to Li Hung-chang (1877)	97
5. Selections from the *Ying-yao jih-chi* (*Journal of a Voyage to England*) of Liu Hsi-hung	110
6. Selections from the *Sui-shi jih-chi* (*Journal of an Embassy Official*) of Chang Te-yi	150
7. Sir Halliday Macartney's Diary of the Voyage	173
APPENDIX	
1. Extract from the *North China Herald*: 'Kuo Sung-t'ao on the Christian Propaganda'	184
2. Official Apology from the Emperor of China to Queen Victoria	186
3. Kuo's Letter *re* Appointment of Consuls	188
4. Kuo's Request for Leniency for John Donovan	189
5. Kuo's Letter *re* Destruction of Mission Property at Wu-shih-shan	190
6. Kuo's Letter *re* Attack upon Missionaries at Wu-ch'ang	193
BIBLIOGRAPHY	195
INDEX	203

58922

LIST OF PLATES

(Between lxiv–lxv)

1. Kuo Sung T'ao
2. Liu Hsi-Hung
3. Sir Halliday Macartney
4. Madame Kuo
5. John Chinaman
6. To the Tottering Lily
7. Li Hung Chang
8. Sir William Jervois

INTRODUCTION

It is something of a truism to say that China has always been very much of an enigma to the West. All the other civilizations of the Asian land-mass—the *Oikoumene* as Alfred Kroeber once styled it in a celebrated monograph[1]—were more or less contiguous. Egypt, Greece, Rome, Byzantium, Islam all shared something of a common heritage, a patrimony from which not even India can be said to have been totally excluded. But China developed and matured in relative isolation. Of late, a great deal has been written about the effects that Western 'discovery' of this unique civilization had upon European thought.[2] The Western debt to Chinese thought and to Chinese technology is now fully established. Surprisingly little, however, has been written about the impact of Western civilization upon China. It is only recently that historians have begun to realize that Europe was no less strange to China than China to Europe; that the Chinese intellectual discovery of Europe, a culture completely alien to and in some respects superior to her own, was a traumatic event for the Middle Kingdom, a cultural earthquake that eventually brought the old order down in ruins.[3]

Other world-orders, notably those of Egypt, India, and Mesopotamia, possessed, as China did, 'a notion of universal kingship linked to a widely shared sense of participation in a high culture'.[4] Yet China differed from all these other empires precisely because she developed in virtual isolation, and so remained unchallenged by any rival, universal state for some 3,000 years. One of the most important consequences of this was that since no neighbour of the Chinese could boast a native culture comparable in size, splendour,

[1] A. L. Kroeber, 'The Ancient Oikoumene as a Historic Culture Aggregate', in *The Nature of Culture*, pp. 379–95. Kroeber uses the term to mean 'the range of man's most developed culture'.

[2] We may instance J. Needham's *Science and Civilisation in China*, 4 volumes of which have appeared to date; Donald F. Lach, *Asia in the Making of Europe*. The bibliographies attached to these works are of especial value for documenting China's influence on the West.

[3] See note 1, p. lxiii.

[4] B. I. Schwartz, 'The Chinese Perception of World Order, Past and Present', in *The Chinese World Order*, ed. J. K. Fairbank, p. 277.

or permanence to their own, the Chinese had come to think of themselves over the course of the years as the only civilization. They styled themselves *T'ien-hsia* ('All under Heaven') or *Chung-kuo* ('The Central Kingdom'), envisaging themselves as the cultural centre of the world. At the apex of their civilization stood their universal king, *T'ien-tzu* ('Son of Heaven'). Around him were ranged barbarians of varying degrees of uncouthness and hairiness, who could yet be brought within the religio-cosmic circle of Chinese enlightenment if they would but 'come to be transformed' (*lai hua*) by the Virtue (*te*) of the universal monarch. This they did by formally acknowledging themselves as tributaries of the Chinese Empire.

Such an outlook naturally determined their foreign policy. The Chinese were set apart from the barbarians by their possession of Confucian culture. It was this moral order which lent an ethical basis to their claims of universal kingship. The Chinese conception of relations between states would seem basically to have been an extension of Confucian ideas about the family, with their emphasis on 'the five relationships' and the virtues of filial piety. China was envisaged as the head of a family of nations, presiding with patriarchal wisdom over the junior members around her. So, Burma, Siam, Cambodia, Champa, Annam, Java, Korea, and even Japan, as well as a large number of smaller states, such as Brunei and Malacca, played for long centuries the part of dutiful sons to their stern but just father, the Son of Heaven. At fixed intervals these states would send a formal tributary mission to China, whose members, after performing the prescribed ritual obeisance to the Emperor, were duly feted, presented with liberal gifts, and—most important of all—accorded the right to trade.

This closed and self-perpetuating system was shattered in the nineteenth century by the challenge not of a universal state, but of the nation-states of the West. The Chinese were slow to realize the power of the forces arrayed against them. This is all the more surprising since their own system of foreign relations, for all its talk of moral persuasion, was firmly based on the Chinese recognition of their own economic and military superiority to those around them. The Chinese are nothing, if not realists. Why then did they take so long to become aware of the full power of the West? One can only conclude that they had eventually fallen victims to the myths they had themselves evolved and had come to believe that all foreign countries were alike in their inferiority to China.

The abortive British embassies of Lord Macartney (1793) and Lord Amherst (1816) bear eloquent testimony to this, since they failed because the Ch'ien-lung Emperor (reigned 1736–95), whose reign had marked the zenith of Ch'ing power, could only regard them as tribute-missions, sent 'in a respectful spirit of submission', and not as embassies from one sovereign state to another. Ch'ien-lung knew nothing of the Industrial Revolution and had never heard of British expansion in India and Canada. For him, George III was an obscure monarch of some petty kingdom, of no more—and no less—importance than other 'external vassals' (*wai-fan*), such as Laos, the Ryuku Islands, or Sulu.

The concept of nation-states was not altogether new to the Chinese: it was simply one which they had abandoned since the days of their own Spring and Autumn and Warring States periods (722–221 B.C.). The establishment of the Ch'in universal state (221 B.C.) had bodied forth the long-held ideas of the Chou philosophers on universal kingship, and this concept, handed on from dynasty to dynasty, had persisted for 2,000 years. Since China was 'All under Heaven', other peoples only existed, as it were, by geographical accident, outside the bounds of civilization. Moreover, the universal Chinese *imperium* was not so much a state as a state of mind: a cultural entity in which nationality took second place to acceptance of the Chinese ethos. How then could the Chinese be expected to recognize and understand Western ideas about diplomatic relations between more or less equal states?

The problem was further complicated by the fact that as late as the middle of the nineteenth century the Chinese had little more information at their disposal about the West than had their ancestors of some 500 years before. In some ways they knew even less: for half a millennium of isolation had undoubtedly left its mark. Chinese culture had grown increasingly narcissistic since the Ming dynasty. True, the seventeenth and eighteenth centuries had witnessed remarkable advances in scholarship, especially in the fields of textual criticism, historiography, and classical studies; but these advances, impressive though they were, had all been confined to the realm of Chinese literary and historical studies. In other fields—notably in world geography—there had been a marked decline.¹ One has only to glance at the map of the world found in Ch'en Lun-chiung's (*fl.* 1730) *Han-kuo wen chien lu* (1744) to see how distorted a picture of the globe the Chinese possessed even at this late date.² What is still more surprising is that this map does not essentially represent much of an advance on those magnificent examples of Yüan cartography, dating from the fourteenth century, which are incomparably superior to any European or Arabic works of that period.³ In fact, the only major differences between the Yüan maps and those of the eighteenth century lay in changes which had been made in the latter on the basis of information provided by the reports of the seven Ming voyages, when for a brief period (1405-33) a great Chinese fleet under the command of the Grand Eunuch, Cheng Ho, ranged the seas as far abroad as the Malayan Archipelago, Ceylon, the Persian Gulf, and East Africa.⁴

It is here that we come to an understanding of the roots of Chinese isolationism. The Ming was undoubtedly the greatest age of maritime exploration that the Chinese had ever known. A stele dedicated to a Taoist goddess at Ch'ang-lo, Fukien, just before the last expedition set sail in 1432, gives a succinct account of the accomplishments of these Chinese sailors, who had by then performed feats of seamanship which anticipated by several decades those of the great European navigators:

From the third year of the *Yung-lo* reign-period (1405) until now, we have seven times received the commission of ambassadors to the

[1] See Needham, *Science and Civilisation*, iii, section 22, especially pp. 583-6, for a good account of the development of Chinese achievements in geography and cartography during the Ch'ing. Needham draws attention to such works as Ku Yen-wu's (1613-82) fine geographical work, *T'ien-hsia chün-kuo li ping shu* (preface dated 1662), and the great Ch'ien-lung atlas of China (1769), which, he avers, show that 'China was ahead of all other countries in the world in mapmaking' (p. 586). This is certainly true; but it in no way invalidates the contention that the lack of interest shown by the Chinese towards the world outside the Empire was reflected in their cartography of those regions, which was of a lamentably low standard.
[2] This map is reproduced in Fairbank, Edwin O. Reischauer, Albert M. Craig, *East Asia: The Modern Transformation*, p. 148.
[3] See Needham, *Science and Civilisation*, iii.551-6.
[4] See J. J. L. Duyvendak, *China's Discovery of Africa* and 'The true Dates of the Chinese Maritime Expeditions in the Early Fifteenth Century', *T'oung Pao*, xxxiv (1938), 341-412; P. Pelliot, 'Les grandes voyages maritimes chinois au début du XVe siecle', *T'oung Pao*, xxx (1933), 237-452; also addenda in xxxi (1935), 274-314, and xxxii (1936), 210-22.

countries of the Western Ocean. The barbarian countries which we have visited are: by the way of Chan-ch'eng [Champa], Chao-wa [Java], San-fo-ch'i [Palembang] and Hsien-lo [Siam], crossing straight over to Hsi-lan-shan [Ceylon] in South India, Ku-li [Calicut] and K'o-chih [Cochin], we have gone to the western regions Hu-lo-mo-ssu [Hormuz], A-tan [Aden] and Mu-ku-tu-shu [Mogadishu], all together more than thirty countries, large and small. We have traversed more than one hundred thousand *li* of immense tracts of water, and have seen in the ocean huge waves like mountains towering to the skies. We have set eyes on barbarian regions hidden far away in a blue transparency of light vapours, while our sails, loftily unfurled like clouds, continued their course with the speed of stars, day and night breasting the savage waves as though we were but journeying along a high road.[1]

The importance of these ambitious expeditions, which were probably intended to bring most of the known civilized world under the suzerainty of the Chinese tributary system, can hardly be over-estimated. Had they continued, the whole history of South-East Asia might well have been entirely different, since it is doubtful whether the European powers, Portugal, Spain, and Holland, would have succeeded in establishing themselves in that region in the teeth of Chinese opposition. By the fifteenth century there were already considerable colonies of Chinese— the nucleus of the present overseas Chinese—scattered throughout South-East Asia. If China had chosen to develop her maritime power, to proceed systematically with the colonization of the rich lands to her south and resist all intruders, the results on both Chinese and European history would have been incalculable.[2] As it was, no such decision was taken. The Confucian *literati*, jealous of the power and prestige of the eunuchs who had been

[1] This stele was not discovered until 1937, by Wang Po-ch'iu. The above translation is taken (with some changes) from Needham, *Science and Civilisation*, iii.557-8. For another translation see Duyvendak, 'The true Dates of the Chinese Maritime Expeditions...', pp. 349–50. In his 'Science and China's Influence on the World' in *The Legacy of China*, ed. R. Dawson, pp. 293–6, Needham discusses the Chinese technological discoveries which made these voyages possible, remarking with truth: 'All too unjustly have the Chinese been dubbed a non-maritime people' (p. 293).

[2] See V. Purcell, *The Chinese in Southeast Asia*, pp. 1–30; N. A. Simoniya, *Overseas Chinese in Southeast Asia—A Russian Study*, pp. 9–12; C. P. Fitzgerald, *The Third China: The Chinese Communities in South-East Asia*, pp. 1–15; P. Wheatley, *The Golden Chersonese: Studies in the Historical Geography of the Malay Peninsula before A.D. 1500* (Kuala Lumpur 1961); H. J. Wiens, *China's March toward the Tropics*.

primarily responsible for these voyages, succeeded in having the expeditions discontinued on the grounds that 'the treasure that was lavished on these undertakings brought no profit in return', dismantled the fleet, abandoned the overseas Chinese to the fate that was later to overtake them at the hands of the Spanish and the Dutch, and, most important of all, forced China into an isolationist policy from which she was not to emerge for close on four centuries and a half. The Confucian bureaucracy, like the celebrated Oxford don, had become convinced that 'what they didn't know wasn't knowledge'. This explains their stubborn refusal to bother finding out more about the rest of the world until the force of the Western impact had already battered down their doors. They had learned too little and too late.

The self-centredness of the Chinese world, even as late as the mid-nineteenth century, is apparent from a glance at its gazetteers, still stolidly dispensing information about the West which had been copied, almost unchanged, from works written three or four hundred years earlier. As J. K. Fairbank has pointed out, Chinese geographers during the nineteenth century were still applying to the Europeans and Americans of the time 'many of the stereotypes that had been developed during millennia of contact with neighbouring peoples in Asia'.[1] Like the nomads of Central Asia, for ever changing their habitat and their names, the nations of Western Europe were believed to spend their time wandering restlessly across their territories, having no firm abode or certain appellation. The Chinese *literati*, fixed in their own conceit, evinced no interest in the West. Even the Jesuit missions of the seventeenth century proved unable to penetrate this fog of ignorance. Matteo Ricci's (1552–1610) great map of the world, which ought to have been known to every educated Chinese, went completely disregarded simply because its origins were Western and therefore despicable.

It is ironic that the first descriptive account of the West to be given by a Chinese who had actually travelled in those regions was largely the work of an illiterate sailor, Hsieh Ch'ing-kao (1765–1821), whose *Hai-lu* (*Record of the Seas*) was to remain for many years the only reasonably accurate Chinese account of Europe.[2]

[1] Fairbank, Reischauer, Craig, *Modern Transformation*, p. 216.
[2] See note 2, p. lxiv.

Hsieh's account, naive and confused as it often is, is yet incomparably superior to the work of the great scholar Juan Yüan (1764–1849), whose provincial gazetteer of Kwangtung (1819–1822) jumbles together places as diverse as Johore, Trengganu, Portugal, Calicut, Cochin, Hormuz, Italy, and Siam as though they were contiguous. To the disdainful gaze of the Chinese gentleman, the states of the Malay peninsula and the states of Europe were equally insignificant. To make confusion worse confounded, no attempt was made to sort out one European nation from another. We may instance, for example, the term Fo-lang-chi (Franks), which was originally applied to the Portuguese and then to the Spaniards. When the French arrived from Fa-lan-hsi (France) they speedily found themselves confused with their predecessors. The Italian Jesuits, incautious enough to use Portuguese Macao as a base, were also christened Fo-lang-chi.[1] With Spain, Portugal, France, and Italy thus arbitrarily huddled together, it is hardly surprising for us to learn that England was but another name for Holland; that Portugal was not far from Malacca; that Cambodia, Johore, Pahang, England, Spain and the Netherlands were all in the South-Western Ocean; that Sweden and Switzerland were identical; and—unkindest cut of all—that America was a small island off the coast of England.

Such ideas persisted until well into the nineteenth century and gravely hampered the operations of the Chinese Foreign office, the Tsungli Yamen. As one observer sardonically remarked: 'Their Excellencies talk glibly of the balance of power in Europe, but Austria still seems hopelessly mixed up in their minds with Holland...'[2] The confusion went further than this. The Tsungli Yamen on occasions proved unsure as to the location of Burma (a tributary state!)[3] and mistook Baluchistan for Peru.[4] They

---

[1] See Earl H. Pritchard, 'Confusion about the Portuguese and other Europeans in Early Ch'ing China: A Case of Cultural Blindness', in *International Symposium on [the] History of Eastern and Western Cultural Contacts*, pp. 117–20. The author attributes Chinese confusion about Western countries partly to the slavish copying of earlier sources, but mainly to 'the profound indifference of Ch'ing scholars... to Western peoples... and their distrust of anything written by a Westerner' (p. 120). In this context we may note the way in which Ricci's famous map of the world (1602) was largely ignored by the Chinese because, as the *Ming-shih* puts it, 'His words were far-fetched and there were no records to verify them.'
[2] V. Chirol, *The Far Eastern Question*, pp. 54–5.
[3] W. A. R. Martin, *A Cycle of Cathay*, p. 341.
[4] Ibid.

refused to negotiate a treaty with Prussia on the grounds that none of their officials had ever heard of its existence.¹ They were similarly ignorant of the existence of the entire French African empire.² The intellectual fog through which they dimly descried the looming outlines of the Western powers was not to be easily dispersed, since it had hung over the Chinese world-order for centuries.

Similar myths existed about the Europeans themselves. Ku Yen-wu (1613–82), a scholar of considerable distinction whom one might have expected to be better informed on this subject than most, nevertheless gravely remarks of the Franks that 'they take babies and cook them in boiling water and then eat them. In their kingdom, only the king may eat a baby every day. A child costs 100 pieces of gold.'³ Even more widespread was the belief that Europeans used the hearts and eyes of Chinese for medicine. This story proved a serious obstacle to the efforts of the Christian missionaries, who were suspected of cutting up their converts on their death-beds in order to obtain ingredients for their potions.⁴

Misconceptions such as these took a long time to dispel. A major step towards resolving the geographic confusion was taken, however, in 1850 when Hsü Chi-yü (1795–1873), governor of Fukien province, borrowed an atlas from the local American missionary, the Rev. David Abeel (1804–46), and on the basis of this produced the first accurate Chinese geography of the world, the *Ying-huan chih-lüeh* (*Brief Survey of the Maritime Circuit*)⁵ This work not only contained many maps carefully copied from Western ones, but also gave an up-to-date account of each Western country, followed by Hsü's own interpretative and generally unfavourable comments. The general tone of the work was hostile, even xenophobic. Yet such was the odium attaching to anything

¹ C. Holcombe, *The Real Chinese Question*, p. 185.
² V. Chirol, *The Far Eastern Question*, p. 55.
³ Quoted in Hsü Chi-yü, *Ying-huan chih-lüeh*, viii.12.
⁴ This belief was firmly entertained by Tso Tsung-t'ang (1812–85), one of the most enlightened statesmen of his day. Tso's ideas about the West were in no way aided by Sosnovskii, leader of the Russian delegation to China in 1874, who informed him in all seriousness that cannibalism existed in Russia, 'though this was a land where angels flew around much as dragons did in China'. See P. Piassetskii, *Voyage à travers la Mongolie et la Chine*, pp. 405 and 415. As late as 1889, Hsüeh Fu-ch'eng (1838–94), then Chinese Ambassador to London, was ordered to make discreet enquiries to ascertain how much truth there was in this story.
⁵ The *Hai-kuo t'u-chih* (1844) of Wei Yüan (1794–1856), though inferior to Hsü Chi-yü's *Ying-huan chih-lüeh*, is also of great importance.

that savoured of the West that its publication played a part in having Hsü recalled from his post, on the grounds of his having been too intimate with foreigners.

In short then, China, even as late as the mid-nineteenth century had no idea of the power or extent of the forces which were threatening her. Despising her enemies and convinced of her own invulnerability, she took no steps to defend herself. Even her defeat in the Opium War (1839-42), which opened her gates to the West, did not succeed in opening her eyes to the plight she was in. It took a further series of catastrophic events to make the Chinese aware of the need to learn something about the barbarians who were menacing her. The Taiping rebellion (1850-64), inspired by Christian ideas, ravaged seventeen provinces and took toll of some 30,000,000 lives. Hard on the heels of this disaster came the second Western invasion of China (1856-60), culminating in the seizure of Peking by the Anglo-French forces, the humiliating flight of the Emperor, and the burning of the Summer Palace. The shock of these upheavals was powerful enough to cause all but the most die-hard reactionaries among the Chinese gentry to realize that China could no longer afford to ignore the West. The force of the Western impact on China was undoubted; all that remained to be decided was the nature of the Chinese response.

Unfortunately for China, the main response took the path which one might have predicted. Westerners, so the line of reasoning ran, were simply barbarians who were lucky enough to have hit upon a superior technology. Reform was therefore simply a matter of gadgetry, of adopting the armaments and machinery of the West, not in order to modernize the country but rather to restore the vanished Golden Age of three millennia before. Paradoxically enough then, the avowed aim of the early westernizers was not progression but retrogression; a steady advance to the rear into an imaginary past firmly palisaded by modern armaments. To achieve this end the barbarians had first to be properly subdued. 'Learn the technology of the barbarians in order to control them,' became the slogan of the day. From this emerged the Self-Strengthening (*tzu-ch'iang*) Movement, inaugurated by Tseng Kuo-fan (1811-72) and Li Hung-chang (1823-1901), which aimed at making China strong enough to resist the West by adopting her technology, while at the same time strengthening and preserving traditional Confucian values.

One of the lines which the self-strengthening system was to follow was based on a diplomatic programme. Under the classical tributary system, the Chinese had never known diplomatic representation. No resident envoys had ever been exchanged between the Chinese Empire and her tributary states. Diplomatic practice ran counter to the whole political and social system of Imperial China. The Chinese resisted Western attempts to install resident ministers in Peking with a desperation which seems to us wholly perverse and unwarranted until we remember that what was at stake was not only China's traditional estimation of her supreme place in the world but the fate of the dynasty itself. As Immanuel Hsü has well expressed it: 'The question involved was not ritual formality, as it might appear on the surface, but the basic fabric of Chinese society and government.'[1]

From the point of view of the Chinese government, foreign relations were simply an extension of its domestic rule. Hence if the barbarians were no longer submissive, the dynasty had clearly forfeited the Mandate of Heaven and would soon come to an end under the stress of rebellion from within and invasion from without. The presence of foreign ambassadors in Peking would be interpreted as a clear sign that the dynasty was losing its hold. The situation was made all the more disturbing by the fact that the installation of resident ambassadors did not fall within any of the recognized categories of measures for keeping down the barbarians—indoctrination with Chinese culture, bribery, or diplomatic manoeuvering—but was itself an unprecedented and portentous departure from tradition. Assertions that the geomantic harmony of the capital would be disturbed by the presence of the ambassadorial residences were simply the Chinese way of formulating an unpalatable truth.

The Western viewpoint that the exchanging of ambassadors was an essential part of the structure of foreign relations between a community of equal nations could hardly have impressed the Chinese. Their own experience had taught them that in multi-state systems some nations are always more equal than others. During the Chou dynasty, when such a system prevailed in China, the big fish had eaten the little fish for centuries, until only the state of Ch'in remained. The system which they were now being invited to join at gunpoint was therefore not only one which they

[1] Hsü, *China's Entrance*, p. 112.

had themselves outgrown, now presented to them on a global scale, but one which was traditionally associated with anarchy, treachery, and violence. Furthermore they were joining at a disadvantage, for China was certainly not equal to the Western powers with whom she was being asked to deal on equal terms.

Nevertheless, China had to yield to Western demands after her defeat at the hands of the European powers. The Convention of Peking (24 October 1860) established once and for all the presence of Western diplomatic representation in the capital. It was not until many years later, however, that the Chinese themselves decided to establish permanent diplomatic missions abroad.

Again, the reasons for this attitude are deeply rooted in the Chinese conception of their place in the world. Under the tribute system, China herself had sent missions abroad only to beg for peace or to ask for alliances with the barbarians at times when she was weak or in need of support.[1] The only exceptions to this rule were the missions of the investiture envoys, sent to bestow rank and symbols of office upon submissive tributaries.[2] Furthermore, since China was largely self-sufficient, she had no need to trade with foreign countries. Nor, since 1727, had China been interested in the protection of the overseas Chinese, many of whom were anti-Manchu and all of whom, by Confucian standards, had deserted their fatherland in defiance of their government's prohibitory laws and to the neglect of their ancestral tombs, in the sordid pursuit of profit. In short then, leaving the investiture missions aside, the Chinese regarded the sending of diplomatic representatives abroad as an act of degradation, weakness, and submission, to be undertaken only as a last resort.

An important consequence of this attitude towards foreign relations was that the Chinese government could hardly expect to find men willing to suffer the humiliation of being sent abroad—a fate considered worse than banishment—without considerable difficulty. Matters were made even more difficult as the encroaching tides of the West washed further into the Middle Kingdom. The behaviour of the traders and missionaries who now thrust

[1] We may instance, for example, the Chinese missions sent to Russia (1729–31) in an effort to counter the rising power of the Zungars in Central Asia. See M. Mancall, 'China's First Missions to Russia, 1729–31', in *Papers on China*, 9 (1955), 75–110.

[2] See Ch'en Ta-tuan, 'Investiture of Liu-ch'iu Kings in the Ch'ing Period', in Fairbank, *Chinese World Order*, pp. 135–64.

their way into the remotest parts of the Empire, always tactless and often outrageous, roused the Chinese to frenzies of xenophobia.

In your last letter you say that the common people are furious when they hear anyone with something good to say about foreign countries, but are exultant when they hear them harshly criticized. They have made up their minds in advance that everything about foreigners must be bad.... The gentry hate all foreigners and when they set eyes on their machines, loathe them with all their heart.[1]

This overwhelming hatred of the foreigners and all their works was to prove a serious obstacle to the establishment of diplomatic relations. All foreigners were red-haired devils (*hung-mao kuei*) and anyone who had dealings with them in any capacity was a devil's slave. This attitude was found among the officials of the Tsungli Yamen itself, even though this institution was popularly regarded as but a stalking-horse for the Western invasion of China. One Yamen minister, Yen Ching-ming (1817–92), petulantly remarked that no gentleman with a sense of honour could possibly bring himself to learn anything about foreign affairs.[2] Hence to be posted to the Chinese Foreign Office was a disgrace and an insult. Wo-jen (1804–72), a leading conservative, is said to have wept with shame on hearing of his appointment and to have resigned from all his posts in order to avoid such a disgrace.[3] Weng T'ung-ho (1830–1904), tutor to the Emperor, several times refused to take up his position in the Yamen and was only very reluctantly compelled to accept it.[4] If merely to work in the Tsungli Yamen was considered humiliating, how much more shameful was it to be sent out as an ambassador!

It is hardly surprising, under the circumstances, that it was not until 1876 that the Chinese sent their first resident minister abroad, and then only as a result of considerable pressure from the British government. It had taken Peking a long time to come round to seeing the usefulness of international law and the functions of

[1] Kuo's letter to Yao Yen-chia, cited in Chih, *L'Occident 'Chrétien' vu par les Chinois*, p. 130.
[2] Min Erh-ch'ang, *Pei-chuan-chi pu*, xv.13.
[3] Weng T'ung-ho, *Weng-kung kung jih-chi* (*ting-mao*), pp. 24–5; *Ch'ing-shih lieh-chuan*, xlvi.22. See also Chang Hao, 'The Anti-Foreignist Role of Wo-jen (1804–1871)', *Papers on China*, 14 (1960), 12–14, who points out that Wo-jen deliberately injured himself to escape appointment.
[4] Wen T'ung-ho, *Weng Wen-kung kung jih-chi* (*yi-wei*), pp. 626–46.

modern diplomacy. Since 1860, a small group of self-styled 'friends of China'—most of whom were British officials—had been urging the Tsungli Yamen to send diplomatic representatives overseas. But such a legacy of hatred and mistrust was not to be overcome in a few years. To the expostulations of men like Robert Hart, Sir Thomas Wade, Rutherford Alcock, and Anson Burlingame, the Peking government replied cautiously that missions were expensive; that good men were hard to find and harder still to persuade to travel; that foreign languages were difficult to understand; and that innocent Chinese, living alone in strange lands, would fall easy prey to Western cunning.[1] Behind these rather lame excuses lay a justifiable fear and suspicion of the West. The Old China Hands of the Treaty Ports, still avidly pursuing the chimera of a vast, unexploited Chinese market, were vociferous in urging the British government to pursue an aggressive, forward policy that would open up China to trade and set the Chinese marching, protest as they might, in the ranks of the nineteenth century.[2] It was to no avail that the British government averred that it had no intention of seizing China in the way it had taken over India. The Chinese, who had no inkling of the animosity that existed between the Old China Hands and the Foreign Office, did not believe it. In such an atmosphere of hatred and suspicion, it is hardly to be wondered at that the majority of Chinese officials saw in Western suggestions that they should send diplomatic representation abroad, only another subterfuge aimed at undermining the dynasty.

Slowly, however, the Tsungli Yamen came to realize that it would be to China's advantage to have resident ministers abroad. As Benjamin P. Avery, American Minister in Peking, put it, a few Chinese statesmen came to realize 'how inconvenient it is for their country, while receiving a large body of ministers and consuls from abroad, who subject her to a constant sharp criticism before the world, to have no representative of her own, who can speak for and defend her'.[3] Between 1866 and 1876, the Chinese sent four roving missions overseas, all of which played their part in

[1] See *Ch'ou-pan yi-wu shih-mo*, 1.32a, for the Tsungli Yamen's opinions on these matters.
[2] See Nathan A. Pelcovits, *Old China Hands and the Foreign Office*.
[3] United States Government Documents (unpublished), National Archives, Washington: China, Dispatches, vol. 38, doc. 78, Benjamin P. Avery to Hamilton Fish, 16 July 1875, quoted in Hsü, *China's Entrance*, p. 176.

paving the way for the establishment of diplomatic representation abroad.[1] The Japanese punitive expedition to Formosa in 1874, which resulted in an indemnity of 500,000 taels being levied on China, led Li Hung-chang to memorialize the throne to the effect that if China had possessed diplomatic representatives in Tokyo, as he himself had advised three years earlier, this humiliating and costly incident could have been avoided.[2]

While China thus stood hesitating on the edge of a decision she found herself unceremoniously pushed over it. In 1875, August R. Margary, a British consular officer in China, was murdered by hostile tribesmen after crossing the Burmese border.[3] The truculent British minister in Peking, Sir Thomas Wade, promptly seized this opportunity to present the Chinese government with a fresh set of demands, among which was one to the effect that a mission of apology be sent to England. The Chefoo Convention, concluded on 13 September 1876, provided among other things for the despatch of such a mission.

Li Hung-chang now determined to convert this deputation into the first Chinese Embassy to England. The time had come for China to have a resident minister at the Court of St. James. It remained only to find the right man.

The man on whom Li's choice alighted was Kuo Sung-t'ao (style Yün-hsien, 1818–91), a native of Hsiang-yin, Hunan.[4] Kuo had been a serious child, endowed, so we are told, 'with all the earnestness of an adult'. As a young man he studied in the Yüeh-lu Academy at Shan-huo (Hunan) where he became a friend of Tseng Kuo-fan, the most powerful statesman of the T'ung-chih period. Hunan scholarship was famous for its blend of Sung Neo-confucian philosophy and practical statemanship. From this scholastic synthesis sprang the ideology of the T'ung-

---

[1] See Knight Biggerstaff, 'The Establishment of Permanent Chinese Diplomatic Missions Abroad', *Chinese Social and Political Science Review*, xx.1 (Apr. 1936), 1–41. The missions in question were: (1) the investigatory Pin Ch'un mission of 1866, (2) the Burlingame mission of 1868–71, (3) the Ch'ung-hou mission of 1870–2, (4) the Commissions of Investigation to Peru and Cuba of 1873.

[2] Ibid., pp. 21–2. This memorial, which was received at Court on 12 Dec. 1874, is discussed in Hsü, *China's Entrance*, pp. 173–4. Text in Li Hung-chang, *Li Wen-chung-kung ch'üan-chi*, Series I, *Tsou-kao*, xxiv.27a–b; *Ch'ou-pan yi-wu shih-mo*, xlix.33b.

[3] See S. T. Wang, *The Margary Affair and the Chefoo Convention*.

[4] See note 3, p. lxiv.

Introduction xxix

chih Restoration, many of whose foremost figures were imbued with the Hunanese ethos. Kuo was particularly influenced by the early Ch'ing materialist philosopher, Wang Fu-chih (1619–92), until recently a thinker highly regarded in Communist China. Wang's philosophy, which laid stress on the intellectual flexibility needed to cope with an ever-changing world, was undoubtedly to play a major role in Kuo's response to the Western impact.[1]

Kuo was a brilliant student. After taking his *chü-jen* degree (roughly equivalent to an M.A.) in 1837 and his doctoral *chin-shih* degree in 1847, he was appointed to the Han-lin Academy, the highest institute of learning, along with his friend Li Hung-chang, later to become Prime Minister. He was prevented from assuming office by the death of his parents, since officials were forbidden to take up their posts during a period of mourning, and only the outbreak of the Taiping rebellion in July 1850 brought him out of his seclusion. In 1853 he helped Tseng Kuo-fan organize the Hsiang Army against the Taipings and also drew up plans for the creation of a naval force which would drive the Taipings off the Yangtze. He went on to distinguish himself by personally leading a force of volunteers to raise the siege of Wu-ch'ang. It was at this time that he forswore his interest in literature on the grounds that: 'The writing of poetry in times such as these is merely an amusement which cannot benefit the self or educate the age. No gentleman could ever bother with it.'[2]

Five years later in 1858, Ch'en Chih-ho (d. 1866), President of the Board of War, commended Kuo's services to the Court, a recommendation which led to his being sent to assist the famous Mongolian general, Prince Seng-ko-lin-ch'in (d. 1865), to build up the defences of Taku against the Anglo–French invaders. It was at this time that Kuo's shrewd assessment of the strength of the Western forces first became apparent, since he wrote to Seng-ko-lin-ch'in no less than seventeen times to try and persuade him that negotiations, not war, constituted the only effective way of dealing with the Europeans. 'The foreigners are above all concerned with trade,' he argued, 'hence we should look for a way to deal with them accordingly and not confront them with arms.'[3] Seng-ko-lin-ch'in ignored Kuo's warnings, only to suffer a

---

[1] P'eng Tse-yi, p. 64; Hamilton, p. 24, n. 9.
[2] Kuo Sung-t'ao, preface to collected poems, *Yang-chih shu-wu yi-chi*, xxv.1a.
[3] Kuo, *Yü-ch'ih lao-jen tzu-hsü*, p. 8.

Introduction

disastrous defeat near Pei-t'ang—a defeat which made Kuo even more certain that his own estimation of the strength of the barbarians had been the right one. This was Kuo's first clash with the military faction. As a result he resigned, on grounds of illness, and was transferred to the Shantung Customs.

Just before Peking fell to the Anglo–French forces in 1860, Kuo scandalized the guests at a social gathering by declaring that the barbarian problem could never be solved by force but only by diplomacy. Such sentiments, always highly unpopular, were positively dangerous to utter at a time when the enemy was almost at the gate of the national capital and patriotic ardour was reaching unprecedented heights of verbiage. As Kuo's friend, Ch'en Chih-ho warned him later, to make statements of this kind in public was to invite disaster upon himself.[1] Nevertheless, Kuo stuck stubbornly to his views, for he was convinced from his own observation of the Europeans that they could only be handled effectively through the medium of international law and the treaty system.

To understand Kuo's position, one must realize that the *literati* and court officials of the time were almost to a man virulently anti-Western, opposed to any sort of reform and passionate advocates of a purely military solution of China's difficulties. The loud-mouthed bellicosity of these adventurist advocates of violence, unsupported as it was by any real capacity for making war, was eventually to result in the destruction of the Chinese fleet during the Sino–French war of 1884, the humiliating defeat at the hands of Japan in 1895, and the follies of the Boxer movement at the turn of the century. Nevertheless, to associate oneself with this group was a sure way of attaining advancement. As the Hunanese scholar, Wang K'ai-yün (1833–1916), remarked to Marquis Tseng Chi-tse (1839–90) in 1877: 'You'll find that advocating war will benefit you both publicly and privately.'[2]

In opposition to this chauvinistic faction stood the advocates of westernization, a much smaller coterie known as the *Yang-wu*, or 'Foreign affairs' group. Bitterly opposed as they were to the die-hard obscurantists, these men had yet no great admiration for the West. For them it was simply a matter of cold logic: China must either modernize or perish. Li Hung-chang himself be-

---
[1] Hsü, *China's Entrance*, p. 180.
[2] Wang K'ai-yün, *Hsiang-yi-lou jih-chi* (1927), vi.18.

Introduction

longed to this group; it was, in fact, largely his powerful support which prevented its members from succumbing to the attacks of the traditionalists. Li was firmly convinced that it was impossible for China to retreat into isolation again and ignore the new forces that were disrupting her. 'It may be all right for you people to refuse to take an interest in foreign affairs,' he announced to his opponents, 'but if I too refuse to discuss them how is the ship of state to be steered?'[1] Li's friendship for and admiration of Kuo was later to save the latter from some of the more unpleasant consequences of his open advocacy of westernization.

In 1860 Kuo resigned from his post to avoid running into further difficulties with his colleagues and did not resume office again until 1862. From then until 1874, when he was recalled to the capital, he held a number of posts, ranging from Grain Intendant in Soochow to Acting-Governor of Kwangtung (1863) and Judicial Commissioner of Fukien. As Acting-Governor of Kwantung his conduct was exemplary. He subdued a group of rebellious aborigines in Ch'ang-ning, put down an army mutiny, and helped to suppress the last flickers of the Taiping rebellion, when a contingent of rebels led by Prince K'ang (Wang Hai-yang, d. 1866) was wiped out at Chia-ying. His work in Kwangtung brought him into direct contact with Westerners at Canton and so gave him the opportunity to study them further. He soon established a favourable reputation among them which was to stand him in good stead later on. At this time, however, he was principally concerned with domestic matters, in particular with the financial problems which the Taiping rebellion had left in its wake. He was deeply concerned with the welfare of the people, who had been stranded homeless and impoverished amid the devastation wrought by the long civil war. In 1864 he sent up a famous memorial, written in collaboration with Mao Hung-pin (1806–1868), Governor-General of Kwangtung and Kwangsi, asking for the continuation of the *likin*. In this memorial Kuo argues that 'the profits of the merchants and traders are great and their influence also is weighty. Their wealth is imposing and their power is formidable.' Hence, he concludes, the collection of *likin* does not harm the merchants, who are well able to afford it. For

---

[1] Li Hung-chang, *Li Wen-chung-kung ch'üan-chi*, Series 12, xvi.30a-b. The un-Chinese 'ship of state' metaphor is drawn from the oratorical repertoire of Li's hero, Bismark.

though 'the merchant pursues an inferior course the flow of his profits is abundant'.[1]

In attacking the merchants in this way, Kuo was evincing the traditional Confucian distrust of this class. Later he was to modify his ideas as he came to realize that European wealth and power were largely built upon the enterprise of the merchants.

In 1866 Kuo was unaccountably discharged from his post in Kwangtung—perhaps because of his reprehensible interest in Western affairs—and remained out of office for the next few years. During this time he continued his study of China's foreign relations, which he had begun after the Allied occupation of Peking in 1860. His approach was based on the methods of *ching-shih* scholarship he had learnt in Hunan.

> The method I consider best is to examine the pattern by which the country was protected and the state governed since antiquity and to see whether the theories of earlier scholars are right or wrong, suitable or not ... and then to investigate the true feelings and outward actions of the various nations—what is seen to be beneficial or harmful, what should be avoided or sought after, that we may distinguish the differences between past and present.[2]

Kuo's thesis, which he expanded in several of his writings, was that 'the grand strategy by which the Han and T'ang Dynasties controlled the barbarians has been lost for over seven hundred years'.[3] During the earliest period of Chinese history down to the end of the Chou dynasty, China's attitude to her barbarian neighbours had been governed by *te* (moral influence) and *li* (protocol). From the Ch'in dynasty (221–206 B.C.) to the end of the Northern Sung (1127), a flexible and realistic foreign policy had been pursued which sought to exert pressure on the barbarians when the country was strong and to come to terms with them when the country was weak. But from the time of the

---

[1] *Kuo shih-lang tsou-shu* in *Yang-chih shu-wu yi-chi*, v. 19–28, hereafter referred to as *Kuo Shih-lang tsou-shu*. A translation of the memorial is found in Edwin G. Beal, *The Origin of Likin (1853–64)*, pp. 125–42. *Likin* was a tax on merchants and travellers, first levied during the Taiping Rebellion.

[2] Letter to Chu K'o-ching in Ch'u Chin, 'Kuo Yün-hsien shou-cha ping pa', *Chung-ho yüeh-k'an*, i.12 (1940), 68–76.

[3] Kuo, *Sui-pien cheng-shih* in *Yang-chih shu-wu yi-chi (wen-chi)*, iii.15b–17b, hereafter referred to as *Sui-pien cheng-shih*. Part of the preface in which the remarks occur has been translated by Yang Lien-sheng, 'Historical Notes on the Chinese World Order' in Fairbank, *Chinese World Order*, pp. 20–33.

Introduction xxxiii

Southern Sung dynasty (1127–1279) a recklessly militaristic policy came into fashion.

The custom of regarding the Yi and the Ti [barbarians] as great evils and peaceful relations with them as a flagrant disgrace really began only with the Southern Sung.[1]

From the Southern Sung our foreign policy underwent a change. Officials throughout the empire indulged in reckless talk of war. When the state was strong they strove to dominate the barbarians. When it was weak they refused to admit their weakness.[2]

It seems to me that during the past thirty years, in dealing with foreigners our officials, both at Court and in the provinces, have imitated the attitude which developed after the Southern Sung dynasty, considering it disgraceful to make peace treaties but excellent to make war.[3]

Such policies may have sometimes been successful in the past, Kuo went on, but now the Chinese found themselves faced with an entirely new situation.

I realize that the strength of the foreigners, their challenge to our country and the harms they have inflicted upon us, surpass all that has happened in the past. Their method of seeking excuses to create incidents, in order to force us to deal with them, is also something new. If we deal with them properly, their management of customs, their teaching in the schools, their training of soldiers, and their making of weapons for us could go well and entail no difficulties or suspicions. If we do not deal with them properly, discussions will increase and incidents will be provoked, a small thing often becoming big, an easy thing often becoming difficult, thus leading to endless troubles.[4]

Furthermore, he noted that the Westerners were far too strong for the Chinese to think of defeating them. 'The foreigners, both kings and officials, pay great attention to the training of soldiers and the making of weapons, and continue to produce an unending stream of new armaments,'[5] thus making it impossible for the Chinese to

---

[1] Kuo, *Shih-hsi chi-ch'eng* in Wang Hsi-ch'i, comp., *Hsiao-fang-hu chai yü-ti ts'ung-ch'ao* (hereafter referred to as *HFH*), p. 152b. See translation below.
[2] Letter to Chu K'o-ching, *Chung-ho yüeh-k'an*, p. 68.
[3] *Kuo Shih-lang tsou-shu*, xii.6b. See translation of the whole memorial below, p.88 ff.
[4] Ibid.
[5] Ibid., xii.4b.

withstand them. The real enemies were within the gates. Those officials who 'with gaping mouths and bulging eyes ... seek their own gratifications, even going so far in their discussions as to say that they would rather see the state destroyed and the dynasty overthrown than talk of peace'[1]—these were the real menace to the security of the empire. Furthermore, it was ridiculous to prattle of war when what the Westerners wanted was not territory but trade. 'Since they do not speak of war,' Kuo reasoned, 'why should we force them to fight?'[2] In short, he concluded,

> I believe ... that the management of foreign affairs requires adaptation to circumstances. This, in turn, involves two things: reason and strength ... We should grant them without hesitation whatever we can as long as it does not injure our national interests and stubbornly refuse them what we ought not to grant them. This is the policy dictated by strength and reason ... When strength and reason are on our side, there can be no fear of defeat.[3]

What Kuo was advocating was a policy known as 'loose rein' (*chi-mi*) which can be traced back as far as the Former Han dynasty.[4] Kuo himself refers explicitly to this policy in the preface to his *Investigation into the Realities of the History of Frontier Pacification* (*Sui-pien Cheng-shih*), where he remarks: '... to control the barbarians our wise kings punished and resisted them when they came bent on invasion, and prepared and guarded against them when they left. If they were attracted by our Chinese culture and came to offer tribute, they would be treated courteously and kept under loose rein without severing the relationship. Hence the blame for any devious behaviour would always be theirs, not ours.'[5] This policy, so Kuo believed was applicable to the Westerners largely because it laid stress on good faith and sincerity. What was needed, he averred, was some degree of mutual confidence. But before this could be attained it was necessary to understand the West and to realize that China was not the only civilization in the world. Failure to do this would bring nothing but disaster in its train.

For Kuo foreign policy and domestic reform were branches of

---

[1] Kuo, *Shih-hsi chi-ch'eng*, p. 153a. See translation below, p. 44.
[2] *Kuo Shih-lang tsou-shu*, xii.4b.
[3] Ibid., xii.3b.
[4] Yang, 'Historical Notes on the Chinese World Order', pp. 31–3.
[5] *Sui-pien cheng-shih*, p. 15b.

the same tree. The military Self-Strengthening Movement was doomed to failure, since it was ultimately political and economic institutions that determined superiority, not the mere acquisition of modern weapons. 'Military matters are of little importance,' he wrote to Li. 'The basis on which the state is established must be that of newly-created institutions.'[1]

From his examination of Western and Chinese history Kuo had arrived at an understanding of the deep-seated malaise that possessed China. From a Confucian point of view, the state exists only to benefit the people. Yet in China, Kuo contended, only lip-service was paid to this ideal. 'The West is active in seeking to benefit the people, while China does precisely the opposite.' Whereas in the West 'if a source of profit is opened up, the state will surely assist in establishing it... in China this is not so. Every effort is made to block the enterprise, and the officials take no notice.'[2] In mining, for example, whereas Westerners were concerned with the most efficient ways of extracting the maximum potential from the earth, Kuo's fellow-countrymen were concerned only with not violating the geomantic principles of *feng-shui* and considered that mining disturbed the 'veins of the earth' (*shan-mai*). As a result, it was impossible to build a stable foundation for wealth and strength in Chinese society. Much the same considerations applied to other Western institutions. The banking and credit systems and the joint-stock company, which Kuo believed responsible for the growth of the European economy, could find no place in China. So he concluded 'the industries which produce wealth and strength for the West are not what China can expect in the near future'.[3]

As a result of his careful researches into history and economics, Kuo was forced to conclude that the only practical measures China could afford to implement were the development of steamships, railways, and telegraphs in order to unify the country and so create the basis for wealth and strength. Superficially, he might have seemed to be advocating the same programme as the 'self-strengthening' reformers, who argued that China should adopt Western technology only to strengthen the traditional state. But Kuo's proposals were aimed not at avoiding further reform but at encouraging it. One writer has correctly pointed out that

---

[1] *San hsing-shih shu-tu*, i.46.   [2] Ibid., i.120.   [3] Ibid., i.104.

Kuo had painted himself into a corner here.[1] He had begun by arguing that wealth and strength were the consequences of having correct principles. But when he came to consider the practical problems of imitating Western methods, he argued that correct principles could be adopted only if the country was wealthy enough. 'In my opinion wealth and strength have been the highroad to order since the Ch'in and Han dynasties.'[2] He was never to solve the conundrum he had set himself.

In 1875, however, at the time of the Margary affair, he was serving as Judicial Commissioner of Fukien, when he was summoned to take up a post in the Chinese Foreign Office, the Tsungli Yamen. Just before he was sworn in, he sent up a memorial requesting the impeachment of Ts'en Yü-ying (1829–89), Governor-General of Yunnan and Kweichow, on the grounds that he had failed to take proper precautions to ensure Margary's safety.[3] Kuo's real motive in making this move was simply to save Governor Ts'en from having to answer the much graver charge of having connived at Margary's murder; but such subtlety was lost upon his fellow officials and the *literati*, who accused Kuo of treachery, alleging that he was trying to curry favour with the Westerners and appease Sir Thomas Wade. By 1876 the campaign against Kuo had mounted to such proportions that Wang K'ai-yün, was moved to write in his *Diary of the Hsiang-i Chamber*: 'We Hunanese feel very ashamed to be associated with Kuo.'[4] When a Catholic cathedral was built in Ch'ang-sha, a place with which Kuo had close connections, the local populace, convinced by the gentry that Kuo had conspired with the missionaries to bring this about, demonstrated against him and threatened to burn down his house.[5] The irony of this was that Kuo himself was strongly opposed to Christianity, which, so his experience with the 'Christian' Taipings had convinced him, was a menace to the stability of the Confucian state.

This, then, was the man whom Li Hung-chang had selected to

---

[1] Hamilton, p. 17.
[2] *San hsing-shih shu-tu*, i.121.
[3] Kuo was sworn in during September 1875; see Henri Cordier, *Histoire des relations de la Chine avec les puissances occidentales, 1860–1900*, ii.50. For Kuo's memorial against Ts'en see Hsü, *China's Entrance*, pp. 182–3, and my translation below p. 85.
[4] Wang K'ai-yün, *Hsiang-yi-lou jih-chi*, v.6.
[5] Chin-liang, *Chin-shih jen-wu chih*, p. 129.

Introduction xxxvii

lead the mission to England. It was a thankless enough task. As we have already indicated, diplomatic assignments, especially those of a humiliating nature involving the presentation of formal apologies, were shunned by everyone. For Kuo to accept such a post after the attacks that had been mounted upon him was, in popular opinion, equivalent to an open admission of his complicity in Western designs against China. Kuo knew well enough that to take on this commission would irretrievably ruin his promising official career. He must have been fully aware of the fate of Chih-kang and Sun Chia-ku, who had accompanied Anson Burlingame on his mission as roving Ambassador to the West in 1868, only to find themselves doomed to spend the rest of their days in minor appointments in remote areas of the Chinese border.[1] Such was the stigma attached to those who associated themselves with the West. In Kuo's case, his acceptance of the leadership of the mission would seem to have cost him the coveted Governorship of Fukien, which should rightfully have been his. Once he did waver, begging the Court to allow him to resign from the mission to England since he could no longer stand the fury of public condemnation levelled against him. He stood, indeed, in some personal danger. When he returned to Hunan, just before he left for Europe, a crowd of his fellow Hunanese assaulted him and burnt his boat. A set of anonymous verses, in circulation at the time indicates the temper of popular feeling:

> He stands out among his contemporaries,
> He is raised above his peers.
> Yet the nation of Yao and Shun
> Cold-shoulders him.
> He cannot serve human beings,
> So how can he serve demons?
> What is the point of abandoning
> His native land?[2]

But in the end his pride, his high idealism, his sense of duty, and his burning conviction that no one else had the qualifications to undertake this task, made him decide to see it through.

As negotiations for the Chefoo Convention drew to an end, Sir Thomas Wade, who prior to the settlement had been anxious to

[1] Martin, *Cathay*, p. 379.
[2] Wang K'ai-yün, *Hsiang-yi-lou jih-chi*, v.6.

xxxviii   *Introduction*

delay the departure of the mission to prevent Kuo from settling the case of his own accord in London, now showed himself equally anxious for the legation to leave. Two months before the departure of the mission, on 1 October 1876, Kuo's assistant envoy, Hsü Ch'ien-shen, was given another posting. His place was taken by Liu Hsi-hung, a fifth-grade director of one of the four Minor Courts, who belonged to the conservative faction, had connections in the Grand Council, and was bitterly prejudiced against foreigners.[1] Kuo had already protested vigorously against Liu's proposed appointment, arguing that he knew nothing about foreign affairs, lacked patience and objectivity, and had a reputation for being stubborn and ignorant. But his protests were in vain. The appointment of this 'arch-reactionary', as Wade styled him, was a victory for the obscurantists and a heavy blow to Kuo, who must have been doubly incensed at this rebuff, since he had already refused to accept Liu in the minor post of attaché and was now compelled to take him on in a much more distinguished capacity.

Attached to the legation staff in the capacity of foreign secretaries were two Englishmen, W. C. Hillier of the Peking Legation,[2] and Dr. Halliday Macartney,[3] who had previously been director of the newly-founded Arsenal at Nanking. Macartney, who was to hold the post of English secretary to the Legation for almost thirty years, made his influence felt right from the start.

[1] See also Hamilton, p. 9, who quotes Knight Biggerstaff, 'The Change in Attitude of the Chinese Towards the Sending of Diplomatic Representatives 1860–1880' (unpublished doctoral dissertation, Harvard University, 1934, p. 187), as saying that Liu 'was totally unknown at the time of his appointment'.

[2] Sir Walter Caine Hillier (1849–1927), son of C. B. Hillier, a former British Consul at Bangkok, had entered the Foreign Office in 1867 as a Student Interpreter in China. He was subsequently appointed 3rd Class Assistant (1872) and 2nd Class Assistant (1874). On his return from his mission to England, he became Assistant Secretary to the Peking Legation (1879) and subsequently Secretary (1885). In 1889, he was appointed Consul-General in Korea, retiring from the service in 1896. From 1904 to 1908 he held the Chair of Chinese at King's College, London. From 1908 to 1910 he was adviser to the Chinese Government, and was thus on stage during the last act of the imperial drama, which ended in 1911.

[3] Dr Halliday Macartney (1833–1906) had been in the service of the Chinese government since 1862 and had for ten years (1865–75) been Director of the Nanking Arsenal. He was no great success in this capacity, since an inspection of the Arsenal in 1874 disclosed that the cannons he cast were fit only for the firing of salutes. As Secretary of the Chinese Embassy, however, he distinguished himself from the start by his able management. See Demetrius C. Boulger, *The Life of Sir Halliday Macartney*.

Introduction xxxix

On his appointment, in November 1876, he found that it had been arranged that the Embassy should undertake its voyage in a *French* steamer. Macartney's patriotic fervour was aroused by this slighting of the traditions of British seamanship, and he very soon succeeded in altering the arrangements. As he planned it, the Embassy was to travel from Shanghai to Southampton by P & O steamers, stopping *en route* only at British outposts of empire— Hong Kong, Singapore, Ceylon, Aden, Malta, and Gibraltar. This, he averred, would have a profound effect upon the members of the Embassy who could not but be impressed at seeing the British flag flying in every port of call they came to and thus girdling half the globe.[1]

At midnight on Friday 1 December 1876, the Embassy sailed from Shanghai on board the P & O mail-steamer *Travancore*, under the command of Captain W. Barratt. We have ample testimony about this journey, since from the moment they got on board both Kuo and Liu began to keep journals in which they recorded their impressions of the brave new world they were entering. Keeping a journal constituted an important part of an ambassador's duties, for all Chinese envoys were under express orders from the Court to record everything of interest they saw. The diaries, when complete, were sent back to the Tsungli Yamen. Only in this way, so it was believed, could reliable information about the ways of these barbarian countries of the West be obtained. Kuo's diary, in particular, is of great interest, because the views it expressed were so much at variance with the viewpoint then prevailing among the Chinese *literati* that its publication caused an outcry. Wang K'ai-yün contemptuously described the book as 'Western poison'.[2] Ho Chin-shou, a Hanlin editor, sent up a memorial alleging that 'Kuo tells lies about England and wishes China to be subject to her'.[3] Passages in which Kuo had spoken favourably of Western civilization were cited as evidence of his traitorous character, the hue and cry eventually reaching such proportions that the Empress Dowager, Tz'u Hsi, ever nervous of public opinion, was forced to yield to popular demand and have the diary banned and the printing plates destroyed. Fortunately, however, a few copies of the book survived the proscription, though in a rather mutilated condition,

[1] Boulger, *Life of Macartney*, p. 265.
[2] Quoted in P'eng Tse-yi, p. 69.   [3] Ibid.

and it is upon this work that we must depend for our knowledge of Kuo's first impressions of the totally alien civilization that was the West.

Kuo's *Shih-hsi chi-ch'eng* [*The Record of an Envoy's Journey to the West*] resumed a long literary tradition, virtually discontinued since the Ming, of records kept by Chinese travellers abroad. China's retreat into isolation in the fifteenth century had put a stop to the colourful succession of travellers' tales which the Chinese scholar had enjoyed since the days of the fabulous *Shan-hai ching* (*Classic of Mountains and Seas*), the *Fo-kuo chi* (*Record of Buddhist Countries*) of the monk Fa-hsien (*fl.* A.D. 414) and the *Ta T'ang Hsi-yü chi* (*Record of the Western Countries at the Time of the Great T'ang Dynasty*) of the celebrated pilgrim Hsüan-tsang (603–64). Amid all the astonishing wealth of literature produced from the sixteenth to the mid-nineteenth century we find few eye-witness accounts of regions outside China. Apart from the *Hai-lu*, the only works extant would seem to be the journals of the investiture envoys, who were sent to places within the traditional Chinese sphere of influence, such as the Ryukyu islands, and so reveal nothing of the world beyond. Not until 1866, with the departure of the Pin Ch'un Mission, do we find the older literary tradition resumed.[1]

One of the members of the Pin Ch'un Mission was Chang Te-yi (1847–1919), then a young student of nineteen, who was later to accompany Kuo to Europe in the capacity of English interpreter.[2] Chang, who eventually became minister to England (1901–5), was a first-class diarist, a born writer with a frivolous almost Pepysian interest in trivia for their own sake which makes his work of absorbing interest to the social historian. Chang's view of Europe has all the naivety and freshness of his youth about it. Everything delights and astonishes him, from the railroad at Suez—the first he had set eyes on—to the gas-lights, the lifts, the water-closets, and the hot-and-cold plumbing systems

[1] For the investiture envoys, see p. xxv, n. 2 above. On the Pin Ch'un mission, see Knight Biggerstaff, 'The First Chinese Mission of Investigation Sent to Europe', *Pacific Historical Review*, vi.4 (Dec. 1937), 307–20.

[2] Chang Te-yi, style Tsai-ch'u, also known as Te-ming and Te Tsai-ch'u, who was a member of the Chinese division of the Bordered Yellow Banner, had been a student in the English department of the T'ung-wen kuan. The *Hang-hai shu-chi* is found in *HFH*, xi.58–101. The diary Chang kept during his service with the Kuo embassy, *Sui-shih jih-chi* in *HFH*, xi.210–92, is also of great liveliness and interest. Passages from the *Sui-shih jih-chi* are translated below, pp. 150 ff.

of his hotels. From his diary we gain a vivid impression of how the mission went jaunting about all over Europe, visiting Paris and London, having audience with the Queen at Windsor, and then dashing off to The Hague, Hamburg, Stockholm, St. Petersburg, Berlin, Brussels, and Marseilles before heading for home. This formidable itinerary, every unforgiving minute crammed with improving visits to parks, zoos, prisons, museums, arsenals, factories, newspaper offices, telegraph stations, and the like, interspersed at frequent intervals with tea-parties, formal receptions, balls, and banquets, almost turned Chang's young head. However his diary, the *Hang-hai shu chi*, (*Record of My Voyage*), like the two journals kept by his superior Pin Ch'un, contains a mass of information about the West, which, garbled and only half-understood as much of it is, must nevertheless have been of considerable importance as the first authentic account of a civilization comparable to that of China.

Kuo himself had certainly read the Pin Ch'un diaries; and we may assume that his own approval of Europe was partly conditioned by them. Kuo's own staid journal, however, is very different from the breathlessly exuberant work of the young Chang. This is not to accuse it of dullness. For all its maturity, it is a work as exciting in its own way as, say, the celebrated *Journals* of Matteo Ricci. The comparison is not an idle one, since in both Kuo's *Record* and Ricci's *Journals* we are confronted with the spectacle of a distinguished mind, steeped in the classical culture of its own civilization, confronting without undue prejudice and yet from the basis of firm belief a totally alien culture, which is viewed with considerable sympathy and understanding. Here however, the comparison must end; for whereas Ricci's *Journals* were the product of many patient years spent in the acquisition of Chinese language and culture, Kuo's work was in essence but the record of his ignorance of the West.[1] Yet it is precisely in this ignorance, in the freshness of response that it evokes, that much of the charm of his work lies.

This naivety is amusingly illustrated by an incident which took place shortly after the envoys had left Shanghai, when their

---

[1] Kuo was keenly aware of his own shortcomings in this respect. As he once wrote to Peking: 'How can I, who know no foreign language and am ignorant of world affairs, fill my post competently?' Wang Chü-ch'ang, *Yen Chi-tao nien-p'u*, p. 7.

vessel, the *Travancore*, was forced to stop its engines in order to avoid being run into by the *Audacious*, flagship of the China Squadron. Captain Barratt, master of the *Travancore*, saved the situation by explaining to Kuo that the entire procedure was but an example of naval etiquette which involved, among other courtesies, his ship's yielding way to the *Audacious*. On hearing this Kuo was prompted to exclaim: 'How refined and civilized are these ceremonial courtesies of theirs! These alone are sufficient to indicate that the wealth and power of this nation was not acquired by mere chance.'[1]

In this passage Kuo is putting forward a thesis which would not have been subscribed to by even the most progressive of his countrymen. He is alleging, in fact, that the West is rich and powerful not merely because it has stumbled upon a viable technology, but because its institutions are solidly based upon ceremony and order, the very virtues upon which the Confucian state itself was supposed to have been founded. Such a statement had revolutionary implications, since it asserted the existence of a civilization morally equivalent to China, and thus undermined completely China's claim to superiority. To admire the technology of the West was dangerous enough, since it was already doubtful whether Confucianism could survive the challenge which it posed. But to admire the *ethical* basis of Western civilization was to sound the death-knell of the Confucian world-order. Over forty years later, during the May 4th Movement of 1919, Ch'en Tu-hsiu (1879–1942), founder-member of the Chinese Communist Party, was to call upon 'Mr. Science' and 'Mr. Democracy' to banish 'Confucius and Sons' for ever. In urging his fellow Chinese to free themselves of the shackles of the old order by adopting the distinctive values of the West, not merely its technology, Ch'en was ultimately indebted to men like Kuo, who had been the first to point out to their sceptical countrymen that Western civilization did indeed possess a firm basis of principle.

It must not be assumed that Kuo's opponents were unaware of the profoundly heretical nature of his views. On the contrary, it was precisely his praise of the moral, not the technological basis of Western civilization, which led them to burn the blocks of his diary, and demand his impeachment as a traitor. One passage

[1] Kuo, *Shih-hsi chi-ch'eng*, p. 1a. See translation below, p. 4.

from the diary has become famous, since it was this which particularly aroused the ire of the conservative faction. It runs as follows: 'The kingdoms of Europe date back for some two thousand years. Their governmental and educational institutions are well-ordered, enlightened, and methodical. They are completely different from such upstart dynasties as the Liao (947–1125) and the Chin (1122–1234), which suddenly sprang up and as suddenly declined... their knowledge and their strength are both pre-eminent...'[1]

Kuo is here arguing that Westerners are quite different from any other barbarians the Chinese have encountered, since they have a civilization which can bear comparison with that of China itself. He develops this theme in several other passages, of which the following are typical:

In Europe people have been competing with each other with knowledge and power for the last two thousand years. Egypt, Rome and Islam have each in their turn flourished and decayed, yet the principles which formed the basis of these states [sic] still endure. Nowadays, England, France, Russia, America, and Germany, all of them great nations which have tried their strength against each other to see who is pre-eminent, have evolved a code of international law which gives precedence to fidelity and righteousness and attaches the utmost importance to relations between states. Taking full cognizance of feeling and punctiliously observing all due ceremonies, they have evolved a high culture on a firm material basis. They surpass by a long way the states of our Spring and Autumn period.[2]

... the nations of Europe do have insight into what is essential and what is not and possess a Way of their own which assists them in the acquisition of wealth and power. In this manner, a state may well last for a thousand years...[3]

What struck Kuo first and foremost about Western culture was not its technical and scientific achievements, but the fact that it was founded on firm principles of justice, order, discipline, honour, and integrity, qualities, which, so he seems to imply, are fast disappearing from China. 'In Europe, commerce is the root of government. Their commercial regulations are orderly and dignified and their methods are exact... From all this we can see that

[1] Ibid., p. 153a. See translation below, p. 43.
[2] Ibid., p. 158. See translation below, p. 72.
[3] Ibid. See translation below, p. 73.

[the European] acquisition of wealth and power is not without a firm foundation.'¹

In these, and many other similar passages which occur throughout his works, Kuo is laying stress on the need for China to emulate the West if she is to become wealthy and powerful. His admiration for the West increased as he came to know it better, so that by the time he was recalled to China he was a whole-hearted proponent not just of the modernization but of the westernization of his own country. Ku Hung-ming (1857–1928), once alleged that Kuo thought so highly of Western culture that he remarked on seeing Europe and its splendours: 'Confucius and Mencius have tricked us.'² This story, which implies that Kuo believed that the Confucian contempt for profit (*li*) had resulted in the impoverishment of Chinese civilization, is probably apocryphal. Nevertheless, there can be little doubt that Kuo, though he remained a firm believer in Confucianism, was of the opinion that some of its tenets had fallen into decay. Hence he reserves his harshest criticisms for his countrymen, whom he accuses time and time again of idleness, ignorance, greed, complacency, chauvinism, corruption, and selfishness. As he remarks despairingly in one of his letters from London: 'Personally, I think there is something in the Chinese mind which is absolutely unintelligible.'³

Kuo's greatest concern was with *kuo-t'i*, the dignity of the state. Even as he lay dying this was in his thoughts: 'While in London whenever I became aware of what would harm or benefit relations between East and West, I spoke up at once because of my concern for the dignity of the state. My criticisms were simple and I had no fear of speaking about matters beyond my competence. But nothing of what I had to say was accepted.'⁴

Kuo's scathing criticisms of the ruin that was China did not blind him to the faults of the West. While fundamentally sympa-

---
¹ Ibid., p. 151b. See translation below, p. 35.
² Ku Hung-ming, *Chang Wen-hsiang mu-fu chi-wen*, p. 3b. On Ku Hung-ming see Liu Ts'un-yan, 'Ku Hung-ming and his interpretation of Chinese Civilisation' in *Proceedings of the Symposium on Historical, Archaeological and Linguistic Studies on Southern China, S.E. Asia and the Hong Kong Region*, pp. 269–81.
³ Kuo's letter to Li Hung-chang from London (1877). See translation below, p. 97.
⁴ Quoted in P'eng Tse-yi, p. 77. This comes from his last letter, written on the twentieth day of the third month of the seventeenth year of *Kuang-hsü* (28 April 1891).

thetic towards the achievements of Western civilization, he never carried his admiration to the point of uncritical acceptance. He was too much of a patriot to remain indifferent to the ravages of imperialism in China. Though contemptuous of his opponent's claims that the European powers were bent on the military conquest of the Middle Kingdom, he was nevertheless keenly aware of the threat to China's integrity posed by Western commercial and missionary interests. He was especially opposed to the Christian missionaries and their doctrines, of which he remarks acidly:

Your servant believes that the Western religions are infinitely inferior to those of our saints. If one considers them from the point of view of profundity and perfection, there can be no comparison between the two. Only imbeciles would be deceived by Christianity. Intelligent people and wise men would never let themselves be taken in by such nonsense. Needless to say, all scholars and gentlemen detest the Christian religion.[1]

While scornful of Christianity, he is even more bitterly antagonistic—and with good reason—to the bullying and aggression that all too often accompanied missionary activity in China. 'The mission stations', he alleges with justice, 'have become just so many sanctuaries for criminals, who behave wantonly, defy the law, and are a source of scandal and concern to honest people. Not only have [the missionaries] failed in their original intention of establishing their religions [in China], but I also fear that when these facts are made known to the countries concerned, they will rouse the deepest shame.'[2]

It is clear then that Kuo reserved his enthusiasm for the moral, and to a lesser extent the technical, achievements upon which Western civilization was grounded. For the attitude of the trader and the missionary, the one intent upon sales, the other on souls, he had nothing but contempt and anger.

Kuo's enemies, however, the *ch'ing-liu* faction, were incapable of making such subtle distinctions. For them, Kuo's very interest in the West, let alone his championing of its civilization, was proof of his treachery. Kuo was saved from the full fury of their attacks only through the friendship of Li Hung-chang who was

[1] Kuo's letter to Yao Yen-chia, cited in Chih, *L'Occident 'Chrétien' vu par les Chinois*, p. 130. See also Appendix, p. 190.
[2] Kuo, *Shih-hsi chi-ch'eng*, p. 151a. See translation below, p. 34.

very sympathetic to his suggestions. In a letter written to Kuo in 1877 Li says: 'I have read through your diary several times. Your opinions and the facts you lay before us have never been mentioned by anyone else. I felt as though I myself were voyaging through the Red Sea to Europe. My horizons have been broadened.'[1]

For all this, Li was unable to afford complete protection to Kuo. The Empress Dowager had a policy of maintaining her own rule by playing off one faction against another. So Kuo's enemies were placed in positions of power from which they were able to harass him continually. Li Hung-tsao (1820–97), a conservative implacably opposed to everything Kuo stood for, was appointed to the Tsungli Yamen shortly after Kuo was sent to England. From this vantage point he was able to support Liu Hsi-hung and eventually have Kuo recalled to China.[2] Li Hung-chang himself was compelled to bow before the storm and advise Kuo to be more moderate in his suggestions for reform. 'I am very impressed with your memorial,' he wrote in 1877, 'but I fear that the Tsungli Yamen will not transmit it and will leave it aside. Please do not send any more memorials in this vein. Your friends in the Yamen say you have too many suggestions for reform.'[3]

It is instructive to compare Kuo's character and outlook with that of his fellow-envoy, Liu Hsi-hung, whose appointment in the teeth of Kuo's opposition had embittered relations between the two men from the start. Liu had a far from prepossessing personality. Henri Cordier, who knew both men personally, refers to Liu as 'ce personnage obtus, jaloux et acariâtre'.[4] Certainly Liu possessed a quite remarkable talent for not getting on with people, particularly with Westerners, and seems to have exercised his abilities in this direction from the moment the Embassy left Shanghai. Halliday Macartney's diary records several instances of the way in which Liu's manners shocked his fellow passengers:

At breakfast he called for an egg, and proceeded to open it in such [an] awkward manner that his fingers went into it, his long nails, or rather claws, meeting from opposite sides. With the yolk of the egg dripping

---
[1] Li Hung-chang, *Li Wen-chung-kung ch'üan-chi*, Series 2, *P'eng-liao han-koa*, xvii.5a.
[2] Ibid., xviii.6a.   [3] Ibid., xvii.35b–36a.
[4] Cordier, *Relations de la Chine*, ii.136.

Introduction   xlvii

from the points of his fingers and streaming over his hands he presented a curious picture of the *corps diplomatique* . . . Having finished his dinner before the rest of us, he retired from the table and entered his cabin. We were still at our wine when his servant was seen to snatch up a lamp and go into his state-room. The captain instantly sent one of the stewards to see what he was doing with it, and in a minute he returned stating that H.E. was enjoying his smoke. The captain sent back the steward for the lamp, and with instructions to put out the Ambassador's pipe. This being carried out, H.E., accompanied by his servant, went upstairs apparently in anything but the best of humours.[1]

Liu's behaviour towards Kuo was motivated by hatred and envy from the start. He seized every opportunity he could to foment trouble during the voyage, even going so far as to complain to Peking that Kuo had sullied Chinese honour by allowing the Governor of Malta to cover his mandarin robes with his raincoat during a sudden shower.[2] Once in England, his behaviour grew even worse. At times, he would humiliate Kuo by leaving him alone in an empty embassy while he took the entire staff out for a walk![3] Liu also kept a diary, the *Ying-yao jih-chi* (*Journal of a Voyage to England*) in which he recorded his impressions of Western culture.[4] It forms an interesting contrast to Kuo's journal.

Kuo presented his letters of credence at Buckingham Palace on 7 February 1877. He seems to have settled down quickly to the hectic social life demanded of ambassadors, attending with diligence balls, receptions, soirées, and other functions where the charm and courtesy of his manner never failed to win the hearts of those who met him. Not for nothing had the astute Cordier referred to him as 'esprit éclairé . . . d'une grande courtoisie, d'un commerce sûr . . .'[5] Even the stern Mr. Gladstone unbent so

[1] Cited in Boulger, *Life of Macartney*, pp. 267–8. References to Macartney's diary will henceforward be cited as *Macartney*.
[2] Martin, *Cathay*, p. 381. Martin cannot resist pointing out that Liu visited a dentist during his stay in Europe in order to have himself fitted with dentures, adding wittily: 'His patriotism was not proof against the seduction of artificial teeth.' (p. 382.)
[3] Chang, *Sui-shih jih-chi*, p. 265a. See translation below, p. 162.
[4] Liu Hsi-hung, *Ying-yao jih-chi*, in *HFH*, x, ch. xi, pp. 160a–209b. See translation of selections below, pp. 110 ff. A few extracts from this diary have also been translated by F. S. A. Bourne, 'Diary of Liu Ta-jen's Mission in England', *The Nineteenth Century* (Oct. 1880), pp. 612–21.
[5] Cordier, *Relations de la Chine*, ii.133.

far as to pronounce him 'the most genial Oriental he had ever met'.¹

The arrival of the Legation created quite a stir, for Chinese mandarins were something of a novelty in London. *Punch*, a highly political paper at that period, celebrated the event with a full-page cartoon depicting Kuo as a grinning organ-grinder's monkey in Chinese dress, come to peer at the British lion.² The offensive doggerel that accompanied this jingoistic daub was very much in the mood of the time. The British Empire, after all, was barely a month old, having officially been called into being by Disraeli on 1 January 1877. The arrival of a Chinese Ambassador on a mission of apology must have seemed to set the seal on Britain's pre-eminence.

Kuo's secondary wife, who had accompanied him on the voyage, also aroused great interest. Kuo had originally planned to take both his secondary wives to England with him, but must have been persuaded by Macartney that such an indiscretion would prejudice his being received in polite society.³ *Punch* addressed a set of verses to the Ambassador's lady, whom it depicted in the guise of a simpering Japanese geisha in an outrageously *décolleté* kimono, expressing the hope that her bound feet would not start a national fashion since

> An inability to stand
> Is not the charm we most demand
> In Western women.⁴

Later a rumour went round that this 'Tottering Lily of Fascination', as *Punch* called her, was not Kuo's principal wife but a concubine. This disclosure almost certainly owed its origin to Liu. Eventually, however, the seal of respectability was set on Madame Kuo when Queen Victoria herself gave her a special audience at Osborne, shortly before the ambassador's return to China in January 1879.⁵

¹ 'A Chinaman in London', *Blackwood's Magazine* (Oct. 1901), p. 492.
² *Punch*, 10 Feb. 1877, pp. 58–9.
³ The Western diplomatic community in Peking was aware that Madame Kuo was not Kuo's principal wife, as we may see from a report submitted by one of the Secretaries of the French legation in Peking, cited by Cordier, *Relations de la Chine*, ii.112: 'Kuo, qui est veuf depuis nombre d'années, emmène cependant avec lui deux petites femmes ou concubines, toutes deux d'un certain âge.' Chang also refers to her as *ju-fu-jen* (concubine), *Sui-shih jih-chi*, p. 379a.
⁴ *Punch*, 10 Feb. 1877, p. 65.
⁵ *Macartney*, p. 291; the *Illustrated London News*, 24 Feb. 1877, p. 171, com-

Londoners soon grew used to the sight of members of the Embassy at social occasions. We may note, for example, that shortly after their arrival the whole Embassy went off to the Queen's Theatre to see a performance of the new opera *Biorn*, which they must have endured with much the same uncomprehending stoicism as an Englishman would have displayed at a Chinese opera.[1] The standing of the Embassy was soon increased by an incident in which one of the Embassy servants, out shopping with Chang Te-yi, was attacked by a drunk.[2] Kuo put in a personal plea on behalf of the accused, which was thought very sporting of him and added greatly to the popularity of these Chinese visitors, who became the lions of London society that season.[3]

Later, this incident had a somewhat melodramatic sequel, when another member of Kuo's staff had his pigtail pulled by a young lout in Oxford Street and retaliated by striking his assailant over the head with his umbrella. The youth slipped and fell under a cart, which injured his foot. On having this matter brought to his notice by receiving a lawyer's letter demanding compensation, Kuo fell into a rage at what he considered the serious misconduct of one of his staff and it was with only the greatest difficulty that Macartney dissuaded him from having the offender summarily beheaded in the cellars of Portland Place![4] But there were also matters of more serious import for Kuo's attention. His original

---

mented: 'Kuo-Ta-jên is accompanied by Lady Kuo, who may be said to be the first lady of position who has ever ventured beyond the shores of the Central Kingdom. During her voyage to England, in conformity with Chinese ideas of propriety she remained during the whole time in the strictest seclusion, never once having even taken a seat on deck.'

[1] *The Times*, 17 Feb. 1877, p. 6b.

[2] Chang, *Sui-shih jih-chi*, p. 222b. See translation below, p. 155.

[3] *The Times*, 2 Feb 1877, p. 11d, reports that John Donovan, an Irishman, was charged before Mr. Knox with being drunk and assaulting Chang A-mao. The prisoner, who admitted that he 'did not like the religion of those people', nevertheless maintained that he was merely playing. He was sentenced to two months with hard labour. See Appendix, p. 189. The *Illustrated London News*, 24 Feb. 1877, p. 171, mentions 'the hearty welcome shown [to the envoys] by the cheering of the people' wherever they went.

[4] *Macartney*, pp. 284–5. Boulger gives a rendering of a letter purportedly written by Kuo which concludes: 'The minister then begged to inform Lord Derby that he had given orders for the immediate execution of the offender within the precincts of the Legation.' (p. 286.) I have found no trace of this letter in the Foreign Office files. Boulger must have come across it in Macartney's papers. It may have been written, but I doubt that it was ever sent.

Introduction

credentials, which had been drawn up by the Tsungli Yamen, were now discovered to be valid only for his position as leader of the Mission of Apology. If he was to remain in England he would need new credentials, as would Liu Hsi-hung, whose name had not been mentioned in the original documents at all. Liu, however, was far from happy at the prospect of staying on to work under Kuo in London and accordingly sent home a memorial asking for permission to return to Peking. Eventually the Court confirmed Kuo in his post as Resident Minister in London but transferred Liu to Berlin, as the first Chinese Ambassador to Germany. Liu received his appointment on 12 May 1877, left England on 13 November and presented his credentials in Berlin on the 26th of the same month.[1] A few months later, on 20 April 1878, Kuo was concurrently appointed Ambassador to France, presenting his credentials in Paris on 6 May.[2] In the space of eighteen months China had established diplomatic relations with three European countries and taken her place in the family of nations. In addition, Ch'en Lan-pin had been appointed envoy to the United States, Spain, and Peru in 1875, presenting his credentials in these countries between September 1878 and April 1880.[3] Ho Ju-chang became the first Chinese Ambassador to Japan, presenting his credentials on 17 December 1878.[4] The Manchu, Ch'ung-hou, in charge of the Ili negotiations, presented his credentials in St. Petersburg on 20 January 1879.[5]

Kuo's two years in London were to be very busy ones. His post was not unduly onerous, but such duties as he had he took very seriously. His correspondence with the Earl of Derby and his successor the Marquis of Salisbury fills two bulky files in the Foreign Office Records.[6] These letters, which show Kuo's noteworthy grasp of the main issues involved, are also remarkable for their careful attention to detail.

[1] *The Times*, 14 Nov. 1877, p. 6f; 15 Nov. 1877, p. 9e; 29 Nov. 1877, p. 9f.
[2] F.O. 17/794, Kuo to Salisbury, 22 April 1878. The actual appointment was made in Peking on 22 Feb. 1878. Kuo had also been promoted from the rank of Senior Vice-President of the Board of Ceremonies to a position on the Board of War even prior to his appointment as Ambassador to France.
[3] Hsü, *China's Entrance*, p. 185. Ch'en, a Senior Secretary of the Board of Punishments, presented his credentials in Washington on 29 Sept. 1878; in Madrid on 24 May 1879; and in Lima on 17 April 1880.
[4] Ho Ju-chang, a Han-lin editor, was accompanied by an associate envoy, Chang Ssu-kuei. Hsü, *China's Entrance*, p. 186.
[5] Hsü, *China's Entrance*, p. 186.   [6] F.O. 17/768 and 794.

Introduction li

Kuo's main concern was with the Chefoo convention, which had been ratified by the Chinese in September 1876, but was not to be ratified by the British until 1885.

The difficulties were caused by two factors: the *likin* and the opium trade. The question of which areas were to be exempt from the *likin* concerned all the treaty powers, whereas the opium problem was a matter for discussion between Britain and China alone. Trade in opium, which had been legalized in 1858 and was still expanding, was regarded with some ambivalence by the Chinese government. On the one hand, Peking professed a moral objection to the use of opium; on the other hand, half the import duty revenue of the Chinese government was derived from taxes on the drug. Under the terms of the Convention, China was to collect both an import tax and a variable *likin* on opium, a measure which would have had the effect of discouraging smuggling, raising revenue, and drastically reducing the import of opium from India, which was costing China £6,000,000 to £8,000,000 sterling a year. The Calcutta authorities found these provisions disturbing, since they were afraid that the Chinese would tax Indian opium at a rate designed to exclude it from China for ever. Their fears were not to be quieted until 1884, when the Foreign Office finally came to an agreement on the opium tax with Kuo's successor in London, Marquis Tseng.[1]

In addition to the problems raised by the Chefoo Convention, Kuo found himself occupied with a number of other matters ranging from the question of the appointment of Chinese consuls in British dependencies[2] to attacks on missionaries,[3] the shooting of two Chinese fishermen at Foochow,[4] a collision between a China Navigation Company steamer and a salt-junk,[5] and

---

[1] D. E. Owen, *British Opium Policy in China and India*, pp. 251–79. Interestingly enough, a rumour–almost certainly originated by Liu–went round that Kuo himself was an opium smoker. This gained such currency that Macartney had to scotch it by writing a letter to *The Times*, 31 Aug. 1877, denying this.

[2] F.O. 17/768, Kuo to Derby, 3 Mar. 1877.

[3] F.O. 17/794, Kuo to Derby, 12 Mar. 1878.

[4] F.O. 17/794, Kuo to Salisbury, 21 May 1878. Two fishermen had been shot by a certain Antonio, an employee of Messrs, Elles and Company, Foochow. In this long and very carefully reasoned letter, Kuo presents his case on the basis of treaty rights, international law, and previous cases of the murder of Chinese by Englishmen.

[5] F.O. 17/768, Kuo to Derby, 14 July 1877.

the reception of a Chinese educational mission.[1] Kuo's handling of these matters was firm, tactful, and astute. This is particularly apparent in his approach to the case of John Wolfe, a missionary of the Church Mission of England, whose mission premises at Wu-chih-shan, Foochow, had been attacked by a crowd of local Chinese infuriated by Wolfe's disturbance of local geomantic harmony through his building activities. In his letter to Salisbury informing him of the destruction of the mission, Kuo pointed out that Wolfe was at fault in this matter, since 'according to the law and usage of nations, the land and houses having been rented and not sold to him he was not entitled to make changes without having first consulted and obtained the permission of the owner'. He then went on to point out that Wolfe was a notorious troublemaker and asked for his deportation.[2] Kuo's growing knowledge of the rules of the game of international law was here put to good service. The tone of this letter contrasts markedly with that of his conciliatory letter to Derby on an earlier occasion, apologizing for an attack on a group of missionaries at Wu-ch'ang by a group of candidates for the local military examinations.[3] On this occasion, Kuo admits, the Chinese were in the wrong and would be punished accordingly. Obviously, he was nothing if not flexible in his approach to the often high-handed British dignitaries with whom he was dealing.

Kuo also spent considerable time and effort in an endeavour to establish Chinese consulates abroad, particularly in Hong Kong and Australia, where he felt their presence was urgently needed. He had already scored a notable success by setting up a wealthy Cantonese merchant Ho Ah Kay (Hu Hsüan-tse) as Chinese consul in Singapore, but met with considerable resistance when he attempted to extend this practice elsewhere. The Foreign Office pointed out that China had no treaty rights to appoint

[1] F.O. 17/768, Kuo to Derby, 25 June 1877. The mission, which consisted of a party of twelve naval students, visited various naval dockyards and ships. Nine of the twelve officers were later seconded to the Royal Navy, six of them attending the Royal Naval College at Dartmouth. F.O. 17/768, Kuo to Derby, 3 Oct. 1877.

[2] F.O. 17/794, Kuo to Salisbury, 19 Nov. 1878; see Appendix, p. 190. We may note that Kuo was elected honorary Vice-President of the Association for the Reform and Codification of the Law of Nations at its Sixth Annual Conference in 1878, his name remaining in every issue of the Association's *Report* until 1922. See Hsü, *China's Entrance*, pp. 206-7.

[3] F.O. 17/794, Kuo to Derby, 12 Mar. 1878; see Appendix, p. 193.

Introduction

consuls abroad and went on to argue, with a certain insolence, that China could not claim the usual privileges accorded to other countries because she had not freely opened her gates to foreigners but had been compelled to do so.[1] Kuo, however, contended soundly enough that the appointment of consuls rested on international law and that it was his country's duty 'to overlook her subjects in foreign countries and to prevent as far as possible disputes and disturbances from arising'.[2] The matter was still unresolved when Kuo left England, though the official notice of the appointment of Ho Ah Kay as Consul in Singapore, which appeared just before his departure, must have given him cause for satisfaction.[3]

In June 1877, Kuo was present at an anniversary dinner of the Royal Literary Fund at which he made a speech in Chinese, with Macartney acting as interpreter.[4] He spoke of the Chinese debt to the early Jesuits, in particular Ricci, Verbiest (1623–88), and Schall (1591–1666), from whom China had acquired a knowledge of mathematics, timepieces, and firearms. He then went on to say that during the three months he had been in London he had met several famous scientists—Tyndal and Owen among them—and had attended their lectures. Since science in England was open to all and was supported by an excellent government, he concluded, it was not surprising that Western nations were superior to China in construction of all kinds.

These remarks of Kuo's cannot be discounted as mere after-dinner bonhomie. He was undoubtedly impressed by Western science, not as mere technology which could be used for the defence of traditional values, but as a means of 'investigating things' (*ko wu*), to employ the famous phrase much used by Chu Hsi (1130–1200). Here again we discern the influence of the materialist philosopher Wang Fu-chih, whose impact on Kuo's thought has been mentioned earlier. Wang's contemporary, Yen Yüan (1635–1704), another philosopher with whom Kuo was certainly acquainted, had attempted to bring about a revolution in Chinese

---

[1] F.O. 17/794, Pauncefote to Derby, 2 Jan. 1878.
[2] F.O. 17/794, Kuo to Derby, 2 Jan. 1878; see Appendix, p. 189. The Chinese in Australia had to wait until 1909 before a Chinese consul was appointed, though from as early as 1861 onwards there were never less than 30,000 Chinese in Australia.
[3] *London Gazette*, 24 Dec. 1878.
[4] *North China Herald*, 23 June 1877, p. 623.

education by introducing science and technology into the classical curriculum. As Joseph Needham has put it: 'The Chang Nan Shu Yuan, as it was called, had not only a gymnasium, but also halls filled with machines of war for demonstration and practice, special rooms for mathematics and geography, an astronomical observatory and facilities for learning hydraulic engineering, architecture, agriculture, applied chemistry and pyrotechnics'.[1] In his admiration for science, Kuo was simply reviving an older Chinese tradition which had fallen into desuetude during the nineteenth century. In this he was very different from his fellow ambassador Liu Hsi-hung, whose philosophical standpoint looked back to the Neo-Confucianism of idealists like Wang Yang-ming (1472-1528), rather than to the revival of Han learning of the seventeenth and eighteenth centuries, with its stress on wide learning careful investigation and clear reasoning.

Liu Hsi-hung's diary, which he kept up throughout his stay, provides us with a viewpoint very different from that of Kuo's journal. Surprisingly enough, Liu's attitude to foreigners and all their works, at first deeply distrustful, seems to have mellowed considerably during his sojourn in London. The early diary entries are openly suspicious of the West. He shows himself especially hostile towards European railway building in China, which he thought would endanger the security of the country and the livelihood of the people.[2] He was also contemptuous of the Japanese reformers, who had recently enforced the adoption of Western law and even Western dress upon their subjects. The Chinese, he maintained, must preserve their own customs or make themselves a laughing-stock and lose their self-respect, as the Japanese had done. Western ways were not for them.[3]

Opposed as he was to the westernization of China, Liu was nevertheless remarkably objective and fair-minded when it came to appraising the achievements of Westerners in their own countries. The Western Tao was not for China; but there could be no denying its successes.

We have been in London for two months. When we observe their politics and customs carefully, we notice that nobles and humble

---

[1] Needham, *Science and Civilisation in China*, ii.515.
[2] Liu, *Ying-yao jih-chi*, pp. 160a-161a. See translation below, p. 111.
[3] Ibid., p. 165a. See translation below, p. 116.

people alike do not make much of the relationship between father and son and the difference between man and woman. Yet there are no idle officials, no unemployed subjects, no barrier between the high and the low, no cruel or inhumane politics, no use of empty words to deceive. From the prime minister down, every office has one chief, four assistants, and several other clerks. Every day, from 12 o'clock on, they all work hard at their job, leaving at 6 p.m. to return home. Not only are the common officials very busy in their work, but even the Prime Minister and other high officials devote themselves whole-heartedly to their tasks and yet appear never to be able to come to the end of their labours. That is why I say how there are no idle officials. Scholars, farmers, artisans, and traders all devote their minds and their energies to their tasks; poor and unemployed persons are taken off to do manual labour. Throughout the whole country, there are no gambling houses and no opium dens. In their free time, the people hold boat races, horse races, and boxing and high jumping contests, all to foster military training. That is why I say there are no idle subjects. Every city, village, town and district elects one or two representatives to Parliament, who can, at any time, communicate the wishes of the people to the officials. Even merchants trading abroad have a central trade association in London, which is also under the charge of a member of Parliament, to act as a mediator between the government and the people. When the wishes of the people are considered inopportune by the officials, they must be interrogated on the facts of the case until agreement is reached; then the necessary measures are taken. That is why I say there is no barrier between them. The penal system is very lenient; there is no capital punishment by beheading, nor flogging. Criminals are put in prison and well fed. Even cattle and horses are not beaten overmuch. The poor and lonely, the disabled and sick, as well as refugees from different places are placed in houses of charity, where the sovereign frequently sends people to inspect their conditions of living. Every few leagues one finds big buildings for the cure of the sick, to which the sovereign also sends the royal physician on visits. During battles, there is slaughter only at the front, but it is forbidden to wound captives and to imprison and harm civilians. That is why I say there is no cruel government. Those who are employed are busy all their lives and very law-abiding. In cases of deceit or unfaithfulness, the whole affair, with all its rights and wrongs, advantages and disadvantages, is very thoroughly debated, in order that everyone may understand the matter clearly and precisely. In taking and receiving, people also behave straightforwardly, without deceit, not pretending to be solicitous, nor affecting false modesty. All men and women act alike in this. That is why I say there is no use of empty words in human relations. During our two months here, when we have visited others or gone to parties we have often passed through the streets, but never have we heard people shouting or quarrelling, nor have we seen anyone looking sad or worried. When we observe the fact that, from Gilbraltar eastwards, going south to Malta, India, Aden, Ceylon, Penang, Singapore, Hong Kong and Australia, the English can travel for thousands of leagues over the sea and have taken over those important places where they can stop their ships and establish cities, but have not gone inland to occupy any territory, it is clear that their intention is only to trade.[1]

The last sentence, asserting that the English had come to China not to conquer but to trade, is a particularly startling one, since it represents a direct reversal of his earlier views. Its effect on the conservative faction at home must have been all the more impressive in view of Liu's known hostility to the West. In the light of this evidence, we must be prepared to modify our opinions of Liu. He was not the stubborn bigot that contemporary Western observers like Macartney and Cordier made him out to be. He may have been an intriguer, a former of factions, a man activated by malice as his critics allege, though even here we must realize that his enmity for Kuo may have been motivated as much by principle as by jealousy and spite, since he saw Kuo as a traitor to his country. But in the light of his diary we can safely assert that he was no hide-bound, blinkered reactionary. In fact, he shows a flexibility of mind which would be surprising in any man of his age and background and is astonishing in that most conservative of conservatives, a Chinese official. Very few Westerners who went to China were able to judge it with as much detachment and objectivity as Liu brought to bear on the West. The intolerance and bigotry of the great majority of the European missionaries, merchants, and officials in China contrasts very unfavourably with Liu's willingness to see things in perspective.[2] There were few things more shocking, for instance, to a Confucian than violations of sexual decorum. Yet Liu comments on the bare arms and bosoms of fashionable society and the promiscuous mingling of men and women (for no Chinese lady would ever have appeared

---

[1] Ibid., p. 178a–b.
[2] Kipling exemplifies the state of mind of many Westerners of the time: 'Now I understand why the civilized European of Irish extraction kills the Chinaman in America. It is justifiable to kill him. It would be quite right to wipe the city of Canton off the face of the earth, and to exterminate all the people who ran away from the shelling. The Chinaman ought not to count.' Rudyard Kipling, *From Sea to Sea and Other Sketches*, p. 306.

Introduction lvii

at any social function or spoken to a strange man) with all the dispassionate detachment of an anthropologist commenting on the sexual mores of a Pacific islander. He was not even scandalized by the statues of naked women scattered around London's galleries, nor upset by what he took to be a full-length nude of Queen Victoria herself hung for public display in the hall of Buckingham Palace![1] One has only to contrast such observations with the self-righteous fulminations of Western missionaries against the 'filthy and odious vices of heathen Chinamen' to realize that Neo-Confucianism, for all its shortcomings, was far less intolerant and uncompromising than Victorian Christianity. There is a certain detachment about Liu's diary which reminds one of that cast of mind typical of the eighteenth century in Europe. We might, perhaps not unfairly, call him a Chinese Burkean.

Liu differed from Kuo in that though he was willing to praise the achievements of Western civilization, he was totally opposed to its introduction into China. Admirable as the Tao of the barbarians may have been in many of its manifestations, it was not for import. Like Marquis Tseng, Liu believed that Western civilization had originally sprung from China, a conviction which undoubtedly made it easier for him to accept it and praise it. But he also believed that during the course of the centuries it had become so modified that it would be impossible, even if it were desirable, to introduce it to China again.

[Such scientific subjects as] electricity... dynamics, and chemistry are what the English call real knowledge, while they consider the teaching of our Chinese sages as empty and useless talk. Chinese officials who are deceived by their words often agree with them. I argue against these beliefs, saying that their real knowledge consists only of petty, miscellaneous tricks, which can be used to make 'a utensil' of but limited capacity...

... They concentrate on such miscellaneous tricks, using boats and vehicles made to bring in profit, and firearms made for killing, trying to produce more and more of such things to become wealthy and strong. How can we call all this useful, real knowledge? Since the beginning of history, China has endured longer than any other civilization, and has produced a hundred and several dozen sages one after another, daily refining and completing their [social and moral] institutions. The depth of our philosophical discussions greatly exceeds

[1] Liu, *Ying-yao jih-chi*, p. 175b. See translation below, p. 128.

those of the West. Foreigners consider material wealth as true wealth: China takes temperance as true wealth; Western nations think brute force is strength: China takes deference as strength. This is the real truth. It cannot be explained in a few hurried words.[1]

Liu's diary shows that Neo-Confucian opposition to Westernization was not based on mere self-interest and irrational prejudice. Once its initial premises are granted, the rest follows logically. Liu realized that it was not possible for China to accept only what it wanted from the West and reject the rest. One either took all or nothing.

The West considers the building of steamships and trains as progress. But I dare not say whether this is real progress or retrogression... If this comes from the Will of Heaven however, a man can do nothing about it. For example, with steamboats we Chinese did not at first want to imitate the foreigners, but now we have about twenty or thirty of boats... Now we have steamboats, we must use coal and make more iron cannons; having to use more iron and coal and not being able to ask for them from Western countries the question of opening mines arises. But then, what will be needed for the transport of coal and iron? What about the cost of labour and the difficulty of the roads? We must naturally then discuss the construction of railways. This shows how things are mutually related. One thing will lead to another, and we will not be able to refuse them.[2]

This is as perspicacious a statement as one could wish. It anticipates the conclusions reached by modern historians that the structure of Confucian China could not be modified by Westernization without bringing the whole edifice down in ruins. There could be no symbiosis between Confucianism and industrialization. As a Chinese Burkean, Liu merits our respect if not our admiration. He was not a reactionary but simply a conservative, and moreover one whose opposition to technology links him with modern Western thinkers like Jacques Ellul.

It soon became apparent that a clash between the conservative Liu and the radical Kuo was inevitable. Carried away by his enthusiasm for European civilization, Kuo was incautious enough to send home a series of outspoken dispatches advocating modernization. All were highly critical of the backwardness of China.

[1] Ibid., pp. 183b–184a. See translation below, p. 135–136.
[2] Ibid., p. 192a–b. See translation below, p. 142–143.

Introduction

The Japanese Ambassador, on meeting me, remarked that Westerners know how to exploit the world. They do the hard part; we do the easy part. How can we therefore continue to neglect such matters? Other countries envy our vast territories and our numerous population, and pity us when they hear that up to now we have not yet made efforts to strengthen ourselves. On hearing such words I felt very ashamed and could find no answer.[1]

Nothing the West has done has been more harmful to us than opium. Even English gentlemen themselves are ashamed of the fact that they have used this harmful trade as an excuse for provoking hostilities with China, and are making a serious effort to eradicate the evil. Yet our Chinese scholar-officials complacently degrade themselves by smoking opium, and do so without remorse. This has been for several decades already our national disgrace, exhausting much money and man-power, and poisoning the lives of our people. And yet there is not one man who feels ashamed of it.

At present, every home possesses such [western] articles as clocks watches, and toys, while Western textiles and woollens are to be found even in the remote countryside. In Kiangsu and Chekiang it is even the practice to neglect our own currency and to make use of foreign money, the value of which is even raised, without any thought whatsoever of right and wrong. And yet, when our people hear of the building of railways and the spreading of telegraphy, they become enraged and crowd together to create difficulties. There are even people who stir up public anger when they set eyes on foreign machines. When Tseng Chi-kang, on account of a death in his family, took a small steam-boat from Nanking to Ch'ang-sha, many officials and important men raised a hue and cry which lasted for several years without cease. Such people willingly allow others to harm us and squeeze the marrow from our bones, and yet with their whole strength close up the sources of our national revenue. It is really difficult to understand their motives. After thirty years of foreign relations, our provincial authorities still know nothing. All they can do is to impose their ignorant ideas on the Court and call this 'public opinion'. The Court encourages them to do this and uses 'public opinion' as a cover for its own purposes. Sad to say, the common people have long been denied an outlet which would permit them to submit their complaints to higher authorities. And yet, the ignorant have been made use of and the unemployed have been stirred up to the attainment of purely selfish ends, all this with the help of many of our officials. The weakening of the Sung and the downfall

[1] Kuo's letter to Li Hung-chang from London (1877). See translation below, p. 97 ff.

of the Ming, were both the outcome of the actions of such irresponsible and ignorant people.[1]

Such radically outspoken opinions brought down a storm of furious criticism on Kuo's head. Foremost among his persecutors was Liu Hsi-hung, his vanity stung by the English refusal to recognize him as Second Ambassador. Even after his appointment as Ambassador to Germany he carried on with his campaign of defamation against Kuo.[2] Chang Te-yi alleges in his diary that one of the reasons for Kuo's recall was that he had allegedly made himself a laughing-stock by his behaviour when having his portrait painted by an English artist.[3] Another excuse was that Madame Kuo, contrary to all Confucian rules of propriety, had received her guests at a soireé in accordance with Western etiquette and shaken hands with all the gentlemen present.[4] These, however, were no more than excuses. The fact was that the publication of Kuo's journal had roused the feelings of Chinese officialdom to such a pitch that his impeachment and instant recall for punishment were both being loudly demanded.[5] Only the protection afforded by such powerful figures as Li Hung-chang and Tseng Chi-tse (1839–90)[6] saved Kuo from his detractors. During an audience with the Empress Dowager in 1878, Marquis Tseng, who was then on his way to take over the post of Minister to

[1] Ibid.
[2] Liu had been promoted to the vacant post of Sub-Director of the Banqueting Court after his appointment as Ambassador, *Peking Gazette*, 2 June 1877, as quoted in *North China Herald*, 23 June 1877, p. 616b
[3] Chang, *Sui shih jih-chi*, p. 287a–b. See translation below, p. 165 ff.
[4] Chang, ibid., p. 379a, records that he dissuaded Kuo from putting Madame Kuo's name on the invitation cards on the ground that since she was a concubine she was not his social equal. Though this would give no offence in Western countries, he argued (sic), it would be bound to give offence in Peking and thus lend Kuo's enemies another stick to beat him with. The reception, held at Portland Place on 19 June 1878, created something of a stir in London Society. Over 790 guests were present.
[5] Ho Chin-shou, a Hanlin reader, impeached Kuo; Chang P'ei-lun, secretary and son-in-law to Li Hung-chang, demanded his recall. See Chang P'ei-lun, *Chien-yü chi*, i.28a–b; *Ch'ing-chi wai-chiao shih-liao*, xii.29.
[6] Tseng Chi-tse was the eldest son of Tseng Kuo-fan. On the death of his father he inherited the hereditary title *hou*, and was henceforward known in the West as Marquis Tseng. He was appointed Minister to England in 1878, presenting his credentials on 20 Mar. 1879. His most outstanding diplomatic achievement was the conclusion with Russia of the Treaty of St. Petersburg (1881), which was generally regarded as a diplomatic triumph for China. He was a close friend of Kuo and Halliday Macartney.

Introduction

England, went so far as to beg the throne to see that Kuo came to no harm, since he was 'an upright and straightforward person' who had 'risked damage to his reputation in order to manage affairs for the nation.'[1] To this the Empress assented.

Thanks to such good offices on the part of such few friends as remained to him, Kuo was eventually allowed to return in peace to his estate in Hunan[2]—though he dared not risk life and limb by going to Peking, as was customary—where he spent some time teaching at the Ch'eng-nan Academy in Ch'ang-sha before retiring into obscurity to write his memoirs.[3]

Blunt, honest, outspoken to the point of tactlessness, Kuo nevertheless towers above all but a handful of his contemporaries in insight and mature wisdom. It was his misfortune to live in an age when such qualities, especially when applied to foreign affairs, could receive no recognition. He would appear to have had only one disciple. This was the future political scientist Yen Fu (1853-1921), at that time a young student in London. In a commentary to his translation (1905-9) of Montesquieu's *L'Esprit des lois*, Yen recalls that he was overwhelmed by the superiority of the British legal system to the Chinese after witnessing the operations of the London law-courts. He told Kuo that 'the reason why Great Britain and the other countries of Europe are wealthy and powerful is that impartial justice is daily extended. Here is the ultimate root.'[4] Kuo entirely agreed with him for he had himself 'admired the pains taken in order to investigate the circumstances of the case, their caution in arriving at a decision, and their respect for human life evinced in their passing sentence.'[5] Thereafter, in spite of their great differences in status, 'they often spent whole days and nights discussing differences and similarities in Chinese and Western thought and political institutions'.[6]

---

[1] Tseng Chi-tse, *Tseng Hui-min-kung shih-hsi jih-chi*, in HFH (*Tsai pu pien*), xi.1a-7a. This passage has been translated in Teng and Fairbank, *China's Response*, p. 106.

[2] Kuo arrived in Shanghai on board the *Anadyr* on 26 Mar. 1879. Cordier, *Relations de la Chine*, ii.133.

[3] His memoirs, *Yü-ch'ih lao-jen tzu-hsü*, are largely an apologia for his political beliefs. Only 54 pages long, they devote little space to his mission to England.

[4] Yen Fu, *Fa-yi*, *Yen yi ming-chu ts'ung-k'an*, vol. v, bk. xi, ch. 6, p. 8.

[5] F.O. 17/794, Kuo to Derby, 21 May 1878.

[6] Wang Ch'ü-ch'ang, *Yen Chi-tao nien-p'u*, p. 7. Quoted in Schwarz, *In Search of Wealth and Power*, p. 29. Schwarz goes on to comment: 'Kuo Sung-t'ao was one of those who had already gone beyond the self-strengthening formula of the T'ung-chih statesmen to a realization that nothing less than a full devotion to

But Kuo was to find no other adherents to his cause besides Yen Fu until after his death in 1891, when he became the idol of the Hunanese reform movement.[1] To appreciate just how far Kuo was ahead of his time one has only to contrast his views with those of his successor in London, Marquis Tseng. Though Tseng was an intelligent and likeable fellow and basically sympathetic towards the West, he had no understanding of the unique nature of Western civilization, which he saw as essentially derivative from that of China![2]

It is obvious that when Kuo contrasted the depth of his own understanding of the West with that of his contemporaries he was not merely boasting. It was for such insight perhaps, as much as his devotion to his ideals that Li Hung-chang paid him belated tribute by having his name inscribed in the Bureau of National History, much against the wishes of his enemies.[3] This posthumous honour was the only reward Kuo was to reap for a lifetime of brave and faithful service to a country which, as he was well aware, was proceeding to its downfall with all the blind assurance of a sleep-walker.

Ultimately, Kuo was a failure. Not only was he unsuccessful in converting the gentry and the bureaucracy to his views, but he also elicited a conservative backlash which played a major part in repressing the reform movement of the *Kuang-hsü* period (1875–1908).[4] History has continued to deal harshly with him. The Chinese Communist regime, exemplifying the old dictum that the views of the extreme left often coincide with those of the extreme right, has also excoriated him as a traitor who was prepared to sell his country to the Western powers. As he once remarked despairingly of himself: 'Half accomplished in scholarship, half successful in his official career, how often were his life's ambitions realized?'[5] The spectacle of the destruction of the repu-

---

the goals of wealth and power would suffice. What is more, his stay in England was leading his thought in the same direction as that of his young fellow countryman [Yen Fu], and well beyond that of Li Hung-chang. Political institutions, legal institutions, social arrangements, and even values and ideas all were involved in the wealth and power of the West.'

[1] Charlton M. Lewis, 'The Reform Movement in Hunan (1896–1898)', in *Papers on China*, 15 (1961), 62–90.
[2] See note 5, p. lxiv.
[3] Hsü, *China's Entrance*, p. 190   [4] Hamilton, p. 23.
[5] P'eng Tse-yi, p. 64: 'Hsüeh-wen pan-t'ung, kuan pan-hsien, yi-sheng huai-pao chi ts'eng k'ai.'

Introduction lxiii

tation of a man whose only 'fatal flaw' was that he was too honest, too courageous, too intelligent, and too far-sighted for his time, is a sobering one. The ironies of history afford no consolation.

This first Chinese mission to England constitutes not only the opening chapter of the diplomatic history of China, but also an important contribution to the history of ideas. Indeed, diplomatically these early envoys on the whole accomplished very little. They were far too busy keeping their diaries, purchasing guns and munitions, looking after the interests of their compatriots abroad and trying to cope with a bewildering, unfamiliar world to have much time left for active diplomacy aimed at improving China's international status. The lasting value of their work is to be found rather in the part they played in introducing the West to China. Their diaries and voyage-journals, though often naive and quaintly ill-informed, continued to be a source of guidance and inspiration to the Chinese for many years after they were written. A careful perusal of these works will prove even more enlightening to the historian anxious to trace the still largely unwritten history of China's discovery of Europe. As Collingwood remarked in that seminal work, *The Idea of History*, we study the past only in order to understand the present.[1] To learn something of what the Chinese thought of the West when they first encountered it, is to go a long way towards understanding how China looks at the West even today.

[1] R. Collingwood, *The Idea of History* (Oxford, 1963), p. 10.

NOTES

[1] We may make a somewhat arbitrary distinction here between the Western impact on China—a process in which China was largely passive—which lasted until roughly 1860 or so, and the Chinese response to the West, which may be said to have begun with the *T'ung-chih* Restoration of 1862–74. Intellectual history is, of course, inextricably woven with political, economic, and diplomatic history. Hence the reader should consult works such as the following: Teng Ssu-yü and John K. Fairbank (with E-tu Zen Sun and Chaoying Fang), *China's Response to the West: A Documentary Survey 1839–1923*; Mary C. Wright, *The Last Stand of Chinese Conservatism, The T'ung-chih Restoration, 1862–1874*; Masataka Banno, *China and the West, 1858–1861: The origins of the Tsungli Yamen*; Immanuel C. Y. Hsü, *China's Entrance into the Family of Nations: The Diplomatic Phase, 1858–1880*; Benjamine I. Schwartz, *In Search of Wealth and Power: Yen Fu and the West*; Joseph R. Levenson, *Confucian China and Its Modern Fate*, 3 vols.; André Chih, *L'Occident 'Chrétien' vu par les Chinois vers la fin du XIXe siècle (1870–1900)*.

Introduction

The best general work on China's relations with the West is Fang Hao, *Chung-hsi chiao-t'ung shih*, 5 vols.

² Hsieh, who came from Chia-ying county in Kwantung, had spent fourteen years as a sailor on a foreign ship travelling around the chief ports of the world. His reminiscences of Europe were dictated to a friend of his, Yang Ping-nan, in 1820. A scholar named Wu Lanh-siu (*chü-jen* of 1808) then used Hsieh's observations to write the *Hai-lu*. See Kenneth Ch'en, '*Hai-lu*, Forerunner of Chinese Travel Accounts of Western Countries', *Monumenta Serica*, vii (1942), 208–26. Ch'en remarks (p. 226) that even though Hsieh's work is 'the best in the period under discussion', we must realize that 'keeping in mind what the Europeans knew about China, the paucity of information contained in the *Hai-lu* about the West stands out in glaring contrast'. It is a pity that none of the handful of brilliant Chinese scholars who visited the West during the seventeenth and eighteenth centuries as Jesuit protégés have left any record of their sojourn. The *Yi-yü lu* (*Description of a Foreign Country*) of K'ang-hsi's emissary, Tulisen, who was sent to meet the chief of the Turyüd tribe in 1714, is probably the earliest Ch'ing account of any Western country.

³ A brief biography of Kuo is to be found in A. W. Hummel, ed., *Eminent Chinese of the Ch'ing Period*, 2 vols. A pioneering article is that of D. Hamilton, 'Kuo Sung-tao: A Maverick Confucian', *Papers on China*, 15 (1961), 1–29. Kuo wrote an autobiography, *Yü-ch'ih-lao-jen tzu-hsü* (*Memoirs of the Old Man of the Jade Pool*), first printed in 1893. His biography, written by Liu Ting-sheng, is found in Kuo's collected works, *Yang-chih shu-wu yi-chi* (55 chüan, 1892), xvi. 1a–10b. Other works on Kuo are those of Yang Hung-lieh, 'Chi Kuo Sung-t'ao ch'u-shih Ying Fa', parts 1 and 2 in *Ku-chin*, xi (1942), 11–5, and xii (1942), 23–32, respectively; Yü Ch'ang-ho, 'Kuo Sung-t'ao yü Chung-kuo wai chiao', *Yi-ching*, xxxi (1937), 21–4; P'eng Tse-yi, 'Kuo Sung-t'ao chih ch'u-shih Ou-hsi chi ch'i kung-hsien', in *Chung-kuo chin-tai shih lun-ts'ung*, vii.64ff., hereafter referred to as P'eng Tse-yi. See also Hsü, *China's Entrance*, pp. 180–5, for a brief account of Kuo's career and his appointment to the mission. The final character of Kuo's personal name can be read as either 'tao' or 't'ao'. I have followed the latter reading.

⁴ Macartney also notes that: 'The passengers and the whole ship, indeed, were much impressed with the bearing and manners of the first Ambassador, but were much less so with Lieu tajen, who on several occasions committed many grave breaches of good manners. During dinner he choked and spat, and on one occasion, after an unusually successful attempt at expectoration, called his servant and ordered him to bring the spittoon into which he spued rather than spat. This was exceedingly disagreeable to the gentlemen sitting on the opposite side of the table, who turned away their faces and manifested the most decided signs of disgust.' (p. 267.) The *Straits Times*, 16 December 1876, carries another story in very much the same vein: 'The Shanghai papers relate the following story of the two Chinese envoys: Both paid a visit of inspection to the *Travancore* and having been offered refreshment they broached a bottle of Champagne like men and enjoyed it amazingly. Kuoh, the Chief Envoy, then asked for a cup of tea which was immediately provided and the Ambassadors courteously insisted upon drinking it in the English fashion with sugar and milk. Li Si-hung [*sic*], however, was for dipping his own teaspoon into the sugar basin, but in this he was stopped by the elder mandarin who told him that was not at all in accordance with foreign ideas of business.'

⁵ Tseng, *Ch'u-shih Ying-Fa jih-chi* in *HFH*, xi.385a–b: 'During the course of a conversation I had with Sung Sheng, one evening he put forward the view that the Western system of government and education was in many respects very similar to that of our *Chou-li*. He maintained that Lao-tzu had been an archivist

1. KUO SUNG T'AO

2. LIU HSI-HUNG

3. SIR HALLIDAY MACARTNEY

4. MADAME KUO

JOHN CHINAMAN.

Air.—"*A Highland Lad my Love was born.*"

"We have to announce the landing at Southampton, (Saturday, January 27), of QUOH-SUNG-TAO, the first Chinese Envoy ever accredited to this country, and suite."—*Shipping Intelligencer.*

A CHINAMAN QUOH-SUNG was born,
The "Foreign Devils" he held in scorn;
But some time ago those "Devils" began
To tread on the toes of John Chinaman.
  So like it or no, John Chinaman,
  You have got to go, John Chinaman,
  To the land of the "Outer-barba-ri-an,"
  An Ambassador, though, John Chinaman!

With his eyes aslant, and his pigtail's braid
Coiled neatly round his close-shaved head,
And his button a-top, Southampton ran
To behold this great Panjanderan!
  And if QUOH-SUNG is scarce so fine a man
  As we hoped for the sample Chinaman,
  How many big things from as little began
  As this Embassy from John Chinaman!

As stubborn as pigs, and as hard to steer,
With a taste for cheap buying and selling dear;
A decidedly difficult sort of man
To deal with, we've found John Chinaman.
  His own way he'll go, will John Chinaman;
  At no lie he'll shy, will John Chinaman;
  And he'll sell you a bargain whenever he can,
  In treaties or teas, will John Chinaman!

You may talk of your Yankee and Hebrew Jew,
But I guess they're small potatoes, and few
In a hill, compared with that yellow man,
After yellow boys keen, John Chinaman.
  He'll outdo our doos will John Chinaman;
  And he'll win where we lose, will John Chinaman;
  The dirt our miners have left he'll "pan,"
  And make it pay, will John Chinaman!

If all this he has learnt without leaving home,
What will it be now that he deigns to roam,
And from civilised Christians learns to plan
New dodges undreamed by John Chinaman?
  If in fits we would throw John Chinaman,
  Stock Exchange-wards show John Chinaman,
  Where promoters he'll study, financers scan,
  And go home an improved John Chinaman.

We'll invite him to dinner, and serve him in state,
On more costly than willow-pattern plate,
Set small-waisted ladies his heart to trepan,
Failing small-footed belles *à la* Chinaman.
  You shall go to crushes, John Chinaman,
  See Drawing-room rushes, John Chinaman;
  In West-End *soirées* be glad of your fan,
  And think of home-odours, John Chinaman.

Our ships, guns, rails, mills, shops, and towns,
From John o' Groat's House to the Sussex Downs,
Let QUOH-SUNG survey, study, plot, and plan,
As an extra-observant Chinaman.
  He may go back a gladder John Chinaman,
  Or, it may be, a sadder John Chinaman;
  But one riddle he'll scarce have read as he ran—
  Why JOHN BULL should despise John Chinaman.

5. JOHN CHINAMAN.

Punch, 10 February, 1877

TO THE TOTTERING LILY.

"WE hear that a Chinese lady (wife of one of the Staff of the Ambassador), whose name signifies the Tottering Lily of Fascination, has accompanied the Chinese Embassy to this country."—*Gossip of the Day.*

FAIR flower from the Flowery Land—
  How national is your *cognomen!*
An inability to stand
Is not the charm we most demand
      In Western women.

'Tis plain you've not been favoured yet
  With a Celestial MARY WALKER.
Ah me! how much you must regret,
Or should do, never having met
      That lively talker!

But pray don't bring in fashion here
  Your pedal fascination.

Of all that's hideous, awkward, queer,
Our Dames are quite too prompt, I fear,
      In emulation.

The Grecian bend, the Roman fall,
  Set all our beauties waddling, wobbling;
Sight of your tootsicums so small,
Fair totterer, might be setting all
        Our beauties hobbling!

The Chinese Totter! Taking name!
  Fancy presents appalling pictures.

Imagine all our Ladies lame,
And modish *bottiers* earning fame
      For ten-toe strictures!

We've lots of fashions, goodness knows,
  Which are—excuse me!—quite as silly.
You're welcome, dear, but don't disclose
To Western gaze those tiny toes,
      Sweet Tottering Lily!

6. TO THE TOTTERING LILY. *Punch*, 17 February, 1877

7. LI HUNG CHANG

8. SIR WILLIAM JERVOIS

of the Chou dynasty. Afterwards, when he went off to the West across the desert, he took the regulations and laws of the Chou along with him and so brought these documents over to the West. Unfortunately, however, we have no proof of this. I found this a novel and pleasing idea.

It was my contention that since in ancient times the inhabitants of Europe were all savages their cultures and political systems must, for the most part, have gradually spread westwards from their place of origin in Asia. This would explain why the people and customs of Europe resemble those of ancient China ... Indeed it is plain that we have already experienced in China all the situations that now confront the Westerners. Take, for instance, their common household appurtenances, all of which are inlaid and decorated, for they insist on luxury. They derived the inspiration for this from our Chinese goblets—carved goblets, painted goblets, inlaid drinking-cups, platters ... Perhaps it may be argued that in ancient times we had no steamships, trains and ingenious machines ... However, it is probable that in high antiquity the Middle Kingdom possessed countless types of machines. But material production gradually diminished as the people became indolent, so the art of making machinery was lost. When we look at the West today, we can see what China was like in high antiquity. When we look at China today, we can see what the West will be like in years to come. For one day the ingenious must be supplanted by the crude and the subtle by the simple ...'

I

Shih-hsi chi-ch'eng
(The Record of an Envoy's Journey to the West)
of Kuo Sung-t'ao

Kuang-hsü, second year, 10th month, 17th day, *chia-ch'en* [Saturday, 2 December 1876]

Mai Hua-t'o [W. H. Medhurst][1] informed me that the P & O steamer *Ta-fan-k'ou-erh* [*Travancore*] was due to depart at the *tzu* watch [11 p.m.–1 a.m.] on the eighteenth day.[2] At 2 p.m. she moved to her moorings at Hung-k'ou. I was informed that

---

[1] Sir Walter Henry Medhurst (1822–85), son of the China missionary Dr. Walter Henry Medhurst (1796–1857), entered the Foreign Service in 1840 as a Clerk in the Chinese Secretary's Office of the British Superintendency of Trade in China. From August 1841 onwards he was attached to Sir Henry Pottinger's Suite and was present at the taking of Amoy and Chusan during the Opium War. He subsequently served as Interpreter at Shanghai (1843); Vice-Consul at Amoy (1848); Chinese Secretary to the Superintendency of Trade in China (1850); Secretary and Registrar to the Superintendency of Trade (1853); Consul at Fuchow (1864), but transferred to Hankow; Acting Consul, Shanghai (1868). In January 1871 he became Consul at Shanghai, retiring from this post on 1 January 1877.

[2] 'Leaving per P & O steamer *Travancore* for Southampton, His Excellency Kwoh Sung-tao and suite, Dr. Macartney and Mr. W. C. Hillier' (*North China Herald*, 1 Dec. 1876, p. 552). The *Travancore* was on the P & O Shanghai to Bombay mail-run under the command of Captain W. Barratt. (See *North China Herald*, loc. cit.) The boat should have sailed at midnight on Thursday, but had been delayed for forty-eight hours at the express wish of Sir Thomas Wade, the British Minister, to allow the Embassy time to catch her. The normal timetable for the Shanghai–Bombay service was as follows: Shanghai (Dep.): 1 Dec.; Hong Kong (Arr.): 5 Dec.; Hong Kong (Dep.): 7 Dec.; Singapore (Arr.): 13 Dec.; Singapore (Dep.): 14 Dec.; Penang (Arr. & Dep.): 16 Dec.; Ceylon (Galle) (Arr.): 21 Dec.

The *Travancore* had been completed in Scotland in August 1867, and was a screw steamer with three decks and two masts. She was brig-rigged, with elliptic stern, was clench built, and had a female figurehead. Her dimensions were 281 ft. long, 35 ft. broad, and 27 ft. depth in hold. She had two direct-acting engines of 400 h.p. built by John Key, Kircaldy. Her gross tonnage was 1899; 1,185 tons register. The *Travancore* was lost off Cape Otranto, Southern Italy, in February 1880. (Information in letter from Public Relations Office, P & O Orient Lines, 16 Feb. 1966.)

we should be on board in good time, for it happened that my friends would be assembled there. In all the business, both public and personal, I had to transact, everything I did was extremely hurried. Kuan Ts'ai-shu and Chou Ying-shih[1] had been so kind as to come several hundred *li*[2] to see me off, yet I was unable to pay them a return visit. At the *wei* watch [1–3 p.m.] I sent a 400-*li* express-memorial from my post-station announcing the time of my departure abroad. I then began to use my official seal. I sent two despatches, one to the Tsungli Yamen, the other to the Senior Officers of the Northern and Southern Foreigners' Board, through the agency of Huang Hui-ho of the China Merchants' Steam Navigation Company.[3] A storm of wind and rain blew up, becoming really severe by nightfall. Li Mien-lin and Cheng Yü-hsien[4] sent a steamer to take us to Hung-k'ou. Over ten of our friends came as far as this with us. By then it was past ten o'clock. Our captain's name was Pa-la-te [Captain W. Barratt].[5]

18th day [3 December]

Raining. We left our anchorage exactly at midnight [on the 2nd]. As we came down the coast of Chekiang the gale buffeted us around so violently that all of my suite and the passengers were sick except four, Liu Yün-sheng, Li Ch'un-chai,[6] Te

[1] Unidentifiable.
[2] A *li* is approximately one-third of an English mile.
[3] Kuo had appointed Major Huang Hui-ho to handle despatches and had put him on the legation payroll. Later, in 1878, the Chinese Government set up a centralized Office for the Transmission of Government Correspondence with the China Merchants' Steam Navigation Company, under the general management of Huang Hui-ho. See Hsü, *China's Entrance*, p. 193. Hsü notes that Liu Hsi-hung entrusted his correspondence to the Shanghai Customs Commissioner. For details see *Yüeh-chang ch'eng-an hui-lan*, Part 2, ii.18–25b. On the China Merchants' Steam Navigation Company (*Lun-ch'uan chao-shang chü*) see Albert Feuerwerker, *China's Early Industrialization*, pp. 96 ff. Li Hung-chang's steamship project had an office in Shanghai which served as an *ad hoc* government agency. See Liu Kwang-ching, 'British–Chinese Steamship Rivalry in China, 1873–85' in C. D. Cowan, ed., *The Economic Development of China and Japan*, pp. 49–78.
[4] Li Hsing-jui, style Mien-lin, and Cheng Ts'ao-ju, style Yü-hsien, were both officials of the Kiangnan Arsenal, Shanghai. See Liu, *Ying-yao jih-chi*, xi.160a–209b.
[5] For Macartney's account of the embarkation see below, p. 173.
[6] Li Shu-ch'ang (1837–97), style Ch'un-chai, was Counsellor to the Embassy. He had distinguished himself when young by presenting to the throne his views on current affairs, which were so perspicacious that he was made a district magis-

Tsai-ch'u, and Liu Ho-po being the only ones able to bear up. I forced myself to sit up, but found my head was spinning, my eyes smarting, and the tip of my nose very painful, so that I was in great distress.

19th day [4 December]

As we ran along the Fukien coast I saw the hills of Amoy away in the distance and realized that we had already passed Taiwan. As the wind grew even stronger, I lay down in misery, finding myself quite unable to rise all day. When the wind and waves abated for a moment, I opened the port and could just make out a faint smudge that marked the hills.

20th day [5 December]

Passing the coast of Kuangtung. Between Shan-t'ou [Swatow] and Chieh-shih, for several hundred *li* lies an unbroken chain of mountains. An English ironclad came up astern of us. The captain told me it was the flagship of Admiral Lai-te [Vice-Admiral A. P. Ryder].[1] When our vessel hoisted a flag the warship also hoisted a flag, whereupon our vessel then lowered the flag. The man-of-war gradually increased her speed until she drew close to us, the two vessels then running side by side perhaps a hundred feet or more from each other. The man-of-war's crew all manned the yards and the ship's band struck up.

trate by way of reward. In 1863 he became secretary to Tseng Kuo-fan, a post he held for the next six years. During the years 1870-1 he was acting district magistrate of Wu-chiang and Ch'ing-pu. After his appointment to the Embassy, he spent four years in Europe, moving from England to France, Germany, and Spain. In October 1881, while serving as Chargé d'Affaires at Madrid, he was appointed Minister to Japan. Li wrote several short accounts of his sojourn in Europe, among them the *Feng-shih Ying-lun chi* (printed 1894). For further details of Li's career, see Hummel, *Eminent Chinese*, pp. 483-4.

[1] Vice-Admiral Alfred Phillipps Ryder's flagship, H.M.S. *Audacious*, of 6,034 tons, was a barque-rigged, armour-plated, double-screw, iron ship. Admiral Ryder (1820-88) entered the navy in 1833 and became Lieutenant in 1841. In 1846 he was promoted to the rank of Commander and of Rear-Admiral in 1866. In 1872 he became Vice-Admiral and was appointed Commander-in-Chief in China 1874-7. He became Admiral in 1877, Commander-in-Chief at Portsmouth 1878-82, and Admiral of the Fleet in 1885. Admiral Ryder was a man of high attainment and made persistent exertions to raise the standard of education in the navy. He devoted much of his time on shore to scientific study, and wrote a number of pamphlets on professional subjects. Ironically enough, in view of the near-collision, he was the author of a treatise entitled *Methods of ascertaining the distance from ships at sea* (3rd ed., 1858).

When our vessel again hoisted a flag, the man-of-war turned her head across our bows and then passed in front of us. Our vessel stopped her engines and waited a while before hoisting sail and proceeding on course at full speed.

I asked the captain the meaning of our hoisting the flag. He replied that this was to inform the other vessel that we carried an ambassador. I then enquired why that vessel also hoisted a flag. He told me that this was by way of reply: that is to say, a respectful acknowledgement that an ambassador was on board. I then asked why the flag was lowered. He told me that once they had conveyed the message the flag could be hauled down again. I enquired the reason as to why the man-of-war's crew manned the yards. He said that this was a mark of respect, much like drawing the men up in ranks, for after they have manned the yards they can be seen at a distance. The band is used for playing martial music to regulate the movement of the ranks. I then asked why the warship turned across our bows as she passed us, and was told that she was hastening to greet us. Our stopping the engines indicated that we were yielding precedence. How refined and civilized are these ceremonial courtesies of theirs! This is sufficient to indicate that the foundation of this nation's wealth and power was not acquired by mere chance.[1]

21st day [6 December]

We reached Hong Kong, latitude 22.12 north, nine degrees nearer the equator than Shanghai. The climate was startlingly different, so that everyone was soon putting on thin cotton clothes. The English Rear-Admiral Lan-po-erh-te (Rowley Lambert] came to pay his respects. Then we went to his headquarters to inspect the detached squadron under his command, which was all ready to sail to its base.[2] As it was, they had

---

[1] Captain Barratt would have made no mean diplomat himself, for he succeeded in turning into an act of ceremonial courtesy what in fact was only a blunder on the part of the *Audacious*, as the account in Macartney's diary makes clear; see below p. 174.
[2] The detached or flying squadron under the command of Rear-Admiral Rowley Lambert, flagship H.M.S. *Narcissus*, also included the *Topaze*, *Newcastle*, and *Immortalité*. The squadron did in fact leave for Singapore on the morning of 6 December 1876, but the *Narcissus* had an accident to her engines and was forced to return to Hong Kong on the 7th. See *The Times*, 16 Jan. 1877, p. 6f.

merely been awaiting my arrival before setting sail. The Governor of Hong Kong, His Excellency K'eng-erh-ti [Sir Arthur Edward Kennedy][1] sent his Aide-de-camp A-k'e-na-heng [Captain Cornelius O'Callaghan][2] with a four-man sedan-chair to meet me. Along with Second Ambassador Liu, Councillor Li, and the interpreters, I took my seat in the ten-oared cutter that had been sent for us. On landing, a salute of fifteen guns was fired from the fort, the troops were drawn up as a guard of honour and military music was played to welcome us. The Canton Consul, Lo Po-sun [Sir Daniel Brooke Robertson], an old acquaintance of mine, was also there to welcome me at the landing-place.[3] After a little ordinary conversation we were carried to Government House, where over twenty civil and military officers were assembled. Among those who were introduced by name were Admiral Ryder, Flag-Captain K'uo-lun-pu [Captain Phillip H. Colomb],[4] and Chief Justice Ssu-mei-erh-ssu [Sir John Smale].[5]

[1] Sir Arthur Edward Kennedy (1810–83) had been knighted in 1868 after a long career in the colonial service. He became Governor and Commander-in-Chief of Hong Kong in 1872, holding that office until 1877, when he was made Governor of Queensland. G. B. Endacott, *A History of Hong Kong*, pp. 160–9, gives a good account of Kennedy's career as Governor of Hong Kong. He concludes (p. 169): 'The governorship of Kennedy was a period of quiescence and showed how much could be achieved by humane, common-sense administration. He had a balanced, friendly approach; he consulted the community, took pains to treat the Chinese with friendliness, and was the first Governor to invite them to functions at Government House ...'

[2] Captain Cornelius O'Callaghan, of the first West India Regiment, was Private Secretary and Aide-de-camp to Governor Kennedy. He later accompanied him to Brisbane in that capacity. (*Hong Kong Directory*, 1877; *Whitaker's Almanack*, 1880.)

[3] Sir Daniel Brooke Robertson (1810–81) was Vice-Consul at Shanghai in 1843 and Acting Consul at Ningpo, Amoy, and Canton. He became Consul-General at Shanghai in 1877, retiring in 1879.

[4] Philip Howard Colomb (1831–99) entered the navy in 1846 and became Lieutenant in 1855. He devised a system known as 'Colomb's Flashing Signals' in 1861 which was fully adopted in the navy in 1866. In 1863 he was appointed Commander, and Captain in 1870. For the greater part of the next four years Colomb was employed at the Admiralty preparing the 'Manual of Fleet Evolutions', officially issued in 1874. From 1874 to 1877 he commanded the *Audacious* on the China station as Flag Captain to Vice-Admiral Ryder (see note 8 above) and then the *Thunderer* in the Mediterranean 1880–1. In 1886 he was retired for age and became Rear-Admiral in 1887 and Vice-Admiral in 1892. Colomb was the author of several books and numerous pamphlets on naval matters.

[5] Sir John Smale (1805–82) was called to the Bar, Inner Temple, in April 1842. He was made Attorney-General for Hong Kong in 1861, and Chief Justice from 1866–81, when he retired on a pension.

When I enquired about educational institutions, I found the Inspector of Schools in this colony, Ssu-chüeh-erh-te [Frederick Stewart],[1] was sitting there. He offered to show us round the school. After taking a little wine we went to the [Government Central] School, where I met Assistant Inspector Fa-na-chien-erh [Alexander Falconer].[2] These two gentlemen have the entire system of education in their hands. There are five halls altogether. Chinese literature—the Five Classics and the Four Books—along with contemporary literature are taught in three of these. There is one hall for European literature. European boys have one hall where they study the Five Classics and the Four Books. Every hall has a hundred pupils to each master. Where the Five Classics and the Four Books are taught, the master is a Chinese. European masters teach European subjects. Each hall is divided into ten rows, with a space in front of each. In every row there is a long desk which can seat ten or more pupils. They are graded, rising towards the back of the class. In front and directly facing the class sits a master. There is another master sitting in the middle of the class with five rows to the left and right of him. The idea is that he can see and hear everything; so not a single boy can escape from or gloss over his work. The Five Classics and the Four Books each have their allotted time for study. There is a limit set for the study of verse, namely one lesson every five days. This is called a minor subject. This is as much as to say that, being an art of little importance, one lesson in five days is enough. The rules are well thought-out and severe, and the viewpoint [of those who made them] is far-sighted. It would appear that the Europeans have inherited something of the ancients' ideal of forming and nourishing the talents of their pupils. I also heard that the school

[1] Frederick Stewart, M.A., first headmaster of the Government Central School (1862–81) is well discussed in Gwenneth Stokes, *Queen's College. 1862–1962*, pp. 19–44. The Central School stood on the lower slopes of the hill above Queen's Road Central, on a site now occupied by Hollywood Road Government School, until 1889. See the map in Stokes, *Queen's College*, p. 49. In 1889 the school was renamed Victoria College and in 1894 Queen's College. For schools in Hong Kong during this period, see also G. B. Endacott and A. Hinton, *Fragrant Harbour*, pp. 136–41.

[2] Alexander Falconer, a teacher at the Government Central School since 1869, had been promoted to Second Master in 1874. (*Colonial Office List*, 1876; Stokes, *Queen's College*, p. 26.) He would appear to have taught chemistry and geometry. For Macartney's account of the reception and the visit to the school see below, p. 175 ff.

had a chemistry laboratory and expressed a wish to inspect it. But Captain O'Callaghan pointed out that the soldiers who were to escort me had been drawn up on the sea-front, waiting, for a long time already. In view of this, I made my way back to the ship, the ironclad again giving me a salute of fifteen guns while the band played martial music to welcome me. The band on the French warship also played martial music in harmony with it.[1]

I remember that in the year *kuei-hai* [1863–4] of the *Hsien-feng* period [1851–62],[2] when I came this way by sea to take up my post as Governor at Canton, the houses I saw in Hong Kong numbered scarcely a third of those today. Now, more than ten years later, streets run in all directions and tall buildings stand everywhere. It has become a veritable metropolis, with what must be now over 130,000 inhabitants.[3] There are 6,000 European households. Two forts stand there, one on the east side, one on the west. Two ironclads are stationed there, one called *Ao-ta-hsi-a-ssu* [*Audacious*], the other *Fei-tuo-erh-jih-man-nu-erh* [*Victor Emmanuel*].[4] The latter is the name of the ruler of Italy which the English bestowed on this vessel in his honour. This evening an English merchant paddle-steamer while anchoring struck our vessel with a noise like thunder, destroying ten feet of our stern lights and cutting in two a small boat that was hanging on our stern. The lights were rather

[1] For Macartney's account of the return to his ship, see below, p. 176 ff. *The Times*, 16 Jan. 1877, p. 6f, carries a report by its Hong Kong correspondent which supplements it: 'The Envoy and his Staff landed at 2 o'clock in the afternoon at the wharf, where a guard of honour of Her Majesty's 28th Regiment with the band was in attendance. His Excellency was received by Capt. O'Callaghan, aide-de-camp to the Governor, the garrison battery firing a salute of fifteen guns. After short delay, the Envoy and his suite being provided with chairs, they left for Government House accompanied by an escort of four mounted troopers... After a stay of nearly three quarters of an hour, during which time his Excellency evinced a great interest in the system pursued in the school, his Excellency proceeded to Murray wharf where he re-embarked for the Peninsular and Oriental Steamer *Travancore*, the guard of honour and band of the 28th Regiment again being in attendance. On his leaving the shore another salute was fired from the *Victor Emmanuel*.'

[2] Kuo became Acting Governor of Kuangtung in 1863, but this was during the *T'ung-chih* period, not the *Hsien-feng*.

[3] The population of Hong Kong in 1876, according to the demographers Behm and Wagner, was 121,985. See *The Times*, 13 Dec. 1876, p. 6c.

[4] The *Victor Emmanuel* was a wooden sailing-vessel of 5,157 tons, according to *Whitaker's Almanack*, 1877, and not an ironclad. It was receiving ship, Hong Kong; captain, George W. Watson.

high, so no water came in.¹ An envoy on shipboard is certainly in a perilous plight!

22nd day [7 December]

We remained another day in Hong Kong to repair the damage to the ship. The Governor, Sir Arthur Kennedy, came in the company of Sir Brooke Robertson to pay me a return visit. When I referred in conversation to the completeness of the way in which the school was planned and administered [the Governor] remarked with a sigh that these pupils were all the sons of poor families; so that after two or three years' study, when their education was only partially complete, they would all too often leave of their own accord to look for a living. As a result, very few of them completed the course. This led to a discussion on European methods being characterized by an undeviating impartiality. An instance of this was prison discipline in the colony where criminals were treated alike, no matter what their nationality. I asked if I might go to visit the prison. The Governor gladly agreed, instructing Captain O'Callaghan to bring a two-man sedan-chair to meet me. Sir Brooke Robertson was to accompany me.²

The prison was administered by a Chief Jailer and Assistant Jailer. The Assistant, Ta-mo-sen [G. L. Tomlin]³ conducted me through the building on arrival. There are three stories, the heaviest offenders being placed in the upper storey. In the lowest storey each prisoner has a cell to himself. In the upper storey there are three men to one cell. All the prisoners have their doors bolted. Each block is self-contained, either standing alone or else facing another one. All the cells have iron bars and doors that lock. In each of them is a small wooden settle, one for each person. Quilts, mattresses, blankets, towels, brooms,

---

[1] 'The *Fleurs Castle* was steaming up to her berth about 2 a.m. when she struck the *Travancore* well aft, cutting clean through the stern boat and cleaving her way into the saloon about twelve feet, leaving a gap little more than two feet wide. The taffrail and all the supports of the wheel were likewise carried along.' (*North China Herald*, 21 Dec. 1876, p. 603.)

[2] Cf. Macartney's account, below, p. 175 ff.

[3] Text reads 森 *sen*, which is clearly a graphic error for 林 *lin*. G. L. Tomlin, a former superintendent of the convict hulk at Stonecutter's Island, Hong Kong, was Acting Superintendent of Victoria Gaol at that time. (*Hong Kong Directory*, 1877; *Colonial Office List*, 1876.) The Victoria Gaol, first erected in 1842, stands between present day Old Bailey Street and Hollywood Road. For Macartney's account of the visit to the prison see below, p. 179 ff.

bowls, plates, and other things are all provided. Every day quilts and blankets must be meticulously arranged on the settle. If anyone fails to do this, his rations are cut down. The prisoners include over thirty Europeans, Philippinos, and Indians, besides some 514 Chinese. As well as these, there are people who have been fined amounts from four or five dollars up to 200 dollars. Prisoners do not remain in prison for the same length of time. Some serve long sentences of five or seven years; some serve short sentences of only five days; some are confined there for life. There are three categories of treatment. Some spend their time in close confinement; some spend a long period weaving rugs; others have to carry stones and cannon-balls. Those who carry cannon-balls are divided into three groups— Europeans, Philippinos, and Chinese. All of them are in squads under military discipline, the file being composed sometimes of five men, sometimes of ten. The work is carried on for two periods a day. Those who carry stones form only one group. This is for those who have committed lighter offences.

For those in close confinement, there is an iron cylinder in each cell which they have to turn by hand fourteen thousand times a day. A dial records the number of revolutions. If they do not fulfil the number, their rations are cut. The prisoners have two meals a day, consisting of rice and a dish of four small fishes. Long-term prisoners eat meat and a better grade of rice. There is also a place for female prisoners, all of them sharing one room. Tomlin took us all over the prison. In the place where they carry stones and cannon-balls there were close on 100 men standing round in a circle in a hall. When he raised his hand as a signal, all of them fell quickly into ranks, in three or four rows, and stood in their right places. Then they all raised their hands to their foreheads as a salutation. When the jailer opened the outside door and shouted loudly, even the prisoners in close confinement stood up by the doors of their cells with their arms by their sides and faced the outside. It can be seen from this what strict discipline they are subjected to.

Outside the prison is a wash-place where every man has to wash once a day. Inside there is a chapel where religious service is held once a week. The prisoners sit round in a ring and listen to sermons. There is a sick-bay for the treatment of the sick, under the management of a physician. There is another prison hall for preparing for burial¹ those prisoners who have died of disease. Besides this, there is a punishment hall. The whole place was sprinkled, swept and spotlessly clean; even the floors were polished with resin. Not only were there no foul odours, but the men themselves were so clean one forgot that this was a prison.

Hsi Tsai-ming [W. C. Hillier] told me that formerly all convicts had been put to work building walls and repairing roads under the supervision of overseers. But Governor Kennedy had introduced for the first time the practice of keeping prisoners in confinement and not letting them do forced labour. The carrying of stones and cannon-balls, as well as the turning of the iron cylinder, are used as punishments. In addition to this, these exercises strengthen the bones and sinews and promote the circulation of the blood, so that it does not stagnate and cause illness. For instruments of punishment they have manacles and chains for fettering the feet. They also use a whip made of cords, which tears open the flesh after fifty lashes. Criminals who are deceitful, unruly, and likely to do harm to the general public are branded on the neck with a circle and then driven away, being forbidden to remain in Hong Kong. Some of them, however, cut out the circle with a knife and then smear the wound with salve. Yet when this heals the scar still remains, thus enabling the police to discover them, arrest them, and throw them into jail. The law must be observed and punishment meted out only in strict accordance with the offence.²

23rd day [8 December]

About the *mao* watch [5–7 a.m.] we got under way. By noon we had made a run of ninety-five *li* and were then in latitude 21.22 north. The captain had a sand-glass to measure the time and a pointed piece of wood attached to a cord wound round a reel. The pointed piece of wood was thrown into the sea and the line allowed to run out until all the sand in the glass had trickled down. Then the line was pulled in and the speed measured by

---

¹ Read 殮 for 斂.
² The year 1876 had seen a great increase in crime in Hong Kong, due largely to the reduction of the steamer fare from Canton to ten cents, which enabled large numbers of vagabonds to make their way to the colony. See Endacott and Hinton, *Fragrant Harbour*, p. 106.

the amount of line that had run out. Our speed was calculated at thirty-four *li* an hour. Every day at noon, the number of *li* travelled is calculated and our distance from the equator worked out by means of a sextant. This information is posted up daily. We caught sight of several score of single-sailed fishing-boats in the distance, tossing up and down on the waves as light as leaves. From this we knew that we could not be far from Wan-chou, in the south of Ch'iung [Hainan].

24th day [9 December]

At noon we had run just 831 *li* [277 miles]. Our position was 17.30 north. I estimated that we were between two and three hundred *li* south of Hainan. The crew called this sea '*Ch'i-na-hsi*', which means 'the Sea of the Middle Kingdom' [China Sea]. I caught sight of many flying-fish in the water, several feet in length. They leapt up to the height of ten feet or so before alighting again. Not far away to port lay the P'ai-la-su [Paracel] Islands, which produce *bêche-de-mer* and coral, though not of the best quality.[1] These islands belong to China, but they are barren and uninhabited. One of our fellow passengers was an Englishman called P'ai-de-ssu-li-hsi-te [Patrick Lister?].[2] He was making a world tour and had joined the ship on his way home. On making enquiries I found that he was a wealthy Englishman who was travelling for pleasure.

This evening was rainy and quite as hot as at the height of summer [in China], so that I could not bear to have even a quilt over me.

25th day [10 December]

Raining. By noon we had run 852 *li* and were in latitude 13 north. We passed Mount Wa-lei-la [Cape Varella] on the south-east border of Annam. The sea is called the Seven Island Sea.

Ma Ko-li [Halliday Macartney] gave me some information about the revenue of England for the year 1875 (this corresponds to the year *yi-hai* in the Chinese cycle). For London, the

---

[1] *Bêche-de-mer* was a delicacy in great demand among Chinese gourmets, who highly prized the soup that it produced. For the Chinese love of coral, a substance known in China since the Han dynasty, see Edward H. Schafer, *The Golden Peaches of Samarkand: A Study of T'ang Exotics*, esp. pp. 246–7.
[2] Unidentifiable.

revenue was over £210,000,000; for India over £160,000,000; for Australia—which the English call the New Gold Mountain—over £10,000,000; for Singapore and the Straits Settlements over £1,000,000. For Hong Kong, the revenue is only a little over £180,000, while expenditure runs to over £190,000.[1]

26th day [11 December]

Rainy. Our run at noon was 939 *li*. We were then in latitude 8.10 north—450 *li* south of Saigon. Saigon is a French settlement and mart under the government of the Annamese prefecture of Chia-ting, in the territory of what was anciently Chen-la, at the mouth of the Lan-ts'ang [Saigon] river.[2]

As we travel south from Hong Kong the weather gets hotter every day and the rain falls more heavily. At Shanghai the thermometer registered 53; at Hong Kong it was 65; now we are in the tropics it is up to 81. We can no longer wear our wadded cotton clothing. The crew are all wearing thin summer clothes.

27th day [12 December]

Raining. Our run at noon was 835 *li*—latitude 4.3 north. I estimate we are somewhere in the Gulf of Siam. We have an Italian fellow passenger by the name of A-la-to-ni [Aladoni?][3] who, I discovered, has a business in London. He has made a voyage through America and Japan and visited our Chinese ports on his tour of the globe. He belongs to the aristocracy in his own country and has received a decoration of the highest class. It may be seen from this just what importance they attach to trade in Europe.[4]

There is another Italian fellow-passenger by the name of Ying-na-chi-ko [Ignazi?].[5]

[1] Macartney had his figures wrong. For the period 1874–5, gross public revenue for Australia was £15,689,994; for India £50,570,171; for Singapore and the Straits Settlements £327,000; while for Hong Kong revenue was £186,818 and expenditure £181,337. (*Whitaker's Almanack*, 1878.)

[2] French forces had first seized Saigon in Feburary 1859, consolidating their position there by the Treaty of Saigon (June 1862), which ceded to them the three provinces of Cochin China.

[3] Unidentifiable. Alatoni, Aratoni, Alladoni, and Allatoni are also possible.

[4] Kuo is contrasting Europe with China, where in theory at least, the merchant occupied the bottom of the social ladder. The background, as well as the practice of such theory, can be traced to the time of Former Han, if not earlier.

[5] Unidentifiable. This is surely Ignazi, but the *ko* is puzzling.

Kuo's Journal

28th day [13 December]

Raining. At 11 a.m. we reached Singapore, latitude 1.20 north, after a run of 720 *li*. Early in the morning we passed an island with a lighthouse on it, named Horsburgh. Horsburgh was one of the first European explorers to come to China.[1] Macartney informed me that our [naval] paddle-steamer *Yang-wu* had already arrived at Singapore.[2] On our arrival, Admiral Ts'ai Kuo-hsiang and his younger brother Ts'ai Kuo-hsi,[3] accompanied by Hu Hsüan-tse of Huang-p'u came to pay us a visit.[4] Li Chao-min had a letter for Mr. Hu and took this opportunity to deliver it.

The English Governor, Che Wei-li [Sir William Francis Drummond Jervois],[5] despatched a military officer with a two-horse carriage to receive me. I was asked, however, to delay my visit until four o'clock while he sent round an order to every commander, requesting a guard of honour. In the meantime I agreed to pay a visit to Mr. Hu's garden to see its exotic flowers, curious plants, rare birds, and marvellous animals, such a collection as has seldom been seen before.[6]

---

[1] John Horsburgh (1762–1836), hydrographer, is best known as the author of the *India Directory, or directions for sailing to and from the East Indies, China, New Holland, Cape of Good Hope, Brazil and the interjacent ports*, 2 vols. (London, 1809–11). The foundation stone of the lighthouse which bears his name was laid on 24 May 1850. See C. B. Buckley, *An Anecdotal History of Old Times in Singapore*, ii.510 ff.

[2] The corvette *Yang-wu* (1,400 tons), launched 23 Apr. 1872, was the seventh of the training-ships built by and belonging to the naval school of the Foochow shipyard. Yen Fu, the great translator of Western writers, had served on this vessel as a young man in 1872. See Schwartz, *In Search of Wealth and Power*, p. 27. After the *T'ung-chih* restoration, the Chinese had taken to the sea again for the first time since the fifteenth century. The *Straits Times* commented on the *Yang-wu*'s arrival in Singapore on 9 December 1876 from Hong Kong bound for Calcutta: 'We have, too, a Chinese man-of-war which purposes going on a long cruise, in our harbour, and which is manned by Chinamen, the Commander and the Engineer being Englishmen. The Celestials, we are glad to see, are advancing.' (Editorial, *Straits Times*, 16 Dec. 1876.) A sketch of the *Yang-wu* may be found in Gideon Ch'en, *Tso Tsung-t'ang*, p. 38. For Macartney's account of the visit to Singapore see below, pp. 173–183.

[3] Ts'ai Jui-an, styled Kuo-hsiang, had been aide to Tseng Kuo-fan, for whom he had built a steamer. Later he was put in charge of training at Foochow dockyard. At this time he was captain of the *Yang-wu*. Liu Hsi-hung had a conversation with him in Singapore in the course of which Ts'ai insisted that Chinese abroad should never adopt western ways. See Liu, *Ying-yao jih-chi*, xi.165a. His younger brother, Yüeh-ch'ing, styled Kuo-hsi, was also an officer on the *Yang-wu*.

[4] See note 1, p. 81.   [5] See note 2, p, 81.

[6] The Chinese scholar's traditional love of the exotic is well illustrated by the

In a large glass case he has an antelope's head with horns still on it which turn down in a triple spiral and then point up again. He also possesses a pair of wild ox's horns, a rhinoceros horn, and a pair of deer's antlers. The antlers are each about three feet long. He has the sword of a swordfish, about seven feet in length, the colour of ivory, spiralling, twisted, hard, and slender; the jawbone of a fish and two white ants about two inches long, which he feeds with water from a glass bottle. They are kept in two stone eggs, with a hole bored in the top of each, through which they are fed. You have to open the egg to get at them. These are called king white-ants.

There are more than ten ostrich eggs, each the size of a peck, as well as four serpents' eggs as big as goose-eggs. There are two ostriches; two brightly-coloured *luan* birds;[1] a six-legged tortoise, over three feet in length; two white-shelled turtles with purple flowers and mottlings on the shell, which rises up like a peak, their heads and feet both white; a small Tibetan bear; a porcupine; a kangaroo. The head and two forefeet of this beast are like those of a hare, but the part between the belly and the two hind-feet is several times larger in proportion. The hind-feet rest on the ground, crooked like knees, yet he cannot stretch them out though they are twice as long as the forelegs. He has a tail two feet long. He moves in bounds, as though he were flying. Underneath the belly is a pouch, from which the animal gets its [Chinese] name of *tai-shu* ['pouch-rat']. I once saw this animal among pictures of strange birds and beasts in the German Legation in the capital.

After this, I went off to Government House, accompanied by Second Ambassador Liu and Councillor Li. Here we saw Sir William Jervois with his Lady[2] and their two daughters. He was much more affable in his bearing than Governor Kennedy. His lady is very intelligent and most sympathetic in her enquiries.

lengthy passage that follows. Even a man as intelligent and perceptive as Kuo could travel 10,000 miles on a steamer without evincing the slightest interest in its construction or its engines. Yet he was completely captivated by what to us would seem a trivial collection of curios. It was this mentality that made the industrialization of China such a difficult task. A contemporary Japanese would have reacted very differently.

[1] The *luan*-bird was purely mythical. Kuo must have thought it really existed.
[2] Lady Jervois (d. 17 Mar. 1895), née Lucy Norsworthy, married Sir William in 1850 and bore him two sons and three daughters.

Kuo's Journal 15

When Mo-li-ya-ssu [Colonel W. K. McLeod],[1] the Officer Commanding the Troops, returned I went over to the fort with him.[2] Two tiers of fortifications have been constructed along the hill, with the general headquarters and four rows of barracks between them, each capable of holding over 100 men. There are two sets of married quarters to house the officers and men with families. Behind the barracks are the kitchens, two armouries, a mess-hall, a reading room, and a military hospital. There are ten large guns, each in its own strong point, and a powder magazine. Small guns, each on its own gun-carriage, are placed at the corners of the walls. A large telescope stands in front of the highest part of the wall before the headquarters, in a building of its own. This is used for keeping watch on the distance. The construction and layout of the place are entirely different from those of Chinese forts. The troops are divided into artillery and infantry. The infantry all carry foreign-style rifles to assist the artillery. The Artillery Commander is called Mi-ko-erh-ssu (Brevet-Colonel O. H. Nicolls).[3] The Infantry Commandant is called Lin-chih [Lieutenant-Colonel W. W. Lynch].[4] Their posts are the counterpart of the Chinese Major (*yu-chi*). The troops are divided into two categories. The upper ranks receive one Straits dollar every three days, equivalent to 0·24 taels of our money a day. The lower ranks receive one Straits dollar every four days, equivalent to 0·18 taels a day. Married officers receive an allowance for their families. The soldiers' families support themselves through their own efforts by taking in washing and acting as seamstresses. Such is the fort on the north side of the hill, overlooking the town. There is yet another fort on the south side.

29th day [14 December]
Raining and thundery. Governor Jervois again sent a carriage for me and dispatched his interpreter, Pi Ch'i-lin [W. A.

[1] The Honourable William Couperus McLeod (d. 1880) entered the Madras army in 1821 and served in India for most of his career. He was made a general in 1877, at which time he was Officer Commanding the Troops, Singapore. See the *Singapore Directory of the Straits Settlements*, 1877.   [2] See note 3, p. 81.
[3] Brevet-Colonel O. H. Nicholls commanded the 9th Battery, 2nd Brigade of the Royal Artillery, Straits Settlements, at this time. See *Singapore Directory*, 1877.
[4] Lieutenant-Colonel William Wiltshire Lynch (1831–88) entered the army as an ensign in 1850. In 1877 he held the rank of Lieutenant-Colonel of the 10th Foot. He was promoted to Major-General in 1887.

Pickering],[1] to accompany me on my tour. We first went out to the *Yang-wu*. The crew all manned the yards and a salute was fired as we went on board. The Naval Instructor La-k'o-ssu-mo [Captain Luxmoore],[2] an Englishman, went to great pains to explain everything to us. He conducted us to his school-room where he has twenty pupils under training. After this there was a display of gunnery and the marines were put through their drill. When we left, they again manned the yards and fired a salute for us.

Pickering then took us along to the Hung Gardens, a public park for Hokkiens and Cantonese.[3] Among the flowering groves of trees was a stream, as crystal-clear and shady as could be. There is a tiger's den and two leopards' dens, all with iron railings around them. I saw two small Tibetan bears and three mountain dogs. There are nine monkeys, some grey, others with red faces; some with long bodies and arms, others with short. All are of different species. There are amongst them one very large and fierce beast locked up in an iron cage. It had yellow fur about four inches long and was called a Golden Marmoset.[4]

There are over thirty iron-meshed cages containing wolves, foxes, weasels, squirrels, beavers, and other animals set around the grounds, with cages of birds interspersed among them in a setting of variegated trees and flowers. There are four kinds of

[1] William Alexander Pickering (1841–1907) had been appointed Chinese Interpreter to the Straits Settlements Government in 1871. In 1874 he was appointed a Police Magistrate and played an important part in the negotiations leading up to the Pangkor Treaty (20 Jan. 1874). On 4 May 1877 Pickering was appointed Protector of Chinese Immigration, a post he held until July 1888, when he was forced to retire on medical grounds as a result of an attack by a member of the Ghee Hok Society, one Choa Ah Sia. See Cowan, *Nineteenth-Century* Malaya, p. 181, who remarks on Pickering's 'outstanding work' and his 'remarkable personal gifts'. For his biography see R. N. Jackson, *Pickering: Protector of Chinese*.

[2] A Captain 'Luxmore' is mentioned in the *Straits Times*, 16 Dec. 1876, as Captain of the *Yang-wu*.

[3] This must refer to the present Botanic Gardens, founded in December, 1859, on a site donated by Hu Hsüan-tse, but not opened to the public until 1874. Henry James Murton—the first man to plant para-rubber trees in Singapore—was Superintendent of the gardens at this time. The formation of the zoo had been suggested by the Governor, Sir Harry Ord (1819–85). By 1877, there were 144 exhibits in the zoo. It was finally wound up in 1905. See Gilbert E. Brooke, 'Botanic Gardens and Economic Notes', in Makepeace *et al.*, *One Hundred Years of Singapore*, ii.63–77. Kuo must have been struck by the fact that the zoo and gardens were open to the public, a practice unknown in China.

[4] *Leontideus rosalia*.

parrots there, one white, one ash-grey, one red, and one emerald green. In addition there is one variety which is emerald green, with red wings. There are three kinds of eagles, one white, one azure, one ash-grey; three kinds of pheasant, one variegated, one azure, one mottled black and dark-brown. There are many varieties of pigeon, quite the oddest of which is a kingfisher-blue dove, a strange bird which looks like a green *luan* bird. There are tits and water-rails too. There is a kind of copper pheasant with variegated plumage and a blue or red head. It sings well. Yet another variety resembles a wild duck with one long, slender tuft of feathers on its head.

I noticed three extraordinary sights there. One was the Lohan Pine,[1] which rose to a height of several score feet and covered the ground like a bell-shaped cloak. In the centre, the trunk of the pine was too big to encircle with the arms, while the connecting boughs were all twisted and bent. Inside there was an empty space, while the branches and leaves on the outside formed the densest possible screen.

Another strange sight which I saw in several places was a network of wistaria shutting out the sky like a huge screen. It was bent like a nine-leaf folding wind-screen. It grew straight up from the ground to a height of twenty or thirty feet or more. All around it were flowers and leaves, quite unsupported, trailing on the ground.

Another sight was that of ten or more pines, so tall they touched the clouds. About a foot or so from the ground, five branches stuck out horizontally, with their needles hanging down and revolving like discs. Every foot or so, several small branches spring out abruptly in this way, so that from afar the trees look like a number of many-storeyed pagodas set in the middle of a forest. These are all very strange sights.

They have also constructed a bowl-shaped iron frame, rather like an umbrella, and set creepers to grow over it. Though they have only just planted them, in ten years' time they will cover the frame completely and will certainly make yet another very curious sight. I have just learned that all the things I have described above were the result of human skill, but have no idea how they were brought about.

[1] *Podocarpus Chinensis*, Wall.

As to palm-trees[1] with long leaves that spread out like great fans, they are to be found everywhere here. There are flowers and trees from every country and every foreign nation, all with cards attached to them for information. One can easily see that this garden is a triumph of human ingenuity. When I was in Hong Kong, there was a public park there which I was told I really must see. At that time I thought I should concentrate on practical administration and not fritter away my time in sightseeing for entertainment. Yet now, quite unexpectedly, I have come across these strange sights which have filled my heart with intense delight.

On our way back we dropped in at the Law Courts, where the Judge, Fei Li-pu [Sir Theodore Ford],[2] was on the bench hearing a case. [Liu] Yün-sheng and I sat down by his side. The judge's bench is shaped like a platform raised five feet up from the floor. Below this is a long bow-shaped table, where two solicitors have their places, while recording clerks and interpreters sit around it. At a higher level, two wooden enclosures stand on either side. Here, I believe, the witnesses take the stand. Inside are eight small stools where those under cross-examination sit while they are waiting. A railing marks off the court so that the spectators can look on and listen. There is no flogging and corporal punishment in court, yet the lay-out of the whole court is orderly and severe and no undue noise is heard.

There is also a high school and five primary schools, one of which is a girls' school; but as the Governor, Sir William Jervois, had arranged to pay me a return call at three o'clock I found I had no time to go and look at them.

The population of Singapore is about 200,000, of whom 2,000 are Europeans, while a good 10,000 are Malays or Hindus.[3] The rest are all Hokkiens or Cantonese, the men of

[1] *Livistonia Chinensis*, Br.
[2] Sir Theodore Thomas Ford (1829–1920) was called to the Bar at the Middle Temple in 1866 and was appointed to the Straits Bench in 1874. He became Chief Justice in 1886, was knighted in 1888, and retired in 1889. For an account of his work in Singapore, see Roland St. J. Braddell, 'Law and the Lawyers,' in Makepeace *et al. One Hundred Years of Singapore*, i.214–15.
[3] The census of 1871, though admittedly unreliable, gave the population of Singapore Island as 97,131. The *Colonial Office List*, 1877, considers this figure about 20 per cent too low. In 1881, five years after Kuo's visit, the population was estimated to be 139,208, of whom 86,766 were Chinese.

Yüeh [Kwangtung] being by far the most numerous. Hu Hsüan-tse avers that the Cantonese already exceed 70,000 in number.

The Governor of Singapore rules over three settlements. To the west lies Ma-la-chia [Malacca]; further west still lies Betel-nut Islet [Penang], which is an island in the sea. West [sic] of Malacca and divided by the sea from Penang is Wei-erh-ssu-li [Province Wellesley]. All are under the government of the colony of Singapore. Two English warships are stationed here. One is named *Ju-na* (H.M.S. *Juno*), under the command of Captain P'o-lan [Captain James A. Poland];[1] the other, named *Ma-ku-pai* [H.M.S. *Magpie*], is under the command of Captain An-sheng [Captain C. V. Anson].[2] Governor Jervois honoured us with his presence at three o'clock. We sailed immediately afterwards.

30th day [15 December]

We have sailed 210 *li* north-west from Singapore, passing Malacca and then heading west towards the Indian Ocean. The P & O vessels veer a little to the north, towards the island of Penang, over 100 *li*[3] distant. Since we were not travelling directly along the recognized sea-route west, the captain did not bother to post up the distance run.

Hillier showed me a copy of *The Times* for [Friday] 10 November, the ninth month, twenty-fifth day of the Chinese calendar, the very day we began our journey from Peking.[4] I gave it to Te Tsai-ch'u and Feng K'uei-chiu, who translated an editorial on the Yunnan case.[5] This copy contained an article on the English Captain, Le Erh-ssu [Sir George Nares], whose arctic expedition set forth in 1874 (Chinese year *chia-hsü*),

---

[1] Captain James Augustus Poland (1832–1918), promoted Vice-Admiral in 1893, was in command of H.M.S. *Juno*, a screw corvette of 2,216 tons, from 1875 to 1879.
[2] Captain Charles V. Anson was captain H.M.S. *Magpie*, a double screw gunboat of 774 tons. He was probably the son of Admiral Talavera Anson (1809–95).
[3] In fact over 1,500 *li*.
[4] *The Times* for Friday 10 Nov. 1876 carries no such article as the one mentioned. Could Kuo have been referring to the *Mail*, a tri-weekly summary of the contents of *The Times*, one number of which did appear on the date mentioned? This would presumably have carried a précis of the first report of the Nares expedition, which had appeared in *The Times* of Saturday 4 Nov., p. 10.
[5] The Margary affair. See Introduction above, pp. xxviii ff.

and returned in July, 1876.¹ He reported that land stretched as far as 82 degrees north; beyond this all was a sea of ice. At first the boats pushed on through ice-floes. When soundings were taken, the ice proved to be up to 160 feet thick. After two attempts the ships could proceed no further. Then they cut a road through the ice. In all there were two ships and over 300 men. Dragging each other along and leaning on each other they made their way north, covering about 3 *li* in one day. They got as far as latitude 83.25, in a journey of over two months. They did not see the sun for over 140 days. Four of them died and several men got frost-bitten feet. Beyond this point they found themselves unable to advance, so they retraced their steps along the route they had come by. When volunteers for the Arctic expedition were originally being sought, over 700 men had come forward. They were sent for a medical examination, which tested their sinews, bones, blood, and veins, as well as their strength and ability to withstand cold. More than 300 men were selected. They were away for over two years. The Queen has issued a proclamation granting handsome rewards to all members of the expedition, while Nares himself has been given a Medal of the First Class.

11th month, 1st day [16 December]

At the *ssu* watch (9-11 a.m.) we reached Betel-nut Islet (which the Europeans call P'i-lan [Penang]), 933 *li* from Malacca, in latitude 6 north. There is an English Resident there, who also bears the name of An-sheng [Sir Archibald Anson].² Hu Hsüan-tse had told us that he knew a Hokkien by the name of Wang Wen-ch'ing in business in Penang, who was also the agent of the China Merchants' Steam Navigation Company. I sent a man to find out where he was, whereupon he arrived, accompanied by six or seven of his countrymen; I noticed that they were all wearing short garments and spoke Malay, for

[1] The Arctic expedition led by Sir George Strong Nares (1831–1915) was one of the chief topics of conversation at the time. The expedition set sail in spring 1875, not 1874. Nares was knighted for his services. For an account of the Expedition, see his *Narrative of a Voyage to the Polar Sea during 1875–76*, 2 vols. (London, 1878).
[2] Lieutenant-Colonel (later Major-General) Sir Archibald Edward Harbord Anson, K.C.M.G. (1826-1925) had been appointed Lieutenant-Governor of Penang in 1867. He was in charge of the Perak expedition during the second phase of British intervention in Malaya after the murder of Birch.

Kuo's Journal

they have been living here for several generations.[1] Since our vessel was only staying a few hours before leaving again, there was not time for me to go on shore.

I was told that the population of Penang is 140,000.[2] Hokkiens and Cantonese make up 100,000 of these; the rest are all Malays. The landscape is sunny and verdurous. To the south it is mountainous and thickly covered with trees. I heard there was a waterfall over 100 feet high, and regretted that there was no time to go and see it. The northern shore is called Wellesley, a long, narrow province running from north to south along the sea-coast for over 900 *li* [*sic*].[3] An English military officer from Wellesley named Tuan Hsi-yi [Tuan Sheehey?][4] came on board to take passage home. Ten or more small boats filled with local people came to see him off to the accompaniment of music and came up to the ship. This officer must have endeared himself to the local people by his good deeds.

We sailed at the *shen* watch [3–5 p.m.]. The evening was windy.

11th month, 2nd day [17 December]

Our run at noon was 684 *li*; latitude 5.57 north. Sumatra was visible to the south, about forty *li* distant. I could see a huge mountain-range stretching out like a landscape-scroll. This was Mount Wan-ku-lu [Goudberg?].[5] Sumatra extends for over 20,000 *li* [*sic*]. It rises south of Hsi-li [We Island?] and runs west from Penang for over a thousand *li* [*sic*], with innumerable small islands dotted along its coast. Holland has been in control of this territory for several hundred years. Recently, however, Dutch power has declined; and the Dutch Resident in Sumatra

---

[1] These were Penang *babas*, Chinese who had been settled in Penang for several generations and had almost certainly married Malay women. They were wearing short jackets and trousers, not the traditional long gowns.

[2] The population of Penang according to the census of 1871 was 71,797.

[3] Province Wellesley, ceded to Britain by the Sultan of Kedah in 1798, was in 1876 a strip of coast forty-five miles long and about eight miles in width, opposite Penang.

[4] Unidentifiable. *Tuan* is Malay for 'Master'.

[5] A close study of all available maps and charts of this region of Sumatra failed to elicit to which peak of the Bukit Barisan Kuo was alluding. I should hazard the guess that it was the peak formerly called Goudberg (5,780 ft.), which is certainly visible from the latitude and distance mentioned.

has proved incompetent to pacify the natives, who have now taken up arms again. The fighting is still going on.[1]

This evening there was a great deal of wind and rain.

11th month, 3rd day [18 December]

Blowing a gale, with rain and thunder. Our run at noon was 774 *li*; latitude 6.16 north. We are now coming into the great sea called the Indian Ocean, the common [Chinese] name for which is the Little Western Ocean. This evening the wind has been blowing more strongly than ever. The captain, seeing a cyclone coming on, hastily stopped the engines to avoid it. As the sail was being set to catch the wind, it proved impossible to loosen sail in a hurry and three of the crew who went aloft to haul at the sheets fell down [on deck] and were injured. Hokkiens and Cantonese call this rotating wind a '*toi-fung*' [typhoon]. Europeans call it a '*sai-ko-luan*' [cyclone]. It rotates in an ascending spiral. It also occurs on land, in which case it is known as a 'ram's horn wind'. Over the oceans it forms a revolving spiral, sometimes over 1,000 *li* or several hundred *li* across; and any ship caught in this is whisked up and whisked down again, almost invariably capsizing. When European sailors see a cyclone rising, they consult the barometer at once, deciding by the height of the mercury whether to go on or turn back. When the atmosphere is heavy and the barometer is rising, they gradually move away from the wind to avoid coming to grief. Macartney told me that all the great states of Europe have set up '*mi-ti-a-lo-chi-ko a-fei-ssu*' [meteorological offices] to keep watch on the force of the wind. The fastest winds travel at the rate of eighty English *li* an hour (an

---

[1] The Atjeh war had broken out in March 1873 because of the piracy of the Achinese, which could no longer be tolerated after navigation through the Straits of Malacca had increased with the opening of the Suez Canal, especially as 'under the treaty of 1824, the Dutch Government could be held responsible for any damages resulting from Achinese piracy'. See Bernard H. M. Vlekke, *Nusantara*, pp. 297–302. The best general work on this war, which dragged on to the end of the century, is that of C. D. E. J. Hotz, *Beknopt geschiedkundig overzicht van den Atjèh-oorlog* (Leiden, 1924). C. D. Cowan, *Nineteenth-Century Malaya*, p. 134, points out that the Atjeh war 'brought some economic benefit to the Straits Settlements' even though all trade with Atjeh was prohibited and a strict Dutch blockade maintained. On the Achinese themselves, the best works are those of C. Snouck Hurgronje, *De Atjehers*, 2 vols. (Leiden, 1893–4), published in English as *The Achinese* (London, 1906), and J. Kreemer, *Atjèh*, 2 vols. (Leiden, 1922).

English *li* being equivalent to three Chinese *li*, this equals 240 *li*): but the telegraph spans 1,000 *li* in an instant. So if the wind gets up in England, this information is at once telegraphed to Germany, France, and other countries. Similarly, when the wind rises in Russia, the news is communicated in the same way. As soon as the news is known at every sea-port, the boats are ready to adjust their times of arrival and departure accordingly. —'*A-fei-ssu*' means 'offices'.

11th month, 4th day [19 December]

Raining and windy. Our run at noon was 546 *li*; latitude 5.54 north. The previous night's typhoon taken in conjunction with our stopping of the engines and our having met with a contrary wind meant that we had not been able to keep to our timetable. The captain remarked that in all his thirty years at sea he had never met with such a cyclone, nor as much wind as he encountered throughout this passage. I remarked jokingly that this was due to my own lack of *te* [Virtue], which had implicated my fellow voyagers. The captain changed countenance and apologized. Everyone in my suite was sick and so distressed that they were often unable to eat. The oppressive heat has increased our distress. At night I have been completely prostrated, wiping away perspiration like rain. By now I have had no proper sleep for more than ten days.

11th month, 5th day [20 December]

Rainy and very windy. Our run at noon was 663 *li*; latitude 5.54 north. Our cook, Liu Shu-jen, has been seriously ill for several days. His hands and face suddenly broke out in an eruption of red pustules. When the Western doctor was called to see him, he said after examining him that he was suffering from smallpox. In European ships everyone is very much afraid of sickness, especially of smallpox. When anyone is struck down by this complaint, a yellow flag is hoisted to warn people that crew and passengers cannot leave or board the ship. In the sick-bay, all suffering from infectious diseases are placed in a separate ward, the ship being put in quarantine for twenty days, or until there is no more danger of infection. After that the people on the ship are allowed to go ashore quite freely. We are now two days' voyage from Ceylon, where we are to

24   *Kuo's Journal*

change to another vessel, so everybody on board is apprehensive. The captain has had the sick man taken to a small cabin near the bows that I have been using as a study for the past few days. He has quarantined the cabins in the saloon [the cook] had occupied, forbidding his room-mates to come out and thus causing inconvenience to many people.

11th month, 6th day [21 December]
Our run at noon was 864 *li;* lattitude 5.40 north. After sailing another 219 *li* we reached Ceylon.

The Judge of this territory, Lu-ssu-ma-li-k'uo [A. H. Roosmalecocq] and the Colonel [?] K'o-la-erh-k'o [Clarke?][1] had been given instructions by the Governor K'o-lei-ka-li [Sir W. H. Gregory][2] to arrange for us to go to a government residence[3] for a short time. Because there was a lot to be done on board, I declined the offer. The ship had anchored at a place called Galle, where an arm of the sea branches into the land, on the extreme west of the south coast of Ceylon.[4] The Governor resides at Colombo, 240 *li* distant.

A doctor from the hospital came to have a look at Liu Shu-jen and ordered him to be sent to hospital. With him went our tea-and-water boy, Ch'en Ping-hsiang, who was also to be detained there. These two men were left behind in Ceylon to prevent the infection spreading among other members of the

[1] Names given by the *Colonial Office List*, 1876. A. H. Roosmalecocq was acting District Judge of Galle. He had been appointed Assistant Commissioner of Roads, Ceylon, in 1845; Assistant Government Agent, Galle, 1846; District Judge of Tangalla, 1853; District Judge, Trincomalee, 1862; District Judge, Jaffna, 1869, and Acting District Judge, Galle, May 1873. See *Colonial Office List*, 1877.

[2] Sir William Gregory (1817–92) had taken up his duties as Governor of Ceylon in 1872. He is considered one of the island's best governors (see H. A. J. Hulugalle, *British Governors of Ceylon*), especially in view of his work in restoring the ancient tanks or irrigation reservoirs. He is probably better known to most readers as the husband of the Lady Gregory (*née* Augusta Perse) celebrated by Yeats and Shaw.

[3] The party actually went to the Oriental Hotel. See *North China Herald*, 18 Jan. 1877, p. 66: 'The Chinese Ambassador landed at 11 with eight attendants. He was received by the officials with a guard of honour and a salute of fifteen guns. He drove from the Jetty to the Oriental Hotel, accompanied by the District Judge. His Excellency visited the Jail, the Hospital and the Buddhist Temple, with the Government Agent [F. B. Templer], and the Mudaliyar. He lunched at the Oriental Hotel and re-embarked at three o'clock.' (Galle, 22 Dec. 1876. Reuter Political Telegram.)

[4] Before the development of Colombo Harbour in 1875, Galle was the main port of Ceylon.

embassy. We arranged with the P & O to advance all expenses incurred, agreeing to refund the money on our arrival in London. This has caused us more inconvenience than I dare to say.

By way of ferries, the Sinhalese use boats hollowed out of tree-trunks, with four or five compartments, each compartment barely large enough to hold one man. You put your feet inside and sit up on top. Lengths of wood stretch out from the sides. At bow and stern, there is a heavy block of wood lashed to them. This enables the boat to go through heavy seas without capsizing. This is a relic of the art of hollowing out boats in tree-trunks which was practised in extreme antiquity.[1]

11th month, 7th day [22 December]

At the *ch'en* watch [7–9 a.m.] we went aboard the P & O steamer *Pei-hsia-wa-erh* (S.S. *Peshawur*), a vessel about double the size of the *Travancore*, built just on two years ago.[2] The Captain, whose name was Huai-te [Captain C. A. White],[3] told me that *Peshawur* and *Travancore* were the names of two Indian provinces, one in the extreme north, the other in the extreme south. Europeans are fond of giving names like this to their ships. The P & O agent, Pu-lai [Captain Bayley][4] sent a boat for us. Roosmalecocq and Clarke came to meet us on shore. A salute of fifteen guns was then fired from the fort. This is how Europeans receive ambassadors. When we arrived at the judge's residence, a military secretary, Tan-pu-lai [F. B. Templer],[5] sent by the Governor to receive us, was waiting there. He came with us to look at Buddhist temples near by and inspect a prison under the jurisdiction of the judge. A local

---

[1] He is describing the Indian catamaran.

[2] The *Peshawur* had been built in Scotland in December 1871, and underwent trials on 9 February 1872. She was a screw steamer with four decks, three masts, schooner rigged, round stern, and was clincher built. She was 378 ft. long, 42 ft. broad, and had 33 ft. depth in hold. She had two compound engines, inverted cylinders, of 600 horsepower. Her gross tonnage was 3,871. She served twenty-eight years with the P & O before being sold to an Indian Company. (Information contained in a letter from the P & O Public Relations Office.)

[3] Captain White retired from the company's service in 1879. (Information from P & O Public Relations Office.)

[4] Captain Bayley, the P & O agent in Galle, was a well-known local character who lived in a house on one of the off-shore islands, the 'Villa Marina', which was famous for its setting. See Ernst Haeckel, *A Visit to Ceylon*, pp. 178–9.

[5] F. B. Templer had served in Ceylon since 1845. He had been government agent, Southern Province, since June 1868.

officer, T'i-hsi-la-wa [Da Silva],[1] was appointed to guide us around.

Though the prison is inferior in model to that of Hong Kong, it is just as clean. The main prison has eight sections, each capable of holding seventeen prisoners. During the day these are all set to work under overseers. Those criminals who have committed serious offences are securely confined in a separate building, one man to each cell. The women's prison is a separate building with two sections, each capable of holding seventeen prisoners. There is also a prison hospital.

There are two Buddhist temples, one on a small hillside reached by a gently winding path; the other near the beach. Both buildings are low and narrow. Each contains a clay image of the Reclining Buddha accompanied by two of His attendants. The priests have been given yellow cloth to cover their bodies. They leave the right shoulder bare. When I asked if I could look at the [Buddhist] canon, I found it was all written on palm-leaves, bound together with string and wrapped up in squares of embroidered silk. The writing looked like so many circles joined together. When I requested the priest to recite a little, I found it slightly resembled the chanting of the Tibetan lamas. I distinguished the two syllables *na-mo* very clearly.[2]

By the side of each of these temples is a white pagoda, in front of which are stone shrines with pennants standing by them. In the West, people believe that Śākyamuni was born in Ceylon. I suspect this should refer to the disciples Mañjuśrī and Samantabhadra, both of whom were said to have been reborn into another world.[3] This island may perhaps have been the birthplace of Mañjuśrī and Samantabhadra, but Śākyamuni himself was reborn in Eastern India. For now the river Ganges flows south-east and disembogues in Bengal; and this is the river that the Buddhist writings refer to as the Heng. Hence Tathā-

---

[1] Unidentifiable.

[2] Pali: *Namo* (Sanskrit: *Namah*) meaning 'to devote oneself to; to trust in salvation' is a word used constantly in the Buddhist liturgy.

[3] Mañjuśrī is a Bodhisattva, a guardian of wisdom, accorded the chief place of honour by the Mahāyāna. One of the eight Dhyāni-bodhisattvas, he is the Lefthand Assistant of Buddha. He is revered as the principal Bodhisattva of Mount Wu-t'ai (Shansi). Samantabhadra (Viśva-bhadra) is another Bodhisattva, the Righthand Assistant of Buddha. He is Lord of the Dhyāna and is generally depicted as riding a white elephant. He is revered as the principal Bodhisattva of Mount O-mei (Szechwan).

gata must certainly have been born in Eastern India.[1] It is because of the very strong hold that Buddhism exerts upon the Sinhalese that this tradition is current among [Sinhalese] Buddhists.

Groves of coconut trees are found everywhere here. The priest of one of the temples split open a coconut and used the juice as tea, which he handed to his visitors. 'The coconut supplies us with drink and the bread-fruit tree supplies us with food,' he remarked, 'so long as we have these we need never fear hunger or thirst.'

On asking the name of the temple by the beach, I was told it was called *Wa-lu-k'a-la-ma* [Vālukārāma]. I asked what this meant, and was told that this was just the name of the priest who built the temple near the beach.[2]

We then went off to the judge's residence where we had lunch and received a visit from Mao Li-sun [C. Morrison][3] who works for a foreign company. The island of Ceylon is over 1,000 *li* in circumference; Galle lies at its westernmost point. A fort stands there, with 400 soldiers in it, under the command of Colonel Clarke. By now I had been roaming around for half the day, yet had not set eyes on a single Chinese. Da Silva pointed out to me a house with an upper storey. This, he said, had once been the palace of a former king and had recently been sold to a merchant. When I asked why the king's palace should be put up for sale, he told me that the family was poor. I asked how it had come about that the palace was surrounded by a huddle of dwellings belonging to the common people, and was told that since the country was governed by the English the king had lost his power and merely occupied the royal palace. When I asked where the king had gone, Da Silva could not tell me.[4]

---

[1] The Tathāgata (Śākyamuni Buddha: the 'Once Released') was, in fact, born in the old kingdom of Kosala, in the modern district of Oudh, on the borders of Nepal.

[2] Buddhist temples are often named after their builders. But here the name simply means 'Sand-Hermitage'.

[3] Unidentifiable.

[4] This garbled story would seem to refer to the 'Queen's House', a residence dating from A.D. 1687, which was used by governors of Ceylon when they visited Galle. Da Silva is presumably referring to the sale of this property by Sir William Gregory shortly after the latter assumed office. See Hulugalle, *British Governors of Ceylon*, p. 114.

Europeans colonize other countries with the intention of settling there and making a profit. All they do they plan with wisdom and strength, so that they monopolize power and roll up the country like a mat. Yet they do not have to overthrow the royal house in order to extinguish the state. Hence they take the country without specially relying on military strength. This is, in truth, a policy which was unknown in past ages.

Today we weighed anchor at the *yu* watch [5–7 p.m.] in a high wind.

11th month, 8th day [23 December]

Our run at noon was 634 *li*; latitude 6.49 north. In conversation with Hillier, we got on to the subject of the Dutch war in Sumatra. The local chiefs, the sultans, who had suffered from the Dutch invasion, tried to raise troops and put up a resistance. From this conversation turned to the Dutch and their colonies in the South Seas. Their rule was characterized by harsh taxation, which was used for the benefit of the mother country.[1] The English do not behave like this. The taxes they levy on a country are spent on that country. So the yearly revenue from India and Australia, which amounts to more than £100,000,000, is spent entirely on those countries and on nowhere else. It is used for cutting canals, making roads, and setting up schools. Using the wealth of the country for that country's own good ensures that all the people have a share in it and thus breeds no resentment. It is because of this that every petty kingdom in Sumatra would be happy to present their country to the English;[2] but none of them wants to be joined to Holland. I said that though the taxes in Europe are ten times heavier than those

---

[1] Hillier's comments on the Dutch taxation system in the Indies have more than a grain of truth in them. In 1867 the total income of the Indies Government amounted to about 137,500,000 guilders, of which nearly 15,000,000 were sent back to the Dutch Treasury. Taxes brought in 25,599,000 guilders. Ten years later, in 1877, income from taxes had increased to 35,000,000 guilders. The budget however closed with a loss of 4,239,000 guilders. On this Vlekke comments: '[This was] a deficit for which the government in the Netherlands was partly responsible, for even while he saw the deficit coming the acting Minister of Finance had managed to siphon off for the home country two and a half million guilders from the Indies treasury.' (Vlekke, *Nusantara*, pp. 291–2.) Vlekke goes on to comment that 'three fourths of the taxes were paid by the Indonesians, and these had little with which to pay'. (Ibid., p. 292.)

[2] A piece of chauvinism on Hillier's part!

in China, Europeans make a point of drawing profits from trade and commerce. They set up ports so that their people may grow wealthy from settling there and exchanging commodities over a distance of 10,000 *li*. Profit and loss, success and failure, are all identified with the prosperity and decline of the mother-country. It is because of this that these countries are so stable.

Dutch income always falls short of their expectations. When the sultans revolt, they lack the military strength to suppress them forcefully and so have for long been unable to pacify the country. In this respect, their rule is far inferior to the way in which England has subdued Indian Delhi and the other states. The strength of a country makes all the difference.

9th day [24 December]

Our run at noon was 750 *li*; latitude 7.55 north. Today is Sunday. Over a score of people attended religious service, and sang hymns in praise of the Great Spirit to the accompaniment of a piano. There was a European lady called Wei-li-le[1] who sang in a clear high voice, which was most agreeable and of great compass. The service lasted for more than an hour, after which the company dispersed.

Three German naval officers named P'ai-sen, Ko-erh-li-mo and Fa-p'ai-erh[2] came to talk to me. I learnt that they were members of a [German] expedition, numbering twenty-one in all, that had been to the South Seas to make astronomical observations, carry out marine surveys and draw up instructions for navigation. The expedition was commanded by a naval officer named A-erh-a-t'a.[3] The expenses of the voyage were all paid by the German government. Each member of the expedition was given three pounds a month as an allowance. They had spent a month or two at Hong Kong, Amoy, and Australia. At every place they visited in the course of their voyage they had to make surveys of the sea-routes and verify them. After they return to their own country they will have to pass an examination before being appointed to any further post.

In answer to an enquiry of mine, I was told that the Emperor, Wei-li-ya-mo I [Wilhelm I] was eighty years old; the

---

[1] Unidentifiable.
[2] I have not been able to identify any of these officers.
[3] Unidentifiable.

Chancellor Pi-shih-ma [Bismarck] was sixty-four; General Mo-erh-k'o [von Moltke] was seventy-five; and the Military Counsellor Lu-te [von Roon] was sixty-five.[1] The wealth of the country and the strength of the army is entirely the result of the work of these four men.

10th day [25 December]

Heavy rain. Our run at noon was 828 *li*; north latitude 9.5. We are exactly in the latitude of Pei-lu-chih [Baluchistan], a country on the west bank of the Indus river. Today is the 25th day of the twelfth month of the Western calendar, which is traditionally reported to be the birthday of Jesus. There was reading of the scriptures and prayers, with hymn-singing to the accompaniment of a piano, for this is a great festival of the Christian church. Our food and drink was better than usual.

Hillier had got hold of a newspaper in Ceylon which contained an article on the Yen-t'ai [Chefoo][2] Convention. I asked him to translate it, along with Liu Ho-po.

11th day [26 December]

Our run at noon was $814\frac{1}{2}$ *li*; latitude 10° 11' 12" north. Yao Yen-chia drew my attention to a passage in the *Chung-kuo kuan-hsi lüeh-lun* [*A Brief Account of China's Relations with Foreign Countries*] in 4 *chüan*, by Lin Lo-chih [The Revd.

---

[1] Wilhelm I (1797–1888); Otto, Prince von Bismarck (1815–98); Helmuth Carl Bernhard, Count von Moltke (1800–91). The last name is puzzling. I suggest it must be Kuo's muddled transcription of Albrecht Theodor Emil, Count von Roon (1803–79), who was certainly one of the makers of German 'power and wealth' at that time. See note 4, p. 82.

[2] The Chefoo Agreement arose out of the murder of A. R. Margary (see Introduction, p. xxviii). Wade had seized this opportunity to force Li Hung-chang to grant Britain further trade concessions, as well as a satisfactory settlement of the Margary case and a refinement of the rules for diplomatic relations between high officials of the two governments. The Conference began on 14 August 1876, and was formally concluded on 13 September. Though the agreement was ratified almost immediately (17 September) by the Chinese government, the British delayed their ratification for nine years: partly because of opposition from British mercantile interests, who were far from satisfied with it; partly because of opposition from the other Powers, Russia, the United States, France, Germany, and Spain, who objected to Britain's unilateral action. Ultimately, however, it was the opium clauses in the Chefoo Convention, which in effect doubled the tariff on the drug, that proved most decisive in bringing about its ratification. See Nathan Pelcovits, *Old China Hands and the Foreign Office*, pp. 125–30; Wang, *Margary Affair*, *passim*, for a full discussion of this Convention.

Young John Allen], the American writer,[1] in which is included the eight-articled 'Memorandum on the Missionary Question' of the Tsungli Yamen.[2] The context of the eight articles is severe, but clear and detailed. I read them with a sigh. In the past, when I discussed the Roman Catholic religion with Wen Wen-chung-kung,[3] he considered it a very serious source of trouble, especially in Kweichow and Szechwan.[4] This trouble assuredly springs from the conduct of the Government officials there, who are so in want of regular procedure that any action they take is counteracted. This has been going on for so long that the practice has become firmly established, and it is now quite impracticable to try to put Government orders into effect. For example, after the Tientsin affair, discussions were held with the representatives of the various [European] states to try to find some way of making sensible regulations governing their activities, so that we could patch things up a bit and save the situation. Wen Chung-kung told me that written drafts had been made and submitted to the various countries concerned, only for them to be treated with complete indifference. This was the Memorandum in question.

I find that the religion of the Lord of Heaven [Roman Catholicism] dates from the time of Moses. The religion gets its name from Jesus Christ. Several hundred years afterwards, the Islamic religion of Arabia arose. More than 1,000 years later, Lu-te [Martin Luther] found the Western [Protestant] religion, and the Protestant religion came into being. Greece is the ancestor of European culture. The Greeks also established their

---

[1] Young John Allen (1836–1907) was a well-known American Methodist missionary, who had first arrived in China in 1860. He was active as an educator and tireless as a translator, with some ninety or so works translated into Chinese to his credit. In 1868 he founded the *Chiao-hui hsin-pao*, a weekly review for circulation among the Christian Chinese, which was later expanded into the *Wan-kuo kung-pao* (*The Globe Magazine*, later called *Review of the Times*), which appeared weekly from 1875 to 1883 and monthly from 1889 to 1907. As J. K. Fairbank puts it: '... this journal, ably edited by Chinese scholars, presented in literary Chinese a wide selection of Western ideas and information, including Timothy Richard's proposals for remaking China. It became in fact one source of the Reform Movement of the late 1890's.' (Fairbank *et al.*, *Modern Transformation*, p. 364.) The *Chung-kuo kuan-hsi lüeh-luan* is found in *HFH*, xi.34a–39a.

[2] This must refer to the circular letter and eight draft regulations, aimed at reducing the power of the missionaries, put out by the Tsungli Yamen on 9 February 1871, after the Tientsin Massacre. See note 5, p. 82.

[3] See note 6, p. 82.   [4] See note 7, p. 83.

own interpretation of the teachings of Christ, thus forming the Greek Orthodox Church. Both these doctrines stem from Moses. Roman Catholicism and Protestantism, both of which emanate from Jesus, are at loggerheads with each other. Thus the Roman Pope explains the origin of Catholicism, pointing to its wide extension and antiquity as an argument favouring the propagation of this religion (which is his own devotion). The Protestants do the same. Among the religions of Europe there are those that are held in common by both ruler and people, while in other countries ruler and people are of different religions, each venerating his own gods and not interfering with anyone else. Only China enjoys the religion of the Sages, which is comprehensive and subtle and sets up no territorial limits. Hence Buddhism, Roman Catholicism, and Islam have been disseminated throughout China; and neither their rites, their beliefs, nor the open profession of these religions has been forbidden.

At the beginning of the T'ang dynasty [618–907], the worship of 'Hsien-shen', which is mentioned in the tablet concerning the dissemination of Nestorianism, was already in existence.[1] The monk, Ching-ching,[2] explaining that this term referred to 'the God of Heaven', said that this religion arose in Fu-lin [Byzantium?], which means that it stems directly from Moses. The tablet says: 'He [God] set out the figure of ten [the cross] in order to establish the ultimate.'[3] Such is the origin of the Roman Catholic custom of setting up crosses. During the *Wan-li* period [1573–1620] of the Ming [1368–1644], Li Ma-tou [Matteo Ricci][4] came out east, and Hsü Kuang-ch'i [1562–1633]

---

[1] Kuo has confused Zoroastrianism (*Hsien-shen chiao*) with Nestorianism, which is the main subject under discussion. The Nestorian tablet found near Sian in Shensi, in 1625, in a spot where it had lain buried for some 800 years, commemorates the arrival of the Nestorian missionary A-lo-pen in Ch'ang-an in 635. The tablet itself dates from 781. After its discovery, the tablet was set up north of the Ch'ung monastery, outside the west gate of Sian. Here it remained until 1907. For a translation of the inscription, see A. C. Moule, *Christians in China Before the Year 1550*, pp. 34–52; P. Y. Saeki, *The Nestorian Documents and Relics in China*, pp. 53–77.

[2] Ching-ching was the Chinese name of Adam, a Persian monk of the Ta-ch'in monastery, who recorded the inscription. See Moule, op. cit., p. 35; Saeki, op. cit., p. 34.

[3] Kuo has misquoted the text, which should read: '.... in order to establish the four quarters'. See Moule, op cit., p. 35.

[4] Matteo Ricci, the great Jesuit missionary, arrived in Macao in 1582.

gave his house for a Roman Catholic chapel.¹ The religion was propagated throughout the empire, yet did no harm. At the beginning of the *Yung-cheng* period [1723–36], laws were made for the suppression of this religion and it was prohibited.² Thirty years ago the prohibition of Roman Catholicism was revoked.³ France, which reveres the Roman Catholic faith, sought by relying on her authority and power to protect it.⁴ Thereupon robbers, bandits, and scoundrels hid themselves among the Catholics so that they could defy the laws of the Government. So the power of the priests began to extend itself. During the *Tao-kuang* [1821–51] and *Hsien-feng* periods, the Government administration in Kweichow and Szechwan fell into complete disorder. There were crowds of scoundrels there who were busy perverting the laws of the land, while the missionaries were taking advantage of the situation to do just what they liked. Thus the misery of these two provinces has been growing more pronounced. So after the Tientsin affair, there had to be consultations with representatives of the [European] countries

---

¹ Hsü Kuang-ch'i (Paul Hsü), biography in Hummel, *Eminent Chinese*, pp. 316–19, was one of Ricci's most important converts. He did not 'give his house for a Roman Catholic chapel' but helped Ricci to buy a residence for the mission in 1605. Later he built a church on the west side of his own house. See the account in L. J. Gallagher, *China in the Sixteenth Century*, pp. 474–5.

² The Sacred Edict of the Yung-cheng Emperor (1724) stamped Catholicism as heterodox. Hence for over a century Christianity in China was relegated to the category of a secret society.

³ In 1844, after the Opium War, the French Government succeeded in having Christianity legalized. However, it was not until after the Anglo–French invasions of 1856–60 that the foreign missionary was permitted to live, preach, and own property in the interior of China.

⁴ The legalization of Christianity was due very largely to the efforts of the French. It was the French envoy, Theodore de Lagrène, who persuaded Ch'i-Ying to legalize the practice of Christianity during the course of the negotiations after the Opium War. By 1853, Catholic clerical pressure had persuaded Louis Napoleon that the protection of missionaries and the restoration of church properties must be an integral part of French policy in China. The murder of the French missionary, August Chapdelaine (29 Feb. 1856) provided France with a convenient excuse to participate in the expeditions of 1856–60. Article 13 of the Sino–French Treaty of Tientsin and Article 6 of the French text (but not the Chinese text!) of the Sino–French Convention (1860) virtually gave the missionaries *carte blanche* in China. By 1870, there were about 400,000 Chinese Catholics, under the care of some 250 priests. Protestants, who had started to penetrate the interior only at a much later date, were far fewer in number. Hence, Cohen has well expressed it: '... When the average Chinese of this time thought of Christianity he generally had in mind Catholic Christianity, its missionary proponents, and its official protector, France.' *China and Christianity*, p. 71.)

concerned. It was pointed out that the mission stations were protecting their converts in every province and that the people of Szechwan and Kweichow were being dragged through fire and water. Just the bare mention of a missionary was enough to drive people wild and start them cursing and swearing, so that they were likely to seize any chance at all to get their own back. The mission stations everywhere had become just so many sanctuaries for criminals, who behaved wantonly, defied the law, and were a source of scandal and concern to honest people.[1] Not only have [the missionaries] failed in their original intention of establishing their religions [in China], but I also fear that when these facts are made known to the countries concerned, they will rouse the deepest shame.

There is an urgent necessity for a proclamation to the effect that no distinctions will ordinarily be made between the adherents of the various religions, but that when it comes to matters of official business, the converts will be judged along with the common people. Governors and Governors-General should strictly enjoin the prefectural and district authorities to carry out these injunctions; whenever they fail to do so, they should be censured and punished out of hand. Only when we are able to subdue the overbearing influence of these converts will the government of their affairs be carried on without undue difficulty.

12th day [27 December]

Our run at noon was 807 *li*; latitude 10.55 north. Our position was about south of the arm of the sea called the A-le-fu Sea[2] [Persian Gulf], into which the Indian Ocean flows after skirting Persia. The two Turkish rivers [Tigris and Euphrates] flow into it. The sea is bordered by Persia and Arabia. It is also called the Eastern Red Sea.

While I was discussing with Macartney the expert way in which the captain took his bearings, he told me that in European countries there were Boards of Trade composed of high-ranking officials and nautical schools as well. When the students have completed their studies, they have to sit for a

[1] See p. xlv, n. 1 above. For an account of the troubles in Kweichow (1865) and Szechwan (1866), see Cohen, *China and Christianity*, chapters 5 and 6.
[2] Hsü Chi-yü's *Ying-huan chih-lüeh*, iii.34a, glosses 'A-le-fu hai' as 'Arabische See'.

Board of Trade examination. Those who are placed at the top of the list are given master's certificates. Those who come out below them are given subordinate posts as officers. Everyone is given a grade. Those who are placed low on the list are examined again, sometimes two or three times, for before you can be a captain you must rank high in the examination. Shipowners are not allowed to make clandestine appointments of captains.

When a ship goes to sea, a surveyor from the Board of Trade inspects her capacity for freight and passengers to see that they do not exceed her dimensions. It is forbidden to carry freight in excess of the registered capacity, or passengers in excess of the number of cabins and beds. Those who transgress against these regulations are punished.

When a ship is built, a high official from the Board of Trade inspects her to see whether the workmanship is strong and the timbers good or shoddy. All this must be according to specification. After this [the official] determines the number of years the ship may serve. It may be for ten or for twenty years; but if she does not come up to specification she is condemned and is not allowed to go to sea. Any contravention of these rules is punished.

When a ship goes to sea, the number of hands employed and the amount of provisions on board are all fixed according to the dimensions of the ship. If the ship does not have her full complement [of men and provisions], she is not allowed to go to sea. Every man has to receive a daily allowance of rice and salt and meat. The food he receives is a fixed amount. If this allowance is not forthcoming, a penalty is imposed.

When a captain puts out to sea, the rewards and punishments to be meted out are all in his hands alone for the duration of the voyage. Every day he records everything that has occurred in a log-book. If any dispute should arise, the high officials of the Board of Trade decide the matter according to the entries in this log-book.

In Europe, commerce is the root of government. Their commercial regulations are orderly and dignified and their methods are exact. So captains on the China run are all specially selected for their posts and have great authority. From all this we can see that [the European] acquisition of wealth and power is not without a firm foundation.

Today the wind, which has been blowing strongly for several days, was higher than ever.

11th month, 13th day [28 December]

Our run at noon was 792 *li*; latitude 11.26 north. We must be close to Arabia. Macartney said that outside the Red Sea there was an island belonging to England called Su-k'o-te-la [Socotra], 1,500 *li* from Ya-ting [Aden]. He estimated that as we were something over 200 *li* distant from it and there was thus a wide stretch of sea in between, we should not be able to see it. He also told me that there was an island called Pi-erh-lin [Perim] 354 *li* outside the Red Sea.[1] A French envoy had arrived at Aden and announced that his government intended to occupy this island, which was no more than a wasteland. While he was making plans for opening up this territory, the authorities at Aden informed the Governor of Meng-mai [Bombay] of this in a dispatch. The Governor then sent off a dozen or so soldiers, who landed on the territory by night and planted the English flag there. Two days later the French envoy arrived, only to see the English flag flying there; so he returned downheartedly. Since Englishmen of all classes scheme with all their might for the profit of their country, [this nation] is certain to prosper exceedingly.

Captain White showed me a time-table for the arrival and departure of English vessels at various ports, beginning from 1 January of this year. According to this, the *Peshawur* was due to leave Ceylon on 25 December. Now we actually left on the 7th day of the eleventh month, i.e. on 22 December by the Western calendar. We are thus three days ahead of schedule. All the hundreds of vessels which come and go between the ports of the world have their times fixed in this way. At the beginning of each year these are all classified and published in a table. If you wish to go to such-and-such a place in such-and-such a month, you may see from this table what vessel you must travel by; and so accurately are the multifarious details arranged that there is not the least fear of mistake.

---

[1] Perim Island, 96 miles west of Aden in the strait of Bab el-Mandeb, had been garrisoned briefly by the British in 1799. It was reoccupied in 1857, in view of the threat posed, so it was thought, by the imminent cutting of the Suez Canal.

Today a high wind is blowing and the weather is somewhat cooler. I find I can wear a light wadded jacket again.

11th month, 14th day [29 December]

Our run at noon was 864 *li*; latitude 12.16 north. In the morning we sighted Mount Ya-te-fei [Cape Guardafui], which means we are now on the northern coast of the continent of A-fei-li-chia [Africa]. At this point the Asian and African sea-routes converge. From here our course turns at an angle into the Red Sea.

Macartney was saying that in European warfare captives are not killed. If they are officers, they carry their commissions on their persons. When they are captured, they show their commissions and are then treated with the courtesies due to officers. Food, drink, and lodging are provided for them in accordance with their rank. Sometimes an agreement is made to release a prisoner on condition that he takes no further part in the hostilities. If the prisoner is unwilling to agree to this, then he is put under restraint to prevent his escaping. When the war is over he is released and sent home. Occasionally [an officer] who has been released under promise to take no further part in the war asks to be given a command again. His commanding officer then reprimands him for his breach of faith and very often he is cashiered. There is a general understanding among all states [of Europe] about the reciprocation of treatment [of prisoners]: hence no breach of faith with the enemy is tolerated. For should a man who has promised to take no further part in hostilities then be allowed to enlist for service again, the enemy would cite his example in the case of prisoners captured later and would refuse to release them. This would not only injure a great number of people but would also cause the country concerned to incur the stigma of want of faith and breach of contract. So in this matter no one dares contravene the code. Here again we see that the good faith and enlightened integrity of the states of Europe is very close to that of the ancients.

An English minister, Fa Lin-ssu [the Revd. Vallings?],[1] died on board, and the captain had the body put in a coffin, dressed for burial, and cast into the sea. Since we were so close to Aden,

---

[1] Unidentifiable.

his widow begged that the burial might take place there. But the captain refused, saying that as in the case of death [at sea] the body was generally covered only with a shroud, to have it placed in a coffin and dressed for burial was to show greater respect than usual: but that it was immaterial whether the burial took place in earth or in water. So with their scriptures in their hands they intoned the praises of the deceased and then cast him overboard.

11th month, 13th day [30 December]

Our run at noon was 777 *li*; latitude 12.38 north. After sailing another $145\frac{1}{2}$ *li* we arrived at Aden. Aden lies on the coast of Arabia. (The *Ying-huan chih-lüeh* is at fault in calling it an island.) It stands on the brink of the sea, a single mountain of bare rock. The English have built a fort at the furthest edge of the mountain. East and west, two mountains project crosswise into the sea, with an anchorage for ships between them over ten *li* across. The English have settled in this spot because they consider it the most advantageous position outside the entrance to the Red Sea. The Europeans have built their houses all around the eastern mountain. Behind the mountain the waters of the sea have swept in and formed a small lake. Another fort has been built there. There are three forts in all, as well as guns placed along the coast. A military officer named Heng-te [Hunter?][1] came on board to pay us the compliments of the Governor of Bombay, for this territory is also under the Bombay government.

There are over 8,000 Arab inhabitants; over 6,000 Indians; between 3,000 and 4,000 Africans, and 100 or more Europeans of various nationalities. There are 1,000 native artisans working here. There are 2,000 troops stationed here, comprising infantry, cavalry, and artillery, most of them Indians. This territory originally belonged to the Arabs, but the English have settled here and made it an anchorage for ships coming and going along their ocean routes. The Arabs are Muslims, fierce robbers much given to plunder and murder, whose actions can never be foreseen. For this reason it is essential to keep a good number of troops stationed here. There is a fighting ship here called the

---

[1] Untraceable.

Po-erh-te [Borderer?], the naval commander being named A-erh-pen [Albert?].[1]

It rains very little in Aden, but there is a great deal of sunshine. I discovered from asking Hunter[?] that during the six years he had been in Aden it had only rained three times. Small reservoirs have been constructed along the sides of the hills to supply drinking-water. Every time it rains the water trickles into them without a drop being wasted. The country produces ostriches which stand sixteen [Chinese] feet high with their necks stretched out. One of their eggs will hold a peck. Their feathers are used as ornaments on the hats of European ladies.

11th month, 16th day [31 December]

We sailed at the *ch'ou* watch [1–3 a.m.]. Our run at noon was 402 *li*; latitude 13.10 north, directly opposite Mu-chia [Mocha], the most thriving seaport on the eastern shore. The place produces coffee, which is exported to England, America, and other countries. The hills along the coast are a reddish-brown colour, hence the name 'Red Sea'. The capital of Arabia is called Mai-chia [Mecca] and is the place where Islam took its rise. It too stands near the coast of the Red Sea.

Today was a day of worship. There was singing, reading of the scriptures, and worship of the Heavenly Spirit. By the Western calendar, today is the thirty-first day of the twelfth month and hence the last day of their year. In China we call the equivalent day '*ch'u-jih*' or 'the day of passing away'.

11th month, 17th day [1 January 1877]

Raining. Our run at noon was 771 *li*; latitude 16.46 north, in Arabian waters. At times we caught sight of lofty mountains byond the sea in A-po-hsi-ni-ya [Abyssinia], a barbarian country. Both sides of the Red Sea are inhabited by Muslims, with the exception of the Abyssinians who profess the Western religion and form a separate tribe having no commercial dealings with the other states. A year or so ago the English sent troops to invade the country because the Abyssinians had imprisoned an English subject. They entered Man-ku-te-lin [Magdala], the capital, and killed the king in the course of the fighting that ensued. After having set up another king, the

[1] I have been unable to discover any ship in the navy list which would correspond to this one, nor the name of any captain which resembles 'A-erh-pen'.

troops went home. The military commander on this occasion was Le Pi-erh [Lord Napier], the present Governor of Chi-pa-ta-ta [Gibraltar].[1]

Today is the European New Year's Day, but they have no congratulatory ceremonies. I have heard that today the English Queen is to be raised in status to Empress of India. All the Indian princes are to assemble in the city of Te-li-eh [Delhi] in northern India, to offer their congratulations. The various Muslim tribes of the Western Regions will come there from afar, as well as Buddhists from Pu-ta-la [Bhutan]. The K'uo-erh-ka [Gurkhas], [the rulers of] Pu-lu-k'o-pa [Punjab?], and K'o-shih-mi-erh [Kashmir], as well as [the King of] Siam in the South Seas, will all send envoys with congratulatory addresses.[2] The king of Bhutan will be there in person, thus making a full gathering of the princes of India. There will be more than 1,000 elephants in ranks. All the states under English rule will fire their great cannon, sing 'Long Live the Queen', and let off fireworks.

A fellow passenger, an English merchant named Ssu-li-wen-sheng [Stevenson?], told me that over 3,000 *mou* of land in India had been planted with tea. In China, the tea-plantations yield two hundred catties a *mou*. In India, three times the number of tea-bushes are cultivated and this amount is being increased annually. Over the last twenty years the yield of tea has been 30,000,000 pounds.[3] I found on enquiry that the tea-planting region is A-sa-mi [Assam] in the north-east of Bengal. The *Ying-huan chih-lüeh* states that the annual yield of tea is over 200,000 catties, but this amount has by now increased more than a hundredfold.

[1] C. D. Cameron (d. 1870), consul in Abyssinia, was imprisoned by Theodore II (r. 1855-68), along with other British subjects and some European missionaries, on the grounds that they had participated in an alleged Egyptian plot. A British expeditionary force under General Sir Robert (later Lord) Napier landed at Zoulah Bay on 2 January 1868, and stormed Magdala on 13 April. Theodore committed suicide in his stronghold. After his death, three rival claimants fought for the crown. Kassa, chief of Tigré was eventually victorious in 1872, assuming the name of John IV (r. 1872-89). For Lord Napier of Magdala, see p. 167, n. 4 below.

[2] Kuo's conservative colleagues, ever fearful of British designs on China, must have been alarmed by this announcement of Queen Victoria's suzerainty over India.

[3] In 1876 India exported 21,392,760 lbs. of tea to the value of £1,963,550. China's tea export for that year was valued at £10,500,000.

Kuo's Journal

11th month, 18th day [2 January]

Our run at noon was 723 *li*; latitude 20.23 north. The captain told me that the Red Sea was about 500 *li* wide. From time to time we sighted islands which are not marked on the map. The only island recorded by the *Ying-huan chih-lüeh* is Ma-su-a [Massawa],[1] which belongs to Arabia. In recent years the English have taken possession of Perim: but there are a great many small islands here which have not been cultivated and belong to no one. Even European atlases do not mention their names.

Since we left Aden, the weather has gradually become cooler as we have drawn further away from the equator every day. The reason for the great heat of the Red Sea is that the African coast to the south is all sandy, uninhabited desert, where the sun scorching down on the sand and rocks raises a burning heat. This is wafted across by the south wind, and the steaming atmosphere is driven over the Red Sea. In autumn and winter the north wind abates the heat. Ch'ung Ti-shan, the [Junior] Guardian[2] of the Heir Apparent, is of the opinion that the oppressive heat from the Red Sea is not dissipated even during the depth of winter. It seems to me he has not properly studied this question.

While I was in Singapore, I obtained copies of *The Times* and while in Ceylon I got hold of a copy of another newspaper. All of them contained several articles on the present negotiations between China and England. I handed them over to Te-tsai-ch'u and Feng K'uei-chiu, who have translated them with the assistance of Hillier. Since the three principles of foreign affairs, national standing, and proper [diplomatic] method are involved, these articles will enable us to learn something of the European standpoint and grasp their methods of handling

---

[1] Massawa, in Eritrea, is not an island.

[2] Ch'ung-hou (1826–93), style Ti-shan, was a member of the Wanyen clan and of the Manchu Bordered Yellow Banner. After the Tientsin affair (1870), he was ordered to convey an official apology to France. He sailed from Shanghai on 16 November 1870, arriving at Marseilles on 25 January 1871. He thus passed through the Red Sea in winter, as Kuo did, and was evidently equally surprised at the heat he encountered there. In 1876 Ch'ung had become military governor of Mukden, after having served as Senior Vice-President of the Board of War since 1872, with a concurrent appointment in the Tsungli Yamen. See Liu's *Journal*, p. 118, n. 2 below. 'Kung-pao' is a short form for 'T'ai-tzu Shao-pao', one of the six titles associated with the entourage of the Crown Prince since Sung times. This title was conferred on distinguished officials as a mark of prestige.

affairs. I then ordered Liu Ho-po, Chang T'ing-fan, and Huang Yü-p'ing to write three memorials on this subject, abridging any matters that might prove offensive.

From the Northern Sung dynasty [960–1127] onwards, troubles on our frontiers increased daily, and those who discussed border conflicts became so rash and importunate that [the government] had nowhere to hide itself for shame. Master Ch'eng,[1] the great Confucian scholar, during a discussion of the five things that had been best performed under the Southern Sung [1127–1279], remarked that one of them was to have treated the Yi and the Ti[2] with complete sincerity. Before the Northern Sung, our statesmen were still broadminded. Hence it is said in the Book of Mencius: 'Those who delight in Heaven use a small state to serve a great one.'[3] Mencius then goes on to quote the example of T'ang serving Ko[4] and King Wen serving the Hun barbarians[5] as examples of those who delight in Heaven. When Han Kao-tsu was besieged in P'ing-ch'eng [200 B.C.], he sent an envoy to the barbarians to make peace through a marriage.[6] T'ang T'ai-tsung [reigned 626–49] yielded to the Gök Turks for expediency's sake.[7] The glorious founder of the dynasty did not consider this a disgrace.

---

[1] This saying is attributed to Ch'eng Hao (1032–85), style Ming-tao, one of the founders of the Neo-Confucian school. The passage Kuo has in mind is found in *Erh Ch'eng ch'üan-shu*, xv.126–32. A note prefacing this chapter on p. 1a says: 'It has been said that these are the words of Master Ming-tso.'

[2] Names used vaguely to denote the non-Chinese tribes of the east and north.

[3] *Meng-tzu*, 1, *Liang Hui Wang* (B), 3; Legge, *Classics*, ii.155.

[4] T'ang the Completer, legendary founder of the Shang state, was said to have lived in Po, which adjoined the state of Ko. T'ang sent a number of his people to assist the peasants of Ko in their farming. Yet the Earl of Ko, far from showing gratitude, attacked and robbed the people of Po as they were carrying provisions to his subjects. See *Meng-tzu*, 3, *T'eng Wen-kung* (B), 5; Legge, *Classics*, ii.271–2.

[5] King Wen, father of King Wu, the reputed founder of the Chou dynasty (1122 or 1027 B.C.–256 B.C.), was said to have served the Hun barbarians. See *Meng-tzu*, 1, *Liang Hui Wang* (B), 3; Legge, *Classics*, ii.155.

[6] Takigawa Kamitarō, *Shih-chi hui-chu k'ao-cheng*, lvi.14, records that when the first emperor of Han reached P'ing-ch'eng, in the course of a campaign, 'he was surrounded by the Hsiung-nu and for seven days was unable to obtain anything to eat. Emperor Kao-tsu, in accordance with an ingenious plan suggested to him by Ch'en P'ing, sent an envoy to the consort of the Shan-yü. The siege was at length raised and Kao-tsu made his escape.' For details of this stratagem, see the early fifth-century commentator P'ei Yin's explanation in the *Shih-chi*. Kuo has this commentary in mind.

[7] The T'u-chüeh, or Gök Turks, first emerged as a force to be reckoned with in

Kuo's Journal 43

From the beginning to the end of the T'ang dynasty, when the Uighurs[1] and the T'u-fan[2] were treated cordially, we bore suffering in patience and endured shame. In this way our rulers protected the country and kept the people happy. The custom of regarding the Yi and the Ti as great evils and peaceful relations with them as a flagrant disgrace really began only with the Southern Sung. The effects of this policy became apparent during the declining years of the Sung and Ming dynasties.[3]

The kingdoms of Europe date back for some 2,000 years. Their governmental and educational systems are well-ordered, enlightened, and methodical. They are completely different from such upstart dynasties as the Liao [947-1125][4] and the Chin [1122-1234][5] which suddenly sprang up and as suddenly declined. They have come to China merely for trade, yet have already firmly entrenched themselves there. They keep pushing forward and oppressing us. Since their knowledge and their strength are both pre-eminent, we must study ways of dealing with them. To engage in such discussions cannot be called appeasement. There are those who baselessly talk of

---

the middle of the sixth century A.D. See W. Eberhard, *A History of China*, pp. 149 ff. Kuo would seem to be referring to T'ai-tsung's treaty with Qadir Khan (626), which led the Turks to withdraw from China.

[1] The Turkish Uighurs had been called in by the Chinese to help put down the rebellion of An Lu-shan (755-63). After the death of Emperor Su-tsung (762), the Uighurs decided to take over China, allying themselves for this purpose with the T'u-fan. Eventually, in 765, they turned on the T'u-fan and came over to the Chinese side. See Eberhard, *A History of China*, p. 186.

[2] The T'u-fan emerged as a new political unit in Northern Tibet at the beginning of the seventh century of our era. They had an upper class of Turks and Mongols ruling a Tibetan lower class. See Eberhard, *A History of China*, p. 177. In 763 they captured the western capital, and were finally defeated only with the help of the Uighurs.

[3] Kuo is making the point that to treat the barbarians badly was to invite invasion, since the Sung dynasty had been overthrown by the Mongols and the Ming by the Manchus.

[4] In 946 the Khitan destroyed the Later Chin Dynasty and founded the Liao dynasty in North China and adjacent areas. See K. A. Wittfogel and Feng Chia-sheng, *History of Chinese Society: Liao 907-1125*.

[5] The Tungusic Jurchen, who were ancestors of the Manchus, founded the Chin dynasty in North China after defeating the Liao (1125). They controlled a larger part of China than the Liao had done and posed a formidable threat to the Sung, who were compelled to pay them tribute from 1141 onwards. The dynasty was eventually extinguished by the Mongols in 1234 after involving itself in exhausting wars.

'appeasement' in order to intimidate the Court. With gaping mouths and bulging eyes, they seek their own gratifications, even going so far in their discussions as to say that they would rather see the state destroyed and the dynasty overthrown than talk of peace. Many times have I heard such words spoken in the capital. Duke Shao's admonition to King Ch'eng said: 'Pray that the Mandate of Heaven may last for ever.'[1] He who prays to Heaven in fear and trembling will be willing to restrain himself and humble himself, for he has set his heart on the tranquillity of the people and the preservation of the state. I certainly never expected that the Sung and Ming literati would do as much harm as they have done by the transmission of their doctrines and discussions; Liu Ho-po has remarked that those who discuss European affairs only see one side of the truth. I personally think that we must look at every side of the truth. If we see only one side, we are looking at this from a selfish standpoint. What we call truth is none other than something that must be applied both to ourselves and to others. Then what we do will be right and what we practise will be correct. When we extend this to others, our hearts [will be peaceful] and we will have hold of the truth. Once we have put this into practice, then the empire will be at peace. Those who have obtained office will carry out their duties through such practices and shoulder their responsibilities without entertaining any doubts. Those who have not obtained office will understand the truth and recognize it in their hearts, and will not dare to be presumptuous. It is the task of the great officers to honour their lord and protect the people. What is the use of leading the country to be vainglorious? A vainglorious man is a foolish man. If an ordinary man were to behave in such a way [as these do] in society, then his fellows would be angry with him and the demons and spirits would punish him. Can one discuss affairs of state with people like these? To act in this way is to stray very far from the truth. I am a very stupid man; yet I shall not spare myself from contending with such people at the top of my voice, speaking to them harshly in order to bring them to their senses. I hope to enlist the aid of all scholarly and intelligent gentlemen in bearing this testimony.

[1] *Shu-ching, Shao Kao*; Legge, *Classics*, iii.436. The full passage reads: 'May the king by means of his virtue pray that the Mandate of Heaven may last for ever.'

11th month, 19th day [3 January]

Our run at noon was 756 *li*; latitude 23.57 north. Early in the morning we passed Mecca, the capital of Arabia, which lies about one day's journey from the sea. On the African coast to the south lay Nu-po-ya [Nubia], another Muslim country. This country is under the control of Mai-hsi [Egypt].

At Singapore, which is not far from the equator, the length of the day was about the same as it is during the spring and autumn equinoxes [in China]. Since we entered the Red Sea and have been sailing northwards, the day is becoming the same length as it was before [when we left Singapore]. The length of the day is diminishing, while the nights are growing correspondingly longer. There is rather more than two hours' difference in time between here and China, while at London the difference is over four hours.[1] For in the extreme west of the globe we naturally see the sun a little later.

Te Tsai-ch'u has been examining the flags of all the nations, and gives the following summary of what he has found:[2]

The American flag is oblong and divided horizontally into 13 stripes, six white and seven red. The section nearest the flagpole has a blue ground with thirty-seven gold stars embroidered on it. The country is divided into thirty-seven states, which are symbolized on the flag.[3] The Union flag is bright blue with thirty-seven stars set round it.

The Russian flag is oblong, the front half being white with a diagonal blue cross on it. The rear half is divided horizontally into three stripes, white, blue, and red.[4]

The Swedish flag is blue, with a yellow cross on it. In the right-hand corner, near the flagpole, is another cross with the horizontal arms yellow and the vertical arms blue, with white edges. The parts around the cross are each divided into two parts, red and blue.

---

[1] Peking is eight hours ahead of Greenwich time, not four.

[2] Chang's summary is on the whole accurate, except that he consistently fails to distinguish between national flags, naval flags, and mercantile ensigns.

[3] Strictly speaking, since Colorado was admitted to the Union as the thirty-eighth state on 1 August 1876, the American flag should have had thirty eight stars, not thirty-seven. But of course, the handbook which Chang was consulting could not have incorporated this amendment.

[4] There appears to be some mistake here. The Russian mercantile ensign was a horizontal tricolour of white, blue and red. The flag of the Imperial Russian navy was a blue saltire of St. Andrew on a white ground.

The German flag is a white oblong with a black cross on it. The arms of the cross are divided into five stripes, three black and two white. In the centre of the cross is a black-framed escutcheon with a golden oriole on it. The upper rectangle in the right-hand angle of the cross, next to the flagpole, is divided horizontally into three stripes, black, white and red. In the centre of these is another black cross, with a white border.

The Danish flag is a red oblong with a white cross on it. The French flag is an oblong divided vertically into three parts. The part nearest the flagpole is blue, the outside red, the middle white.

The English flag is a blue oblong. On one quarter, the upper corner next to the flagpole, there are two crosses, one rectangular and one diagonal with a white edge, like a six-petalled flower.

The Spanish flag is an oblong with five rectangular stripes, three yellow and two red.[1]

The Austrian flag is an oblong divided horizontally into three sections. The upper and lower parts are red and the middle white. Right in the centre of the upper band is a golden royal ceremonial hat [i.e. a crown] surrounded by twelve silver stars. In the very centre of the middle section is an escutcheon, of which the upper and lower sections are red and the middle white. This escutcheon has a yellow border.[2]

The Italian flag is an oblong divided vertically into three sections. The middle is white, the left-hand side red, the right-hand side green. In the middle is a red escutcheon with a blue border and a white cross on it.[3]

The Portuguese flag is an oblong, the left half white and the right half blue. There is a red ground in the centre on which is a golden royal crown. Below the crown is a small escutcheon with a yellow border. At the top and down the two edges of the escutcheon are seven small yellow turrets. In the middle is another small, white escutcheon in the centre of which are five small blue squares in the form of a cross.

The Belgian flag is an oblong divided vertically into three sections: the middle one yellow, the left one red, the right one black.

[1] This was the Spanish mercantile ensign.
[2] This was the flag of the Imperial Austrian navy.
[3] This was the Italian mercantile ensign.

Kuo's Journal

The Dutch flag is an oblong divided horizontally into three sections: the middle one white, the upper one yellow, the lower one blue.[1]

The Greek flag is an oblong divided horizontally into nine stripes, four white and five blue. On the upper half next to the flagpole there is a quadrangle with a blue ground on which is blazoned a white cross.

The Turkish flag is a red oblong. On the upper half nearest the flagpole there is a red quadrangle bordered with white, in the middle of which is a white star.[2]

The Mexican flag is an oblong divided vertically into three sections: the middle white, the left red, the right green.[3]

The Peruvian flag is an oblong divided vertically into three bands: the middle white, the right and left both red.

The Egyptian flag is a green oblong with a white crescent moon in the centre of it.

The Persian flag is an oblong with a white centre bordered with green. In the centre is a yellow lion holding a blue sword in its left forefoot, and bearing on its back a sun emitting golden rays.

The Japanese flag is a white oblong with a red sun in the centre.[4]

The Siamese flag is a red oblong with a white elephant in the centre.

The Swiss flag is a red oblong with a thick, white cross in the centre.

The flag of the Spiritual Ruler of the Roman Religion [i.e. the Papal States] is a white oblong. In the centre of this is a large ornament which looks like two keys interlocking and forming a cross. On top of this a golden, ornamented crown rests on a blue background. Underneath is an oval figure with a gold border, the inside of which is divided into four parts, two with obtuse angles. There are two golden lions on a blue ground; two red bands and two white, the upper and lower bands to left and right differing in length. Underneath this there

[1] The Dutch flag is a horizontal orange, white, and blue tricolour and contains no yellow stripe.
[2] The Turkish flag had a white crescent moon and a white star on a red background.
[3] This was the Mexican mercantile ensign.
[4] This was the Japanese mercantile ensign.

are two branches with flowers and leaves curving upwards to the rings of the keys. Under the keys is an ear of wheat. Under the cross and branches there are flying ribbons, red in colour.

Every country has different flags for its warships and its merchantmen. The rank of the officer commanding the warship is also denoted by the colour and number of the marks [on the flag]. Small states and dependent territories also sometimes have different flags and pennons. But it is difficult to distinguish these clearly, so I shall refrain from giving details of these. The important thing is that all these flags are oblong and flown horizontally. Since the flagpole is vertical the flag is horizontal. Hence the horizontal dimension forms the length of the flag while the upright strip forms the vertical part. The horizontal length is about seven or eight feet, while the vertical height is about four or five feet. In general, flags flown from the mastheads of ships are longer vertically and shorter horizontally than others. Because it flies in the full force of the wind up at the masthead, the length of the flag is fastened to the flagstaff to prevent the wind from wrapping it around the mast. Sometimes warships fly long flags which are divided at the end like a fishtail. There are also flags which taper away to a point; flags in the form of triangles; and triangular flags divided into two at the apex. The flags are all more or less squarish in form, the acute angles never being formed by oblique lines. In case of sickness, a yellow flag is flown. When the ship arrives at port it has to wait until a doctor comes aboard and until then the people on the ship are forbidden to go ashore. Every sea-going nation observes this rule.

When we come to examine the nine flags mentioned in the *Chou Li* we find that those made of one piece of silk are all of one colour, while those made of several pieces joined are of all five colours interspersed.[1] The *Erh-ya* says: 'A full length pennon of eight feet is called *chao*. The divided streamer added to the end of the pennon is called *p'ei*.'[2]

Now Cheng K'ang-ch'eng says that the divided streamer

---

[1] *Chou Li*, xxvii, *Ssu-ch'ang*, Ch'un-kuan tsung-po Shih-san ching ching-wen ed., p. 41, contains a description of the nine standards used during the Chou dynasty.
[2] *Erh-ya*, *Shih-t'ien 8*, *Erh-ya yin-te*, Harvard-Yenching Institute Sinological Index Series, Supplement, No. 18, p. 20, 8/11.

added to the end of a pennon was shaped like a swallow-tail.¹ This is like the long [European] flag with its divergent points. Yet the Europeans were certainly not influenced by our ancients. It is just that the spontaneity of Heaven and Earth makes no distinction between China and the rest of the world when it comes to questions of design. The nine flags [of the *Chou Li*] were distinguished by their dimensions. All of them were oblong in shape. None of these ancient flags had oblique edges; but when they were formed to acute angles this was simply because it made them more convenient to roll and unroll.

When the flags of our nation are cut to acute angles this makes them unsuitable for a model of respect. I think that the ancient [Chinese] flags all had fringes, though these have now disappeared. This would explain the origins of their borders.

When we send embassies to Europe we should naturally avoid doing anything which they may regard as objectionable. We should use fringes of red silk on our flags and follow the ancient model in having images of mounting and descending dragons on them. I am keeping these notes for future consultation in case the question of the patterns of our own flags should be raised.

20th day [4 January]

Our run at noon was 726 *li*; latitude 27.32 north. By now the sea has gradually grown narrower. Close at hand on either side are mountainous coasts. From time to time we sight islands almost touching the coastline. I realize that now we are in the waters of Mai-hsi, which Europeans call Ai-chi [Egypt]. The farther end of this sea divides into two branches. The eastern outlet is called A-k'a-pa [Aqaba] and belongs to Arabia. The Western outlet is called Su-erh-shih [Suez] and belongs to Egypt.

Each is several tens of *li* across at the place where they divide, with a great mountain between called Mount Hsi-nai [Sinai]. This is traditionally said to be the spot where Mo-hsi [Moses] founded the religion of the Ten Commandments. A little to the east lies Turkish Yü-t'ai [Judea]. This is what the *History of the*

---

¹ Cheng Hsüan (A.D. 127–200), style K'ang-ch'eng, biography in *Hou Han-shu*, lxv, was the most famous of the Han commentators on the Classics.

T'ang Dynasty refers to as Fu-lin.¹ It is the native land of Moses. European culture has its origins in Egypt. Judea is where the founders of the [Christian] religion came from.

The biography of Pan Ch'ao in the *History of the Eastern Han* [A.D. 25–220] records that he sent Kan Ying on an expedition to Ta Ch'in.² When he arrived at T'iao-chih [the Crimea], he came to the sea. But when he wanted to cross over to reach the western borders of An-hsi [Parthia], the sailors prevented him from going with tales of how vast the sea was. Ta Ch'in is present day Rome, which is part of Italy. An-hsi is now Persia. T'iao-chih is now Arabia. The sea at which he arrived is the present-day Mediterranean. During the Han dynasty this country belonged to T'iao-chih, while the western boundary of Persia came right up to the Mediterranean. During the Han and T'ang dynasties and even earlier, Europeans trading with China got no farther than the farthest [eastern] boundary of the Roman empire. Communication between An-hsi and T'iao-chih on the one hand and China on the other, was first effected about the beginning of the Western Han dynasty [206 B.C.–A.D. 25]. These countries were those which had the earliest contact [with the East] and were culturally highly cultivated. Wherever there is motivation enough, civilization will certainly manifest itself. These Egyptian hieroglyphics, said to be the origin of European writing, are indeed a spontaneous creation of Heaven and earth.

21st day [5 January]

By the *mao* watch [5–7 a.m.] we had run 513 *li* and reached the port of the bay of Suez, where Asia and Africa are joined by a single thread about three hundred *li* long, between the Red Sea and the Mediterranean.

In the third year of the *T'ung-chih* period [1864], Lai Sai-p'u [Ferdinand de Lesseps], a Frenchman, used machines to start digging a ship-canal sixty feet wide and not more than thirty

---

¹ Fu-lin (Ancient Chinese: *p'jut-ljam*) was the Chinese name for Byzantium. On this name see R. Blake, 'Note supplémentaire sur Fou-lin', *Journal Asiatique*, 2nd ser., 202 (1923), 83–8; A. von Gabain, 'Ein Beitrag zur Fu-lin-Frage', *Sinica*, 8 (1933), 195–7. The T'ang histories recorded four embassies from Fu-lin to China, between 643 and 719.

² See note 8, p. 83.

feet deep.¹ The work was completed in seven years at a cost of seventy or eighty million [dollars]. Merchants from many [European] countries took shares in the enterprise.² As the territory belongs to Egypt, she was given one third of the shares. All ships going through the canal pay a toll, and the profits are divided among the shareholders. In the thirteenth year of *T'ung-chih* [1874], Egypt sold shares worth 12,000,000 [dollars] to England. Because of this, the amount of shares taken up by the English, including both the government and private holdings, amounts to about half the total.³ A railway runs to the Egyptian market-town of Suez, some eight *li* away. Accompanied by Liu Yün-sheng, Li Ch'un-chai, Liu Ho-po, Chang T'ing-fan, Te Tsai-ch'u, and Feng K'uei-chiu, I made a trip on it to see what it was like.⁴ When we arrived in Suez we spent a short time at a European business house, the manager of which was named T'e-erh-le [Taylor?]. Both the European houses and the native dwellings are mostly built of mud-brick, and all have flat roofs. The place cannot compare for business with the sea-ports of Europe. The local people wear long gowns without lapels. Their heads are swathed in cloth. The women cover their heads with a cloth fastened in front. Over the nose they wear a cane fastening which fits on a button attached to the tip of the nose. Only their eyes remain uncovered. Even beggars are dressed like this.

¹ Ferdinand de Lesseps (1805-94) was the creator of the Suez Canal. See his *Recollections of Forty Years*, trans. C. B. Pitman. The canal was begun on 25 April 1859, and formally opened on 17 November 1869. In 1876 the average width of the canal at the surface was 325 feet, its bottom width 72 feet and its average depth 26 feet. For details, see the report by Captain Richards and Colonel Clarke (Feb. 1870) in Percy Fitzgerald, *The Great Canal at Suez: Its Political, Engineering and Financial History*, i.217-25.
² Shares were taken up by France, the Ottoman Empire, Spain, Holland, Tunis, Piedmont, Switzerland, Belgium, Tuscany, Naples, Rome, Prussia, Denmark, and Portugal. Neither Britain nor the U.S.A. took up shares initially. See de Lesseps, *Recollections*, ii.120. The cost of the canal, as stated in the official report of 30 May 1870, submitted to the shareholders, was 432,807,882 francs or £17,312,315. Pierre Crabitès, *The Spoliation of Suez*, pp. 133 ff., discusses these figures and decides they are correct.
³ On 25 November 1875, Britain bought 176,602 Suez Canal shares from the Khedive for £3,976,582, a price of approximately £22. 10s. a share. See Crabitès, *Spoliation*, p. 172. Britain thus held almost half of the original 400,000 shares.
⁴ Kuo was one of the very few Chinese officials of this period who was in favour of introducing railroads into China. See Wright, *Chinese Conservatism*, p. 177; Kuo, *Yang-chih shu-wu yi-chi*, xxviii.11b-15b.

There is only one well of drinking water here.¹ A Frenchman has laid out a garden in the neighbourhood which has water brought to it by machinery from five *li* away. Since we could not visit this place, we hired a small boat and went back to the port. Here we saw two dredgers and went up to have a look at them.² This one is a device consisting of two boats joined together, with a machine over thirty feet high set on top of them. In the middle is an iron bridge six or seven feet across. The two boats are set far enough apart to accommodate the bridge. By raising and lowering the bridge it can be made to descend over ten feet [*sic*] into the water. For taking up the mud, there are over thirty iron baskets which turn around the bridge on pulleys like the 'dragon-bone' [square-pallet chain-pump trough] of a water-wheel.³ The top of the bridge is connected with an iron cistern, by the side of which is an iron gutter about fifty or sixty feet in length. This projects horizontally and is kept up by iron pillars. On either side is a fence made of meshed iron, like an openwork trellis. As the mud is scooped up, it passes to the top of the bridge, is shot into the iron cistern and then sent flowing along the iron gutter until it comes out again. What a marvellous display of earth-lifting machines! Each of these consists of a mechanism over thirty feet high set on a boat.⁴ By the side of each machine is a very wide, short iron pipe. Macartney said that these machines are used especially for scooping up sand, but I fear that I must disagree. I suspect that they use them for digging out the earth on both banks of the canal that it is not necessary to cart away. The boats work in pairs to assist each other.

Close at hand to the left stands a stone statue of a man, over

---

¹ Before 1863, the town of Suez had been forced to depend for its supplies of fresh water on the Wells of Moses, an oasis three miles distant. After 1863, however, the town was supplied by a fresh-water canal from Cairo. See A. T. Wilson, *The Suez Canal*, p. 28.

² Kuo is describing the trough-dredger (*drague à long couloir*) designed by the French engineers Borel and Lavalley in 1865. See note 9, p. 83.

³ Needham in his *Science and Civilization*, iv.2, p. 339, calls the square-pallet chain-pump 'the most characteristic of Chinese water-raising machines'. Kuo was right in comparing these dredges to the Chinese machines he knew so well; for as Needham has shown (ibid., p. 349) the chain-pump was originally a Chinese invention which had found its way to Europe.

⁴ This was simply a variant of the dredges described in note 148 above. These dredges discharged their load through the short iron tube into a barge. See Fitzgerald, *Great Canal*, i.203–4.

Kuo's Journal

ten feet high. It is said to be that of a Frenchman named Wa-ch'en-han* [Thomas Waghorn], who lived two centuries ago.[1] He was the first to ascertain the distance between the two seas, so the statue has been raised to commemorate him.

The Red Sea derives its name from the colour of its coasts. The reflection of the evening sun on the stony hills makes them glow red and purple, like a picture painted with rouge. This is certainly a strange sight!

22nd day [6 January]

The captain has been waiting for the *Wei-ni-ha* (S.S. *Venetia*) from Bombay, which has just arrived this morning, at the *hai* watch [9–11 a.m.].[2] These steamers all run to scheduled times. The *Venetia* was running from Bombay to Ye-le-san-te [Alexandria]. Those who are scheduled to take passage for London are transferred here. Since she was overdue, we had to wait for her.

Hillier has gone on by train to Alexandria, where he will join the steamer for Po-lin-ti-hsi [Brindisi], in Italy. From there he can reach London by rail in three days, so he left us at once. We have received a telegram from the Company's London Office informing me that Chin Teng-han, [J. D. Campbell][3] with the help of an official letter from Ho [Sir Robert Hart],[4] the

---

[1] Thomas Waghorn (1800–50), an English naval lieutenant, was the promoter of the overland route to India. During the years 1831–7, he established a regular caravan service between Cairo and Suez, turning a once dangerous route into a secure highway. He spent his life in attempting to prove to an apathetic British public that the best route to India lay through the Suez. For de Lesseps's admiration of Waghorn, see Percy Fitzgerald, *Great Canal*, i.6–11. The statue of Waghorn at Suez, which was raised at de Lesseps's instigation, was executed by Vidal-Dubray and inaugurated on 12 November 1869. See Wilson, *Suez Canal*, p. 10, n. 2; *The Times*, 30 Nov. 1869, p. 7f.

[2] For the *Venetia*, see *The Times*, 9 Jan. 1877, p. 7f.

[3] James Duncan Campbell (1833–1907) joined the Chinese Customs Service in 1862, becoming Auditor and Chief Secretary at Peking. In 1868 the Tsungli Yamen sent him to Europe on a special mission in connection with the proposed purchase of Macao from the Portuguese. In January 1874 he was appointed Non-Resident Secretary to the Chinese Customs Service in London, a post he continued to hold until 1907. He acted as Hart's confidential agent in London, and played a major role in the parleys with the French Government which concluded the Franco–Chinese War of 1884–5. The Chinese Government accorded him Civil Rank of the Third Class (1878), Civil Rank of the Second Class (1882), and the Order of the Double Dragon, 2nd Division, First Class (1897). In 1885, he was created a C.M.G. See *The Times*, 5 Dec. 1907, p. 4a.

[4] Sir Robert Hart (1835–1911) was largely responsible for the development of

Inspector-General of Customs, had already rented a house for us in Po-k'o-lun-po-li-ssu [Portland Place], all complete with the necessary furniture.¹ On hearing this, I wrote a letter [to Campbell], which I entrusted to Hillier.

We sailed at the *yu* watch [5–7 p.m.]. After leaving the port of Su-sai [Suez], we entered the newly-opened canal. It is barely large enough to accommodate a single vessel; but along its course are several lakes in which ships going through can pass each other when they meet. Mile-posts have been set up along the banks of the canal to show the distance travelled. A telegraph wire runs along the southern bank of the canal, and every ten *li* or so there are wooden huts for the telegraph operators. By the side of the canal, at intervals of several *li*, or several tens of *li*, as well as at the entrance and the exit, balls as big as gourds are hung up on poles to act as signals. When a ship is coming from the east, her arrival is announced at the western entrance, whereupon these balls are hung up to inform eastward-bound vessels that they must make room by stopping at some convenient place to wait for the [other ships.] When ships arrive from the west, the fact is announced in the same way.

No vessel may travel at night. As the canal is just wide enough to hold one ship, it is free from all blockages and hubbub.² At night ships have to stop their engines and wait in the wider parts of the canal. In all this they follow fixed rules which no one dare break.

Today we have travelled thirty-six *li* and are anchored in the Little Bitter Lake.

---

the imperial maritime customs service and the postal service in China. Since 1863, he had been Inspector-General of Customs. The standard biography is S. F. Wright, *Hart and the Chinese Customs*.

[1] In a private letter dated January 1877 (cited in *Macartney*, p. 277), Macartney writes: 'Mr. Campbell, an agent of the Commissioner of Customs, has been asked to look out for a house for the embassy.... Have just received telegram from Campbell. We are to live in Portland Place.' No. 49, Portland Place has remained the Chinese Embassy down to the present day. For Campbell's Chinese name, see D. N. Rowe, *Index*, p. 126.

[2] *Regulations for the Navigation of the Suez Canal* (in force on and after 1 July 1872), Article 3, states that 'navigation by night time is authorized only under exceptional circumstances....'

Ships were allowed to pass each other in the canal, providing they were proceeding in opposite directions, by having recourse to the sidings (*gares*). See *Regulations for the Navigation of the Suez Canal* (1870), Article 6; Stokes Report (January 1874), cited in Fitzgerald, *Great Canal*, i.247–8.

Kuo's Journal

23rd day [7 January]

At the beginning of the *mao* watch [5–7 a.m.] we weighed anchor. When we entered the Great Bitter Lake—also known as the Salt Lake—we were informed that a vessel named the Na-mu-tan [S.S. *Hampton*] had already come through the western entrance.¹ So we stopped our engines and waited. We then passed through Lakes A-mei-ta [Tussum]² and Sai-la-pin (Serapeum) and entered Lake T'i-mu-sa [Timsah]. Here we crossed by the head of another vessel and passed two ships, one named A-mu-no-erh [*Galley of Lorne*] and the other named T'i-ko [*Tigre*].³ At the side of the lake was a dredger.

At noon we passed Jih-ssu-ma-li-ya [Ismailia], half-way through the canal. The railway to Alexandria runs through this place, which is a busy market-town.⁴ When we entered the Suez Canal we had taken on a pilot, who had to be replaced when we got to Ismailia. Yet we did not have to stop, for when we looked out we saw the steam launch of the Company's pilot coming towards us from the town.

On entering the canal again we saw the palace of the Empress of France. In the ninth year of T'ung-chih [1870],⁵ when the canal was completed, the Pasha of Egypt sent out invitations to the sovereigns of every country,⁶ requesting their presence at the opening. The kings of Italy and Austria both put in an appearance. The Emperor of France sent the Empress, for whom a travelling-lodge was erected by the side of the canal. This is still standing there, perfectly preserved.⁷

The canal has been growing narrower, with sand heaped up

---

¹ S.S. *Hampton* was a Commercial Steamship Company vessel, from Southampton, bound for Java, which had left Port Said on 6 January. See *The Times*, 8 Jan. 1877, p. 6c.

² 'A-mei-ta' must be a mistake. Kuo can only be referring to Tussum, which lies between Serapeum and Lake Timsah.

³ *The Times*, 9 Jan. 1877, p. 7f.

⁴ Ismailia, called after the reigning Khedive, Ismail Pasha, was a new town which had sprung into existence in 1862, as a result of the construction of the canal. For a description of Ismailia as it was about the time Kuo passed through it, see Fitzgerald, *Great Canal*, i.186–8.

⁵ The canal was officially opened on 17 November 1869, i.e. in the eighth, not the ninth, year of the T'ung-chih period.

⁶ For a description of the opening ceremonies, to which some 6,000 guests were invited, see *The Times*, 18 Nov. 1869, pp. 10a–b.

⁷ This palace, which had cost 40,000 *livres* to build, actually belonged to the Khedive Ismail.

on both sides of us to a height of over 100 feet. Ships going through the canal are no more than a few feet away from its banks. There are many bays and indentations. We passed through another small lake called Pa-la [Ballāh] and reached Man-sa-lei [Lake Manzala], where we anchored. Today, Sunday, we have travelled 220 *li*.

24th day [8 January]
At the beginning of the *mao* watch [5-7 a.m. we weighed anchor and sailed fifty-four *li* to Po-sai [Port Said]. On the northern bank stood a dredging machine and a sand-pressing machine. On the south bank stood two more dredging machines and a crane. Since the digging of the canal, the sand has been drifting across to the river Ni-lo [Nile], where it piles itself up, sifting several feet deeper every year. The captain told me that a lighthouse which formerly stood on the coast overlooking the sea is now 700 paces away from it, owing to the sand that has been washed up by the tide. Because of this, long piers made of heaped-up stones have been constructed, which project into the sea from both sides of the canal at its mouth, to break the force of the waves and keep back the sand. The pier on the northern side is over 680 yards long; while the one on the southern side is several times more lengthy and looks like a long bridge floating far out among the waves. Since stone cannot be found in the desert, a machine has been used to compress the sand, into oblong blocks about seven or eight feet long and over two feet in height and thickness. These bear an English inscription stating how many *li* the pier extends. All in all, this is a fine example of how the strength of man can combat the forces of nature.[1]

In the town of Port Said there are tall houses ranged in rows. I discovered on enquiry that these had been newly built since the opening of the canal. On the banks of the canal stands a water-pump which brings Nile water from the south for the people to drink. There is a gas-works which supplies gas for the houses and street-lights in the town. There is also a cylindrical reservoir of red wood, measuring several tens of feet in circum-

---

[1] For the Port Said breakwater see Fitzgerald, *Great Canal*, i.160-71. The blocks of which the piers were formed, each of some twenty-two tons in weight, were manufactured on the spot from a mixture of sand and lime. See ibid., pp. 170-1.

Kuo's Journal

ference around the top, standing on a circular mound, and a gasometer which has a separate iron-framed cover over its top.

On the summit of a hill to the east of the town I noticed a windmill revolving in the wind like a fly-wheel. At the furthest end of the town, where it touches the coast, stands a lighthouse, fifty or sixty feet high, looking like a square pillar. At night the lamp is lit for the guidance of ships at sea.[1]

From a vendor of pictures of Egyptian antiquities we bought a number of plates, among which were two views of *K'e-li-a-pei-Ni-te-erh* [Cleopatra's Needle].[2] This is a quadrangular stone-pillar, seventy or eighty feet high, each of the four sides of which are over seven feet across. Macartney acquired a front view of it while Liu Yün-sheng got views of the back and left side. On each side is an inscription, whose upper line consists of pictures of three birds. Beneath this, the inscription is divided into three columns, each column containing over ten characters. Each character is two feet and more in height, and looks very much like the writing on our bells and tripods, as well as different forms of our ancient seal characters. Huang Yü-ping made a copy of them for me. Many of them are surrounded by a square cartouche, like the characters on our stone drums. For example, we have: 🔲 🔲 🔲 🔲 , while the character 🔲 appears as often as four or five times. Some [hieroglyphics] look like birds, thus: 🔲 ; while others look like horses, thus: 🔲 . There are also others which merely represent a horse's head, while still others resemble an eyebrow or an eye, as for example: 🔲 🔲 🔲 🔲 . Some resemble claws, like 🔲 . Among those resembling our seal characters are 🔲 🔲 🔲 🔲 🔲 🔲 🔲 🔲 🔲 🔲 .

The date of the pillar is uncertain. The tradition in Egypt is that in ancient times there lived a wise empress named Cleopatra. Since the top of the stone pillar is pointed, it is eulogized as Cleopatra's Needle. '*Ni-te-erh*' means 'needle'.

---

[1] This was the light which stood at the inner end of the western breakwater. See Fitzgerald, *Great Canal*, i.217.

[2] This might perhaps have been the very one which now stands in London on the Thames embankment, having been brought from Caesarum, Alexandria, in 1878. We may note, however, that two mock obelisks had been erected at the entrance to the canal in 1869. (See *The Times*, 30 Nov. 1869, p. 7f.) The photographs may perhaps have been of these.

We may thus see that the invention of writing cannot be traced back further than the 'Images' and 'Logical Combinations'. When writing was invented in Egypt, it was based on exactly the same principles as in China. In China, as writing has developed, the differences between the six categories of script have become obscured. Similarly, the twenty-six letters of the European alphabet represent only the phonetic class, while the 'Images' and the 'Logical Combinations' have been lost by now.[1]

This stone pillar is not far from Chia-yi-lo [Cairo], the capital of Egypt. I have heard that a great many characters of more or less similar form may still be found in the port of Alexandria.

At the beginning of the *wei* watch [1 p.m.], we weighed anchor and sailed into the Mediterranean sea. This is a place where three continents converge—Asia, Europe and Africa. The Mediterranean is bounded on the north by Europe and on the south by Africa. Central and Eastern Turkey stretch northwestwards for a distance of 2,000 *li*, forming the remote western boundary of Asia. The Europeans have divided the territory around this single sea into three continents; but this is also one of the great natural boundaries of our world.

At night we twice sighted a lighthouse on the coast to the south. Later we passed the Nile, which flows into the sea through three mouths, at Ta-mi-yeh-te [Damietta], Lo-se-te [Rosetta] and Alexandria.[2] The captain has told us we are still over 100 *li* from Alexandria.

---

[1] 'Hsiang-hsing' or 'Images' is the name given to that type of Chinese character which is basically a sketch representing an object. 'Hui-yi' or 'Logical Combinations' are characters formed by bringing two or more simple pictures into logical relation, the resulting compound then having a metaphorical meaning. The six categories of Chinese writing are images, indicative symbols, phonetic compounds, logical combinations, turnings (*chuan-chu*), and borrowings. An interesting comparison between the ancient Egyptian script and the Chinese is found in Chiang Yee, *Chinese Calligraphy*, pp. 36–7.

The eleven Egyptian hieroglyphs Kuo reproduces here are, with two exceptions, more or less decipherable. Their meaning is: (1) door; (2) mouth; (3) imperfect active participle of verb 'to do'; (4) Lord of Everything; (5) friends? (6) giraffe? (7) Ramses; (8) indecipherable; (9) vulture; (10) horse or jackal; (11) indecipherable, possibly part of one of the royal names of New Kingdom. (Personal communication from Dr. Boris de Rachewiltz, October 1971.)

[2] There were actually three iron-pile lighthouses standing at the Rosetta mouth, Brulos point, and the Damietta entrance of the Nile. See Fitzgerald, *Great Canal*, i.217.

25th day [9 January]

Our run at noon was 789 *li*; latitude 32.51 north. It was rainy and oppressively hot, with occasional glimpses of sunshine. As the sun sank westwards a rainbow appeared in the east, several tens of feet in length. We are over a degree higher in latitude than Shanghai, but you could never guess it was winter.

The captain showed us a Port Said newspaper which reported that delegates from England, Russia, and other countries had convened to discuss the military situation in Serbia on behalf of Turkey.[1] The Sultan of Turkey has been unwilling to divide the country up but is inclined to institute major reforms in the government which would bring it nearer the European model, such as convening a popular assembly and instituting a parliament, setting up officials charged with special responsibilities, and establishing courts to settle the people's suits within a definite period of time. But the most important of all these articles [under consideration] is that providing for those in authority to make no distinction between Muslim and non-Muslim Turkish nationals, so that the people might practise any religion they please, whether the Turkish, the Protestant, or the Catholic, each at his own discretion, without let or hindrance. In my opinion, the Sultan of Turkey should bear a repentant heart. Would that the trouble were settled![2]

Macartney believes that it all depends on how he behaves, for the disturbances cannot be settled by simply issuing a proclamation or sending out orders to appease the people. His words have the smack of truth about them.

As you sail west from Port Said, Turkey lies to the north, while to the south lies Ti-li-po-li [Tripoli], which is also a dependency of Turkey.

---

[1] This was the Constantinople Conference, proposed by Lord Derby in 1876, in an attempt to impose reforms on the Turks. The reforms agreed on by the Conference were rejected by the Turks, who evaded them by the device of proclaiming a constitution (23 Dec. 1876) and insisting that all changes should be referred to a constituent assembly—an institution which lasted only a few months. See A. J. P. Taylor, *The Struggle for Mastery in Europe, 1848–1918* (Oxford, 1954), pp. 228–54, for the general background to the eastern crisis of 1875–8. A more detailed study is R. W. Seton-Watson, *Disraeli, Gladstone and the Eastern Question* (London, 1935).

[2] See *Tso-chuan*, 17th year of Duke Hsüan, for the use of *chih* 豸 in the sense of 'to dissipate'.

26th day [10 January]

Our run at noon was 840 *li*; latitude 34.4 north. A gale, which eventually became unbearable, has left me prostrate. In the Mediterranean, with islands all around us, the wind and waves in their rush and eddy make the force [of the sea] stronger than ever.

Captain White said that the English commander Nares got as far as latitude 83 north in his expedition to the North Pole.[1] He cut his way through the ice for 1,200 *li*, till he met with towering mountains of ice through which no road could be cut, or at the most only one *li* or so of the roughest of tracks. For over 140 days they did not see the sun. Many of the sailors in the expedition fell sick. When their resources were exhausted they returned. It now appears that the cause of the sickness was the lack of fruit; and the Admiralty has been blamed for not providing enough fruit-juice for their stores to last out the voyage. They have resolved to organize another expedition in order to explore those frozen seas thoroughly. According to [the captain], there are people living on the ice who carve out houses for themselves from the very ice, using snow for the doors and sealing up the entrance once they are inside. They catch fish and hunt animals to provide themselves with food and clothing. They clothe themselves with the skins of deer and use them as mats when they sleep. When they go fishing, they bore through the ice for anything up to 100 feet or so. When the fish find an opening in the ice at which they can breathe, they all crowd together under the hole. [The hunters] then catch them with a piece of iron fashioned into a blade and lashed to a long pole with a hook attached. They use fish-oil for fuel, burning it at night to give light. As for their dwellings, they move their igloos about in order to hunt and catch fish and animals, just as the Mongols wander around with their herds. It is not so extraordinary when one reflects that all this takes place in a sadly desolate region!

Today we passed Greece to westward. The sea of Ma

---

[1] See p. 20, n. 1 above. Nare's ship, *Alert*, reached the extreme point of her journey on 1 September 1875, having attained latitude 82° 24 north, further than any vessel had ever been before. The *Alert*'s commander, A. H. Markham (1841–1918), reached 83° 20′ 26″. See Article V, 'Geographic and Scientific Results of the Arctic Expedition', *Quarterly Review*, cxliii (Jan. 1877), 146–86.

[Marmora] off Eastern Turkey, marks the border between Asia and Europe. Greece lies across this strategic area. We have now reached the border of Europe.

27th day [11 January]
Our run at noon was 804 *li*; latitude 35.24 north. The English used to hold the A-ni-ch'ün [Ionian] islands, to the west of Greece. At that time Greece belonged to Turkey; but since [her people] found Turkish rule oppressive, they revolted and took to arms. The English seized this opportunity to take possession of the islands. Later, England, France, and Russia undertook to protect Greece and support her claim for independence. A few years later, England returned the islands to Greece: for the Ionian islands are so close to Greece, with their forts all facing the mainland, that Greece could never feel secure [without them]. Moreover, as the territory was of no strategic importance, the English did not want to start a dispute over them.[1] Today we passed these islands and reached the border of Italy.

28th day [12 January]
By the *ch'ou* watch [1–3 a.m.] we had sailed 384 *li* and reached the island of Ma-erh-ta [Malta], in latitude 37 north. To the north lies the Italian island of Hsi-chih-li [Sicily]. It stands opposite the capital of Tripoli, which lies to the south. The island [of Malta] is shaped like a mortar, with a mountain in the centre that is encircled on all four sides. The island measures forty-five *li* from north to south and thirty *li* from east to west, with projecting spurs. There are four or five bays for anchorage. The island possesses a machine factory, which has eleven forts set around it. It is England's most important strong-point in the Mediterranean. Originally it belonged to Fa-lan-hsi [France]; but the English settled here and took possession of it.[2] Warships from every port put in here for repairs.

---

[1] The Ionian islands had belonged to Venice for many centuries; but on the fall of the Venetian republic in 1797, they were annexed to France by the treaty of Campo Formio. The Treaty of Tilsit (1807) declared them an integral part of the French Empire. After their capture by the British during the Napoleonic Wars, the Treaty of Paris (1814) made them a British protectorate. In 1864 they were finally ceded to Greece.

[2] The French captured Malta from the Knights of St. John in June 1798, losing it to the English after a long siege, in September 1800. In 1814 it came under British rule through the Treaty of Paris.

The governor of this territory, Ssu-te-lo-pan-hsi [General Sir Charles T. Van Straubenzee],[1] sent two military attachés, Na-erh-ssu [Nares?] and To-sun [Dawson?],[2] to meet me with a carriage. A salute of fifteen guns was fired from the fort. We passed two heavy gun emplacements on our way to Government House, which is an imposing and spacious residence. The streets of the town [Valleta] are clean, and in good order; the houses, of five or six storeys, stand closely together, the one overlooking the other, like the teeth of a comb. They have a quite different air about them from those of Ceylon or Aden.

When we arrived [at Government House] we found a gathering of officers there, the highest in rank being [Rear] Admiral Lu-a-te [W. E. Luard][3] and General Ko-lan-te [J. T. Grant?].[4] Governor Van Straubenzee, a white-haired man of sixty or so, spent many years in Kuangtung. His lady,[5] who is also very intelligent, detained us to drink wine. Afterwards, they came with us on a stroll. Close by and to the left is a fort containing 120 guns, six of them weighing eighteen tons a piece. (A ton is equal to 1,800 catties, which would make its weight equivalent to 32,400 catties.) The body of the gun measures over ten feet in circumference. One of the forts stands high up on the crest of a hill. This fort held three enormous guns, but we had no time to go and inspect them. (One gun weighed thirty-six tons, while the other two weighed twenty-five tons each.) In front of each gun stood a pile of several hundred shells, ready for defence in case an enemy should appear. There are 6,000 soldiers on defence service and three ironclads stationed here. One was named *Te-fa-ssu-te-shen* [H.M.S. *Devas-*

---

[1] General Sir Charles Thomas Van Straubenzee (1812–92), who was himself born in Malta, was appointed Governor and Commander-in-Chief at Malta in June 1872, after a long and distinguished army career. He had been in command of the British land forces in China during the Second Anglo–Chinese War, and was thus responsible for the bombardment and subsequent capture of Canton (28 Dec. 1857–5 Jan. 1858).
[2] Both unidentifiable.
[3] Rear-Admiral Sir William Luard (1820–1910) had arrived in Malta on the flag-ship *Hibernia* on 8 January 1877. See *The Times*, 16 Jan. 1877, p. 6e.
[4] Lieutenant-General John Thornton Grant (1810–86) entered the army as an ensign in 1828. He eventually became Colonel of the 94th Foot in 1879, and was promoted to General in 1880.
[5] In 1841 Van Straubenzee married Charlotte Louisa, youngest daughter of General John Luther Richardson of the East India Company, and of the Cramond family.

tation], one *Ho-te-ssu-po-erh* [H.M.S. *Hotspur*], and one *Lu p'ai-erh-te* [H.M.S. *Rupert*].[1] In view of the recent Turkish troubles, troops have been moved here to stand guard against Russia. Therefore, there are twenty-five [British] ironclads in the Gulf of La-pi-li-ya [Nauplia] in Greece.

Government House is reached by a winding staircase. It has been laid out on a grand scale, with two audience-halls. One of them is lined with mirrors, the other with sixteen large tapestries, executed in the western style, each of them over ten feet long, depicting lions, elephants, and other strange beasts, all represented in a most life-like fashion. There is also a long gallery containing ancient weapons such as knives, swords, muskets, and clubs, which are hung around the four walls. There is one of the earliest cannons ever made, wrought of iron with a lining of brass, bound with cord and lacquered over. Above this hang several score small guns, framed by four swivel guns which look rather like gingalls, each over ten feet long and made of wrought iron. They are breech-loaders, almost like the modern military weapons, though they were made over 300 years ago. This made me realize that the European breech-loading musket was already in use in the middle of the the Ming dynasty. There are also over ten stone cannons, each as large as a peck in circumference. In the centre [of the gallery] stand five glass cases. One contains knives and axes taken as spoils of war from the Maltese aborigines by the Muslim Arabs, when they were in their first flush of power. A case contains revolving trumpets also used by the Muslim Arabs. Another case holds prayer-books used by priests 700 years ago. Yet another contains the seal and ribbon of the kings of Malta, along with various documents. The last one holds ancient pottery: innumerable bottles, curled tubes, and jars all decorated with painted patterns and made from some coarse, light material.

From the stone staircase we circulated through several galleries, in shape like our raised pathways. Their sides were lined with figures of ancient warriors clad in armour and holding weapons in their hands. These are also to be found in the

[1] H.M.S. *Devastation* was an iron turret-ship of 9,387 tons, under the command of Captain Frederik W. Richards. (*The Times*, 7 Nov. 1876.) H.M.S. *Hotspur* was an ironclad ram of 5,444 tons, consort vessel of H.M.S. *Rupert*, under the command of Commander W. J. Hunt Grubbe, C.B. See *The Times*, 16 Jan. 1877, p. 6e.

armoury, in the centre of which stands a square pillar bearing a bust of the French ruler Na-po-lun [Napoleon I].[1]

I learned on enquiry that there were two high schools on the island and thirty-four primary schools.

There are two prisons, one of which is reserved for the military. Since there are over 6,000 troops on the island, billeted among the local people, some trouble is inevitable. As the captain was pressing us to leave at once, we could not go to look at the prisons.

Governor Straubenzee told me there were a great number of antiquities on the island, which made me greatly regret that I could not linger for a day or so to go with him to see them. We weighed anchor during the *wei* watch [1–3 p.m.].[2]

29th day [13 January]

The day was rainy and windy. Our run at noon was 699 *li*; latitude 37.28 north. Towering ranges have appeared on the coast to the south. This is T'u-ni-ssu [Tunisia], another country belonging to Turkey. The country thrusts itself out into the Mediterranean. From within its borders a single mountain projects boldly into the sea. At its feet a shelf [of rock] lies hidden, so that a large warship can pass only in mid-channel. Even European vessels look on this as a dangerous spot to pass. Once past this place, the coast to the north adjoins France.

---

[1] For a description of the Palace (Government House), coupled with some excellent photographs, see Allister Macmillan, *Malta and Gibraltar—Illustrated*, pp. 199-204. The hall lined with mirrors is the Hall of St. Michael and St. George; while the tapestried hall is evidently the Council Chamber, the walls of which are covered with Gobelin tapestries purchased by Grand Master Perellos (1689-1720), made after paintings given by a Prince of Nassau to Louis XIV. The glass cases which Kuo saw in the armoury contained, among other things, the original Bull of Pope Paschal II (1099-1118) in which he receives under his protection the Hospital of St. John of Jerusalem (1113) and the original Act of Donation of the islands of Malta and Gozo to the Order by Emperor Charles V (1530). A photograph of the pillar mentioned by Kuo can be found in Macmillan, op. cit., p. 203.

[2] Martin, *Cathay*, p. 381, mentions an incident which occurred during Kuo's visit. 'Touching at Malta on their way to England, [the envoys] were invited by the governor to inspect the fortifications. During a sudden shower the governor threw his cloak over the gay robes of the Chinese Minister. Kuo's acceptance of this kindness was represented as a disgrace to his country [by Liu] not less than if he had allowed the English flag to be raised above the Chinese.' This is highly revealing, since it shows that Liu's machinations against Kuo had already begun before they landed in England.

12th month, 1st day [14 January]

Our run at noon was 720 *li*; latitude 31.20 north. A gale has laid me prostrate. Last night I could not sleep, for it was oppressively hot, as though it were the third month of spring. The captain remarked that there was fighting between the Turkish troops and the Serbians, who are in revolt. The Russians intend to stir up a quarrel and then sit by and reap their reward. Since England, France, and Germany see that it would be to their detriment if Russia were to have free access to the Straits [Dardanelles], they have been earnestly deliberating as to how they might protect them. They are relying on Chün-shih-tan-ting [Constantinople], the capital, to keep watch over this vital area of the Black Sea, for this will be sufficient to keep the Russians at bay. Since the English are the most concerned about this affair, they have sent more than a score of ironclads to the Sea of Marmora. In their hearts the Russians fear the assistance that the English might render to the Turks, so do not dare to act presumptuously. Since the Turks have recently agreed to settle the trouble in Turkey, their joint efforts make it seem unlikely that the various powers of Europe will be embroiled in a general war.

Westwards from Tunis, the terrain consists of a long broken range of mountains thrusting northwards, some distant, others close. From time to time we sighted islands in the sea. Judging from the course of our voyage, the southern coast of France lies to our north. By now we must be somewhere off the coast of A-erh-chi-erh [Algeria], which is also a Muslim country. This is now a French dependency.[1] Today is a Sunday.

2nd day [15 January]

Our run at noon was 723 *li*; latitude 36.51 north. (According to the longitude, we are now exactly in the meridian of London; but the kingdoms of Spain and Portugal lie between. Their territory projects irregularly into the Atlantic Ocean, while London lies to the east of them. Hence by taking the train from Ma-sai [Marseilles], in France, to London, you not only travel by a more direct route but shorten your journey by several thousand *li*.)

---

[1] The French had first intervened in Algeria in 1830, embarking on its complete conquest and colonization in 1840.

The strong wind has made me giddy. I have been sick all day and cannot stand properly. During my ten-days' sojourn in Shanghai I was overburdened with work. Since I embarked, I have not been able to ward off my sickness. At this moment my teeth are aching and my gums are swollen, the pain shooting up to both my ears. My throat is sore, my breathing painful, and my head swimming. I feel intolerably restless and disturbed.

I caught a glimpse of a shadowy mountain away in the distance, which the captain said was in Spain. Macartney told me the mountain was called Hsi-ai-la-ni-wa-ta [Sierra Nevada]. The mountain has pointed peaks which rise up like the teeth of a saw. They are covered with snow which never melts throughout the year. 'Hsi-ai-le' means 'a saw', while 'Ni-wa-ta' means 'snowy'.

A Portuguese fellow-passenger named Mo-k'o-li-a [Signor Machalia?][1] joined the ship [recently] on his way home. He is a highly cultured man. When I asked what office he held, I found he was a judge in Mo-san-pi-kei [Mozambique], in East Africa. The Portuguese have divided the territory into seven parts and appointed a governor of Mozambique who controls the whole country.[2]

In the evening we saw a lighthouse on the coast to our north, flashing suddenly and then suddenly going dark again. In the province of Chia-la-na-ta [Granada] in Spain, which we are now passing, there are two ports, Ya-erh-mei-li-ya [Almeria] and Ma-li-ya [Malaga]. Macartney said there were two good reasons for setting up lighthouses. One was to guide ships towards their ports; the other was to warn them away from dangers. Danger beacons have a red light. Those meant to guide ships to port have a revolving light which either lights up and goes dark by turns, or else just stops shining for a few moments. All of them are timed in their flashes so that people may know what port is indicated. Where there are several ports not far distant from each other, each light has a fixed flash-time, to point out the different places.

[1] Unidentifiable.
[2] Portuguese East Africa acquired its first independent Governor in 1752. In Kuo's time it was divided into four provinces and nine districts.

Kuo's Journal

3rd day [16 January]

Our run at noon was 837 *li*, bringing us to Gibraltar, in north latitude 36.7. This is a rock which rises abruptly to a height of over 14,000 feet and is over seven *li* in length.[1] The English call it a 'no', which means 'a great stone'. It stands over against the Kuei-mei-a-fei-ssu-pei-yin mountain [Guadalquivir valley] in Spain, from which it is separated by only a foot or so, with just a strip of land in between. When the tide comes in, it becomes an island, with the Kua-ta-erh-chi [Guadarranque] river on the right.[2] To the south, on the African coast, the Erh-pu-ssu Ho-te [Ape's Head Rock] thrusts forward into the sea opposite Gibraltar. This leaves only a narrow sea-strait in between, which thus forms the gateway to the Mediterranean. 'Erh-pu-ssu Ho-te' means 'Ape's Head'.

Since the English settled here and took possession of this territory,[3] they have made the mountain into what is said to be a most cleverly constructed fortress.

The governor of the territory, Le Pi-erh [Lord Napier of Magdala],[4] sent his military attaché Pei Le-ssu [Major-General R. S. Baynes][5] with a carriage to meet me. (Recently [Napier] invaded Abyssinia and entered Magdala, the capital. Hence he was given the title of Baron of Magdala.)[6] Troops were drawn up at the landing and a salute of fifteen guns was fired from the fort, as on previous occasions. General Sa-ma-ssu-te [Major-General Somerset] was also there.[7]

I discovered on enquiry that there are 5,000 troops in Gibraltar, divided into seven regiments.[8] There are five brigades of

---

[1] The Rock of Gibraltar attains 1,398 feet.
[2] The Guadarranque is a small river which debouches about five miles west of Gibraltar.
[3] England took possession of Gibraltar in 1704, during the War of the Spanish Succession.
[4] Lord Napier, First Baron of Magdala, G.C.B., G.C.S.I. (1811–90), might well have been known to Kuo, since he had commanded the second division in the second Anglo–Chinese War. This division had attacked and captured the Pei-ho forts (Aug. 1860), subsequently entering Peking on 24 October of that year. He was Governor of Gibraltar from 1876 to 1883.
[5] No biographical details available. [6] See p. 40, n. 1.
[7] Major-General Edward Arthur Somerset (1817–86) entered the army as an ensign in 1836 and served in the Kaffir War (1852–3) and the Crimean War (1854–6). He commanded a brigade at Gibraltar from 1873 to 1878. He was promoted to General in 1883, when he retired.
[8] In January 1877, Gibraltar was garrisoned by six, not seven regiments,

artillery and 500 troops to guard the fort, all of whom are artisans. There are 1,500 riflemen, who are in infantry regiments. Each regiment has a school of its own and there is also a high school. There is a library with 40,000 books. The town is built round the inner flanks of the mountain overlooking the Guadarranque river. The population numbers 19,000. Governor Napier sent Colonel Ti-lung [Dillon?][1] to accompany me around.

The walls of the fort are all made of stone. The inside is hardened by cement, while the outside is protected by two small walls. This is meant to enable the riflemen to throw back an assault from close quarters. The walls of the fort surround and protect the foot of the mountain. Up on top, the guns are ranged, while down below are the barracks. Every barrack-block holds one company of soldiers. All of them are built along the side of the mountain. Houses with upper stories have been built near the barracks to accommodate the families of the troops.

The largest guns weigh eighteen tons, while the shells weigh as much as 400 pounds. (A ton is equal to 1,800 catties: a pound is equal to twelve Chinese ounces.) From the fort we went round to the western side of the rock of Gibraltar, where we saw in an angle of the rock, what is called the hill-fort. Gun-embrasures have been cut through the solid rock in three tiers, one above the other. The guns there weigh 5,400 catties each, and the shells are stacked up by them in readiness. Round three sides of the face of the rock run winding stone galleries, one above the other. On the southern face, where a precipice 10,000 feet high rises straight up from the sea, no guns have been placed. My trip, however, extended no further than the west corner of the mountain. I heard that they were tunnelling through the rock to make a council-chamber in the interior, over 100 feet broad. They are also making a stone cistern to catch the rain water as it runs down. This will hold enough water to keep the garrison supplied with drinking-water for one year. There are a thousand and several hundred guns in the fort.

namely: 69th Regiment; 1st Battalion 3th Foot; 2nd Battalion 23rd Regiment; 2nd Battalion Rifle Brigade; 102nd Regiment; 3rd Company, R.E. Details from Macmillan, *Malta and Gibraltar*, p. 461.

[1] Unidentifiable.

Nowadays they are all being changed to the new breech-loading type, of which 535 have already been installed.[1] This is the most important English stronghold in the Mediterranean.[2] (The *Ying-huan chih-lüeh*[3] calls the port 'Pa-la-erh-ta' and also 'Chih-pa-lo-to'. It styles the town built by the English 'Yi-jen-ta-ta'. All these are only variants of the sound of the four characters 'Chi-pa-la-ta'.)

We were guided around the citadel by the [garrison] commander, Mo-erh-kan [Morgan?], while the artillery commander, Fei-erh-ting [Fielding?], took us round the hill fort.[4] Fielding pointed out a gap in the Sierra Nevada where, he said, there still existed at Luan-t'o [Monda] the ruins of an ancient encampment where Chia-fei-sa-erh [Caesar], when he occupied Spain, fought a desperate battle with the great Roman general Pen-p'iao [Pompey]. This was in the time of the early years of the Western Han dynasty, over 2,000 years ago.[5]

The Sierra Nevada runs crosswise like a wall, commanding an unbroken view of the surrounding country for several hundred *li*. None of the imposing views of those mountains I have seen before is comparable to this one in grandeur.

There was a German warship anchored in the harbour, whose commander, Lo-pi [Captain Livonius][6] paid us a visit.

At the *yu* watch [5–7 a.m.], on our way out of port,[7] we

---

[1] Breech-loading cannon of fair efficiency had been introduced as early as the 1840s, but the system was not perfected until the 1870s. See *The New Cambridge Modern History* (Cambridge, 1962), i.206–8, for a general account of technical developments in artillery at this time. We may note that the increased range and power of these new guns radically altered the strategic value of the rock, a point which escaped Kuo's notice. See G. T. Garratt, *Gibraltar and the Mediterranean*, pp. 143 ff.

[2] Garrat, *Gibraltar*, p. 142, points out that during this period Gibraltar had become secondary to Malta in importance.

[3] Hsü Chi-yü's *Ying-huan chih-lüeh*, vii.20b, styles Gibraltar 'Jih-pa-la-erh-ta'. The first syllable has been omitted in our text.

[4] Both officers unidentifiable.

[5] This must refer to Julius Caesar's defeat of Gnaeus Pompeius Magnus (*fl.* 76–45 B.C.) at the battle of Munda, on 17 March 45 B.C. The site of the battle is uncertain, but it did not take place in the Sierra Nevada.

[6] Otto Livonius (1829–1917), rose to the rank of Vice-Admiral and was well-known in later years as a naval historian. At this time he was in command of the *Kronprinz*, an ironclad screw frigate which had left Malta for the Baltic on 7 January 1877, calling at Gibraltar *en route*. See *The Times*, 30 Jan. 1877, p. 6a.

[7] The party left at 5 p.m. 'The Chinese Ambassador to England and his suite have landed here, and been received by Lord Napier of Magdala, Governor and Commander-in-Chief. The reception was held at the Government House, in

observed another lighthouse. The captain said these waters were called Te-la-fa-erh-gan [Trafalgar Bay]. This was where the English officer Wei-te-lin [Wellington] won his battle with Napoleon III.[1]

4th day [17 January]

Our run at noon was 594 *li*; latitude 37.14 north. After leaving the port of Gibraltar we came to Portugal, whose southern borders face Mo-lo-ko [Morocco] in Africa, another Muslim country. Its territory is still adjacent to the Mediterranean. We had by now reached Hsing-tzu-wen-sheng [Cape Vincent], the southernmost part of Portugal, where we entered the Atlantic Ocean. Europeans consider the end of this mountain [St. Vincent] to be very dangerous; for when the seas meet at this cape after rushing along the coast from opposite directions, the waves are lashed into greater turbulence than ever. The rugged mass of Cape St. Vincent juts out into the sea, dividing its waves, so that our ship was thrown about in the most violent fashion. The land on the western coast of Spain is rather steep towards the north. While the sea is running southwards, it is hindered on its way. For several score *li*—perhaps for even as much as a hundred *li*—the roaring waves boiled and bubbled around us. European ships consider this a most dangerous place.

In the evening we sighted a lighthouse marking a port. The captain said that this was the port of Li-ssu-po-ya [Lisbon], the capital of Portugal, at the mouth of the Te-jen [Tagus] river.

Today the heat was more oppressive than ever. I have heard that it is normally burning hot in the Red Sea even during the depth of winter; as hot, in fact, as at the height of summer. My heart was very much awed on hearing this. Yet on the six days' voyage from Aden to Suez the weather was mild, the wind gentle and the sea quite calm, making it the most pleasant part of the trip. But for the other 30,000 *li* we travelled, we were generally tossed about by the wind and waves. Now that we have come out into the Atlantic we have found that the

presence of the staff and the heads of the Civil and Military Departments. His Excellency and the members of the Embassy afterwards drove round the Rock and visited the galleries. They leave at 5 p.m. today for England.' (Telegram of 16 Jan. in *The Times* 17 Jan. 1877, p. 5d.)

[1] This schoolboy howler leads one to suspect that somebody had perhaps been having a little fun at our Ambassador's expense!

Kuo's Journal

weather is far more oppressively hot than it was in the Red Sea. Weather is certainly unpredictable!

5th day [18 January]

Our run at noon was 780 *li*; latitude 41.30 north. On our way north we passed the two rivers Tou-lo [Douro] and Mi-hsü [Minho]. Here stands the north-west capital of Portugal [Oporto], which takes its name from these two rivers [*sic*].[1] Further northward, we came to the west coast of Spain. In the evening we passed K'ai-p'o Fei-ni-shih-t'e [Cape Finisterre]. Away in the distance we sighted a lighthouse, where the waves were surging with redoubled fury. At this point Spain ends its northward sweep and the land recedes inwards, the whirling waters forming a vast gulf which adjoins French territory. At the mouth of the river Lo-ya-erh [Loire] the coast thrusts out laterally once more. For more than 1,000 *li* across the sea comes hurtling down, rushing into the gulf where its current whirls round then spins about and hastens south. So this ocean has contending currents for over 1,000 *li*: and it needs but a breath of wind to set the clamorous waves and raging billows to urge on the scudding swell. This sea is at its most dangerous off Cape Finisterre. 'Kai-p'o [Cape] means 'a pointed place'; 'Fei-ni-shih' [finis] means 'end'; and 't'e' [terre] means 'land'.

The day was gloomy, with wind and rain; danger and perils lay all around; the oppressive heat was worse than before, and I have severe pains around my heart. When we left Shanghai on the present voyage, my eyes hurt and their pupils were painful. On board ship, the tip of my nose has been smarting for over ten days and on top of that I have had toothache and earache as well. Now I am suffering from a pain round the heart. It is certainly strange that I should be afflicted with ailments in all my five sensory organs at once.

6th day [19 January]

Rainy and windy. Our run at noon was 846 *li*; latitude 46.1 north, 9.52 west of London. Since we entered the Atlantic we have been heading northwards, with a slight tendency eastward. We are now making more easting.

[1] Oporto, the second city of Portugal, on the Douro river is the commercial and industrial centre for the zone north of the Mondego river, including the provinces of Douro and Minho.

In Europe people have been competing with each other with knowledge and power for the last 2,000 years. Egypt, Rome, and Islam have each in their turn flourished and decayed, yet the principles which formed the basis of these states still endure. Nowadays, England, France, Russia, America, and Germany, all of them great nations which have tried their strength against each other to see who is pre-eminent, have evolved a code of international law which gives precedence to fidelity and righteousness and attaches the utmost importance to relations between states. Taking full cognizance of feeling and punctiliously observing all due ceremonies, they have evolved a high culture on a firm material basis. They surpass by a long way the states of our Spring and Autumn period.[1]

Today, Russia, whose territories are situated in the bleak lands of the far north, has penetrated to the Hei-lung [Amur] river by way of the Hsing-an [Great Khingan] mountains, annexed the north-eastern regions, reached the Sung-hua [Sungari] river, and made itself a neighbour of Japan.[2] Starting from the far west, England has penetrated the Mediterranean and gained supremacy over all the peoples of India. They have monopolized the Southern Seas [the Straits Settlements] and established a colony on the island of Hong Kong, with a strong garrison in possession of it.

[1] The Marxist historian, Hu Sheng, in his *Ti-kuo chu-yi yü Chung-kuo cheng-chih*, pp. 47–9, points out that Kuo was quicker than the rest of the *literati* to see that traditional China could only survive if it submitted to the imperialist world-order of international law. Yet Kuo was certainly not alone in his understanding of the importance to China of a knowledge of international law. Li Hung-chang and Hsüeh Fu-ch'eng (1838–94), for example, both claimed that China could have avoided a great deal of misery had her officials been acquainted with international law. For a discussion of this question, see Hsü, *China's Entrance*, 121–45. In this passage, however, Kuo seems to be asking his countrymen to subscribe to the doctrines of international law, not on the grounds of mere expediency, but rather because it represents a new Tao, the understanding of which is responsible for the high state of civilization attained by Europe.

[2] Russia's steady advance into Central Asia, at the expense of what had traditionally been Chinese-controlled territory, had been going on since the seventeenth century. The Treaty of Nerchinsk (1689), the Treaty of Kiakhta (1727), the Treaty of Aigun (1858), and the Treaty of Peking (1860), had given her some 1,648,000 square miles of Chinese territory. In 1871 the Russians had occupied Ili, in Sinkiang. In 1879, only a couple of years after Kuo expressed these fears in his diary the Manchu envoy, Ch'ung-hou (1826–93), foolishly gave away most of the Ili region to Russia by the Treaty of Livadia. See Fairbank *et al.*, *Modern Transformation*, esp. pp. 43–5; Immanuel Hsü, *The Ili Crisis: A Study of Sino-Russian Diplomacy, 1871–1881*, pp. 1–15.

When we compare the territories of these countries and estimate their power, we are justified in looking upon them as the two leading nations of the day. They have surrounded China and press close upon her from spots where they may spy out the land. With their hands reaching high and their feet travelling far, they rise up like eagles and glare like tigers, day by day broadening their basis of wealth and power. Yet for all this, they have not the slightest intention of presuming on their military strength to act violently or rapaciously.

When they do deploy their forces, they do so circuitously and indirectly, proceeding by argument and reasoning, never taking any overt action until their position is a strong one. Surely this is not the time for China to indulge in highflown talk and vain boasting in order to aggrandize herself! This is no time for me to embark on an elaborate discussion of the gravity and urgency of the matter. But [we must realize that] the nations of Europe do have insight into what is essential and what is not and possess a Way of their own which assists them in the acquisition of wealth and power. In this manner, a state may well last for 1,000 years. On the other hand, if a state does not grasp the Way, then disaster will come upon it. Hence Pan Ku,[1] [A.D. 32–92], in his Appreciation appended to the chapter on the Hsiung-nu, remarks: 'If the barbarians approach us [wanting us to civilize them], then receive them with the appropriate rites. If they prove refractory, then overawe them with military power.'[2] We must make it a rule that every wrong movement will be on their part. If this is so in the case of petty contentions, then how much truer must it be when we are dealing with people who show far greater ability in the management of their affairs and whose plans are more deeply laid! Liu Yün-sheng, who considers himself an expert on foreign affairs, has indeed revealed the shallowness of his knowledge at this juncture.[3] He says: 'To deal with the present situation we must

---

[1] Pan Ku, the author of the *Ch'ien Han-shu*, is one of the greatest of Chinese historians. *Tsan* (*Appreciation*) is a style of Chinese eulogistic prose usually composed of lines of four characters and appended to a biography in a dynastic history.

[2] *Han-shu*, xcivb.32b, actually says '*Lai tse ch'eng erh yü chih. Ch'ü tse pei erh shou chih.*' ('If they approach, then control them by force. When they depart, be prepared to stay on guard against them.')

[3] One of Kuo's few public thrusts at Liu Hsi-hung!

be extremely sincere in our dealings with other states: otherwise we shall not be able to establish ourselves.'

Now I have often been sharply criticized by my contemporaries. Yet Yao Yen-chia is of the opinion that I possess scholarship and insight surpassing that of others. But how can I have any pretensions to scholarship and insight? The histories of the Sung and Ming dynasties are still extant; yet the hearts, the minds, the eyes, and ears of our contemporaries have been captivated by the vain and empty discourses of several hundred years, for they never once bother to examine the facts of the case.

I once overheard Ho Yüan-ch'uan[1] talking of foreign affairs, and was astonished at his profound understanding of these matters. In answer to an enquiry of mine, he replied: 'The Six Classics and the ancient writings of the Chou [*ca.* 1027–256 B.C.] and Ch'in [221–206 B.C.] dynasties, as well as the works of our Confucian predecessors are all clearly justified by their consistency with historical facts. Commonplace observations are no more than boastful talk. They lack historical foundation.' This can really be called learning and insight!

7th day [20 January]

Our run at noon was 731 *li*; latitude 49.11 north. We passed the province of Loire in France, and found ourselves directly opposite the point where the coast runs out at an angle far into the sea and the waves dash together more violently than ever. Westerners call this place Erh-sheng [Ushant]. There is a lighthouse to guide ships on their way. Once we had passed this point we could see the county of Ko-erh-nu-wa-li-ssu [Cornwall], in England directly across the water from us.[2] When we reached here we began for the first time to feel the cold a little.

This evening at dinner, ten or more of the diners amused themselves cracking walnuts. Somebody cracked one with his forehead, whereupon they all began to bang them with their

---

[1] Ho Ch'iu-t'ao (1824–62), style Yüan-ch'uan, scholar and historian, is best known for his *Shuo-fang pei-sheng*, the first comprehensive work on Sino-Russian relations. See Tu Lien-che's biography of Ho in Hummel, *Eminent Chinese*.

[2] Text reads 'London'; but since Cornwall is clearly marked on the map of England in the *Ying-huan chih-lüeh*, it is clear that 'London' here is but a synechdochism for 'England'.

foreheads. Some succeeded and some failed; but they all made a great noise in doing so. Some placed a finger on the walnut and then broke it at first try by striking the finger with their fist. Others put the walnut under the elbow then stretched out the wrist, opened the hand, and broke the nut at once by a blow on the open palm. The onlookers put out their tongues in astonishment.

During the day there are generally a dozen or so passengers playing at leap-frog, with a dropped stone acting as marker. One man stands with his back bent, while the others take their stand ten paces or more away. They take it in turns to run up, place their hands on the man's back, and leap over with their legs apart. Then they mark off a line three feet from the man and drop a stone there as a marker. No one is allowed to put his feet over that mark. Gradually the distance is increased to five feet. From that distance only two of them succeed in making a flying leap over the man's back. All the others put one foot over the line. Six or seven of them then take up their positions with backs bent, about five feet from each other while about a dozen others leap over them one after the other, without taking a single step in between jumps. They are all completely carefree and obviously enjoy themselves immensely. Most of the participants were German military officers. They are fair-skinned and refined [generally] spending the whole day reading, without a break. That country certainly produces admirably talented men. Admirable!

The captain pointed out that according to the shipping timetable, the *Peshawur* should have left Ceylon on the twenty-fifth day of the twelfth month by the Western calendar, and reached the port of Su-shih-a-mu-tun [Southampton] on the twenty-first day of the first month. However, though on this trip we had left Ceylon three days earlier than scheduled, we were to be in port the next day at noon, which would be the twenty-first day of the first month by the Western calendar. For after we had entered the Red Sea, the engines had been slowed a little to give the *Venetia* from Bombay time to catch up with us. Since then there had been only a little variation in our speed; so that we were finally arriving right on time.

I estimate that we have passed eighteen different countries during the course of this voyage. We have passed five Asian countries in all, namely: Annam, Siam, Baluchistan, Persia, and Arabia.[1] Annam is Confucianist; Siam is Buddhist; the rest are all Islamic countries. In Europe we have passed Turkey, Greece, Italy, France, Spain, and Portugal, six countries in all. We passed the south-east coasts of France and Spain on our way through the Mediterranean, and then passed their western coasts after we had come out into the Atlantic. Turkey is a Muslim country; the rest are all Catholic countries, though Greece belongs to a separate branch of the Catholic Church.

In Africa we passed the seven countries of Abyssinia, Nubia, Egypt, Tripoli, Tunis, Algeria, and Morocco, all of them Muslim except Abyssinia which professes Catholicism.[2] In recent years the French have settled in Algeria and made it a colony. We passed fourteen English colonies, six of which are in the Southern Seas, namely, Hong Kong, Labuan,[3] Singapore, Malacca, Wellesley, and the island of Penang. Labuan lies to the south of the Chi-hsing-chou [Balabac Island], Malacca adjoins Singapore, and Wellesley lies opposite the island of Penang. None of them is a shipping terminus. Five of the Colonies are in India. The English have settled throughout India, but chiefly in three great coastal regions, namely, Bengal, Ma-ta-la-sa [Madras], and Bombay. With them go the two islands of Ceylon and Socotra. Only Ceylon is a shipping terminus. Madras lies opposite the island of Ceylon; the others are all very far away from it, but the sea-routes leading to these territories could be pointed out [during our voyage]. There are two settlements in the Red Sea, namely Aden and Perim; but ships do not call at Perim. There are two more in the Mediterranean, namely, Malta and Gibraltar. At all these places Protestant churches have been established and all the natives adhere to that religion. In India, which is a Buddhist country [sic], the Muslim religion is also practised. In O-li-sa [Orissa], which comes under the jurisdiction of Bengal, and in Ceylon, the people are all Buddhists and join their hands together when they worship.[4] In

---

[1] Kuo has forgotten to include Ceylon, Malaya, and India.

[2] Abyssinia, a Christian country since the fourth century, has its own Orthodox Church.

[3] Labuan, six miles of the north-west coast of Borneo, was ceded to Britain by the Sultan of Brunei in 1846. In 1876 it was still a Crown Colony.

[4] A curious error. Orissa was not a separate state in 1876 but was still part of Bengal. Its Buddhist population, according to the Census of 1881, numbered

Bombay, one may still see the Zoroastrian religion of ancient Po-ssu [Persia] being practised. (In Europe, every religion acknowledges a Supreme Ruler. When Persia was occupied by the Muslims, who prohibited the original religion, the Zoroastrians all fled to Bombay.)

The South Sea Islands [of South-East Asia] come under the government of several countries. After passing Hainan and coming through the China Sea, you find yourself opposite Lü-sung [Luzon], which belongs to Spain. Further south, after passing the Bay of Kuang-nan, with Saigon lying to the west, is the port of the province of Chia-ting, in French Indo-China. To the east, opposite Wen-lai Island [Borneo],[1] the territory belongs to Holland. Further south, and stretching away westwards past Sumatra, the territory also belongs to Holland. I have made no mention of the other small islands adjacent to these, nor have I recorded those islands which lay too far off our course, nor the countries to which they belong.

8th day [21 January]

By the *wei* watch [1–3 p.m.] we had run 495 *li* and reached Southampton. As we passed P'o-tzu [Portsea] and Lun-tun [Landport], we noticed two very strange and beautiful lighthouses overlooking the anchorage for British warships. As we came into port past the Ni-lo-ssu [Needles], we passed an island called A-lu-wei-te [Isle of Wight], where the Queen has a winter residence called A-ssu-pen [Osborne]. Our ship ran aground and a thick fog came on. We expected the tide would float us off a little later; and after an hour or so we got into port.[2]

only a few hundred. However, until as late as the fifteenth and sixteenth centries there *were* relatively large numbers of Buddhists in Orissa. Was Kuo perhaps recalling something he had read in an old gazetteer? He seems to have been unaware that the Muslim invasion had destroyed the last flickers of Buddhism in India by the late twelfth century.

[1] 'Wen-lai' (Brunei) is the name given to the north-east coast of Borneo by the *Ying-huan chih-lüeh*, ii. This name is not listed in any modern dictionary or gazetteer I have come across. It does however occur in Chang Hsieh's *Tung-hsi-yang k'ao* (1668), v.67. The term is geographically exact, as long as we remember that it refers to the old state of Brunei which once encompassed what is now Sarawak and Sabah and was not restricted to its present narrow domain.

[2] *The Times*, 22 Jan. 1877, p. 6c: 'The Peninsula and Oriental Company's steamship *Peshawur*, Captain C. A. White, from Calcutta *via* the Suez Canal arrived at Southampton yesterday, bringing the heavy India and China mails, 112 first- and second-class passengers, 106 troops....'

Hillier and J. D. Campbell were kind enough to meet the boat. The customs inspector, Phillips, came to convey the good wishes of Te-erh-pi [The Earl of Derby], the Minister for Foreign Affairs, who had sent him a dispatch that morning,[1] which said that the Chinese Ambassador, who was to arrive that day, was to be exempted from all examination by customs. The Peruvian consul Chi-lo-mu [Herbert Guillaume],[2] the agent of the P & O Lines Na-tan [Nathan?],[3] and the Shanghai editor of the *North China Daily News* Mu Ssu-man [Samuel Mossman],[4] all came to meet me. T'u Mai-lun [T. L. Bullock] whom I had formerly known when he was consul at Tientsin [was also there].[5]

At the *yu* watch [5–7 p.m.] we took the train for London.[6] Since this was a Sunday, there were only two trains running during the day, one in the morning and one in the evening.

We passed the two market-towns of Po-hsing-ssu-to-k'o [Basingstoke] and Wo-to [Woking], where the lamps were shining bright as day. As we came nearer to London, the lights were even brighter. J. D. Campbell had previously ordered carriages for us, which were waiting on the right-hand side of the road. The street-lamps were like myriads of bright stars, while the horses and carriages rolled past in an unending stream, with the horses' breath rising like mist. The liveliness of the commercial centres and the beauty of the mansions and houses could scarcely be excelled. After a drive of an hour or so we reached our residence in Portland Place, where we asked Campbell to stay and eat dinner with us.

[1] Edward Henry Stanley (1826–93), fifteenth Earl of Derby, was Foreign Secretary from 1874 to 1878 in Disraeli's second ministry.
[2] Herbert Guillaume had been Peruvian Consul at Southampton since 23 June 1873. See *Foreign Office List*, July 1876.
[3] Unidentifiable.
[4] Samuel Mossman came to China in August 1861 as an assistant to C. S. Compton, editor of the *North China Herald*. He held the editorship of that paper 1861–3. He must have joined the *North China Daily News* (*Tzu-lin hsi-pao*) some time later. In addition to his journalistic activities, Mossman attained a modest fame as a writer. See Frank H. H. King and Prescott Clarke, *A Research Guide to China-Coast Newspapers, 1822–1911*, p. 139.
[5] Thomas Lowndes Bullock was Acting Third Assistant at Tientsin from 24 June 1872 to 13 May 1873. See the *Foreign Office List*, 1877.
[6] This was actually a special train which had been laid on for the embassy by J. W. Dyson, the South-Western Railway Company's Superintendent at Southampton. See *The Times*, 22 Jan. 1877.

Kuo's Journal

I learned on enquiry that the Queen had gone to her palace at Wen-tse [Windsor] and was to leave Windsor for Osborne. She has two palaces in London, one called Sheng-ch'üan-en-hsieh-ssu Pa-lei-ssu [St. James's Palace] in which she holds her drawing-rooms. 'Pa-lei-ssu' means 'Palace'. The other, called Po-chin-ko-en Pa-lei-ssu [Buckingham Palace] is where the levees are held. For the drawing-rooms, court-dress must be worn; but at private audiences ordinary clothes are permissible.

The representatives of foreign nations residing in London fall into three grades and come from thirty countries in all. There are five Ambassadors in the first rank, namely, the Russian Shu-wa-lo-fu [Count Peter Shuvalov]; the French Ta-la-ku [Marquis d'Harcourt]; the German Min-ssu-ta-erh [Count George Münster]; the Austro-Hungarian Fu-ssu-ta [Count Beust] and the Turkish Mo-la-she-ssu [Musurus Pasha].

In the second rank are the American Pi-lo-erh [Hon. Edwards Pierrepont]; the Japanese Wu-yeh-na-ou-chia-chen-no-li [Ueno Kagenori]; the Spanish Chia-sa-lei-ko-lai-hsi-ya [Marquis de Casa Laiglesia]; the Swedish Ho-shih-ch'ih-la-ta [Baron Hochschild]; the Dutch Te-pi-lan [Count C. M. E. George de Bylandt]; the Persian Prince Na-sai-mu-ma-la-k'e-mu Khan [Mirza Malcolm Khan Nazim-ul-Moulk]; the Belgian So-la-wan [Baron Henri Solvyns]; the Danish Pi-lou [Lieutenant-General J. Ohan de Bülow]; the Portuguese Sa-la-ta-ha [M. E. T. de Sampayo]; the Peruvian Ka-la-wei-ssu [Don Pedro Galves] and the Brazilian P'ei-no-tou [Baron de Penedo].[1]

The others are all small states in South America and Africa—eighteen of them in all. Seven states have chargés d'affaires. Ma-t'i-na-ou [Montenegro] in Italy [sic] is represented by an attaché. There is sometimes just one attaché, sometimes three or four. This office is filled by an earl or a baron.

The Earl of Derby is assisted in his general administration by four secretaries, namely, Ting-te-tun [Lord Tenterden],[2] Pang-ssu-fo-te [Sir Julian Pauncefote],[3] Li-ssu-te [T. V. Lister],[4]

---

[1] Names from the *Foreign Office List*, January 1877.

[2] Charles Stuart Aubrey Abbott (1834–82), third Lord Tenterden, was Permanent Under-Secretary to the Secretary of State for Foreign Affairs, 1873–82.

[3] Sir Julian Pauncefote (1828–1902), was Legal Assistant Under-Secretary to the Secretary of State for Foreign Affairs, 1873–94.

[4] Sir Thomas Villiers Lister (1832–1902), was Assistant Under-Secretary of State to the Secretary of State for Foreign Affairs, 1876–82.

and Te-le-erh [Robert Bourke].[1] The Prime Minister of England is Pi-ken-shih-fei-erh-te [Lord Beaconsfield].[2] He has authority similar to that of a Chancellor during our Han Dynasty. The Upper and Lower Houses of Parliament are divided into parties which attack each other. The adherents of the Ministry are called the *T'e-le-shuo-li* [Treasury] benches, and the Ministry must have a majority in either House in order to retain its power.

At the Shanghai rate of exchange, 30,000 taels is equal to £8,939 sterling. One English gold piece weighs two mace, two candareens and is called a pound.[3] One pound is equal to twenty small, silver coins called *shih-ling* [shillings], weighing one mace four candareens each and worth two taels eight mace. However, to exchange the English gold piece cost over three taels three mace in standard silver. Hence 20 per cent has been lost in exchange at the expense of the Chinese currency.

The following is a general outline of the currency: one pound English is called a *se-wu-lun* [sovereign] and is equal to two small gold coins called ha-fu-se-we-lun [half-sovereigns]. The latter is equal to two silver coins called *k'o-lo-en* [crowns]. (The crown is equal to two coins called half-a-crowns, which are not much used.) The crown is equal to five small silver coins called shillings. (There is another silver coin of two mace, four candareens in weight, called a *lo-fun-lun* [florin], which is equal to two shillings.) The shilling is equal to two smaller coins called *hsi-p'an-ssu* [sixpences]. The latter is equal to two still smaller coins called *sa-li-hsi-p'an-ssu* [threepences]. The latter is equal to two [sic] copper coins called *p'ei-ni* [pennies]. The latter is equal to two middle-sized copper coins called *hai-p'ei-ni* [halfpennies]. The latter is equal to two small copper coins called *fa-erh-ying* [farthings]. There are altogether two gold coins, six silver coins, and three copper coins. Notes issued by the Government are also in general circulation They range from five pounds up to thousands, hundreds and ten-thousands. They are called *pan-k'o-pi-la* [bankbills].

[1] Robert Bourke, Baron Connemara (1827–1902), was Under Secretary for Foreign Affairs, 1874–80 and 1885–6.
[2] Disraeli had been Prime Minister since January 1874. As he had been created Earl of Beaconsfield in Aug. 1876, his place as leader of the House of Commons had been taken by Sir Stafford Northcote.
[3] The weight of the English sovereign was 123,274 grams.

NOTES

¹ Hu Ch'iung-hsien, style Hsüan-tse, known as Ho Ah Kay (1816–80), was a wealthy Cantonese merchant known to the European community in Singapore as Whampoa, from his place of birth. He inherited his father's flourishing business on the corner of Bonham Street and Boat Quay, which was principally concerned with the supply of victuals to ships and European residents. He spoke excellent English, was on friendly terms with many influential Europeans, and was the first Chinese to be appointed an Unofficial Member of the Straits Settlement Legislative Council on its formation in 1867. In 1870 he was made a Justice of the Peace, and was awarded the C.M.G. in 1878. On Kuo Sung-t'ao's suggestion, he was made the first Chinese Consul at Singapore, in 1877. He held this office with the help of only one assistant, unti his death. He was then succeeded by a formal Consul-General in the person of Tso Ping-lung (1850–1924), who was at the time of his appointment serving Kuo's successor, Marquis Tseng Chi-tse, as his interpreter in England. His residence on Serangoon Road, two and a half miles from the city, known as Whampoa House, was renowned for its gardens (called in Cantonese *Nam-sang Fa-un*). Famous for his hospitality, he figures prominently in many anecdotes about Singapore in the sixties and seventies. Isabella L. Bird, who was in Singapore briefly during January, 1879, refers in *The Golden Chersonese*, p. 113, to 'Mr. Whampoa, C.M.G., a Chinaman of great wealth and enlightened public spirit who is one of the foremost men in the colony'. The best account of Whampoa's life, together with a photograph of him and his sons, is found in Song Ong Siang, *One Hundred Years' History of the Chinese in Singapore*, pp. 51–6. See also Roland St. J. Braddell, 'The Merry Past', in *One Hundred Years of Singapore*, eds. W. Makepeace, Gilbert, E. Brooke, and Roland St. J. Braddell, ii.498–500.

² Major- (later Lieutenant-) General Sir William Francis Drummond Jervois, R.E., G.C.M.G., C.B., F.R.S. (1821–97), was commissioned in the Royal Engineers in 1839, soon making a name for himself as an expert on fortifications and the strategic outposts of the Empire. Between 1863 and 1872 he reported on the defences of Canada, Nova Scotia, Bermuda, Malta, Gibraltar, Aden, Perim, Rangoon, Moulmein, Bombay, and the Hooghly. On 7 April 1875 he was appointed Governor of the Straits Settlements, a post he held until 6 July 1877 when he became Governor of South Australia (1877–82). From 1882 to 1889 he was Governor of New Zealand. C. D. Cowan, *Nineteenth-Century Malaya; The Origins of British Political Control*, p. 225, gives a brief biography of Jervois. He describes him as 'an ambitious man with a brilliant career behind him and a reputation for getting things done.' On his record as an administrator in Malaya, see Cowan, op. cit., pp. 225–32 and 238–43. Interestingly enough, Jervois was in favour of allowing Chinese immigration to Australasia, a policy becoming increasingly unpopular in Australia at the time. He believed 'that, as half of the Australian continent lies within the tropics it can only be fully developed by coloured labour of which the Chinese is the most valuable'. His pro-Chinese sentiments seem to have been reflected in his genial reception of our Ambassadors.

³ The construction of Fort Canning was begun in May 1859 on the hill originally called Bukit Larangan, and completed in 1861. John Cameron gives the following description of it as it appeared in 1864: 'Fort Canning is a redoubt, following the contour of the top of Government Hill, which stands near the centre of the town about half a mile back from the beach. The hill rises abruptly from the level land around. . . . Its apex is of considerable extent, the ramparts measuring nearly 1,200 yards. It mounts at present seventeen heavy pieces, namely, seven

68-pounders, eight 8-inch shell guns, and two 13-inch mortars; there are also in course of construction, platforms for eight more heavy pieces. Besides these, the ramparts of this fort are furnished with a number of 14-pound carronades. Within the ramparts are barracks, hospital and accommodation for 150 European artillerymen.' (*Our Tropical Possessions in Malayan India*, pp. 240-1.) See also Makepeace et al., *One Hundred Years of Singapore*, i.378. Fort Canning formed part of a defence system, inspired partly by local disturbances, partly by fears aroused since the Indian Mutiny (1857), which was designed 'rather for the safety of the European residents ... than for defence against an outside enemy'. (Cameron, op. cit., p. 242.)

⁴ Von Roon became War Minister in 1859 and Minister of the Marine in 1861. His army reforms, adopted after 1866 by the whole North German Federation, not only ensured Prussia the leadership of Germany, but led to the emergence of the German empire as the foremost military power in Europe. (See A. W. Ward, *Germany 1815–90* (Cambridge, 1916–18), ii.52.) In December 1871 he succeeded Bismarck as President of the Prussian ministry, resigning the same year on grounds of ill-health. In January 1873 he was promoted Field-Marshal. In 1876, von Roon was 73, not 65; but this can only be constructed as another mistake on Kuo's part, or that of his informants. If one rejects von Roon, the only other possible candidate is Ludwig II of Bavaria (1845–86), who reigned from 1864 to 1886 and was in command of the Bavarian armed forces. However in view of Ludwig's youth and relative unimportance, it seems highly unlikely that he would have been the man whom Kuo referred to as 'Lu-te', in spite of the fact that his name is a closer approximation to the Chinese than that of von Roon.

⁵ The articles, briefly summarized, recommended the implementation of the following measures:

(1) The abolition of Catholic orphanages.
(2) A prohibition forbidding Chinese women to enter foreign churches and female missionaries to work in China.
(3) The placing of all missionaries under the control of Chinese officials.
(4) Missionaries not to be allowed to conceal or protect converts who are guilty of crimes.
(5) French missionaries to be allowed to travel only within their own specified district. Holders of missionary passports to be excluded from disaffected areas.
(6) Only persons without a criminal record to be received as converts, any convert committing an unlawful act to be forthwith expelled from the Church.
(7) Missionaries to adhere faithfully to Chinese institutions and customs.
(8) Before erecting buildings or making property transactions, missionaries were to lay the matter before the local authorities to make sure that local geomantic conditions were not disturbed.

Since these demands were aimed chiefly at Catholic missionaries, most protestant missionaries—like Young John Allen—did not find them too objectionable. On these proposals put forward by the Tsungli Yamen, see P. A. Cohen, *China and Christianity*, pp. 247-61.

⁶ Wen-hsiang (1818–76), posthumous name Wen Wen-chung-kung, was a Manchu, a member of the Gualgiya clan in Mukden. His family belonged to the Manchu Plain Red Banner. He became a *chü-jen* in 1840 and gained his *chin-shih* degree in 1845. His exemplary conduct during the Taiping rebellion brought him to the notice of his superiors, who soon secured his promotion. By 1855 he had become an official of the third grade, and by 1859 had reached the rank of Vice-President of the Board of Revenue. In 1860, when the Allies occupied Tientsin during the Anglo-French war with China, Wen-hsiang was one of the three officials in charge of peace negotiations. After the departure of the allies, Wen-

hsiang and his two colleagues submitted a memorial recommending the establishment of the Tsungli Yamen, or 'Office for General Administration' of China's Foreign Relations (13 Jan. 1861). In 1861 the Tsungli Yamen was set up, with Wen-hsiang acting as one of the controlling board. In 1865, he was given the task of putting down banditry in Manchuria, an assignment which he carried out with complete success. On his return to Peking in 1866 he was appointed President of the Board of Civil Office. In 1871 he was made an Associate Grand Secretary and in 1872 became Grand Secretary. In his biography of Wen-hsiang in Hummel, *Eminent Chinese*, ii.854–5, Fang Chao-ying characterizes him as 'one of the enlightened officials of the time' who 'won the respect of foreign diplomats by his straight-forwardness and honesty'. Martin speaks very highly of him in his *Cycle of Cathay*, p. 17.

[7] On 26 June 1869, after the Yangchow riot of August 1868, Wen-hsiang sent a note to Sir Rutherford Alcock 'in which he observed that the principal cause of the missionary trouble in the interior lay in the fact that the Western missionaries, taking advantage of their immunities from local jurisdiction, sought indiscriminatingly to protect Chinese Christians, many of whom were making their religion a pretext for extorting money from honest people....' (Quoted from T'ang Liang-li, *China in Revolt*, p. 62.) For an account of the favoured position enjoyed by the French Catholic missionaries at this time and the troubles they stirred up, see Cohen, *China and Christianity*, especially pp. 65–70. Cohen points out that in 1870 'estimates put the total number of Chinese Catholics at anywhere from 369,441 to 404,530, with about two hundred and fifty European priests. Szechwan ... was still in 1870 the leading province in terms of total numbers of Catholics (about eighty thousand) and foreign missionaries (forty-four).... By 1874, the total [Protestant] missionary force was claimed to be four hundred and thirty six ... [but] the total number of Chinese Protestant communicants in the summer of 1869 was a scant 5,753....' (p. 70.)

[8] *Hou Han-shu*, cxviii, p. 9a: 'In the ninth year of the *Yung-yüan* period of Emperor Ho [A.D. 98], the Military Governor [of Central Asia] Pan Ch'ao, sent Kan Ying as an ambassador to Ta-ch'in (Roman Syria). He wanted to get as far as T'iao-chih (the Crimea), but when he was about to take his passage across the Great [Black] Sea, the sailors of the western frontier of An-hsi (Parthia) said to him: 'The sea is wide and vast. With the help of favourable winds you can cross in three months; but if you meet with unfavourable winds it could indeed take you two years. For this reason those who cross this sea take with them provisions for three years. There is something about this sea which makes a man homesick, several have lost their lives through this.' When Ying heard this he went no further.' An alternative version of this passage, found in *Chin-shu*, xcviii.9a, says '... there is something about this sea which makes one homesick. Those who sail out on it cannot help being overcome with melancholy. If the Chinese envoy has no regard for his parents, his wife, and his children, he may venture forth.'

For my translation of T'iao-chih as 'the Crimea' rather than the usual 'Mesopotamia', see C. P. Fitzgerald, who quotes from an unpublished paper by Yang Hsien-yi in his *China: A Short Cultural History* (p. 198), pointing out that the Chinese name was derived from the Greek 'Taurica'.

[9] 'There is a different kind of mechanical apparatus, called the *drague à long couloir*, which is used in immediate connexion with the dredging vessels, where the banks are not so high above the water. The dredges are furnished with iron buckets fastened to an endless chair revolving over two drums: one being fixed by the end of a long moveable arm, regulated by the depth at which the mud is scooped up; the other being at the top of a strong iron framework mounted upon the hull of the dredging-vessel.... The boxes or caissons have each a capacity of

four cubic yards, and seven of them fit into one of the attendant punts. One end of the box is made to open like a door on hinges, so as to let its contents run out when lifted by the elevator, and carried up the tramway to the other end, when it is discharged. The elevator is an inclined plane, about fifty-two yards long, carrying two lines of rail. It is supported in the middle by an iron frame, which rests on a carriage, moveable upon rails, laid for the purpose along the bank of the canal at a height of six feet above the water. The lower end of the elevator reaches over the water and is supported by a steam float . . . *The long couloir*, or long duct, is of curved or half-elliptical form, sometimes seventy-five yards long, but often smaller, with a slightly inclined channel five feet wide and two feet deep, which is supported by an iron framework on the deck of a barge; a steam-pump keeps a stream of water flowing through this channel, by which the dredged-up matter, when dropped into its upper end, is carried off and cast ashore on the bank of the canal; this process being aided in some cases by the action of the *balayeur*, an endless chain passing along the centre of the channel and bearing a number of iron scrapers to remove the half-liquid slime and mud. By means of the *long couloir*, which has a reach of seventy-five yards, the dredge can work in the very middle of the canal. . . .' (*Illustrated London News*, April 1869.)

2

Kuo Sung-t'ao's Memorial Requesting that Ts'en Yü-ying, Governor of Kweichow, be Submitted to Judgement by Due Procedure (1875)[1]

(SUMMARY) With regard to the killing of Margary in Yunnan, the Governor who failed to prevent the occurrence of this tragedy should be submitted to judgement. I beg for the consideration of Your Majesty in this respect.

The Book of Chou Kuan (*Chou Li*) pays special attention to the duty of hospitality. At that time, our country won the allegiance of nine barbarian nations. The Court arranged for regular interviews with their representatives, and had people appointed to look after them and to protect them, taking care to avoid discourtesy, and setting down the best pattern of three dynasties. Now the various countries of the West have been trading with us for over forty years. Westerners are in charge of the training given in schools in different provinces along the sea coast, and of our soldiers equipped with Western weapons. They are also responsible for the opening of our ports and harbours, and of our customs offices. Westerners wish to render service to China and have no suspicious intentions. According to treaty rights, they are allowed to travel everywhere, and are granted permission to do so under escort. The case of Margary, however, happened over ten months ago, and still has not been dealt with. Governor Ts'en is certainly not blameless. I realize that when Margary came from Burma with over 100 Burmese soldiers into our country, the Governor certainly had the right to order the local authorities to pay attention to this. The Brigadier-General, Yang Yü-k'e, is responsible for local defence, and the Commandant, Li Chen-kuo, is charged with

[1] *Kuo shih-lang tsou-shu, Yang-chih shu-wu yi-chi*, pp. 1a–3a.

defence of the frontier. When news came concerning the entry of foreign soldiers, they too had to take certain defence measures. Soldiers are hard to control, and so fighting occurred. This was something the Governor could not have foreseen, nor had Yang and Li, who sent the soldiers over, expected such conflict. After investigation, I discovered that the Governor had ordered Yang to be stationed at T'eng-yüeh and Li at Nan-tien, hundreds of leagues away from the barbarous region where Margary was killed. It is easy to see how soldiers left without control and direction acted, causing the murder of the foreigner. Now Governor Ts'en had failed to act upon orders received from Tsungli Yamen, and to communicate them to Yang and Li, so that they were unable to control those underneath them, thus giving rise to the incident. Yang and Li are both famous for their military valour and patriotism, but have been unable to clear themselves on this issue. I feel especially sorry for them, and so beg Your Majesty to bring Governor Ts'en to trial, to ascertain his guilt in not having taken the necessary preventive measures, and then to try the criminals who killed Margary, in order to satisfy the demands of foreigners, and show forth the justice with which our Government handles this affair. Since, by your gracious favour, I work for the Tsungli Yamen I have the responsibility of reporting this affair to Your Majesty. Having entered office, I ought to discuss everything with my colleagues, rather than take it upon myself to make the decision. Therefore I wish to present in advance my humble opinions, and beg Your Imperial Majesty to see to it that the Governor of Yunnan be judged first. I humbly prostrate myself, submitting this Memorial to Your Imperial Majesties, the Empress Dowager and the Emperor, and I humbly await your instructions.

NOTE: On account of this Memorial, I suffered unwonted slander, and was blamed by the officials at the capital. A Secretary to the Privy Council also attacked me for beginning the Memorial with a quotation from the *Chou Li*. However, I do not agree with them. These people wished to protect Ts'en after the death of the foreigner. Actually, in my Memorial, I had sought not only to protect Ts'en Yü-ying, but also to excuse Yang Yü-k'o and Li Chen-kuo. I only asked that Ts'en Yü-ying be tried and punished on the relatively light charge of not having taken certain preventive measures, so that the anger of the foreigners might be appeased. To punish one or two persons would have been enough to let the Privy Council understand the affair. Trading at T'eng-yüeh, Yi-ch'ang, and other places could have continued, and the present misfortune with the French[1] could have been avoided. Nowadays Governors are frequently removed from office for a single transgression, and yet, in this case of the murder of a foreigner, not the slightest blame was placed on the culprit. No wonder we could not win the confidence of the foreigners. In a country ruled by such people, how can we expect anything other than a fiasco? In presenting the draft of my Memorial here, I record also this note, in order to make clear the intention I had when I submitted it. If our foreign policy was a failure, it was certainly due to the ignorance of our officials.

[1] The Sino–French war of 1883–5, which eliminated Chinese suzerainty over Vietnam, was brought about partly by the bellicosity of the *ch'ing-liu* (purification) party at court.

3
Memorial on Foreign Affairs Submitted on the Occasion of the Termination of his Leave of Absence (1875)[1]

ALTHOUGH I am still unwell, I shall soon, in obedience to orders received, terminate my vacation. Now, I humbly submit my opinions on foreign affairs.

Sickness has twice caused me to beg for leave of absence in order to return to my home town, and Your Majesty has graciously granted me this vacation. Actually, as long as the Yunnan case was progressing well, I felt I should keep away from official affairs, especially as I was an invalid. However, on the twenty-fourth day of the fifth month [3 April 1875] the English envoy Wade left the capital suddenly, and so the negotiations on the Yunnan case could not continue.[2] How could I, in this situation, remain uninvolved? I feel obliged to apply for cancellation of my leave, and force myself to do something in spite of my bad health. It seems therefore, on this occasion, that I should submit some general ideas about the handling of foreign affairs. Since ancient times, our country has always suffered from foreign intrusions. Only three reactions are possible: attack, defence, or treaty. There has been a regular pattern in the invasions the country has experienced, as well as in the rhythm of the enemy's growth or decline. It is more than sufficient if we react according to changing times and circumstances. Foreigners use trade as a pretext and encircle all our ports. They have penetrated several thousand leagues up the Yangtze River, seeking for excuses to provoke incidents which would further their advantages. Al-

---

[1] *Kuo shih-lang tsou-shu, Yang-chih shu-wu yi-chi*, 12, pp. 4a–12a.

[2] Wade's departure for Shanghai was intended to throw the Chinese ranks into confusion, as it did. '[Wade's] departure from Peking, simultaneously with that of several of his secretaries and their families and of a number of other foreigners, was the cause of many exciting rumours among the Chinese.' H. B. Morse, *The International Relations of the Chinese Empire*, ii.297.

though we call it an external invasion, we must resist them inland. Although they are called enemies, they really use only diplomatic means to settle disputes. I therefore feel that in today's foreign affairs there can be no question of attack, of defence, or of making treaties. Two things are involved in a war: defence and attack. But the Western countries are several tens of thousands of leagues away, and we cannot therefore go to invade them. Besides, although the foreigners, both kings and officials, pay great attention to the training of soldiers and the making of weapons, and continue to produce an unending stream of new armaments, they will not lightly start a war since they regard the treaty ports as capable of yielding them real profit, and therefore wish to preserve them. Since they do not speak of war, why should we force them to fight? As for peace treaties, these may involve one of three things: annual monetary payments, exchange of envoys, or distinctions between the degrees of honour to be used in forms of mutual address. After over twenty years of trading, foreigners have never spoken of this. In 1857 there was war in Kwangtung but trade went on as usual in Shanghai and Ningpo. The next year, there was war in Tientsin, but trade went on in Kwangtung as usual.[1] Foreigners demand large amounts of 'military compensation' but only in order to cover the expenses of war. Their constant interest has been trade. After every incident, they force us to open more ports, and occupy all the strategic places, bringing about serious consequences. Hence, there can be no question of 'making a treaty'. As to defence, this is something which we could never afford to neglect, from the earliest times till today, whether it involves a single family or the whole country. Along our sea coast, which stretches over 9,000 leagues, there are more than 100 ports. I-tu-men and Ta-ku are both known as strategic points. Since 1845 three ports have been opened to trade, and administrative machinery set up to handle foreign affairs. The strengthening of the Hu-men forts for future defence cost us several million. And yet in 1857 the foreigners were able to penetrate there and destroy everything. In 1859 Tientsin was well prepared for defence, but our best soldiers, fortresses, and cannons could still not resist long in battle. Things went badly in Kwangtung, and Ningpo was lost. Things went badly too in Chin-ling, and Chen-chiang was lost. The war continued till

[1] A reference to the Anglo–French War with China (1857–60).

1857, when the capital city of the province of Kwangtung was taken by foreigners, and the handling of foreign affairs in Tientsin was gravely affected.[1] That was certainly enough to show us what they were capable of. At present, foreigners have reached the interior of our country, and have established embassies in our capital. We have no means of keeping them away. That is why I believe that while national defence should be the constant concern of the Government, it is not advantageous for us at present to try to defend our coastline. I believe, in a word, that the management of foreign affairs requires adaptation to circumstances. This, in turn, involves two things: reason and strength. Strength is a relative term: there is the strength that they wish to attain, and also that which we wish to attain. Weighing the importance of the factors involved, as well as the urgency of the situation, we ought first to understand clearly how matters stand. We must deal with foreigners on points on which they insist though what they wish to insist on is precisely what we must desist from. So we really cannot yield to them. We should grant them without hesitation whatever we can as long as it does not injure our national interests, and stubbornly refuse them what we ought not to grant them. This is the policy dictated by strength and reason. From the earliest times on, whenever our country has fought with other nations, we have always had first to examine questions of right and wrong. When strength and reason are on our side, there can be no fear of defeat, but when our strength is insufficient, we have no other support besides trying to convince the other party by reason. After all, former emperors who appeased and conquered the Dzungars and the Buruts[2] were careful enough to punish evil men, to manifest open-mindedness and sincerity, and to seek to draw others to us not only by gentleness but even by self-humiliation. . . . This is really the established rule of our sage emperors in their domestic and foreign policies. They sought a deep understanding of the successes and failures of past and present in order to learn by observation and experience how we should

[1] For a useful though often inaccurate account of these campaigns see John Selby, *The Paper Dragon*, pp. 46-87.
[2] The Western Mongols, led by the Dzungar tribe of the Ili region, were a thorn in the flesh of the Manchus until the middle of the eighteenth century, when Ch'ing forces under the command of the Manchu general, Chao-hui (1708-64), finally subdued them in the years 1755-7. After this, the Kazaks and Buruts to the west of Ili recognized the suzerainty of China.

respond to other peoples—all this may be called reason. I realize that the strength of the foreigners, their challenge to our country, and the harms they have inflicted upon us, surpass all that has happened in the past. Their method of seeking excuses to create incidents in order to force us to deal with them, is also something new. If we deal with them properly, their management of customs, their teaching in the schools, their training of soldiers, and their making of weapons for us could go well and entail no difficulties or suspicions. If we do not deal with them properly, discussions will increase, and incidents will be provoked, a small thing often becoming big, an easy thing often becoming difficult, thus leading to endless troubles. It seems to me that during the past thirty years in dealing with foreigners, our officials both at Court and in the provinces, have imitated the attitude which developed after the Southern Sung dynasty, considering it disgraceful to make peace treaties, but excellent to make war. This habitual attitude has been formed over a period of several hundred years. And yet, no one has studied the frontier and defence policies of the period before the Northern Sung dynasty, as far back as the Han and the T'ang, though these are recorded in our histories. We know nothing about the foreigners of today and are unable to guess at their motives or appreciate their strength. While our Government has established the office of the Tsungli Yamen to deal with foreign affairs, it still has to be careful of what people are saying and to look around constantly, lacking the courage to deal directly with the issues at hand. Many people think I am foolish, and I would hardly dare to submit any more propositions, except that I am aware that there is nothing more important today than foreign affairs. Of course, Li Hung-chang, Shen Pao-chen[1] and Ting Jih-ch'ang[2] all have a great deal of experience in dealing with foreign affairs, do their best to seek to strengthen our country, and are also very capable diplomats. I, however, am of limited ability, having dealt with foreign affairs only since 1842. Yet

---

[1] Shen Pao-chen (1820–79), style Yu-tan, is best known for his work in developing the Chinese navy during his directorship of the Foochow Arsenal. In 1785 he was promoted to be Governor-General of Kiangsu, Kiangsi, and Anhwei. He had a reputation for probity and strictness, and was noted for his intolerance of corruption and slackness in administration.

[2] Ting Jih-ch'ang (1823–82), style Yü-sheng, a distinguished member of Tseng Kuo-fan's staff during the Taiping Rebellion, is best known as the founder of the Kiangnan Arsenal. He was also famous as an expert on foreign affairs.

what I have seen and heard, as verified by the lessons of history, has taught me much of the meaning of diplomacy, and has given me the strength of deep conviction. Yet, on account of sickness and ineptitude, I have not been able to accomplish much. So I wish at least to present my opinions, as far as it is possible. I herewith put forward four suggestions concerning foreign affairs, and humbly submit them to the judgement and decision of Your Majesty.

1. Our country established the Privy Council, as an executive organ, with power of deciding on internal and external policies. However, in 1864, the Tsungli Yamen was established on the model of the Privy Council, so that we now have two parallel organs.[1] At that time Prince Kung[2] was in charge of the Tsungli Yamen, and could decide everything. He was also very just in his handling of foreign affairs, yet did not wish to have others know of it. Since then, over ten years have lapsed. I believe that where foreign affairs are concerned, the Tsungli Yamen ought to decide our policies, but the issuance of edicts, and other executive measures must remain the work of the Privy Council. Yet the Privy Councillors, having no office in the Tsungli Yamen, do not understand the reasons behind these measures, and have no means of judging whether these are right or wrong. In my opinion, the Privy Councillors ought to hold office also in the Tsungli Yamen in order to participate in discussions of policy-making and therefore learn to make better contributions.

2. Trading with foreigners was at first limited to one port in Kwangtung. Later, many ports were opened along the sea coast, right up to Feng-t'ien [Liaoning], and foreigners penetrated into Kiangsi and Hupei. France now occupies Annam [Tongking] right next to Kwangsi.[3] Russia is penetrating the cities of the

[1] The Tsungli-Yamen was first set up in 1861. In 1864 it underwent a radical change in its organization and a great increase in personnel on the secretary level. See *Ch'ou-pan yi-wu shih-mo* (*T'ung-chih*), 28.13–17.

[2] Yi-hsin (1833–98) was the sixth son of Emperor Hsüan-tsung. In 1850 he became a prince of the first degree and was designated Kung. Though he was at first hostile towards all foreigners, his attitude towards them changed after the convention of Peking (1860), swinging from appreciation of the British to admiration for them. For his part in the establishment of the Tsungli Yamen, see Banno, *China and the West*, pp. 219–23.

[3] France was already claiming sovereignty over Tongking on the basis of a Franco–Vietnamese treaty of 1874, though she did not set up a formal protectorate in the north until 1882.

north-west, reaching Shensi, Kansu, and Shansi. England is demanding the right to trade in Yunnan. There have been many incidents in Szechwan, Kweichow, and Honan, as well as many cases involving the missionaries, so that at present, there is only one province untroubled by incidents relating to foreigners, namely Hunan. They must know how to deal with foreign affairs, in order to remain such an exception. If we have slight doubts, we would feel very uneasy. We might well begin with correct attitudes, but later become confused and even lost. That is why it is extremely important today to understand foreign affairs. Ever since foreign trade was opened, many incidents have happened, usually arising out of our dealings with foreigners. Such arguments have often concluded in our having to pay compensation and open still more ports. This is really the goal of their activities. Yet those who do not know how to take preventive measures easily provoke incidents which offer them more excuses. This is due to the fact that local officials do not understand the intentions of the foreigners, and, being afraid of their ability to provoke incidents, try to cover things up to avoid trouble. This, in turn, only encourages the foreigners to continue in their ways, while the common people often have to suffer injustices and have no means of making appeals. Since foreigners are always provoking incidents, I feel that in dealing with them we must make a special effort to understand this situation. In the Han dynasty, ambassadors enjoyed the same dignity as prime ministers and generals, even though the questions at hand were only minor in comparison with what we are facing today. I therefore beg Your Majesty to seek and use able men, and look for better ways of dealing with foreigners, so that our officials will no longer look down on foreigners, but will do their best to understand the reasons for our successes and our failures. Then they will humbly carry the burden of the task at hand, encouraging the hearts of the officials as well as earning the good will of all our people. Thus we shall create a proper foreign policy while at the same time establishing the basis of national strength and prosperity. And all this depends on one decision only on the part of our Government.

3. We have no urgent need today to send many ambassadors abroad. Only in San Francisco do we find tens of thousands of

Chinese immigrants, living in a region close to Peru and Spanish Cuba. Besides, there is also a question there of the employment of Chinese workers, which requires some control. Apart from this, we have no reason for establishing ambassadors in other countries. In any case, it is hard to depend on an ambassador, at such a remove, to deal with foreign nations. He would only suffer disgrace in case of any mishap. And it is not right to waste talented men by sending them to places where they can achieve nothing. We may as well wait until our merchants can travel by sea to different countries and do business there, before we send important officials away as envoys. But at the present moment, there is no such urgent need. Since we are already sending an ambassador to England, we might be obliged to do the same for other countries. I have been worried about the increased expenses this would lead to. I think that all officials should pay attention to the understanding of foreign affairs, and then almost anyone could be sent as an ambassador. In all departments, officials below the second and third grades who can understand the systems of governments and know how to deal with other peoples, will certainly do their best if sent out by the Government to make peace with foreigners. So I suggest that in future, when ambassadors are nominated, we should follow the custom by asking the Department of Rites to provide a list of officials below the second and third grades and under the age of fifty, who can then await Imperial orders. They should be given the same standing as ordinary envoys or ambassadors, so that our officials may get used to this method of procedure without getting incorrect ideas of the importance or unimportance of the office in question. They would then have to devote themselves to the study of foreign affairs and the international situation, so as to be of service to the country in times of urgency. This should certainly bring us much profit.

4. According to Western customs, every nation follows its own trade laws. We have thousands of laws, and foreign countries cannot follow them. When treaties were made, we were unable to add agreements concerning trading in accordance with the regulations of the Board of Punishments, so that our courts of justice now follow Western laws in their judgements, and we can do nothing about it. We should, however, try to act in an open-minded and just manner. Western law should be invoked in cases

occurring in the 'concessions', while Chinese law should be followed in the incidents which take place elsewhere. In this way, we can treat foreigners as though they were citizens of China, and handle cases involving foreigners as though they were Chinese cases. We might thus hope first to dissolve prejudices, and preserve the attitude of regarding all as one. And so, in cases of dispute, official reports and memorials should be made known to the public in order to let everyone see clearly that justice is being done. Any important details on these cases would then be brought to light. Thus we shall manifest the sincere intentions of our Government, and put the matter in question into perspective. This should not only allay the doubts of our own people, but also win over the foreigners themselves.

I have not discussed in detail these four propositions concerning foreign affairs. It is especially important to understand the policies of both the past and the present, in order to acquire the art of adapting ourselves to circumstances. We must also study well the situations in which we find ourselves, in order to stop the criticism of others. Then we can gradually find out a way of control, and promote a policy of strength and prosperity. Actually, everything comes back to two things: reason and strength, and even the deepest study and best-laid plans do not surpass these. The great Sung scholar, Ch'eng Yi, could always help others to arrive at the same conclusions in the discussion of affairs. He mentioned five things which the government of that time did not do. One of the things he mentioned was that it did not treat enemy nations with perfect sincerity. For if we are sincere towards others, others will be sincere with us too. If we regard others with suspicion, others will be suspicious of us too. This kind of reasoning never fails. Today, we are facing hard times and experiencing financial difficulties. Every bad turn in a case dealing with foreigners must involve some loss in our national strength. To preserve our country, we must take preventive measures; it will be too late if we wait for the occurrence of incidents, which would cause our relations with foreigners to deteriorate beyond remedy. I am an invalid and have no talents. I cannot help to solve the urgent problems of our country, and dare not hope to serve by my words, which can only arouse criticism. Yet, when I reflect on the situation in which we find ourselves, I really cannot stay quiet just to avoid trouble. So I have been audacious enough to submit my opinions. I know that what I have to say is bluntly and clumsily framed, and I feel most perturbed at this. But I have nevertheless disclosed all that I know on the subject of foreign affairs. I beg Your Majesty, the Empress Dowager, to read this and to send me your instructions.

NOTE: At that time the British envoy, Wade, left the capital, and the case of the murder of Margary, which the Court had ordered Li Hung-chang and Shen Pao-chen to discuss with him, could not be concluded. I was then trying to avoid being sent abroad, and, considering the difficulty of the case, sought to apply myself to it. In submitting my Memorial on the occasion of the termination of my leave, I discussed the handling of foreign affairs quite thoroughly, in order to prevent criticism. But an officer in the Board of Punishments, Liu Hsi-hung, kept the Memorial for three days, and so prevented it from reaching Her Majesty.[1] Later I found out that Sir Thomas Wade went to Shanghai and asked for armed intervention, but the British Government refused. When Li Hung-chang went to the meeting at Yen-t'ai, he was able to obtain what I had asked for, receiving a Court order to send me to Shanghai to negotiate with the foreigners in order to help improve the situation. Liu Hsi-hung tried very hard to go along as a member of the party. There were then many discussions concerning the case at the capital, and the Central Government found it hard to see who was right. Liu argued that such a Memorial, if submitted, might provoke displeasure, and even affect him, if he went abroad. He was fearless in all he did, and quite selfish. On account of his actions, I was prevented from making manifest my sincere intention of serving the country. I very much regret that I allowed him to betray me. When I reached Shanghai, I attempted to submit the Memorial anew, but the propitious moment had passed, and nothing I said could have any more effect.

[1] This incident would appear to have marked the beginning of the feud between Kuo and Liu.

4
Kuo's London Letter to Li Hung-chang (1877)[1]

I BELIEVE you have received my third letter, written on the eighth day of the second month [March 22, 1877]. Here, the administration, education, and social customs manifest every day many signs of change and renewal. If we study the origin and development of the [English] state, we find out that in the beginning there was a struggle for power between the King and the people which caused much bloodshed, and disturbances which lasted dozens and even hundreds of years. These were settled only after a period of confusion. They did not, at first, have a long and accumulated tradition of high virtue and culture [as does China]. For over a century now, their officials and their common people have collaborated in the discussion of national policies, have reported these to the King and put them into application, thereby making daily progress. And now their sovereign is beloved for her wisdom, and their way of life becomes better and better. And yet, if we look back, the work of building up their national strength really began only after the Ch'ien-lung period (1736–95). Steamships were first built during the Ch'ien-lung period, but at first they were not very profitable. Not till 1801 did they begin to use them on the sea.[2] From 1813 onwards they followed the same method in building railways.[3] From then on, they promoted

---

[1] *Yang-chih shu-wu yi-chi* (*wen-chi*), XI, pp. 1a–11a.

[2] John Fitch of Connecticut produced the first working steamboat in 1787. By 1790 he had a boat that ran to a printed schedule between Trenton and Philadelphia. The first practical steamboat in the British Isles was the *Charlotte Dundas* (1802). Robert Fulton produced the famous *Clermont* in 1807. See J. T. Flexner, *Steamboats Come True*.

[3] The world's first public railway was opened in 1803. It ran from Wandsworth to Croydon. The first carriage of passengers took place in 1807, on the Oystermouth railway. The first public railway to use steam traction was opened in 1825. The Liverpool and Manchester railway, which may be called the first modern railway in operation, was opened in 1830. Kuo's choice of the year 1813 for the opening of the railway system is inexplicable. Possibly he had learned that this was the year in which William Hedley built the famous 'Puffing Billy', the first locomotive to run on smooth wheels along smooth rails.

the science of electricity, first using magnetic machines to transmit messages, and then, in 1838, establishing a telegraph service in their capital,[1] extending it gradually until it reached India in 1865. With the Opium War (1839–42), their steamships came to the east of Kuangtung, while the war of 1860 saw their telegraph service extended from India to Shanghai. Hence, although the enterprise was only invented a few decades ago, the British have been able to take advantage of our weak political position to come to us as if instantly over a distance of some seventy thousand *li*. This is enough to show that the process of the mechanism of the universe, when once begun, cannot be stopped. Our Chinese gentry, who rely on themselves, and seek to put a stop to this, have not been able to do so. Since my arrival here a few months ago, I have actually seen the convenience of having these trains, which can make a round trip of three or four hundred *li* in half a day. The local gentry here also advise us to build railways, saying that marked the beginning of the foundation of British power, though originally they too had been suspicious of these railways and tried to stop their construction, fearing that they would be detrimental to the people's livelihood. For example, thirty thousand horses were formerly used to maintain communication between the port of Southampton and London. However, with the opening of the railway, over sixty or seventy thousand horses are now used. This has happened because the convenience of the railway has led to a daily increase in trade, and since the railway only follows a route, people from a distance of several dozen *li* or less, who come to take the train, must first travel by horse to get there, and do so in increasing numbers. Last winter, on my way through Shanghai, I saw a railway map in the Academy of Natural Sciences, showing railroads from India to Yunnan, one going out east of Lin-an to Canton, one coming out north of Ch'u-hsiung, proceeding through Szechwan to Hankow, and then heading out from Canton across the (Five) Mountains to come out into Hunan, meeting the other branch at Hankow. Another one ran fron Nanking to Chen-chiang, coming out east in Shanghai. From Shanghai it branches off in two directions: one coming east to Ningpo, the other going north to Tientsin to reach the capital. I was very surprised to see that no sooner had trade rela-

[1] The first telegraph line was installed between Paddington and Drayton by the Great Western Railway Company in July 1839.

tions with Yunnan been opened than the railways were already planned. Afterwards, when I came across this map in London, I found out that it had been made ten years ago, which proves how far-reaching are the foreigners' plans. The railway in India only goes as far as Assam. To reach China, it can take two routes: going north or south around the mountains. The northern route would run from Assam directly to the [upper reaches of the] Irrawaddy. The southern route would run through Burma, turn northeast, go to the Irrawaddy, and from there continue to Manyün. Generally speaking, these two railways are to be built a year or two after the opening of trade in Yunnan. The Japanese Minister,[1] on meeting me, remarked that Westerners know how to exploit nature. They have done the hard part; we should do the easy part. How can we therefore continue to neglect such matters? Other countries, he went on, envy our vast territories and our numerous population, and pity us when they hear that up to now we have not yet made efforts to strengthen ourselves. On hearing such words, I felt very ashamed and could find no answer. Last year, when I came to the capital, I had the intention of examining the events of the past and the present, in order to find out differences and similarities, successes and failures. Since the time of the Sui (581–618) and the T'ang (618–917) we have been trading with the West for some thirteen hundred years. The prohibition of the opium trade led us into war, obliging us to open many ports which lead into the Yangtze River. The foreigners' power has become more and more oppressive and harmful. We should carefully investigate the origins and development of such events, and the reasons why these foreign nations became rich and strong, as well as their intentions towards us. We must also find out for ourselves how our country should face this crisis and deal with others. We can find out everything that needs to be known about these matters, and use them to compile a book which can be submitted to the Tsungli Yamen and distributed to the schools of the Empire, in order to clarify the doubts of our scholar-officials. Government policy towards foreigners has a great deal of foresight and magnanimity about it,

---

[1] Ueno Kagenori (1844–88) was one of Japan's earliest diplomats. In 1868, after the Meiji Restoration, he was made Commissioner of Foreign Affairs. Later he was sent as High Commissioner and Minister Plenipotentiary to several countries in Europe as well as to the U.S.A.

which should be made known to our people. Once this is clarified, the long-term foundation of our state-policy, which should enable our country to continue for millions of years, could then be certainly established. I had already spoken to you about this when I passed through Tientsin; but when I reached the capital, I did not dare mention it, on account of the noisy discussions and criticisms which I encountered.

Personally, I think that there is something about the Chinese mind which is absolutely unintelligible. I refer here to opium-smoking. Nothing the West has done has been more harmful to us than opium. Even English gentlemen themselves are ashamed of the fact that they have used this harmful trade as an excuse for provoking hostilities with China, and are making a serious effort to eradicate the evil. Yet our Chinese scholar-officials complacently degrade themselves by smoking opium, and do so without remorse. This has been for several decades already our national disgrace, exhausting much money and manpower, and poisoning the lives of our people. And yet there is not one man who feels ashamed of it.

At present, every home possesses such [Western] articles as clocks, watches and toys, while Western textiles and woollens are to be found even in the remote countryside. In Kiangsu and Chekiang it is even the practice to neglect our own currency and to make use of foreign money, the value of which is even raised, without any thought whatsoever of [right and] wrong. And yet, when our people hear of the building of railways and the spreading of telegraphy, they become enraged and crowd together to create difficulties. There are even people who stir up public anger when they set eyes on foreign machines. When Tseng Chi-kang (Chi-tse), on account of the death of his parent, took a small steam boat from Nanking to Ch'ang-sha, many officials and important men raised a hue and cry which lasted for several years without cease. Such people willingly allow others to harm us and squeeze the marrow from our bones, and yet with their whole strength close up the sources of our national revenue. It is really difficult to understand their motives. After thirty years of foreign relations our provincial authorities still know nothing. All they can do is to impose their ignorant ideas on the Court and call this 'public opinion' as a cover for their own purposes. Sad to say, the common people have long been denied an outlet which would permit them to submit their complaints to higher authorities. And yet, the ignorant have been made use of and the unemployed have been stirred up to the attainment of purely selfish ends, all this with the help of many of our officials. The weakening of the Sung (960–1276), and the downfall of the Ming (1368–1644), were both the outcome of the actions of such irresponsible and ignorant people. I am a man of Ch'u (i.e., Hunan and Hepeh) who grew up in the backward and foolish countryside. I know nothing about trade, nor have had contact with foreigners. Nevertheless, I have studied a little, and have reflected upon the principles of things. My investigations into past and present events have given me insights, which, in spite of the criticism and contempt of the whole world, I still maintain as principles for the defence and the government of the country, to help us to become independent and strong. I have openly spoken of this without fear, but have never encountered real understanding, being obliged to come here, seventy thousand *li* away from my own country. After less than two months here, having been twice impeached, and considerable reflection, I have come to regret my previous behaviour. However, though at first I did not dare to say anything more, still there are certain things which I have seen and heard that I must tell you. Japan has sent over two hundred people here to learn special skills. They are living in different ports, about ninety being in London. Of the twenty and more I have met, all know English, and one, called Nagaoka Ryōnosuke, was a former feudal lord, who governed a fief. He has now been degraded to the status of a hereditary nobleman, and has come here to study law. Their Minister of Finance, En-lou-ou-mu (Inoue Kaoru), has been sent here to study the management of such (financial) affairs, and hopes to imitate and put into practice all that he learns here.[1] The telegraph offices which the Japanese have established afford another practical example of what these people have learned in London. Only very few are here as military

---

[1] Inoue Kaoru (1835–1915) was one of the five elder statesmen of the Meiji period. In 1863 he left Japan secretly and made his way to England as a sailor. On learning of the bombardment of his native fief, Chōshū, in September, 1864, he hurried home to urge that peace be made, earning only a savage beating from a group of reactionary samurai for his pains. With the overthrow of the Tokugawa in 1867, Inoue became a leading member of the government and held important posts in the ministries of finance, industry, and foreign affairs. In 1877, at the time of his visit to England, he was Minister of Finance.

cadets. After all, war is the most minor of sciences, while the establishment of systems is the root and foundation of the state. You wish especially to have others receive military training, since you are in charge of defence. But it is my opinion that the military system in the provinces lacks an effective method of re-organization, while the recruitment of volunteers cannot be relied on as a constant practice. For the next few decades there will be no danger of war with the West, and this can be seen both by reasoning and by close observation of the present trends. As to the system of military recruitment in London, I have discovered that all recruits must first study and understand military science, before they are selected. Doctors are sent to feel their pulse and examine their health and make sure that their bones are solid, before they are taught systematically to jump and climb and to handle guns and cannons, after which they are organized in army units. Hence their military power rests on a very good foundation, which is more than ours does. One man cannot do very much, however skilful. I am afraid that we may waste much money in 'learning how to kill dragons',[1] complete this training, and never be able to use it. I would like to tell the Government-sponsored students who went abroad with Li Tan-ya, to learn instead how to survey and refine coal and iron, how to build railways and understand the science of electricity, in order to be able to put their knowledge into practice. I recommend that we ask our viceroys and provincial governors to select talented youths, give them financial help, and send them first to Tientsin, Shanghai, and Fukien, to learn the skills of the technical officer and study languages, and then have them sent abroad, to learn various skills according to their different abilities and dispositions. Our technical offices should also employ two or three more teachers each, to wait for the increasing number of students. Once this has started it may be possible to influence the public to do more things of this nature. There is a man here named Stephenson,[2] who says that he has built many railways in different countries. He is very earnest, and advises us to do this quickly. I therefore submit a summary of his plans. For, according to my opinion, we cannot always ask foreigners to do everything for us. We

[1] An expression denoting the acquisition of completely useless knowledge.
[2] Sir Rowland Macdonald Stephenson (1808–95) was a noted railway engineer. He was for many years managing director of the East Indian Railway Company.

ought to order our own people to learn these methods. For example, the country of Egypt, which is in Africa, first sent men to learn railway building in England, and then asked them to do this in their own country. This is a good example for us. I beg therefore for your instructions, in order to discuss this matter with Li Tan-ya. I feel that of the many necessary things which would help us to govern our country well and establish a solid base for national wealth and strength, these two [railways and telegraphs] would enable us to establish a state which would remain strong for a thousand years without any degeneration. It is hardly necessary to mention the great and far-reaching advantages involved. Among these advantages, there are two which are easily seen. Firstly, China is a vast country of over ten thousand *li* in area, because of which it is necessary to wait for many weeks to get a letter from a distant place, and people often suffer for lack of news. With these two things [railways and telegraphs], places ten thousand *li* away become as the hall or threshold of one's house. In times of flood, or drought, or robbers, incidents occurring in the morning will be known by the evening. So we need not worry about disloyal subjects who might exploit such situations to cause trouble. Secondly, there is too much of a distance between our officials and the common people. Yet both these groups seek to hide things from the Court in order to promote their private interests. Hence people often have complaints which they cannot submit to higher authorities. When we have railways and telegraphs, our wealthier citizens would be obliged to make contributions to the service of the country, and would do so with enthusiasm. Furthermore, the railroads will pass through the country much as blood circulates in the human body, so naturally local political situations—better or worse—will not be hidden any longer, and we no longer need fear those corrupt officials who exploit and suppress the people in order to gain unjust profit. Even during the most prosperous days of the Three Dynasties,[1] the highest accomplishment consisted in the officials doing their duties, and the common people communicating their feelings. Nothing can really be added to it. Those who can only allege that foreign machines will damage local geomantic harmony wherever they go, are quite in the wrong. Railway and telegraph lines have to be built on flat surfaces, and need involve no digging

---

[1] The Hsia, Shang, and Chou dynasties.

or destroying. As to mechanical coal-mining, the deeper we go to draw water, the better water we shall find; the deeper we penetrate into the mines, the better coal we shall find also.

The digging method used by the Chinese aims at width while the digging method used by the Westerners aims at depth. Yet both mine coal regardless of the method used. I can see no reasons for opposing such a practice. Taking Hunan as an example, the iron mines are mostly in Pao-ch'ing and the coal mines mostly in Heng-chou, and yet, these two places have produced the greatest number of successful scholars in the state examinations. Both Hsiang-t'an and Shih-t'an produce coal; they are also known for being the home towns of many famous families and clans. Hsiang-hsiang also produces coal, and is especially well known for its successful men in political careers.[1] The best way to show the fallacy of the current criticisms and discussions is to show factual proofs. When our own Chinese manage these things, we shall gain profit, and there can be no reason for such opposition as we are now meeting. If we wait for several decades, the foreigners will have built these things wherever they go, and will have accumulated enough influence to control the situation, and enough profit to induce rascals and outlaws who used to create troubles to work for them, and we shall no longer be able to stand on our own feet. Mencius says: 'Heaven's plan in the production of mankind is this: that they who are first informed should instruct those who are later in being informed, and they who first apprehend principles should instruct those who are slower to do so'.[2] But the responsibility for foresight and perception must lie in our court officials. Thus politics will become clear, and the criticisms of scholars be appeased, only when the Court makes its firm decision. As to our fundamental, national policies, there are certain things which we shall find difficult to do on account of our present situation and strength. But there are also certain pressing measures, which do not pertain to our fundamental policy, but which must first be done if we wish to apply other political measures. Otherwise, even if we get splendid inspirations every day, we shall never accomplish anything. I am referring here above all to the prohibition of opium smoking.

[1] Kuo is arguing that mining cannot have destroyed local geomantic harmony, since these places still produce successful men.
[2] Mencius; Legge, *Classics*, II, Pt. V, 1, VII, p. 363.5.

This was first prohibited at the time of Yung-cheng (1722–36), when it was used as medicine only. As politics were then stable, and officials law-abiding, the people did not dare smoke it. Opium-smoking became more wide-spread during the reign of Tao-kuang (1821–50). In my youth, however, I had not heard of such a practice, since at that time we were living a prosperous life, the people having enough to eat and remaining careful and law-abiding. Only later did opium bring so many calamities upon us, causing the morale of the people to change for the worse. Floods, droughts, and rebellions followed. Our present difficulty with the foreigners also began with the prohibition of opium. The chiefs of the Chin-t'ien rebels [the Taipings] also gathered the dispersed coastal militiamen in the valleys, and started the great disturbance. Therefore, opium not only brings harm to the people, ruining their health and their wealth, but also was the source of the Rebellion. Foreigners are still ashamed of this, although we Chinese have become used to it. I believe that as long as opium-smoking is not eradicated, we can accomplish nothing. There is really a very simple method of prohibiting it, consisting in the officials abstaining from it first, and then extending the prohibition to the commoners, the literati setting an example for the ordinary people. Counselling can be accompanied by punishment, in our attempt to waken a sense of shame in people's hearts, to encourage them to reform themselves. Thus, in twenty years at the most, opium-smoking could be completely eradicated, without leaving any ill effects, and we need fear no more trouble afterwards. I have already spoken of this at great length in my last memorial and have nothing further to add. This is one thing.

Another matter is the cultivation of unused land in Kiangsu and Chekiang. I had first heard that foreigners are only concerned with trade, and do not promote agriculture. Now I have found out that it is not true. Their motive in trade is to enrich the people; hence they only tax a few items, such as tea, wine, and tobacco, leaving all other trade commodities untaxed. Every year, an account is drawn up to show the profits made by the traders, which are then taxed at the rate of one and one quarter per cent. Houses and property are also taxed, somewhat as we collect our household taxes. Those whose annual income is under £300 are exempt from taxation. Medals and other emblems are taxed; house-dogs and other animals are taxed. Leaving aside ordinary taxation, the revenue of the country comes entirely from land tax, which shows how diligent they are in the exploitation of the land ... At present, twelve or thirteen years after the end of the rebellions in Kiangsu and Chekiang, there are still many fields left uncultivated, for the people are no longer used to hard work and wish to husband their strength, and the officials find it too troublesome to make detailed reports on land utilization, so as to avoid the responsibility of submitting to the government the amount of taxation inflicted on their people. The uncultivated land is thus left to grow weeds while the farmers try to hide the facts. This also should be taken care of by the Board of Revenue and Population, and directed and guided by the viceroys and governors. This is another matter of concern.

Furthermore, the land of Kashgaria ought to be ceded to Yakub Beg.[1] However, the land of Kashgaria is close to Andijan, and we are unable to turn the Pamirs into another Great Wall to prevent their people from coming in. The tribes of Khokand are attached to Russia. The remnants of the Moslems took advantage of the revolt in Kashgaria to attack and occupy the territory. However, fearing Chinese power they are thinking of becoming our dependants and last year Wade interceded for them.[2] I think we should follow their wishes and swear a treaty with them, ordering them to restore all the cities, while receiving a Mandarin to be stationed in Urumchi, whose faithfulness and might would be enough to keep them in submission, and so guarantee a century of peace. If we rely on military strength and invade them, we shall waste much time and money, and even if we are fortunate enough to obtain a victory, the remainder of the Moslems will certainly submit themselves to Russia, and continue making war and looting all year round. This would only permit

[1] Yakub Beg (1820–77), was a Khokandian soldier of fortune who had established a Moslem kingdom in Sinkiang between 1866 and 1870. The British government, attracted both by the prospect of increased trade and 'a common front between Britain and Islam against Russia' granted Yakub Beg official recognition in 1873 and urged the Chinese to recognize him. Though the Chinese conservative faction favoured recognition, Tso Tsung-t'ang (1815–85), a veteran general as well as a statesman, advanced into Kashgaria and decisively defeated the rebel forces. By December, 1877, Yakub Beg was dead and the whole of Sinkiang was in Chinese hands, except for Ili, which remained under Russian control. See Hsü, *The Ili Crisis*.

[2] Wade had urged the Chinese to recognize Yakub Beg, arguing that the presence of a weak Northern state in Sinkiang was preferable to that of Russia.

the Russians to profit from the situation, and we would merely suffer losses, without knowing what to do afterwards. Ruling a country demands long term planning, whereas the military and their adherents think only of staging invasions. That is why we cannot expect our generals to propose the cession of territory. Only the Court can weigh the various issues at hand and make plans which are for imminent issues. Then the generals will gain in reputation, and the generosity of the Court be also experienced by distant peoples, inducing them to yield and become docile. That is why I consider Wade's intercession an opportunity we ought not to miss. This is another important matter.

Furthermore, we ought to negotiate with the Russians to determine the position of Ili. England and Russia are powers of equal status. The English wish to open the country up for the sake of profit, but the Russians invade other countries merely to widen their territory. They have unjustifiably used the occasion of the disturbances, to occupy Ili, showing that they are only intent on seizing territory. I feel that in this Sinkiang business, a great deal of discussion will be needed to make the Russians restore Ili to us. There is no regulation in international law which permits a nation to occupy another country's territory during local disturbances. It is possible that the Russians will ask for a war indemnity, before they restore us the land, and they will not be satisfied with anything less than a fortune. So I suggest we turn the tables on them. We should not ask them to lower the price they demand for restoration of this territory, but rather ask them how much they will pay us to acquire it. The desert island of Sakhalin, which belongs to Japan, affords a good example of Russia's intention. They have occupied it and will not easily give it back.[1] All the more so with Ili. Instead of vaguely postponing the affair, and eventually bringing on a war, it is better to negotiate a proper treaty with Russia, which will assure several decades of peace. As a last resort, we can always ask the Russians to take Ili in exchange for the land south of the Amur.

There is still another matter to discuss, namely, the abolition of *Likin*. I am well acquainted with this practice of raising taxes for

[1] Russia and Japan were in joint occupation of Sakhalin until 1875, when a treaty was signed at St. Petersburg stipulating that Japan was to give up her claims to the island in exchange for the Russian cession of the Kuril Islands. Japan eventually gained control over the southern half of the Sakhalin after the Russo-Japanese War (1904–05).

defence purposes, and have practised it myself, having promoted it almost single-handed in Hunan, and also reported on it from Kwangtung, citing examples from the past to prove our present needs. I feel therefore that I understand this business. But I also feel that such ways of raising support for our troops in time of emergency ought not to be undertaken by the Government. Besides, it is unjust, over ten years after the end of the fighting, not to arrange for its cessation. Such methods of taxation always bring complications in their train with the passage of time. The provinces have no urgent needs and do not pay much attention to the collection of such sums, so that the longer the practice continues, the less money they collect. If we should suddenly find ourselves at war, and need to raise money for defence, this would prove highly inefficient. In fact, such a method is doubly embarrassing. Last year, following the case in Yunnan, we decided on the cessation of such taxation in the foreign concessions, thus freeing foreigners from this duty. This is like chasing a fish into deep water, or pursuing a bird into thick forest. It not only causes a diminution of confidence among our own merchants, but is also a national disgrace. My opinion is that we ought to abolish this method of taxation in the provinces, and therefore also cancel the clause concerning the exemption of the foreign concessions from such taxes. Then we should negotiate a treaty which provides for the possibility of raising money for the purpose of defence when the need arises. Local products such as Fukien tea, Chekiang silk and other commodities can be made subject to a regional tax, the revenue from which is to be used locally, and so it will be exempted at the same time with the *likin*. All this can be done reasonably. Formerly, there was a levy of eight taels on every box of tea. Since the opening of the five Ports to foreign trade, this has been suddenly reduced to two and a half taels ... The sources of national revenue ought to be under the control of the Court. Ignorant as I am, I find this disturbing. This is yet another important matter.

As Minister abroad, I have seen something of the negotiations between our country and the foreigners, and have wanted to submit my views, in accordance with the common practice, for a long time. However, I have so far not dared to put forward my own opinions for fear of bringing further disgrace upon myself. For though I am but a low-ranking official who has had little experience abroad I have nevertheless been subjected to such criticism by certain circles in the capital, whose opinion the Court cannot ignore (to say nothing of many other censures I have encountered), that, flee where I may, I cannot escape condemnation. However, I realise that Your Excellency is the most important official in China and ought to be informed of matters affecting our vital interests. That is why, after due consideration, I have thought fit to comment on a few issues of major importance. My proposals can be reasoned out, found logical and put into practice without difficulty, for I have not suggested anything difficult or recondite, which would be merely pompous talk to please myself.

Some time ago, when Pao-chün and I were discussing foreign affairs we decided that while Your Excellency could discern the major issues, Ting Yü-sheng could deal with the finer points and Shen Yu-tan could put proposals into operation, other high-ranking officials were totally ignorant of the matters involved. But when Pao-chün laughingly remarked that I myself was aware of both the major issues and the finer points I told him that I hardly dared think so, since my knowledge was quite philosophically inclined and was concentrated on the understanding of Emptiness and so could hardly be put to practical purposes, remaining thus very far behind that of Yu-tan. However, my study of the past enables me to comprehend the present, and so I understand the important aspects of foreign policy, especially the important policies of Han and T'ang, going back all the way to the Three Dynasties, and the differences and similarities between such issues and those facing us today. I believe that this knowledge has been lost to the world for over seven hundred years already, ever since the Southern Sung. This knowledge I believe I do possess, and so I beg Your Excellency to weigh my proposals, and advise the Court to adopt them for the benefit of our country.

5
Selections from the *Ying-yao jih-chi* (*Journal of a Voyage to England*) of Liu Hsi-hung

[November 1876]

The English Ambassador Wade, when we first met at the capital, often said that since the goal of government is to enrich the people, we ought to consider as our present, urgent business the opening of coal and iron mines and the building of railways. This time, when we came south from Tientsin, the foreigners on our boat put forward identical views. I informed these people of the fact that we Chinese base our culture on the pursuit of righteousness rather than the pursuit of profit, preferring to suit the taste of the people rather than to disturb them. We never grew tired of debating the matter back and forth. At first, I did not understand what satisfaction they could find in China's gaining wealth and power, that they should give us such earnest and intimate advice. After our arrival in Shanghai, on 10 November, we paid a visit to the School of Investigation and Application where Intendant Feng[1] showed us a railway map presented to them by the foreigners, displaying the proposed route from the Five Indies, which ran through our western provinces to reach the capital, so that one line stretched from north to south. Then I realized that the foreigners' intention was not just to occupy the treaty ports and engage in commerce.... If we do not determine to refuse their plans firmly, the people working at the sea ports will be so delighted by novelties and pleased with exotic arts that they will fall into their dark designs without realizing it. (Merchants scheming for profit would support these schemes to deceive the officials, and

---

[1] This Academy was established in the British Concession in 1875. It was financed by Chinese and Western businessmen and had a small museum attached to it. Intendant Feng is unidentifiable.

officials who seek merit would exaggerate their advantages to tempt the Court, and the danger would become impossible to curb, although it is not yet sufficient to worry us. The methods of the market place cannot be used to govern the empire: crafts and tricks are not sufficient to be considered the best administration. How could things today be suddenly different from the past?) Once the railroad is built, the security of the country might change in a minute. So this is not an unimportant matter. I think that we ought to hold to our opinions and say outright that the building of railways would not only be harmful to China but would also affect England, since the common people have not yet been appeased in their anger. If suddenly, in the construction of railways, we had to destroy their fields and houses and destroy the graves, their anger would grow, and the rebels in hiding in the wilderness would use the killing of the English as an excuse to incite the people's hearts to rebellion. Then, not only would the merchants' marts along the coast be overrun, but the very railway to India would be made use of by the rebels, and so be turned against them. When the people's hearts are thus united, their power would be as the waters of the Yangtze and the Yellow River. Even the best-made firearms would never be able to hold them back. What happened long ago to [George] Washington in America,[1] or what happened recently in San-yüan-li, Kwangtung,[2] can all serve as a warning to the British. We must not try to start a fire and forget that the fire may turn with the wind and burn us. When the sun reaches its zenith, its begins to set; when the moon becomes full, it begins to wane; when we pull the bow too hard, it breaks easily; when the tree yields too many flowers, it easily withers. All this shows that progress carried to excess becomes regression. The principle that every situation contains the seeds of its opposite can be discovered with a little thought. The sage kings and wise ministers of China's successive dynasties have not been inferior to those of the West in their talents and wisdom, but they never had the presumption to use clever tricks to scrape the heavens and dissect the earth, competing with Nature in order to attain wealth and strength. For they feared an extensive

---

[1] He is referring to the American Revolution, 1775–83.
[2] An incident in the Opium War, when local militia harassed the British as they withdrew. This was regarded as a victory for the Cantonese population.

danger wherever they saw a deep principle of Nature. They were quite unlike the English who only calculate profits, rushing ahead without ever looking back. Since I have pointed this out to them fully, might they perhaps not learn to see their faults?

What the *Great Learning*[1] said about investigation and application was meant to apply to the Way, not to manufactured goods. The body, the heart or mind, the family and country, and the universe have principles which may be independently correct or mutually related. If we did not investigate their inherent rightness in depth, we would not know how to pass these principles on and put them into practice; if we did not investigate their mutual relations, we would not know how to master their essential points. Without true knowledge, we cannot act properly and so our thoughts or intentions cannot be sincere. And if we do not make our thoughts sincere in our practice, then it will be impossible for us to rectify our minds, we shall have no way of rectifying ourselves, or of cultivating our persons. And so, the regulation of our families, the ruling of our country, and the pacification of the world will all lose their foundation. That is why our holy Classics teach us, when we begin our studies, first to investigate clearly the inherent rightness and the mutual relations of principles, in order that, with understanding, we shall attain to the state of no longer entertaining doubts when we face confusing differences, of not being distracted by external business, and of not limiting ourselves to shallow tasting. Then we may really apply ourselves to the work of rectifying the heart, cultivating the self, ruling the country, and pacifying the world. The so-called 'objects' or 'things' are precisely the self, the heart, the family, the country, and the world. This does not mean that we must first investigate the workings of machines and gadgets. How can machinery and technology be compared with rectifying the heart and cultivating the personality? That would only confuse meanings, so that the further we investigated, the worse matters would become. Since Western countries are known to be wealthy and strong, people who do not study the roots of their politics say that their wealth and strength actually come from manufacturing. Thus, the scholars who admire the West

---

[1] *Ta-hsüeh*, 4. 'Such extension of knowledge lay in the investigation of things,' Legge, *Classics*, i.358.

are like ants admiring the fat of mutton. They establish schools to house machines and call this 'Investigation and Application', seeking to make use of this sentence in the *Great Learning* to lend lustre to the name, and so attract crowds to come to learn. But how can something like that be made use of? After all, scholars are esteemed and placed above the common people because their ambitions and conduct are above the conventional. ...

Today, those who study are like the common craftsmen who carve out and make clay bricks. Those who work as officials are like the merchants who seek new plans of making more profit. How can we hope to gain anything by picking from the ranks of craftsmen and merchants officials who must rule the people and govern the world? And so, if we wish to remedy our poverty and weakness, we ought to begin by reforming officialdom. To begin this reform we ought to commence by the rectification of the scholars' habits, which in turn ought to begin with the study of righteousness and the understanding of the Way. If we still tell our students to apply their hearts to Western learning and to crafts and to learn from merchants, we shall only increase the ranks of the merchants. Then, when the ranks of the officials take in one more merchant, the country gets one more worm, the people one more thief. How can we allow the orders of the government to be set aside and the economic life of the people to be neglected, relying only on ships, cannons, and machines to rule the world? On the other hand, does this mean Western learning ought not to be pursued? No! Western learning is no more than technology. We should change the name of the 'School of Investigation and Application' to the 'Hall of the Forest of Arts', and gather clever craftsmen to teach there, so that students may learn to manufacture instruments well, and take orders from officials, as ordinary craftsmen do. Then things would conform to righteousness. If scholars would only govern their own bodies and minds in order to be able to govern the world, even though weapons were lacking, they could still command artisans to make them, without having to do so themselves. So how can we consider this practical technology as investigation and application?

[pp. 160a–161a]

[7 December 1876]

Today was the first time that I saw a train.[1] The four wheels, both front and back, are covered on top by several rooms made of boards (when used to carry cargo, the rooms are opened to make up one space only); the machine is in front. (It can move backwards too.) The carriage is about six foot high, its depth and width being the same as those of the train. When one vehicle is not enough, several are joined together. Their length extends to a hundred steps and yet they can move without stopping. The rails are about four to five feet wide, the two sides jutting up as small paths in the fields do, in order to hold the wheels. Even travelling slowly, the train can still go over 100 leagues an hour, hence it can often cover a distance of 10,000 leagues in several days and nights. The wonder of such a trick surpasses the magic art of diminishing distances. But if we apply it to China, then the people who bare their thighs and forearms, who hold to the whip and the cord, who row the boats, who pull the carriages, to carry people or cargo, would all lose their jobs. Dynasty after dynasty has always avoided disturbing the people. The work of digging into the mountains to open the mines is difficult to put in practice constantly; a myriad mouths are waiting to be fed, and what method have we to cure poverty? If we daily press more people into becoming bandits, commerce between China and the West will never become peaceful, and even the reliance on force and the use of soldiers cannot stop the flame of hunger. Besides, China does not have as many travelling tourists and rich merchants as does Europe, nor does she reap as much profit from trade. The building of railways would require a great deal of capital, and unless we made the price of transport high, we should not get enough to repay the invested capital and the accumulated interest. But it is Chinese custom to practise economy in travelling and in the transport of goods back and forth, owing to economy in daily life. So there is really very little profit in this business. Now if for the transport of 100 bushels of rough goods over 10,000 leagues, several hundred or a thousand dollars would have to be paid, who would be willing to cut through his own flesh and blood to feed himself no matter how rapid the means of transport? Hence, apart from a dozen rich

[1] At Suez.

merchants in different provinces, the tradesmen and passengers definitely would not take the train or transport their goods by it. Since our most holy Court does its best to keep the multitudes of the people in peace, to rejoice in our happy land together, the farmers, craftsmen, and workers are not very willing to leave their villages, while even the richer families which sometimes arrange with friends to visit different places together, go only to the neighbouring villages, and satisfy their desire to see and hear more by casting quick glances at the towns and cities. They do not resemble the foreigners who want to go to distant places, and often cover several tens of thousands of leagues on one trip before they can satisfy their curiosity. That is why when the railway is first constructed, those who take pleasure at its wonderful efficacy will be in a hurry to try it, and go one after another to take the train. After less than half a year, however, there will be very few who will continue to take the train, so that it will not even be possible to get enough profit to pay back a day's use of coal and labour, not to say of the invested capital and the interest. Besides, economy is a constant need in the governing of a country, and [our Government] therefore would certainly not wish to disturb hundreds of millions of living beings, to spend thousands of billions of silver dollars to begin such a work, which might seem able to bring us quick profit. Hence, the fact that trains cannot be used in China resembles the fact that a tranquil policy cannot work in Europe. We cannot force people to adopt the same methods. As I was leaning against the railing on the boat, and staring ahead of me, the foreign interpreter, W. C. Hillier, came and stood next to me. So I looked at him and told him my opinions. This Hillier has been sent by Wade to travel with us. He has been with us since he boarded at Shanghai. Hearing my words, he nodded agreement. If, in future, there are Englishmen who advise us to construct railways, we ought to explain the matter to them in this way. Even if they exert pressure on us, we ought to tell them directly that this is a matter of domestic policy, and no outsider ought to intervene in the domestic policy of an independent country. Since this is clearly stated in international law, how can they exert pressure on us? Thus can we invoke their own laws to dissuade them and prevent them from pursuing such a policy. [p. 164a–b]

In Japan, the government has ordered that the country change to the use of Western law and that the people must dress like Westerners and adopt their rules of etiquette. Westerners however, despise them for doing so, saying that such an imitation for the sake of conformity causes them to lose their original nature. The commander of the *Yang-wu*, Ts'ai Kuo-hsiang, said that, at parties, the foreigners should learn to use Chinese implements. When they remove their hats, we ought to join our hands in response. If we abandon our own customs to imitate them, they would only laugh at us. Jung Hung [1828–1912][1] is a Chinese mandarin in Western clothes. Macartney considers this disgraceful. Our Chinese officials who are concerned with international relations ought to learn from this.

[p. 165a]

[25 January 1877]

Wade came with his wife at the *hsü* watch [7–9 p.m.]. We received a letter from the Foreign Ministry, asking us to give them our credentials for examination, for the Ministers from different countries always bear Instructions resembling the Imperial edicts from a Chinese court. But our Chinese Government did not know this, and so had not issued us with them when we were sent out. We must submit a special Memorial to ask for them.

[p. 167a]

[26 January 1877]

The next day, the Ambassador met Wade to discuss this matter with him. Wade said that he would inform the Ministry of the matter. That day, I was writing a letter home and so did not see him.

[p. 167a]

[1] Jung Hung (Yung Wing, 1828–1912) was the first Chinese to graduate from an American university (Yale, 1854). In 1875, he was made Associate Minister to Washington, though he did not take up the post until 1878. He came under heavy criticism at home for favouring a policy by which Chinese students in the U.S. were encouraged to adopt the dress and manners of Americans. He himself took an American wife and became a naturalized American citizen. See Yung Wing, *My Life in China and America*.

[27 January 1877]

Gordon visited us. Gordon is the brave general who helped Li Shao-ch'üan [Li Hung-chang] when he was governor of Kiangsu. He is an Englishman by origin, with a brave expression on his face. Ten years ago, he left the south of the Yangtze to go and work as an official in the country of Egypt, governing its new territory. Now he has long been home on vacation, and is now going back to Egypt. He heard of the Chinese ambassadors and so came to call on us.[1]

Between 3 and 5 p.m. Li Shu-ch'ang went to the Foreign Ministry to present to them a second copy of our Letter of State and of the words which we are to read aloud when we submit this Letter of State. This is also a Western custom. We also sent in a written request for an appointment for audience with the Queen. This was done several days ago, but we have not yet received any reply.

[p. 167a]

[5 February 1877]

London has no city wall, but the bridges over which the trains pass are strong as city walls. Since the population is so dense that the trains cannot pass through the streets, bridges are made from huge stones, high over the tops of thousands of houses and chimneys. On these iron plates are laid, and sand and earth piled between them, in order that the trains may travel to and fro. Even when sleeping in a building a hundred feet high, one can often hear the ceaseless thunder overhead made by passing trains. Sitting in the train and looking into the distance, you see from afar the pedestrians below moving about as though on a loom. The city streets and alleys seem small and abysmal, so that you almost begin to wonder whether you are looking into a pit dug into the earth, forgetting that you are up on a bridge.

---

[1] Charles George Gordon (1833–85) had distinguished himself in China as commander of the 'Ever Victorious Army', which inflicted heavy losses on the Taipings. Shortly before his return home in 1865 he was made a mandarin of the first class. Gordon did not go to Egypt until 1874, when he passed through Cairo on his way to take up the governorship of Central Africa. He resigned from this appointment at the end of 1876 and returned to England. On 31 January 1877 he left for Cairo where he received the combined appointment of Governor-General of the Sudan, Darfour, the equatorial provinces, and the Red Sea littoral. His main mission was the suppression of the slave trade.

You also pass high above the tops of towers and can almost bend down and touch the tops of the masts of boats. When I first came to this place, I was very frightened at heart by all that I saw, for everything was strange. People tell me that travelling southwards to the ports, and northwards to Scotland, is taken care of by several dozen railways, and for going 100 leagues one has only to pay one shilling, which is several times cheaper than it used to be before there were trains. That is why the trains for travelling merchants have rooms for groups and also other rooms, always furnished with soft, leather seats next to bright, glass windows, very comfortable for sitting or for lying down. The rich and noble ride in railway-carriages with gilded walls, embroidered curtains, couches, and small tables provided with bottles of clean water and vases with flowers. Though the train goes quickly as the flying wind and thunder, the noise of which penetrates the ear, it makes no difference to the pleasant feeling of being in one's study where one can relax at leisure.

[p. 168b]

[6 and 7 February 1877]

During the *shen* watch [3–5 p.m.] a letter came from the Foreign Ministry arranging for us to go tomorrow [7 February] at 2.45 p.m. to Po-chin-ha-mu Pa-lei-shih [Buckingham Palace] to submit our Letter of State. The Vice-Ambassador could go also. For the Sovereign has returned from Osborne. 'Po-chin-ha-mu' means 'foretelling tranquillity'. 'Pa-lei- shih' means 'palace'. At 7 p.m. the Ambassador sent Te-ming and Macartney to see Wade, to ask him about the etiquette involved in audience with the Sovereign. He told them that he did not know. On the morning of the seventh, someone was sent again to ask the Master of Ceremonies, Sir Francis Seymour,[1] who also answered very vaguely, for they wanted to test us. We looked up the *Hsing-yao chih-ch'ang* [*Handbook of Diplomatic Procedure*] which clearly recorded three bows as being required. The three ambassadors, Chih Kang, Sun Chia-ku and Ch'ung Hou,[2] who previously visited other countries,

---

[1] Sir Francis Seymour (1813–90) had become Master-of-Ceremonies in the Queen's Household in February 1876.

[2] Chih-kang and Sun Chia-ku had accompanied Anson Burlingame on his

did no more than this when they had audience. If the English had said clearly that nothing else was required, would it not have been sincere? Buckingham Palace has a gate made of white stone; it has an imposing appearance, being a palace gate. There are iron railings around the gate. Inside the gate is a big court, some several hundred paces broad, with buildings arrayed on both sides. After this is a garden, which stretches on for over a league. Then one comes to the inner Palace Gate. That day, at 2.15 p.m., the Ambassador and I went together to the gate of the inner palace, where we alighted from our carriage. Te-ming and Macartney followed us. The officers guarding the gate wore helmets and had on short, red uniforms with golden flowers on them. They directed us up three flights of steps to a hall so ornate that our eyes were dazzled. The Foreign Minister Derby, Chien-erh-k'an-shih [the Earl of Caernarvon],[1] Seymour, Wade, Hillier, and Yu Ya-chih[2] were all there. At 2.45 p.m. the glass doors in front of the hall opened, and the three men, headed by Derby, went in first for a while and then came out to conduct the envoys in. We descended one flight and walked along a balustrade to a small room. The Sovereign, dressed in a black robe with a veil made of white cotton cloth on which there were flowery designs, stood there in the middle, facing the door; the Princess named Pi-a-t'a-li-ssu [Beatrice][3] stood behind her, while the others stood on the sides. The Ambassador entered the door and bowed, the Sovereign also bowed; there were three bows all together till we arrived in front of her. Te-ming passed the Letter of State to the Ambassador, who held it respectfully in

mission to the West in 1868. The Manchu official, Ch'ung-hou (1826–93), was twice sent as envoy to the West. The first time he went to France to convey China's apology for the Tientsin affair (1870). The second time he was sent to St. Petersburg to negotiate the Treaty of Livadia (1879). This treaty was so unfavourable to China that Ch'ung-hou was dismissed from office and sentenced to death, being subsequently reprieved only as a result of the intercession of certain Western powers. See Hsü, *The Ili Crisis*, pp. 47–94.

[1] Henry Howard Molyneux Herbert (1831–90), Earl of Caernarvon, was Secretary of State for the Colonial Department, 1866–7 and 1874–8.

[2] A. R. Hewlett, Assistant Chinese Secretary to Sir Thomas Wade. See *The Times*, 8 Feb. 1877, p. 9f.

[3] Princess Beatrice (1857–1944) was the favourite (fifth) daughter and the youngest (ninth) child of Queen Victoria. She married Prince Henry Maurice of Battenburg in 1885 and bore him three sons and one daughter, Princess Victoria, who on her marriage to King Alfonso XIII in 1906 became the Queen of Spain.

both hands and read aloud what he had written. After that, Macartney also read it aloud in English. Then the Ambassador submitted the Letter of State to the Sovereign, who took it and passed it on to Derby. She said to the Ambassadors: 'Your Excellencies have come from far away to establish good relations with us. From now on, let us live in peace and harmony together for ever.' We both replied, 'Yes!' She then asked how the Emperor of China was. We replied that the Emperor was well. She also said that since she had received a letter from the Emperor, she would give us a letter in reply. We again said, 'Yes!' And then we bowed and left her, with Wade conducting us back to a large hall, where we sat for a while, looking at the objects of art placed there, before we went home. The Queen is the niece of Wei-lien [William] IV. Her name is Wei-to-li-a [Victoria], and she has reigned thirty-nine years, being this year fifty-eight years old. Her face is plump but dignified and firm. As Westerners wear black for mourning, she wears black now, as a sign of perpetual mourning for her dead husband Po-ya-na [Albert]. Albert [1819–61] was the son of the Marquis [*sic*] of Sha-ho-pao [the Duke of Saxe-Coburg-Gotha] in Germany. He died over ten years ago. The Queen has built a terrace in the garden, where she has erected a bronze statue, facing the palace. Underneath the terrace, stone has been chiselled into statues of famous officials of this country. On the four corners around the terrace, stand four stone porches, representing the four great continents; the figures of men and animals are all life-size. We went to see them the other day.

The speech which Ambassador Kuo composed and read aloud said:

The Imperial Ambassador of the Great Ch'ing, Kuo Sung-t'ao, and the Vice-Envoy, Liu Hsi-hung, present a Letter of State to the Sovereign of Great Britain and the Empress of the Five Indies. Regarding the case which happened during a previous year, in the region of Man-yün [Manwyne] on the border of Yunnan, of the murder of an official interpreter, Margary, we wish to inform Your Majesty that the governor of Yunnan was immediately ordered to investigate it and to send in his report. And then, under imperial order, the Governor-General of Hu-Kuang, Li Han-chang,[1] was

---

[1] Li Han-chang (1821–99) was the elder brother of Li Hung-chang. He served as Governor-General at Wu-chang (1870–5; 1876–82) and Canton (1889–95).

sent there to collaborate with him on the case, and the Nan-tien [Nantin] Commandant, Li Chen-kuo,[1] was imprisoned and questioned. Furthermore, the Governor-General, Li Hung-chang, was also sent by imperial order to Chefoo, to discuss the affair with your honorable country's royal envoy, Sir Thomas Wade, who took as his principles of action the forgiveness of past mishaps and concern for the future, and hence resolved to forget everything without discussion. However, the Emperor of China was greatly grieved, and has ordered us, his ambassadors, to come especially, to communicate his sentiments to your country, and has therefore made us his ambassadors in residence here in order to establish relations between our two countries and to express his wishes for an everlasting and peaceful friendship. Since we know how Your Imperial Majesty, the great Queen, enjoys a widespread reputation for generosity, forebearance, benevolence, and righteousness, we are sure that you will be able to appreciate the intentions of the Emperor of China, so that we may all hope for ten thousand years of harmony and everlasting joyous peace. We, the ambassadors, under orders, express our Emperor's sentiments of regret in this Letter of State, which we humbly offer to Your Majesty to read, and which also gives an account of the intentions of our coming here as proof that we wish to establish trust and harmony.

[p. 169a–b]

[10 February 1877]

The harm done by opium is not limited to the annual expense of a few dozen millions. When our officials and gentlemen become morally corrupt, the foundation of the government becomes perverse; when our farmers, workers, and merchants neglect their work, the source of wealth and production is cut off; when generals and soldiers grow weak, our powers of defence are weakened. All this is brought about by opium. Hence we ought definitely to prohibit it. When our boat put into Hong Kong, I received from my fellow friend and fellow graduate, Kuei Hao-t'ing (personal name, Wen-ts'an),[2] the petition for the prohibition of opium signed by our fellow townsman, T'ang Te-chün,[3] and others, as well as the treatise on the prohibition of opium published by the English minister,

[1] Li Chen-kuo (d. 1888), a native of Teng-yüeh, born of a Chinese father and a Burmese mother, was perhaps the official responsible for the attack on the expedition. Wade, however, refused to accept his guilt as proved. See Wang, *Margary Affair, passim.*
[2] Unidentifiable.   [3] Unidentifiable.

Tan-na [F. S. Turner].[1] He asked me to do something about it when we reached England. I have been so busy that I have not yet had time to think of it. On [Chinese] New Year's Eve [12 February], Professor Legge[2] of Oxford came to visit me, and spoke about opium. He said that England calls itself a nation of benevolence and justice and yet shows itself on this issue lacking in these two virtues. That is why the gentry have formed a Society[3] to eliminate the evils of opium. If we, the ambassadors, speak eloquently in the Upper House and request the prohibition of opium we need have no fear, for the English themselves will help us as much as possible. Legge has lived in Kwangtung for over thirty years and can speak Cantonese. His English translation of the *Four Books* and of the *Book of Poetry* has already been completed.[4] He hopes to use them to change the customs of society. We do not know whether they are free from mistakes. As to the opium, I have heard that the members of the Society have already drawn up a joint petition, and have elected a leader who is to make an appointment with us to come and discuss the matter.

[p. 171a–b]

[13 February 1877, Chinese New Year's Day]

Facing east, we did reverence to the Imperial Tablets by the usual prostrations, kneeling down three times and making each time a triple kowtow. In the afternoon I went with the Ambassador and the Attachés to visit the Museum of Wax Figures [Madame Tussaud's]. Inside the entrance, the first statue at the right is that of Lord Lin Wen-chung (Lin Tse-hsü).[5]

[1] F. S. Turner, Secretary of the Anglo-Oriental Society for the Suppression of the Opium Trade, was the author of a treatise entitled *British Opium Policy and Its Results to India and China*.

[2] James Legge (1815–97) published his translations of the Chinese classics between 1861 and 1872. In 1876 he became the first Professor of Chinese at Oxford.

[3] The Anglo-Oriental Society for the Suppression of the Opium Trade.

[4] Legge's translation of *The Analects, The Great Learning, The Doctrine of the Mean*, and *The Works of Mencius* had appeared in 1861 as volumes i and ii of *The Chinese Classics*. His *Book of Poetry* (*The She-king*) appeared in 1872 as volume iv.

[5] Lin Tse-hsü (1785–1850) was appointed Imperial Commissioner at Canton in 1838, with plenipotentiary powers to eradicate the opium trade. The actions he took against the British opium merchants eventually led to the outbreak of the Opium War, on 4 September 1839. See Chang Hsin-pao, *Commissioner Lin and the Opium War*, especially pp. 120–60.

From Liu Hsi-hung's Journal

The Museum has three floors; the first two floors contain statues of the good kings of the successive dynasties and also of the famous men of various countries; the top floor contains statues of criminals. All are very life-like, and, when mixed with living men, cannot be told apart. In front of the statue of Lin is a small table with an opened book: it refers to the clauses prohibiting opium. The top lines are in Chinese, the bottom in English. By his prohibition of opium, Lin caused trouble several times to the English, but they still respect him for his loyalty, righteousness, courage, and determination, and for not being careless, lacking in foresight, or trying to gain a moment's respite. It shows they know whom to respect.

[p. 171b]

[14 February 1877]

Our Court always sends two ambassadors, one chief and one subordinate, who are appointed together in order to support and control each other. But in foreign countries, the vice-ambassador is called a counsellor, and must obey the orders of the chief ambassador. Since we left our capital, we have always followed the manners of the foreigners. According to Western custom, documents are addressed to the Chief Ambassador. Hence there is no occasion for me to discuss affairs with the Ambassador, so that all I do is receive my salary without doing any work. On this account, I have prepared a memorial, requesting that I be relieved of my office and allowed to return home. After finishing my draft, I told the Ambassador of it at once, and begged him to stamp it. On the morning of 15 February, this Memorial was sent out.

[p. 172a]

[15 February 1877]

An invitation came from the English Queen, inviting all foreign ambassadors to go with their subordinates to the Palace of St. James, where she had ordered her eldest son and heir, the Prince Wei-erh-shih [of Wales], to receive them in her name.[1] St. James's Palace was built several hundred years ago. Its layout is simple. It stands very close to the markets and

---

[1] *The Times*, 16 Feb. 1877, p. 9f.

shops, so that it is not a convenient place for the royal carriages to go in and out of. That is why, during the Tao-kuang period [1821-51], Buckingham was built for royal use. However, big gatherings still take place in the old palace. Outside this palace there is a gate made of white stone. Several hundred soldiers dressed in red and holding guns stand in a row inside. The guards at the gate are all officers clad in gilded armour. After entering the gate, we ascended two flights of steps, and reached a big hall, where someone held a pencil to note down the number of persons there. (When Westerners take notes, they all use pencils.) His name was Marquis Ho-fu [the Marquis of Hertford].[1] In another great hall all the ambassadors assembled in court robes. However, as this is a death anniversary for the Chinese Court, our envoys were merely dressed in ordinary clothes. At two o'clock, the inner palace gate was opened, and those who are called their great officials and chief ministers first went in. Then followed the various ambassadors in rank, according to the time of their arrivals rather than the size of their countries, in order to avoid dispute. The Prince of Wales had a pleasant, open countenance. He was dressed in a short, red costume with golden flowers, and stood at the foot of the throne. At his left was the German Prince Ke-shih-tien [Prince Christian of Schleswig-Holstein].[2] Also to his left stood the royal relative Sha-ho-shih-kuai-ma [Prince Edward of Saxe-Weimar].[3] Next on the left stood the Duke T'i-ho [the Duke of Teck][4] and the Marquis of Hertford, who stayed in front to receive the names and announce them aloud. Every name was written in Western letters on a Western-style card, about three by two inches, which clearly stated the reason for the interview. Those who came for the first time had cards with red on two sides and on the back, while those who had come before used what were really ordinary Western visiting cards. (Even the Chinese ambassadors use Western visiting

[1] Francis Hugh George Seymour (1812-84), fifth Marquis of Hertford, was Lord Chamberlain of the Queen's Household from 1874 to 1879.
[2] Prince Frederick Christian of Schleswig-Holstein (1831-1917) married Princess Helena (1846-1923), the fifth child of Queen Victoria, in 1865.
[3] Prince Edward of Saxe-Weimar (1823-1902) was the nephew of King William IV and a cousin of Queen Victoria. His whole career was spent in the British army.
[4] Francis Paul Charles Louis Alexander (1837-1900), Prince and first Duke of Teck.

cards, since people here are not able to read Chinese characters, of which they are ignorant. So we have to follow their custom.) Our Ambassador only wrote: 'The Ambassador from such-and-such a country'. The Ambassador and I introduced Li Shu-ch'ang, Te-ming, Feng-yi, Liu Fou-yi and Chang Ssu-hsün in turn, and bowed to the Prince of Wales, who also bowed in reply. He told the Ambassador that he was happy to receive him. Then he stepped back. Other officials, both civil and military, came in after us. Some had met the Prince of Wales before, and shook his hand to show respect. The three halls which we passed through that day were all magnificent and gorgeous, so ablaze with gold they dazzled the eyes. When we returned to the apartment, we were told of an invitation to a party by a Chamber of Commerce. English traders do business in many countries, and have a central trade association at their capital, which is run by some gentry elected from members of their Parliament. When the traders meet with problems, they inform the board, which confers with Parliament. After the matter has been discussed and considered by the Parliament, British ambassadors stationed in various countries are asked for their opinions. Hence the relationship between government and traders is always open, and is in no way impeded. As there are many English traders in China, they very much wished to invite us to dinner. When we found out that diplomats from other countries were not invited and Wade was not going, we turned the invitation down.

[p. 172a–b]

[26 February 1877]

We went to St. James's Palace again to see the Prince of Wales. Envoys and dignitaries from various countries were also assembled there.[1] We made bows as before, but without exchanging words, or using visiting cards. (These cards are not used on a second visit.) Then we went home. The master of the Bank [of England] A-la-po-ssu-na-te and his employers Po-an-ssu [Barnes?] and Wo-la-chin-se came to see us.[2] Barnes helps with shipping business, and asked us personally to go to his works to see ship-building. We have not yet settled on the date. I asked

[1] See *The Times*, 27 Feb. 1877, p. 10, for an account of this levée.
[2] All unidentifiable.

A-la-po-ssu-na-te how much his bank has to pay each year in taxation. He answered that this is not a fixed sum, but depends on the profit made each year; for every golden sovereign, he pays three pence.

[p. 174b]

[2 March 1877]

We went to Buckingham Palace to see the Queen again. The ambassadors of various countries and their wives were all assembled there. All made a bow and then retired. Then came the local officials' wives.[1] Beside the Queen sat the wife of the Prince of Wales, and the Princess Lü-yi-ssu [Louise].[2] All the women wore dresses which exposed their bodies, and did not mind being in a place crowded with men. They held garlands in their hands, and wore dresses of different colours. Behind the dress was a train folded in several layers, looking like a beehive, which dragged for five or six Chinese feet on the floor. All the men and women who knew one another shook hands. Those who were going to see the Queen went up to her, and the attendants lifted their gowns a little, passing from one to another, holding on to them in this way to help the women walk and prevent them from falling through being stepped upon, which would cause embarrassment.

[p. 174b]

[7–9 March 1877]

At eight o'clock on the 7th Lord Derby gave a dinner to the Chinese envoys at the Foreign Ministry. At ten o'clock his wife also gave us a tea-party. According to English custom, the husband and wife must personally be present at the parties. Those who attend also bring their wives. The seats for hosts and guests are all fixed in advance and well marked, so there is no need to stand on ceremony. The hostess does not sit with the husband, but with the most honoured of the gentlemen. The others follow in rank, flanking the wives of the guests.

---

[1] He is referring to the débutantes. See *The Times*, 3 Mar. 1877, p. 10.
[2] Princess Louise (1848–1939) was the fourth daughter and sixth child of Queen Victoria. She was remarkable for her beauty and her artistic talents as well as for her interest in higher education for women. In 1871 she married the Marquess of Lorne, who in 1900 became the ninth Duke of Argyll.

In honour of the host the ladies wear clothes which expose their bodies. Near the end of the party, the ladies rise first, while the gentlemen sit drinking for a little while longer before dispersing. As to the tea-party, it consists of offering coffee and tea, with white sugar and cow's milk, as well as biscuits. These are placed near the side of the hall, awaiting the coming of the guests. When the guests are numerous, they all stand and talk. That night, the wife of Lord Derby had invited over 200 guests. The women all wore elaborate clothes and jewels. They displayed half of their upper body, bosom and back, and rubbed shoulders and feet in the hall with the men, with whom they often shook hands.

Since coming to London, we have visited Buckingham Palace twice: for the English were afraid that we were in a hurry to see the Queen and so had not seen much of the beauty of this palace. On 8 March, the Chamberlain Pa-la-fo-erh-te [Earl of Bradford][1] came for a visit, and arranged to go there with us the next day, saying that he himself had no time that day, but would order his assistant Fan-sun-pi-wei-yin [Ponsonby-Fane][2] to act as our guide. On 9 March, at the *wei* watch [1–3 p.m.], we went to the palace. We saw about six or seven of the halls, as well as the guest-rooms, the rooms where the Sovereign gave private audience to her officials, the rooms where she ate, and the rooms where the princesses lived. Only the bedroom of the Sovereign herself was barred to us. Guests who had stayed in the palace included the Kings of Russia and Turkey, who came personally and who once slept here for two nights only a few feet away from the Sovereign's bedroom. In the halls and rooms all the walls are full of gilded, flowery paintings, in four colours: red, green, yellow, and blue. The tables, beds, and beddings and cushions match the walls. The floors are covered with various carpets with inlaid designs, also in different colours. On the walls hang Western paintings with glass over them and guilded frames; some are square, some rectangular—the more there are the better they like them. They all portray rulers and officials of the past and present, and

[1] The Earl of Bradford held the post of Master of the Horse in the Queen's Household. He was not the Lord Chamberlain. Liu may have confused him with Viscount Barrington, the Vice-Chamberlain.

[2] Spencer Cecil Brabazon Ponsonby-Fane was Comptroller of Accounts and a Gentleman Usher Daily Waiter in the Lord Chamberlain's Department.

the various sovereigns—their faces, figures, and episodes relating to their command of the army and their enjoyment of leisure. In the front court is a painting of Victoria herself (the name of the English Sovereign), lying down quite naked [sic]. There is also a beautiful glass mirror, over ten Chinese feet high, in a gilt frame. On the ceilings are more gilded, flowery designs, from them different kinds of chandeliers big and small hang down. The tables and couches are all gilded; there are more than ten objects made of ivory. Even the fireplace is gilded. For ornaments, there are many porcelain jars and urns with gilded mouths. There are also carved, gilded seats along the corridors, on both sides. Here and there are articles of old bronze and porcelain, and three ivory ships resembling the flower boats of Kiangsu and Kuangtung, with carved human figures and oars. There are also several pagodas of nine floors, over ten Chinese feet high, beautifully carved, in bronze or ivory. There are also flowers and plants made of various gems, covered in glass, and also white stone statues of nude women, lying or standing, in places where all eyes could see. (In every palace and wealthy home there are statues of nude women carved in white stone, standing in the front court; some are even on the side of the streets. I think this practice must be encouraged by the Queen.)[1] There are also many other objects and small tables in jade or stone; we cannot give the names of all. When standing in the midst of all these, we feel the dazzling light of gold, which reaches the limit of human luxury, and pomp. After our visit, the Chief Groom, No-tun [Norton?], was told to conduct us to see the Royal Stables and Mews, where eight horses are kept in each stable. These horses are all of good breed, beautiful and strong, with different colours of hair—red, yellow, black, and white—which distinguish them. The saddles and bridles are all in different colours: the red and yellow ones are given gold, and the black and white ones given silver, so that there can be no confusion. The royal carriages are big and high as in China; the wheels, the top and the columns are all gilded; at front and back stand two golden sea-

[1] Probably to encourage the female (*yin*) element, which would be especially strong since a woman was on the throne. It was widely believed among the Chinese that Christianity was a religion which sought to foster sexual depravity in women. The nudes which Liu saw would only have confirmed him in this belief.

gods, with scales, holding weapons like guards. Yet during a reign of forty years, the Queen has not once ridden in it. On grand occasions, she rides in a high carriage, the top of which is gilded in the centre, with four golden 'paws' stretching out, holding the four corners. The other eight carriages are all ordinary official carriages, only slightly higher.

[pp. 175b–176a]

[16 March 1877]

The railway architect, Stephenson, is over seventy years old. On 16 March 1877, he came to visit us, and said that he had built railways in both England and India. The English railway system extends over 51,000 leagues, and cost £630 million. Every year they carry 507 million passengers and 200 million tons of goods [sic]. For such transport, 62 million in gold money has been received, and, except for 33 million in gold money paid out to cover the cost of coal and labour, they have gained a profit of £29 million....

Now considering the great population of China, and the wealth of our products, if we build a railway from Canton to Swatow, Ch'ang-sha, Yüeh-chou, and Hankow, all along the Yangtze River, and turn east to Nanking and then north to Chen-chiang, Yang-chou, Huai-an, Lin-ch'ing, Ching-chou, Tientsin, and up to the capital, it would involve a distance of 6,000 leagues at the cost of only 20 million in gold. (In Chinese silver money, approximately 60 million taels.) We are sure to gain much profit from it. When this railway line works well, we can go on to open branch routes to reach every town and city, and so change the face of China. He then displayed to us a very workaday map. The Ambassador asked him whether, at his advanced age, he could still build railways. He answered that he could not do the work himself, but could direct others and plan such a project. After giving us the map, he took his leave.

[p. 177b]

[17 March 1877]

The fifty-nine members of the Anglo-Oriental Society for the Suppression of the Opium Trade came to see us. Two days before coming to see us, their chief, To-erh-te [J. F. Talbot?] and his friend Te-erh-na-erh [F. S. Turner] wrote to ask for an appointment and also sent us the manuscript copy of the Petition they intended to submit. Macartney told us that such a task could not easily be carried out by Chinese officials. We were only to thank the members with vague words, and give them no firm promises.[1] My opinion is that it all depends on the English. If the English really want to prohibit opium, it will certainly be prohibited. But since several millions in taxes are at stake, the English will not be willing to give this trade up simply in order to enrich their neighbours. They ought therefore to inform the other countries of this, and make a treaty with them stipulating that the whole world ought to attack and punish any country which still lets its people plant and sell opium. After such a treaty, the prohibition can then be announced, and men be sent to keep watch over the coasts, and to make investigations among the Chinese people so that this evil may really be completely eradicated. . . .

[pp. 177b–178a]

[Undated]

. . . According to Western custom, all nations who join the comity of nations cannot be attacked without cause by their allies. Russia once tried to occupy Turkey in order to have access to the sea, using the confusion of Turkish politics as an excuse. But the English notified other nations of their opposition to this, so that Russia did not dare to use its military might openly.[2]

On the seventh day of the second month [21 March 1877], I wrote letters to various important officials in the capital and to

[1] *The Friend of China*, April 1877, pp. 151–6. The Earl of Shaftsbury read an address enquiring whether Kuo or Liu believed opium-smoking to be 'so great a national calamity as we believe it to be' and expressing the 'earnest hope that some means may be discovered whereby Great Britain and China may unite in a mutual effort for the suppression of the trade'. Legge then addressed Liu, in Cantonese, urging the Chinese Government to take strong measures to restrict the trade. Kuo replied that 'the Chinese Government are exceedingly anxious to put a stop to the trade but . . . unless they are assisted not only by England but by other countries, they would find it difficult to do so.'

[2] The Constantinople Conference (December 1876 to January 1877) was an attempt to conclude a peace between Turkey and Russia. The Treaty Powers failed in their attempt to reconcile the two nations, as war broke out in April, 1877. See *The Cambridge History of British Foreign Policy* (Cambridge, 1923), iii.107 ff.

the Governor of Chihli, Li Hung-chang, about the things that I have observed since I came abroad.

Confucius said that in government, it is essential to be frugal.[1] If we are not frugal, even the resources of the entire world will not be enough for our use. This applies to England. While in matters of government the English try very hard to do everything, sparing no money especially in everything that pertains to education, to enriching the people, and to the armed forces, still they often spend money when they need not and ought not to spend it. For example, this year, on the occasion of the proclamation of the Queen as Empress of India, the English government ordered a general amnesty, and the Sovereign paid the debts of all those imprisoned for debt, freeing more than 10,000 people. This is an example of unnecessary expenditure. Again, they use ships and trains to transport rare objects and precious articles, plants and stones, over thousands of leagues. This is an example of unjustifiable expenditure. Since the accession of Victoria, there have been many military victories and the country has grown stronger and stronger. Yet till now, every year expenditure has exceeded income, so that the national debt has attained 800 million pounds, that is, in Chinese silver, more than 2,672,400,000 taels.[2] On the seventh of this month, Chang Ssu-hsün and Yao Yüeh-wang went to the Li-ju Bank,[3] and were given this information by the treasurer. For every tael an interest of 0·3% is charged. Hence, there is a yearly interest of over 80,170,000 taels.

[p. 178b]

[29 March 1877]

The Japanese, Inoue Kaoru,[4] came to London at the age of fourteen to learn crafts, and returned to his own country ten years later. He told his countrymen of the British use of boats, cannons, and trains, but they hated what he told them, and ostracized him. Some even accused him of improper relations

---

[1] *Lun-yü*, l.v. 'The Master said: "To rule a country of a thousand chariots there must be ... economy in expenditure and love for men."' Legge, *Classics*, i.140.

[2] In 1876 the National Debt stood at £776,970,544. See *Whitaker's Almanack*, 1877, p. 116.

[3] Unidentifiable.

[4] Liu, unlike Kuo, uses the correct characters for this name. See Kuo's letter to Li Hung-chang (1877), p. 101, n. 1 above.

with the West, and induced others to beat him up. This happened before the British invasion of Japan,[1] at which time, the Japanese, not being strong enough to resist, begged Inoue Kaoru to make peace for them, and promoted him to the office of Minister of Finance. He then proposed a reform of the principles of government, bringing them into conformity with those of the West. He has now returned to England to study the policy of taxation. On the 29th, the Ambassador and I paid him a visit on our way back from the Bank of England. He told us that the British tax regulations require only the taxation of imported goods, never taxing their exports, since exports are products of the country, which, if taxed, would discourage the people from selling them abroad. And yet, when sold in the country, very little profit can be made on such goods, so that there would be no way of encouraging the people to apply their craftsmanship to work in order to enrich the population. Hence, exports are not taxed. Instead, the government waits until the trade brings in a profit, and then asks for three pence in every pound. Since the people can make a profit, they do not find taxes difficult to pay, and are therefore happy to sell their goods to distant places. With the increase in exports, commerce and industry are encouraged and prosper, and the farmers and workers need no pressure to work hard to provide industry with what it needs. This is how the British make their people wealthy. He also said that when the construction of railways began in London, the people of England criticized the move, saying that it would throw the carriage-drivers out of work. Many, indeed, rose up to hinder the construction of railways. However, with the use of trains, the carriage-drivers became even more prosperous. For, before the use of trains, the volume of travel and transport was very small, but, with the coming of trains, merchants and travellers are always on the road. Wherever the railway cannot penetrate, ordinary horse-drawn vehicles must be used, so that this business has in fact prospered. The Ambassador asked him which book to read, in order to

[1] On 15 August 1863 British warships bombarded and demolished much of the city of Kagashima, the capital of Satsuma in South Kyūshū, in retaliation for the murder of an Englishman who had failed to show proper respect for the *daimyo*, Shimazu Hisamitsu. The following year a combined fleet of English, French, American, and Dutch vessels demolished the Chōshū forts in retaliation for attacks on foreign vessels in the Straits of Shimonoseki.

study the British system of taxation. He recommended *The Wealth of Nations*. This book was written by Adam Smith, and is very hard to translate, so that only those who learn English can read it. According to Macartney, it would be easier to read a translation of *Political Economy*, written by James Mill.[1]

[p. 181b]

[30 March–1 April 1877]

The Tower of London is an ancient royal palace, built in A.D. 1078. The stone walls are fifteen Chinese feet thick. Around the palace a moat filled with water was dug while forts were built for defence. After three hundred years it ceased to be a palace, but became a prison for officials who committed crimes. Now it has been changed into an armoury, with 2,000 soldiers stationed there. In the Tower are several dozen iron statues of kings, nobles, and generals, some standing, others riding. There are also over 100 boxes of gunpowder, 60,000 modern guns, and countless weapons and armour of past and present. In another place the ceremonial crown of the present sovereign is kept. This crown is as big as a winter melon. It is made of purple satin. There are huge pearls basted on it. Four rows of thread divide it into four petals. On the top is set a diamond, as large as a pigeon's egg. Its sides are thickly ornamented with glistening diamonds.

On 1 April 1877 I visited the Tower and then went to the Thames to see the railway underneath the river.[2] One goes underground, down some eighty-seven stone steps to reach it. The walls on the left and right are made of huge rocks, and iron pieces are used on the top to keep away the river water, so that it resembles the courtyard between the inner and outer gates of a city. Trains run underneath the river, with coal-gas lamps illuminating the whole place. This is certainly a clever construction, but far from indispensable.

[p. 182a]

---

[1] *The Wealth of Nations* was subsequently translated by Yen Fu, who began this enormous task in 1897 and finished it in 1900. No Chinese translation of James Mill's (1773–1836) *Elements of Political Economy* (1821) existed in 1877.
[2] The first stage of the London underground was opened on 10 January 1863. This was the first underground railway in the world. See T. C. Barker and M. Rollins, *A History of London Transport* (London, 1963), i.99–135.

[10 April 1877]

Inoue Kaoru visited us. The Ambassador and I spoke with him. He said that China has rich natural resources, and ought not to let them lie in the earth. Why did we not imitate Western methods and make use of them? Before the Ambassador had time to answer, I asked whether, as Minister of Finance, he had reformed the abuses in his own department. He answered that he had very much wanted to do so, but could not get the others to follow his wishes. I said that this was not due to the others wanting to present obstacles. Rather, the systems and regulations laid down by our ancestors contain deep meaning, and, although with the passage of years, abuses inevitably set in, these are the work of men who try to draw private profit from the system. If only officials could seek the true meaning of the old systems, and try their best to put it into practice, eliminating all that did not exist in the past and restoring all that used to exist in the past, it would be then possible to have good government. If we tried to change systems and develop resources, we would disturb and shock too many people, and so provoke rebellions. Our Imperial Chinese Government should learn a lesson from his country, Japan. While gold, silver, coal, and iron mines are profitable, they also give rise to great harm. Such things are not what a sage Emperor would covet. He listened acquiescently, and after some more friendly talk about poetry took his leave. . . .

[p. 183a]

Concerning the case of the murder of a foreign interpreter in Yunnan, Secretary Ko [T. G. Grosvenor] returned to England about a month ago, after having gone there to investigate the matter.[1] When it was asked why the real facts had not been published in the newspapers, the Foreign Ministry replied that it was due to the fact that Wade has not yet given his report. I do not know whether there are not other complications. The official is called P'i-k'e [Frederick], his surname is Po-lan [Bourne].[2] Macartney often says that China prefers deceit, and does not tell the truth and act honestly, but at every negotiation

---

[1] T. G. Grosvenor, then Second Secretary at Peking, was dispatched by Wade to make an investigation of the Margary murder.
[2] F. S. A. Bourne. See *North China Herald*, 23 June 1877, p. 623.

dissimulates (approving by word of mouth externally what the heart does not really approve) and then does not carry out her promises. Foreigners especially are angered by this attitude. After all, he argued, people all have their real thoughts, as events all have their real meanings. When we ourselves are wrong and others right, we cannot change the situation by force of argument. If we really find that what others say is wrong, why do we not plainly tell them their errors so that they may clearly know and really see our points? If, when we have had our say, the other party is still not convinced, we can always find other explanations and continue the argument. We can either think harder, and continue the debate at once, or else arrange to discuss it later on, so that the foreigners might become thoroughly conversant with our way of looking at things. Since foreigners are not wild beasts or tigers, and will not swallow us savagely, why should we put things so vaguely? I answered that this method was superior, but that debates may easily lead to anger, and perhaps even become occasion for a war, so that we practise patience and keep a gentle expression in order to stop disputes and pacify the world. Macartney said that dissimulation itself, as well as our not keeping promises, would be enough to cause disputes. If we speak reasonably, even when others do not agree with us, they will be sure to behave reasonably. While, during debates, we may appear to be arguing and competing, actually, we are being frank, and our hearts will stay in peace, without fear of provoking any quarrel. I listened and showed approval. Now, I have observed their parliamentary debates, and have seen how each side was eager not to let the other win, until the whole business was settled, lowering their heads without holding any prejudice on account of victory or defeat in the debate....

[Such scientific subjects as] electricity, heat, astronomy, air, light, dynamics, and chemistry are what the English call real knowledge, while they consider the teaching of our Chinese sages as empty and useless talk. Chinese officials who are deceived by their words often agree with them. I argue against these beliefs, saying that their real knowledge consists only of petty, miscellaneous tricks, which can be used to make 'a utensil' of but limited capacity....

... They concentrate on such miscellaneous tricks, using

boats and vehicles made to bring in profit, and firearms made for killing, trying to produce more and more of such things to become wealthy and strong. How can we call all this useful, real knowledge? Since the beginning of history, China has endured longer than any other civilization, and has produced a hundred and several dozen sages one after another, daily refining and completing their [social and moral] institutions. The depth of our philosophical discussions greatly exceeds those of the West. Foreigners consider material wealth as true wealth: China takes temperance as true wealth; Western nations think brute force is strength: China takes deference as strength. This is the real truth. It cannot be explained in a few hurried words.

[pp. 183b–184a]

[May 1877]

During my sickness,[1] some London gentlemen wrote a Petition about the six ways in which the English have bullied China: (1) They have poisoned the people with opium; (2) They have propagated their religion unnecessarily, since China already enjoys the finest teaching of the sages; (3) Their merchants are not controlled by local officials, but by their own consuls, which causes partiality and makes for injustice; (4) They took upon themselves the construction of the Wu-sung railway, and then asked for compensation for their expenses; (5) The Margary case in Yunnan was not settled as a case in itself, but used as an excuse for opening other ports; (6) They have shown lack of courtesy in the reception of our ambassadors.

These gentlemen said that if the Chinese Ambassador would allow them to finish what they have to say, they would gather their friends together to debate the matter in Parliament, and so on. The Ambassador turned them down very kindly, which was the right thing to do, since, as ambassadors in this country, we ought not to listen imprudently to what the people and gentry say, and so cause trouble to their Sovereign and country. But the English really love and respect China in their hearts. Every day, we are invited out to tea-parties in several places. We have more invitations than we can cope with. Whenever we meet their officials and gentry, we hear them earnestly counselling us to strengthen ourselves and keep peace for ever with England.

[1] Liu fell seriously ill with an intestinal complaint on 28 April and was confined to bed for a month.

Sometimes they even say that what their countrymen have done in China makes them feel ashamed.

[p. 187b]

[5 June 1977]

A telegram from Hart informed me that I have been transferred as Imperial envoy to Germany....[1]

[p. 189a]

[10 June 1877]

A letter from the capital informed me that the German Ambassador Pa-lan-ta [von Brandt],[2] during the amendment of the treaty this year, caused extra trouble by insisting that the former treaty only had clauses concerning separate taxation at the various treaty ports, meaning that foreign goods to be transported to the interior need only to be taxed at the ports, and ought not to be required to pay *likin* again. Since foreign goods coming from different countries are already being taxed at the ports both for customs duties and for transit dues, when they pass the *likin* stations they ought only to have to show the bills of lading, and then be free to move on without having to pay any heavy *likin*. However, by the time the goods have passed into the hands of Chinese, what happens is that the Chinese officials, in order to raise military funds for China, tax the Chinese people themselves.[3] Why should this be of any concern to the foreign merchants? Not only need this regulation not be applied to foreigners, but other countries should not intervene in such an affair. We have our own sovereignty and this *likin* is being collected from among our own people. It is therefore our own business, and is no concern of foreigners.

[p. 189b]

[Undated]

At balls, the man and the woman face each other and hold on

---

[1] Since at that time no means of sending telegrams in Chinese had yet been devised, Hart must have been requested by the Tsungli Yamen to draft the cable for them in English.

[2] Max Auguste Scipio von Brandt (1835–1920), the German Ambassador, took up his post in Peking on 10 March 1875, and remained there until 1893. He was a notorious troublemaker, best known for his remark that one could 'always fish something from troubled waters'. He was of the opinion that all the Christian powers ought to come to an agreement to crush China simultaneously, so that each one could derive from it what would be suitable for itself.

[3] Cordier, *Relations de la Chine*, ii.157–60.

to each other. The man holds on to the waist of the woman with one hand, while the woman holds on to the man's shoulder with one hand. They dance this way in the middle of the hall. Usually there are four or five pairs who dance at the same time, going several times around the hall before stopping. The women expose much of their bodies while the men are neatly dressed. But in this country, the men wear formal suits with pants of flesh colour, tightly fitted to their legs, so that, when looked at from afar, they seem to expose the lower parts of their bodies, which is not at all nice to see. They say that this custom has come down from very ancient times, and that the whole Western world follows it. In various Ministries of this country, there are always ballrooms for solemn gatherings, as if they consider dancing an essential part of their official business. Since the fourth [lunar] month, more than ten English families have invited us over to attend such balls. On account of my illness, I have not gone to any of them. On the evening of 22 June, the Queen invited us to a tea-party, so I went to attend it at Buckingham Palace. That night, the ambassadors from various countries all gathered there; high-ranking men and women were all assembled together. Music was played in the front of the hall to accompany the dancing. Even the Crown Prince and his wife took part in the dance. The Prince took another woman as his partner while his wife danced with another man, for husbands and wives are not supposed to be each other's partners.

During the last two months, we have been receiving several invitations every day to go to tea-parties. At each tea-party there are long tables provided with tea, wine, fruit, and cakes for the guests to take and drink, and the whole room as well as the doors are delightfully decorated with fresh, fragrant flowers. . . .

At parties at night many lamps and candles burn. Men and women mingle together, rubbing elbows and shoulders. Sometimes actors and singers are called in to perform plays, to sing and to play music to amuse the guests. (Some people sing and play themselves. European ladies play the piano to amuse the guests. No one finds this strange.)[1] Each party costs over £100.

[1] Chinese ladies never took part in social functions, let alone entertained guests with musical performances. In China, such entertainers were always attached to

When there are five or six hundred guests at a party all stand round the tables to drink. However, the host personally offered the Chinese envoys tea and wine with his own hands. The English are very hospitable and quite used to spending money. Furthermore, when they know some tricks, they always perform these in public to show their abilities. When they have collections of precious objects, tapestries and the like, they exhibit everything in the room, showing every piece to the guest, fearing only that he has not seen everything. The Chinese prefer to hide their abilities and their wealth and never let them be seen; the English like to show everything to the outside world, without hiding a fraction of an inch. When we Chinese see talented people and wealth often, we get used to such things and are heedless of their attractions. But when an Englishman suddenly possesses talents and wealth, he finds it very unusual and keeps boasting about them to others. When we consider these attitudes, we realize it is difficult to urge people to change their pettifogging manners. Every year, the tea-party season lasts from the third [lunar] month to the middle of the sixth [lunar] month.

[p. 191a–b]

[27 June 1877]

On the night of 26 June we attended a ball at the Scottish Association. The Emperor of Brazil[1] and wife were there. (Brazil is in South America.) He wore an ordinary Western suit, for his is a democratic country where it is the custom to do so. The Emperor has visited Africa and Europe, having gone through Egypt, Germany, Austria, France, and other countries before reaching England. He and his wife go together to see every beautiful place and every party. They are almost like strolling Immortals roaming round the world. That night the dance music was even noisier than at Buckingham Palace. The Scottish costume is different from that of London. Both men and women wear red checkered woollen pieces on their

houses of ill-fame. It is hardly surprising that Liu was astonished by this European custom.
[1] Dom Pedro II (1825–91), the second and last emperor of Brazil, was distinguished for his learning and his democratic attitudes. He was deposed in 1889. See M. W. Williams, *Don Pedro the Magnanimous, Second Emperor of Brazil* (Chapel Hill, 1937).

left shoulders, and use the rest to bind their waists. Men do not wear trousers, but have long boots on. Some bind up their lower legs from the knees down with red bands, right down to their feet, a practice like our 'leg binding'. (That night, there were women dressed in the Greek national costumes, in long tunic-like robes with big outer garments rather like the Chinese robe. That is because Greece was the first country to be sinicized.)[1] Women bare the upper parts of their bodies and men expose their lower parts; they cling tightly to one another as they dance, their heads and bodies glued to each other.

[p. 191b]

[Undated]

The people of London love to practise charity. They build large houses for the old, the infants, the orphans, the poor, the handicapped, and refugees from different places, who are well provided for. There is a so-called Old Scholars' Society which gives meals to poor students, and, in case they may regard it as a disgrace to accept food, sends grain and meat to their residences. There is a so-called Embroidery Office, composed of noble women, who can no longer support themselves on account of family misfortunes and who are gathered in large houses, where they are provided with meals and servants.[2] They are made to weave and to embroider, and their products are sold. But men are still forbidden entry to prevent any scandal. When I was sick, the Ambassador and others went there on a visit. There is also a hospital, which I already described on 16 February. But London has other institutions besides these. Every few leagues there are big buildings where the poor are kept and cured of their sicknesses. Other cities and villages have similar places too. For such purposes, the funds are collected from among officials and by the rich. To make up any deficiencies, grounds are cultivated, flowers are planted, and fish are kept, or else plays are performed and other games enacted to attract spectators who pay to gain admission

[1] The Chinese firmly believed that every civilization had its origin in their own. See Introduction, p. lvii.
[2] Presumably the Ladies' Work Society, which was strongly supported by Princess Louise.

and to have a seat, the money then being used for charity. On 26, 27, and 28 June, at South Kensington, noble ladies and gentlemen are exhibiting miscellaneous goods and have invited the Queen, the royal family, hereditary nobles, high officials, ambassadors, and rich men to go there. Pretty girls have been chosen to take charge of sales. The prices have all been raised to a hundred times the original. All the visitors buy a few things before coming out. Such income goes to the care of the sick. On 26 June, they collected two thousand and several hundred taels. On 27 June, Liu Fou-yi, Chang-Ssu-hsün, and Macartney went there with me. We also contributed about sixteen golden sovereigns. That night the Queen invited us to a tea-party with music and singing. The Emperor of Brazil and his wife were there. In the main hall were high officials and wives; on the right were ambassadors and their wives; on the left were hereditary nobles and their wives. (Western custom regards the right as the honoured place.) The Prince and his wife entertained the guests in place of the Queen. The party finished at 1 a.m.

[pp. 191b–192a]

[28 June 1877]

Bourne, our interpreter, came. I asked him about things in England. He said that English customs entail too much luxury, pomp, and enjoyment, and cannot go on very long this way. Women especially waste a lot of money, a thing that does not happen in China. An evening gown often costs over 100 taels in silver. After wearing it twice, a woman no longer considers it fresh, and must change into a new dress. Every day, visiting and entertainments require much money for carriages, horses, wine, and food. Unless one spends 300 or 400 gold sovereigns every month, one cannot get along. So in choosing a husband, a woman must hope for a man from a rich family. But men suffer from having to support them, and dare betroth only women of wealth who can afford such luxuries. That is why there are men and women who never marry all their lives. The Chinese rejoice in having many sons, the English suffer from having many sons. Recently, many more baby girls than baby boys have been born. (This is quite true. Every time we go to a party given by gentry or merchants, we find families with three or four daughters, but seldom a family with two sons.) Such customs are very annoying. One does not know how to correct them. England now relies on trade to make her wealthy, and her commerce extends to the four seas. But in future, if the routes are obstructed and the goods can no longer circulate, the country could easily find itself in trouble. I agreed with him heartily. Then we discussed trains. I said that there are fewer travellers in China so that the building of railways and the making of trains will definitely cause us to lose money, and ought not to be done. He did not agree. He argued that the advantage of having trains lay in transporting goods, not in transporting people. China had the most goods and the greatest amount of trade so that if railways were constructed interest would surely double, and taxes increase. This would certainly be a means of enriching the country and the people. Besides, it could help us to spare our armed forces. Wherever there were rebellions in the provinces, the government, on hearing of these, could send soldiers there within a few days, and then, as quickly as the wind sweeping away leaves, defeat the rebels. Therefore we would only need to keep 100,000 soldiers in the capital, and choose able generals to lead them, while the Son of Heaven himself could review them, and have them ready for any emergency, without having to station many armed forces outside in the provinces. We could save in this way, every year, over 10,000,000 taels of silver.

... But everything in this world has advantages and disadvantages. The West considers the building of steamships and trains as progress. But I dare not say whether this is real progress or retrogression. When one country constructs such a thing, other countries will gradually follow suit. If this comes from the Will of Heaven however, man can do nothing about it. For example, with steamboats, we Chinese did not at first want to imitate the foreigners, but now we have about twenty or thirty boats. Now we have steamboats, we must use more coal. To make more iron cannons we must have more iron. Having to use more iron and coal, and not being able to ask for them from Western countries, the question of opening mines arises. But then, what will be needed for the transport of coal and iron? What about the cost of labour, and the difficulty of the roads? We must naturally then discuss the construction of railways. This shows how things are mutually related. One thing will lead to another, and we will not be able to refuse them. I asked what we ought to do if bandits take the trains to invade us. Bourne answered that these things ought to be controlled by the officials; while the bandits can take the trains, they cannot occupy the whole railway. If the railway is cut, the train cannot run. I said that a railway would cost sixty or seventy million silver dollars. If we must pull it up completely to defend ourselves against bandits, it would not be easy later on to repair. If we only remove a hundred rails or so, the bandits could easily fix things up to transport their own soldiers. This shows there are both advantages and disadvantages to having a railway. Besides, where could China find enough money to enable her to start construction? Bourne said we could borrow from other countries. Since other countries all borrow money, why should China fear to do so? If we borrowed a lot, the creditors would try to protect China and not want to resort to arms against us, since this would make them lose both capital and interest. So this would also be a way of keeping one's friends. I asked what we should do if we could not pay back the capital and interest, and others used force to oblige us to pay? He said that Western nations never used force to recover their debts. Turkey owed most to other countries, but her creditors kept postponing the date of repayment, and helped her to plan ways of raising money for the country, which shows how such matters are arranged. I said that this was not the right way to rule a country, and was not to be relied on. When foreigners treat a diseased foot, they often cut through the tendons and replace the foot with an artificial one. But how can this rude method of treatment produce lasting results?

[pp. 192a–b]

[23 July 1877]

Wei-shih-min-shih-te-erh-a-pi [Westminster Abbey] ... was built 900 years ago. Hsin-p'o-erh-shih [St. Paul's] was built over 200 years ago. These are all Protestant churches. From top to bottom they are made of carved, polished white stone. These buildings are very imposing. Many meritorious officials and famous men of different dynasties are buried here. Their statues are carved in stone, in a sitting or sleeping posture, to show their virtue and ability. Along the London streets there are many iron statues of meritorious officials, which serve the same purpose. Westminster Abbey preserves the country's ancient writings, paintings, coins and other relics. St. Paul's has a big clock and a tall tower from which one can see the whole of London. On 23 July we went to visit it. On our way back Bourne and Liu Fou-yi talked about the rigour of Chinese traditional teaching concerning women. Bourne said that women are also human beings, and ought not to be left alone shut up in rooms and forbidden to come out. Liu could say nothing in reply. I told Liu that he could have said that both the chest and the back are parts of one's body. Why is the chest in front and the back behind? For the chest is *yang* and the back is *yin*. The head is part of my skin, so is the part underneath my belly. Why do I show the skin of my head and cover the other part? For the head is *yang* and the other is *yin*. Later, Liu used this argument, and Bourne could say nothing in reply. (On account of the Westerners' temperament, when we can find reasons to debate with them, the clearer we are, the more they respect us. Otherwise, they think they are right and their pride increases.) . . .

[p. 197a]

[Undated]

Westerners do not consider descendants important. Millionaires often give up everything on their death-beds in order to build charity schools or homes for the aged and the poor, saying that with such arrangements, they can die without regret. When asked who will offer sacrifices to them, they say that since they have given their wealth to charity, their memory will be cherished even after a thousand years. So why should this business of sacrifice worry them? When asked about offering food to their ancestors, they say: 'It is a Chinese superstition to say that ghosts still need food. When a man dies, his vital spirits disperse into heaven and earth. The spirits will soon be gathered to produce another body. Ghosts do not exist. Since our grandfathers or fathers died several decades ago, their vital spirits dispersed long ago, and do not require food. Besides, our grandfathers only begat us as individuals and then brought us up. Now we are using their wealth to help millions of people to live, which is a great act of filial piety.' This way of thinking approaches that of Mo-tzu.[1]

[p. 198a]

[6–8 August 1877]

Macartney came to tell me that Westerners are asking for a discussion of the *likin* on Western goods, not in order to harm China but to profit both China and the foreign merchants. For if there are goods sent from England, through Shanghai to Szechwan, then besides paying the two taxes—regular duty and transit duty—the traders still have to pay so much *likin* in Hupei and so much in Szechwan. Even if this should cause them to pay three to five times more than they should they must still pay a fixed sum. If this fixed sum is paid in Shanghai, and a paper is given them with the provinces of destination marked on it, then when the goods pass through the Customs bureaus in the provinces, the Inspectors will not tax them further. A fine could be imposed on goods sent to places outside those marked, and the goods confiscated. If we did this, we would not change the principle of imposing *likin*. Western traders would have first to estimate the original cost of their goods to establish the price and then entrust them to others in the transport trade. This would be much more convenient for commerce, and would take away the fear of embezzlement of revenue needed for paying the army in China. Hence it would be beneficial to both sides. If there is no fixed rate of *likin*, it is impossible to estimate the price of goods in advance. People often think they can sell a certain amount of goods at such and such a price, but, after transport, find out that on account of the unexpected *likin*, they have lost their capital. One does not know whether the Customs took too much or whether the Chinese agents who transported the goods on their behalf gave a false account. No wonder the Western traders criticize such a system! Now the English Trade Association also wishes to ask for a fixed sum for *likin*. In fact, this cannot harm China. So it seems we ought to approve of it. If we consider *likin* as funds

[1] Mo-ti (470–391 B.C.), generally known as Mo-tzu, taught the doctrine of universal love, enjoining his followers to love their fellow men and not limit their affection to the family. Confucians criticized his doctrines for their neglect of the special claims of parents and offspring.

which the provinces provide out of their own budget, and which ought not to be assigned only to Shanghai, we can order the Customs at Shanghai, in imposing *likin*, to put aside the amounts that ought to go to the provinces in order to transfer them there later. This would be easy too. I remarked that his idea was a sensible one but that we had to study the matter further.

Men and women here all select their own partners in marriage. When a woman likes a man, she invites him to her house to entertain him. (It seems to me that women here are encouraged to be unchaste, while men are not. When a woman likes a man, she often asks whether he already has a wife. If not, she brazenly arranges a rendezvous. The man does not dare to make the first move.) They often talk intimately together, away from others, and go out together. Their parents do not forbid them. After a long period of acquaintance, if the two like each other, they tell their parents. Then they investigate each other's financial situation. If they are unequally matched, they do not marry. (When incorrect reports are made and someone is cheated, then even after marriage, the woman still does not consider the man as her husband, nor does the man consider the woman as his wife. Instead, one will treat the other as no more than a servant.) If they are well matched financially, then they are informed of this and allowed to decide whether or not to marry. After their engagement (a ring is used for engagement to control the other party, so that he or she will not look for someone else), they have even greater freedom to go out together. At marriage (men marry at thirty) the family of the bride go to a Christian Church and ask a clergyman to chant prayers. Many guests are assembled. A crucifix is placed on the table. The bride and groom enter and kneel in front of it. The bridesmaids also kneel. (Their number is not fixed. The Mayor's daughter had sixteen of them.) The clergyman also kneels down, and then gets up to perform the marriage ceremony for the bride and groom, after which he blesses them, and conducts them to a room at the rear, where they write their names in the registry. Then they go together to the official registry of that district where they write down all their particulars. Later, they often travel several hundred leagues to consummate the marriage in an hotel. Those who see them would at first not know they were newly-weds. The bride wears white, with a white veil on the head.[1] (When going out, women often wear a black or white veil to cover their heads, in order to avoid the dust. This is not unique to the bride.) The groom wears everyday clothes. Often when people marry off their daughters, they give them as dowry good thick clothes, useful articles, and all kinds of other necessities. The groom's family and friends also contribute to the bride's dowry, but give nothing towards the groom's wedding expenses. On 8 August, I went to the house of the Mayor of London to see this ceremony for myself.

According to English customs, the daughter-in-law does not live with the father and mother-in-law. Even old people of seventy or eighty are often without children to serve them food and drink, and do their laundry. How to behave as a daughter-in-law should, and understand the virtue of feminine obedience is not known here at all. According to Hillier, after her engagement, the woman often visits the house of her future parents-in-law. But no other formalities are observed as part of the wedding ceremony. As Tai Sheng remarked, when the difference between man and woman is observed, the affection between father and son is established; when the father and son have mutual affection, then comes righteousness; when there is righteousness, there will be ritual propriety; when there is ritual propriety, all things will be in harmony. These few words clearly express all there is to say about the propriety and order that govern heaven and earth. It is very clear and very deep. Westerners do not understand what it means to have parents. Some say that the religion of Jesus considers Heaven as Ancestor, and does away with everything else. When their sons grow up, they each seek their own livelihood, without asking their parents. Some who serve as officials leave their parents for more than ten years, and do not even go to visit them on their return to their home town.

[pp. 199b–200a]

[4 September 1877]

When I first went from Tientsin to Shanghai, there was an

[1] Since white was the colour of mourning in China, this must have seemed extraordinary to Liu.

Englishman on the same boat, over seventy years old, who was speaking with his fellow countrymen. He said that in the West people do not care a rap for their ruler.[1] Now I see that in this country, before playing music and chanting prayers, or having parties and games, the people always first wish the Sovereign well.

In theatres, the Queen's picture is displayed at the beginning and that of the Prince shown at the conclusion. Even a firework display concludes with the picture of the Queen. I also heard that when the Prince was sick over ten years ago, the whole country prayed to Heaven for him. When he was cured, the whole country thanked Heaven. Even in outlying cities, they all love [the Royal family], so that one cannot say the Queen is considered unimportant.[2] We have asked about the reasons for this. It could be because during the reign of Victoria, the English have won every war, and the country has grown stronger day by day, so that although there is no question of her having wrought all this good by herself, she has never gone against public opinion, therefore everyone wishes her good fortune. England is actually a democratic country, and needs no sovereign to rule it. If successive monarchs would only be content to enjoy themselves, and not cause trouble to the Upper and Lower Houses they would be doing all that their people pray them to do. . . .

[p. 202b]

[4 September 1877]

Everything in England is the opposite of China. In politics, things move from the people to the Sovereign; in family regulations, the wife is honoured and the husband has a lower position. (Family decisions are always proposed by the wife and followed by the husband. The wife sits in the position of honour, the husband in a humble position. The same happens when they go out to parties. Ordinarily, the husband serves his wife much as the filial son in China serves his parents. Otherwise every-

---

[1] Literally: 'They consider the sovereign of no more importance than a small Chinese loaf.'

[2] In 1871, a republican movement swept Britain, led by Sir Charles Wentworth Dilke. When the Prince of Wales caught typhoid in November, 1871, the resultant wave of public sympathy extinguished the nascent republican movement. See Tom Cullen, *The Empress Brown* (London, 1969), pp. 148–65.

one would criticize him.)¹ At births, girls are esteemed and not boys; at parties, the host is honoured and the guest humbled. (The host sits in the middle, flanked by his guests.) In writing, they begin from right to left [sic]. (Words and writings are all reversed; for example, London's Tower is called the 'Tower's London' [the Tower of London]; Father's garden is called the 'garden's father' [the garden of father]. That is why it is difficult to translate.) With books they begin from the back and work up to the front. (Every book begins with the last page.)² In eating and drinking, they first take their main meal and then wine. This is because their country is situated below the centre of the earth. Over them hangs the sky above the far side of the earth. That is why their customs and systems are all topsy-turvy. Even the day and the night are reversed. The time in London is eight hours later than that in China, and in Ireland it is twenty-five minutes later than in London. Their evening is our noon in China. Their dawn is our evening in China. The English often rest in the day time and work hard at night. Perhaps it is with night time that the principle of *yang* becomes dominant here!³

[p. 207b]

---

¹ Clearly, even Victorian England was not patriarchal enough for Liu! He has confused deference with subservience.

² The front page of a Chinese book looks like the last page of a European book and vice versa.

³ The *yang* element was associated with day as the *yin* element was associated with night.

6

Selections from the *Sui-shih jih-chi* (*Journal of an Embassy Official*) of Chang Te-yi

[21 January 1877]

There was thick fog in the morning and since one could not tell land from water, at 1 a.m. we stopped our engines. By 8 a.m. the fog had cleared. The pilot came aboard and we entered the Needles. (The meaning of Ni-te-erh-ssu is 'needles'.) It derives its name from the many pillar-shaped stones along the coast. There is an island named the Isle of Wight which is a summer resort for the Queen of England. She has a palace there called Osborne—a scenic spot which she visits while on tour. At 9 a.m. the fog came in again, and the ship went off course for over twenty *li*. After lying at anchor for a while we sailed on for another ten *li* or so, till we ran aground and had to wait for the tide to take us off. During this time Hillier and Campbell, Commissioner of Chinese Customs [*sic*], came aboard, having come down from London to meet us. Then the British Customs Commissioner, Phillips, appeared and told us that he had just been informed by the Foreign Minister, Lord Derby, that the Chinese Ambassador was arriving that day and that none of us would have to go through customs. After that the Peruvian Consul, Guillaume, came to pay his respects, as did Nathan, director of the shipyard, and Mossman, former editor of the *North China Daily News* in Shanghai. By noon the tide was rising and the ship sailed on for forty leagues. To starboard we spied a tall, red-brick building over 400 feet wide and more than 100 feet in height. It was a barracks. We were informed that the building cost 50,000,000 pounds. The current rate for the pound is 3·5 treasury-scale taels. We also saw a smaller but ancient building which was built, so we were told, a thousand years before. The sea was dead calm, the hills emerald green, the breeze cool, and the clouds fleecy-white—a beautiful spring-like scene. Men and women were walking to and fro, and many of them pushed their way forward to see their Chinese visitors.

From yesterday noon until 1 p.m. today our run was 495 *li*. We arrived in Southampton, in south Hampshire, a county in the south of England. The area of the city is twenty-nine miles, and it has a population of 72,000. There are two rivers, one on either side of the entrance to the port. The one on the left is called the T'ai-ssu-t'a [Test] and lies ninety *li* to the north. The one on the right is called the Yi-li [Ely] and lies sixty *li* to the north-west. Neither is very big. This region is fertile, producing fat cattle and fine vegetables. This is one of England's medium-size ports. From Southampton to Gibraltar is 3,446 *li* by sea; from Southampton to Hong Kong is 28,268 *li*.

When the ship dropped anchor the local officials and gentry came to greet us, but most of them were strangers to us. Two or three of them had been in China, but only one of them spoke Chinese. He was known as Chou An-ssu [Jones?]. He told us that he had once worked in the foreign Customs in Shanghai.

At 3 p.m. we checked our baggage and transferred ourselves from ship to train. I said good-bye to the captain, the first mate, the ship's doctor, and other people on board. Then we boarded the train, which left at once. Since this was Sunday, there were trains to London only in the morning and evening. The train headed north at first, then turned east.

We passed through Basingstoke at 5.15 p.m. and turned east. At 6 p.m. we arrived in Woking. We stopped there briefly, then headed for Po-k'o-shai [Berkshire] and entered Mi-te-sai [Middlesex]. The total distance covered was 210 *li*. At 7.15 p.m. we arrived in London, the capital of England. During our journey I saw fields traversed by paths and prospects of green hills and fair rivers. The buildings were magnificent. It was like another world.

When we arrived at Ch'ai-ling-k'o-lo-ssu [Charing Cross station], we alighted from the train and found that the Englishman T'u Mai-lun [T. L. Bullock], Commissioner of Customs [*sic*] in Tientsin, who was now on home leave, had come to welcome us. J. D. Campbell's wife, Madame Wu, had also come to meet us in her carriage. Officials' families ride in two-horse carriages. We travelled for over ten *li* through streets bright with street-lamps like myriad stars. Horses and carriages were everywhere, and the air was full of mist and fog. When we arrived at 45 Portland Place, we went inside and rested for a while. W. C. Hillier, Bullock, and Madame Wu took their leave, so we invited J. D. Campbell to have dinner with us. By midnight all our baggage had arrived, and after checking and sorting out our luggage we settled down temporarily and finally got to bed at 4 a.m.

J. D. Campbell is an Englishman who has been sent by Ho Lo-pin [Sir Robert Hart?],[1] the Inspector-General of Customs, to take charge of the purchase of ships and weapons in London. He is also in charge of the accounts. Before the Envoys left Peking, we wrote to him asking him to rent a house. So he rented this house for us and supplied us with all our needs. This is a four-storey building with a different number of rooms on each floor. Each room is neat and clean, and equipped with all necessary utensils. Although the blinds, curtains, furnishings, beds, couches, fireplaces, and stoves are plain and unadorned, they are all very imposing. The landlord is a Marquis called Ho-shih [?],[2] a Scotsman. The rent was £105 a month, i.e. 367·5 taels. The men-servants comprise a butler, a door-keeper, a footman in charge of the drawing-room, a footman in charge of the library, and a footman in charge of lighting the lamps and taking care of other articles. The maidservants comprise one housekeeper, two general maids, one kitchen-maid, and a cook. There is also a four-wheeled carriage drawn by two horses with a groom and a driver. Portland Place is located in the south-east of the new city in London. Oxford Street lies to the north, Regent's Park to the south [sic], Bond Street to the east and P'u-lan [?] Lane to the west.

The streets here are smooth and clean, and the buildings in good repair. Carriages throng wheel to wheel, and people rub shoulders with each other all day. At night the lights are as bright as day. This is one of the quietest and most fashionable spots in London.

[p. 221a-b]

---

[1] Hart's Chinese name was Ho Te. Lo-pin may have been his style. See Senda Masao, *Kan'yaku Kammei Seiyō jimmei jiten*.
[2] Unidentifiable.

[25 January 1877]

Thick fog in the morning, full of miasmas that rose like vapour. The *Po-wu chih* [*Record of Natural Sciences*][1] reports the case of three people who went out in such a fog. One of them was unscathed, one fell sick, and one died. The one who was unscathed had drunk some wine; the one who fell sick had eaten; and the one who died had an empty stomach. So before venturing out in such a fog one must drink a few glasses of wine as the ascending fumes of the wine can combat the poisons in the fog. This seems reasonable enough. I mentioned the matter to my colleagues, who were of the same mind.

By 2 p.m. the fog had cleared, and a drizzle had set in. Wade and his wife came to call on us. These last few days we have had strong winds and bitter weather. We are hemmed in by miasmas. The woods are deserted, the grasses blighted. I am beginning to feel depressed by the cold.

[p. 222a]

[26 January 1877]

Cloudy. Gordon[2] called on us in the morning. We had met twice before. He said he was soon leaving for Egypt to take up a post there. The German Ambassador, Count George Münster,[3] visited us. The former British Ambassador to Peking, Alcock,[4] paid me a visit with his wife and daughter. We had never met before. At 2 p.m. I went to the Foreign Office with Councillor Li and Macartney to present copies of the Letter of State and the Ambassador's statement.

[p. 222a]

[30 January 1877]

When I got up in the morning the weather was fine. By 6 a.m. it had clouded over and a storm of wind and rain blew up. Between 7 and 9 a.m. it hailed. By 10 a.m. the sky was clear again, though by noon it had clouded over once more. Ho Cheng [James H. Hart],[5] younger brother of the Inspector-General of Customs Ho [Sir Robert Hart], called on me. At

---

[1] By Chang Hua (*fl.* mid-3rd century A.D.).

[2] Liu notes Gordon's visit under his entry for 27 January.

[3] Count George Herbert Münster, Baron von Grothaus (1820–1902), was German Ambassador in London from 1873 to 1885.

[4] Sir Rutherford Alcock (1809–97) was Ambassador at Peking, from 1865 to 1871.

[5] James H. Hart, who succeeded Sir Robert as Inspector General in 1885.

2 p.m. I went off in a carriage with Macartney and the two Envoys to visit Alcock, Campbell, Gordon, and Hart. In the evening Li Ch'un-chai, Liu Ho-po,[1] and I walked a couple of miles to call on the lawyer, Wu T'ing-fang,[2] who lives at 6 Park Lane, Mayfair.

He told us that on the previous day he had received a telegram from Ambassador-Designate, Ch'en Lan-pin,[3] ordering him not to return to Kwangtung but to proceed to the United States. He was not to be a Counsellor but a Consul-General. The two Envoys, Kuo and Liu, wanted him to stay here as an interpreter, since he was familiar with the English language and customs. But he adamantly refused. All that evening we tried to persuade him to accept the post, telling him that he would be appointed either as an interpreter or a second secretary. But he still refused: firstly, because Ambassador Ch'en had already invited him; secondly, because he had now booked his passage; thirdly, because the salary of an interpreter or second secretary was only 200 dollars a month at the most, and even the salary of a Counsellor was no more than 300 dollars a month to begin with. He argued that even if he should lack opportunities in the United States he could still practise as a lawyer over there and earn 1,000 dollars a month. Furthermore, he went on, a lawyer in England could rise to the rank of Vice-President, Chief Censor, or some comparable rank. There was simply no comparison between the posts we could offer him and his expectations. We tried to persuade him again and again to stay on. But he told us he could work for his country just as well in one place as another and still refused firmly.

All the way home an icy wind pierced us to the bones. I learned that the Queen had returned from Osborne, which is 280-odd *li* from London.

[p. 222a–b]

[1] Text erroneously reads 鴻 for 鶴.

[2] Wu T'ing-fang (Wu Tingfang, 1842–1922), late Chinese Minister to the United States of America, Spain, Peru, Mexico, and Cuba; also Minister of Justice for the Provincial Government of the Republic of China, and author of *America through the Spectacles of an Oriental Diplomat* (New York, 1914).

[3] Ch'en Lan-pin (*chih-shih* of 1853), a conservative official renowned for his devotion to Chinese learning, is best known in his capacity as supervisor of the first group of Chinese students in the United States (1872). In 1875 he was appointed Ambassador-Designate to the U.S.A., Spain and Peru, but did not arrive in Washington until September 1878.

From Chang Te-yi's Journal 155

[31 January 1877]

Early morning fog. By 1 p.m. the sun was breaking through.
... Today our footman went shopping with the servants A-mao and Yen Hsi. On the way they suddenly met a drunkard, who gave A-mao a playful blow on the head. Both A-mao and his hat were knocked to the ground. A-mao thought that Yen Hsi did it and was going to hit back, but the drunkard was seized by four passers-by, who called a policeman to arrest him and lock him up in the police-station. The police asked the four passers-by, as well as A-mao and Yen Hsi, to sign the register, telling them they were to come to the Mayor's [sic] court at 10 o'clock the next morning to give evidence. A Mayor is the head of a town. Under English law, all local affairs are under the jurisdiction of a Mayor.[1]

It rained that night.

[p. 222b]

[7 February 1877]

Fine weather. At 9 a.m. Macartney and I drove five or six *li* to St. James's Palace to see the Master of Ceremonies, Sir Francis Seymour, about the etiquette to be observed when presenting credentials. We were told that protocol would be the same for us as for the other ambassadors.

At 2 p.m. the two Envoys set off in an official carriage drawn by two horses. Macartney and I accompanied them. I was wearing court dress and holding the credentials. Two military officers, Chou Ch'ang-ch'ing and Lo Yün-han, stood behind the carriage. After a drive of eight or nine *li* we arrived at Buckingham Palace. This magnificent building was one that I had been to before with our Envoy Pin. When we alighted from the carriage, the officer at the gate who was wearing a helmet, a sword, and a red jacket with golden flowers escorted us in. We ascended three flights of stairs before reaching the main hall. This carpeted room was hung with tapestries whose colours dazzled the eye. The British Foreign Minister Derby, the Grand Chamberlain K'ai-erh-lun [the Earl of Caernarvon], the Master of Ceremonies Sir Francis Seymour, the British

---

[1] See Introduction, p. xlix, n. 3.

Ambassador Sir Thomas Wade, Hillier, and Yu Ya-mei[1] were all there.

At 3 p.m. the glass doors of the hall were opened. The three Ministers, Derby, Caernarvon, and Sir Francis Seymour, entered the hall first. After a moment they returned and led the way to the main door where we turned right and climbed three more flights of stairs before coming to a small room where the Queen stood, dressed in black with an ornate bonnet embroidered with white thread. She held herself erect and faced the door. The fifth princess, Beatrice, stood behind the Queen wearing a grey dress. The three Ministers entered first. Derby stood at the Queen's right and the others at her left. The Ambassadors bowed on entering the room, and the Queen curtsied in reply . . .

The Letter of State which the Ambassador presented said:

The Emperor of the Great Ch'ing dynasty asks after the mighty Sovereign of Great Britain and the Empress of the Five Indies. We received from birth the Heavenly Mandate and are succeeding reverently to the heritage handed down by our ancestors. We are ever mindful of friendly nations and wish to keep everlasting peace and preserve good relations with all. During the first month of the first year of our reign [February 1875], an interpreter from your country, Margary, in possession of a passport, went from Burma to the borders of Yunnan where he was killed, and his companion Colonel Browne was also struck dead [sic].[2] We specially appointed the Governor-General of Hu-Kuang, Li Han-chang, to go to Yunnan, investigate the affair, and see that justice was done. We also ordered the various provincial Governors to instruct their local officials to take proper care of people entering the territory with passports in accordance with the provisions in the treaties. Li Han-chang investigated the case and sent up his report, requesting the punishment of the Commandant, Li Chen-kuo, and others. During the sixth month of the second year of our reign [August 1876], We again specially appointed Li Hung-chang, Grand-Secretary of the Wen-hua Tien, Governor-General of Chihli and Earl Su-yi of the

[1] A. R. Hewlett, see Liu's *Journal* above, p. 119, n. 2. Liu refers to him as Yu Ya-chih, while Chang consistently calls him Yu Ya-mei.

[2] Margary's passport, valid for travel in China, had been issued by the Tsungli Yamen in July 1874. Colonel Horace Browne, deputy commissioner of Thayetmy, was appointed to lead the Western Yunnan expedition. He was not killed in the attack on his party. See Wang, *Margary Affair, passim*. It is sobering to realize that the officials of the Tsungli Yamen were apparently ignorant even of the basic facts of the Margary affair.

From Chang Te-yi's Journal

First Class, as official with full powers to proceed to Yen-t'ai [Chefoo] in Shantung to meet with your Royal Ambassador Sir Thomas Wade to conclude this most important case. Li Hung-chang has reported that your Royal Envoy Wade considers it more important to ensure future peace than to inflict punishment for the past.[1] We have given special orders approving his request, and have remitted the deserved punishment of Li Chen-kuo, but We still ordered the various provincial governors to obey with care our order of last year whereby they were to protect all foreigners according to treaty stipulations. We have also instructed the Tsungli Yamen to draft proclamations to be issued in the different provinces, in order to keep peace between our country and other countries. Now Margary, who came under passport to the Yunnan border, met with a tragic fate, which not only cost him his life but in addition came near to injuring the good relations which exist between us. We regret this very much, and have especially appointed Kuo Sung-t'ao, Acting Vice-President to the Board of Rites and one of the Ministers of the Tsungli Yamen, to come to Your Majesty's country to present our sentiments as a proof of our sincere desire for peace and friendship. We know that Kuo Sung-t'ao is very capable, loyal, peace-loving and perspicacious, and possesses a good knowledge of the management of domestic and external affairs. We hope that Your Majesty will also believe in his sincerity, so that we may have everlasting friendship and enjoy real peace together. We believe this will bring joy and pleasure also to Your Majesty. Second year of *Kuang-hsü*, ninth month, seventeenth day [2 November 1876].[2]

[pp. 223a–224a]

[13 February 1877]

[Chinese] New Year's day, today being the first day of the third year of *Kuang-hsü*. Clear. At 7 a.m., together with others, wearing our official gowns and led by the two Ambassadors, we faced north and made obeisance towards the tablet of the Emperor and the Empress Dowager, kneeling three times and making each time a triple kowtow. After that ceremony, Macartney also paid tribute wearing official dress. His costume included a black felt hat in the shape of a dumpling, with white

---

[1] Wade held the Central Government directly responsible for the Margary affair and protested against any provincial officials being punished. Wang, *Margary Affair*, p. 94.

[2] An English rendering of the Apology is found in F.O. 17/768. It may well have been translated by Wade or Hillier. See Appendix, pp. 186 ff.

dove feathers attached to its rim, and a black felt suit,[1] to the collar and sleeves of which a golden strip about four-tenths of an inch wide was attached.

At noon I went with the two Ambassadors and my colleagues by cab to Madame Tussaud's to see its collection of statues. They are the same as those I saw during my previous three visits. At about 3 p.m. it started to rain. At 6 p.m. Ambassador Kuo invited us to dinner. We were ten at table, and chatted happily together until late at night, when the weather cleared up again.

[p. 225b]

[30 March 1877]

Today is 30 March by the Western calendar, and a Friday. It is the anniversary of the crucifixion of Jesus, and is called Good Friday by the people of this country. Most rich men and officials go out of town on vacation. Those who do not leave, and the poorer men and women, all wear new clothes and walk in the streets and parks. Shops are closed, or are given a holiday, and churches hold services with music, day and night. Their Parliament also closed yesterday, and will not open till next Tuesday. At 5 p.m., a member of Parliament, A-shih-po-li [J. L. Ashbury],[2] invited us to go and listen to music in the Royal Albert Hall, for this Hall is in front of Hyde Park, facing the metal statue of the Queen's late husband, Albert. Hence this name...

The Hall could hold 22,000 people. That day over 10,000 men and women, old and young, were there. The singing and chanting of the scriptures shook our ears. At the end, all present in the Hall stood up to pray for the Ascension of the Lord of Heaven, and also for blessing on the Queen. When the service ended at twelve midnight we left. Men and women were crowded as bees, and many carriages and cabs gathered there. But everyone was quiet and orderly, no one trying to rush ahead, for there were policemen watching...

[p. 236a]

[2 April 1877]

Fine weather. Since the anniversary of the Resurrection of Jesus is always a Sunday, people are all too tired to work on the

[1] By 'felt' he must mean 'velvet'.   [2] M.P. for Brighton.

following day. Two years ago Sir Lu Po-k'o [Sir John Lubbock][1] asked Parliament to give an extra day free from work, since Sunday would be a holiday anyway, and the Resurrection of Jesus was a holy feast. When these two days coincide, one cannot satisfy one's desire to enjoy oneself thoroughly. Hence this day is called the Lubbock's holiday, or Easter Monday, the meaning of which I am not sure. At 2 p.m., together with the rest of the embassy, I accompanied the two Ambassadors by cab to go to see the Tower of London ...

[p. 236a–b]

[26 July 1877]

Clear morning, turned cloudy after noon. At 9 p.m. Macartney, Yao Yen-chia, Feng K'uei-chiu, and I accompanied Ambassador Kuo in his carriage, travelling for six or seven *li* to Pan-ssu-tun-fang [Brompton?] to attend Lady Pien-te's ball.[2] There were several hundred ladies and gentlemen there, in a large and commodious house of several stories. Fresh flowers of exceptional fragrance were placed all around the four walls. The candlelight dazzled the eyes and the music of the piano delighted the heart. When the dance was going on, it struck me that in China dancers have narrow waists, fine feet, and long sleeves, while in this foreign country women display their arms and bosom, and dance in sleeveless dresses. This is another difference between China and other countries.

[p. 254b]

[7 October 1877]

Fog in the morning, although it cleared towards 1 p.m. An English inventor of a farming machine Lang-fo-lou [Longfellow?][3] came to visit us. He said that China has many fields, and could well use such machines to spare human labour. He presented us with a picture of his machine to look at. We saw a knife and the teeth of a harrow which turns around. It removes grass blades and pulls out the roots for the user and then separates them and lets them get dry underneath the sun. There is also a piece of iron bent into twenty-four huge hooks, placed very closely together like human ribs. These can collect the dry grass together. There are also single, double and triple knives which

[1] M.P. for Maidstone. [2] Unidentifiable. [3] Unidentifiable.

dig the ground up, going to various depths according to the case. While every article has iron wheels and catches, they are all pulled by horses, to replace the labour of more than ten men. Some machines use six steel knives to dig up the ground. On both sides of these are steam engines with cords attached. By pulling on the cord, it can move automatically. Only one man is needed to work it, instead of six horses. There is also a machine for pumping water, with leather tubes on its side which sink successively into the water. When the machine moves, it can pump water to places several leagues away. On top of this machine, there is a steam engine which burns not coal, but grass. The engine moves automatically, putting the grass into the fire, without needing a man to push it in. In a light machine, a single piston can do the work of six horses, while a double piston can take the place of twenty horses. The single or double piston is used according to the size of the ground on which the machine works. It can dig up the ground and pump water, thus sparing much human labour. It is really a contrivance clever enough to emulate the work of nature.

[p. 261a–b]

[26 October 1877]

... Around 11 a.m., a man whom we had met before, a scientist [?] of the family of P'i-t'i [Petty?],[1] invited us to go to see the new electric machine. So, Macartney and I accompanied Ambassador Kuo by cab to the old city, to No. 105 Ku-an-nan [Cannon?] Street. Petty [?] showed us inside. Two men, Hsi-la-wo-erh [Silver][2] and Ko-lei [Grey?][3] are the manager and the assistant-manager. They showed us everything. One was an electric light, i.e. a wooden box with switches inside. Even if a building is a few hundred feet high, one only needs to push the handle with one hand to light up all its ten thousand lights.[4] There is also an instrument for curing phlegm. It is a wooden box with sixty bottles of electrified water, attached to two copper threads which connect them to the outside. To the end

[1] Unidentifiable.
[2] Messrs. S. W. Silver were the proprietors of the Silvertown India Rubber, Gutta Percha and Telegraph Works Co. Ltd. See F. G. C. Baldwin, *A History of the Telephone in the United Kingdom*, p. 27.
[3] Unidentifiable.
[4] Electric lighting was introduced into London in 1878.

From Chang Te-yi's Journal

of the threads is attached a copper tube. The patient holds these with both hands, while someone else turns the handle around, so that the blood circulates all over the body of the patient, causing the sickness to leave him. There is yet another box about four or five feet all around, and about five inches thick. Inside is a round wooden disc, as big as the box. When this disc turns, electricity is automatically produced.[1] It is used to set off torpedoes. There was also a newly invented instrument which transmits telegraphic messages to the ear. It is the same as that which we saw earlier at the house of Ssu-t'i-yi.[2] The factory which makes these things is thirty leagues outside the city, in a place called the 'Yin-ch'eng', in English 'Silvertown'. (Translated, the first word means 'silver', the second 'town'.) It used to be a piece of unused ground. The owner, whose surname is Silver, chose this spot to build his factory on. For over ten years now, he has employed about 2,000 workers. There are many houses all around the factory, which makes it resemble a town. That is why it is called Silvertown after him. We have arranged to visit it the day after tomorrow.

[p. 263a]

[28 October 1877]

Fog in the morning, clearing around 11 a.m. Macartney and I accompanied Ambassador Kuo by cab, first to Cannon[?] Street to the Electric Company, to meet Grey, and then with him to Fu-yin-che-erh-ch'ih [Fenchurch] Street station waiting room where we took the train and travelled twenty-nine leagues to Silvertown. Silver welcomed us into his factory, which manufactures electric cables. The factory is quite big, over ten leagues all around, with more than 100 houses. It makes electric cables, some of which are as long as 3,000 leagues, for use in the ocean. Around the copper cables which

---

[1] In some of the early dynamos, wooden cores were used with iron wire wound around them. See P. Dunsheath, *A History of Electrical Engineering*, p. 113.

[2] A surprising statement! Bell arrived in England in August 1877, bringing with him a complete set of telephones. The first telephone was presented to Queen Victoria, for installation at Osborne Cottage in January 1878. The instrument Chang saw must therefore have been an early mechanical telephone, which was in vogue some ten years prior to the date of Bell's device. See Baldwin, *The History of the Telephone in the United Kingdom*, pp. 15-17 and 153-4. The owner, Ssu-t'i-yi, is unidentifiable.

From Chang Te-yi's Journal

have a diameter as thick as a finger, there is an external layer of coarse hemp, over which are tied six iron wires. Then the whole is covered with six coarse, hemp cords and painted outside first with black turpentine, and then with another layer of oil paste. When ready, the cables vary from over an inch thick to three or four inches, depending on the distance to be covered and the depth of the sea.[1] The binding with hemp and iron, and the painting with turpentine and paste are all done by iron machines, far quicker than any man could do it. . . .

[p. 263a–b]

[13 November 1877]

Cloudy and foggy. At 7 a.m. I went with Li Hsiang-p'u, Feng K'uei-chiu, Yao Yen-chia, and Huang Yü-p'ing by carriage to see off Ambassador Liu and the other three, Li, Liu, and Chang, from the waiting-room of Victoria Station, from which they left for Germany. At 5 p.m. Ambassador Kuo arranged for the four of us, Bullock, Macartney, Lo Ch'i-ch'en [Yün-han], and I, to drink with him in the evening and talk about the past. At 11.15 a.m. a circular from the Ambassador had come down for all of us to read. It ran:

I wish all of you to know this. Since we embarked in Shanghai, Vice-Ambassador Liu grew prouder every day and caused many disagreements and was opposed to me all the time. Since I was often ill, and have a sense of shame, I did not wish to bring matters to a head with him, for our quarrels would only have exposed us to the mockery of foreigners, and so I kept everything to myself patiently. Furthermore, Liu often boasted to all of you of receiving his orders from the Privy Councillors. That is why people here only knew of the existence of Liu in his pride and looked down on my instructions about matters. Liu was also very self-willed in all he did, and would brook no control, so that many of you went out all day with him, with the result that sometimes, when there was work to be done and I needed you, there was no one in the Embassy. More often than not I was confronted with this situation. Fortunately, Liu has now gone to Germany, and the situation here can return to normal. I must therefore request you all to prepare those detailed translations of news reports which are your task, and not to waste a single day. You

[1] The latest ocean cables at that time were designed with a stranded conductor of No. 18 gauge wires covered with four coats of gutta-percha and ten armouring wires. See Dunsheath, *A History of Electrical Engineering*, pp. 209 and 220.

ought to work conscientiously every day, and even if work increases, you ought not to find excuses to avoid it. Since foreigners use the constitutional as a means of preventing sickness, you may also go out once daily after your meal, to do your shopping and so on as you wish. You may leave the office only in turn and you must not take your colleagues with you, and your hours of recreation must not exceed your hours of work. In the evenings you must be sure not to venture out unless on business. You must all control your servants and observe the regulations. I have already been much criticized. I often feel sorry that I can find no words to explain matters to you. Now I have decided to ask permission to retire. You all face a bright future. If, in time to come, you again read incidents in the newspapers similar to what has been reported about Liu, whatever position you hold, you must investigate the matter carefully, and leave nothing unresolved. You are good people, who need not wait for my instructions. Because Liu has done so much harm to our morale and caused confusion in people's hearts, I find myself compelled to lay down these regulations, with which I wish to exhort both myself and all of you to do good.

[p. 265a]

[12 December 1877]

Weather brightening. At 1 p.m. we took the Letter of State[1] and set off with the Ambassador and Macartney, travelling by carriage for eight or nine *li* to the railway waiting-room, where we met Sir Thomas Wade and the Minister for Salvador,[2] who was also on his way to present his Credentials. We took the train together to Windsor. The Queen sent two carriages to take us inside the palace gate. We alighted and met Lord Derby, the Foreign Minister, as well as Sir Francis Seymour. We waited till 2.15 p.m., when the gates opened and we entered the main hall and had audience with the Queen. We presented the Letter of State as we did before, but prior to doing so, the Ambassador said: 'The Imperial Ambassador of the Great Ch'ing dynasty, Kuo Sung-t'ao, now presents his appointed Credentials, which he was unable to offer earlier, to the Sovereign of Great Britain.' Then Macartney translated it into English. The Queen took the Credentials and replied: 'I am

[1] Actually the Letter of State and the Credentials, both of which had arrived on 10 November.
[2] The Liberian and Hawaiian envoys also came with them on a special train from Paddington, which left at 10 a.m. *The Times*, 13 December 1877, p. 9f.

very happy to see the Imperial Ambassador of the Great Ch'ing dynasty who will be in residence here. We hope that there will always be an Imperial Ambassador from China here, as a proof of the friendship between our two countries.' When she had finished her speech, Wade translated it into Chinese. Then we retired. At 3.15 p.m. we had afternoon tea together, sitting with four ladies-in-waiting. After tea we took our leave of everybody and left the palace, riding in an official carriage drawn by four horses to the railway waiting-room, where we lingered a while before boarding the train, which left immediately. At 5.15 p.m. we reached London, and then took a carriage to the Foreign Ministry to express our thanks to the Foreign Minister, Lord Derby, and the two Secretaries, Tenterden and Pauncefote. The weather turned cloudy at night.

[p. 267b]

[16–25 December 1877]

Clear. As their New Year and the birthday of their Lord of Heaven [Christmas] are approaching, the city shops have put many new goods on display, such as candy dolls, candied fruits, toy birds and animals, boxes, cases, and other things. All are beautifully made and nice to look at. Over the doors a horizontal sign is hung in the form of a white cloth with red words written on it, saying: 'Newly made Christmas gifts and New Year gifts for sale.'

[p. 268a]

[25 December 1877]

Clear. Today is 25 December in the Western calendar. As it is the birthday of their Lord of Heaven, all the shops are closed and men and women walk through the streets in new clothes. At 6 p.m. our neighbour Ko-la-li[1] and his mother invited Feng K'uei-chiu and me to have dinner with them. A Dr. and Mrs. P'u-a-t'e [Porter?] and Ko's nephew Ko-wan-nien[2] were also present. We talked and drank happily. At 7 p.m. it turned cloudy. During the night over an inch of snow fell.

[p. 268b]

---

[1] Unidentifiable.   [2] All unidentifiable.

From Chang Te-yi's Journal

[26 September 1878]

Fine weather. Last year, before Ambassador Liu left for Germany, he once went with Ambassador Kuo to the National Gallery to view the paintings. Ambassador Liu saw a painting there of the Virgin Mary which was very good; he asked about the price and was told it was £70. After returning to his apartment, Ambassador Liu ordered Macartney to find a painter who was skilful but inexpensive, to make a copy of the painting. Seven or eight days later, a certain friend of Macartney's found a painter named Ku Man [Walter Goodman] who promised to paint a picture four feet long by two feet wide for a fee of £20. He finished it in just over a month, and received his fee, though by that time Ambassador Liu had left.[1] Ambassador Kuo heard of this, asked to see the work, and admired it very much. He told two orderlies to carry it upstairs to show it to the ladies of his household, and kept it with him. The painter, Goodman, said that he was grateful for the appreciation shown him, and professed himself willing to paint a portrait of the Ambassador. He would not ask for his usual set fee, but only payment for the materials used. The Ambassador was very happy to hear it, saying that he wanted a portrait of himself, but lacked the patience for long sittings. Goodman said that he could first use a photograph as a blueprint. However, when he looked at the one given him, he said it would not do, but asked that another photograph be made for him to use as a model. The next day, the Ambassador went with Macartney and Goodman to the photographer's. The Ambassador said that the photograph ought to show his buttons of rank as otherwise people would not know the significance of the hat he was wearing;[2] furthermore, the face should not be a full front view nor yet should it be too much to one side. When the photograph was ready, the painter took it with him to paint the portrait. Afterwards, the Ambassador twice took Macartney to view the portrait, when the painter was adding colours to it in order to make it more lively. The painter, Goodman, had asked the Ambassador to put on his court robes, but the

---

[1] *The Times*, 15 February 1878, p. 9f. 'Mr. Walter Goodman has just completed a copy of Sassoferrato's "Madonna in Prayer" in the National Gallery.' The report goes on to comment with surprise on Liu's unusual taste in art.
[2] The insignia on a mandarin's official cap varied according to his rank.

Ambassador considered that wearing a court robe would be very much like the practice of painting a dead person's portrait in China, and this suggestion was not carried out. When the painting was finished, the National Gallery happened to be open; hence it was hung there, and all who saw it admired it very much. Then it was moved to Liverpool[1] when a gallery opened there. It was exhibited there for forty days. Afterwards it was sent to the Embassy, and the price demanded was £20 for the colours and £6 for the gilded wooden frame. The Ambassador paid altogether £20; neither party had any disagreement. However, quite unexpectedly, on the twentieth day of the sixth lunar month [20 July 1878], the Shanghai paper, *Shen-pao*, suddenly published a paragraph entitled 'Recent Doings of the Ambassador in England'. According to this source, the newspapers in England often found the actions of the Chinese Ambassador rather amusing. Recently, according to one daily, an exhibition was held in England, and a small portrait placed in the gallery was actually that of the Chinese Ambassador. The painter, Goodman, was reported to have said:

When I wanted to paint his portrait, His Excellency showed much hesitation, and agreed only after quite a while. I also had to persuade His Excellency with many soothing words before I could make him sit down. I asked to see his hands, but His Excellency kept them in his sleeves and refused to show them. When I insisted on his displaying them, His Excellency showed even greater embarrassment. After settling down, His Excellency gravely remarked that the portrait must show both his ears, otherwise, if the viewers only saw one ear, they might say the other one had been cut off.[2] He also said that his feather tassel must be painted in. I pointed out that it was covered up by the brim of the hat, and the feather itself was at the back of his head, so that it was impossible to paint. Then His Excellency bent his head down to his knees and asked if I could see it now. I said that I could of course see the feather, but could no longer see his face. Then we laughed together. Afterwards, His Excellency proposed to sit hatless, but have the big hat painted at his side. I

---

[1] Probably to the Walker Art Gallery. Liverpool had long-standing connections with the China trade and Liu—but not Kuo—had visited the city in September 1877. *The Times*, 5 September 1877, p. 6d.

[2] The *Chin-chung Yüeh-chuan*, a novel depicting the patriotic deeds of Yüeh Fei during the early 12th century, tells how a certain Ha-mi-ch'ih, an envoy sent by the Juchen to the Sung camp, had one of his ears cut off by the Chinese as an open insult to his mission.

also asked His Excellency to wear his court robes, but His Excellency said gravely that if he wore his court robes, he was afraid the people of England who saw the portrait would not have the time to kowtow in front of it. So he did not wear them.

The above remarks were all attributed to the painter Goodman. That newspaper also said that when the portrait was done, His Excellency admired it very much for its extreme fidelity, and wanted also to invite Goodman to portray his wife. When the *Shen-pao* arrived here by mail during the early part of this month, the Ambassador happened to be in France. He saw it and was angry, saying that these must be words that Goodman had uttered in jest and were later published in the papers. Actually, nothing of the sort had occurred. He was at a loss to understand how such stories had been invented, unless, when he went to have the photograph taken, Macartney had interpreted incorrectly, and so given rise to such gossip. He ordered Macartney to write to Goodman about it, but so far has received no answer. Last night, I received the Ambassador's instructions to go and ask Goodman for an explanation personally. So I went there by carriage at 2 p.m., only to be told that the artist had gone out of town with his family, and nobody was sure when he would be home.

[p. 287a-b]

[11 October 1878]

Cloudy. In the morning the Ambassador informed everybody that though the report in the *Shen-pao* had astonished him, he had not tried very hard to investigate the affair. Yesterday, however, Yao Yen-chia had told him that a telegram which came on a certain day last month intimated that he might return home. Now the *Shen-pao* came out on the twentieth of the sixth lunar month [20 July 1878]; hence it must already have reached the capital, eventuating in this letter about his return to China. On carefully unravelling the expressions in the *Shen-pao*, he went on, one discovers many detestable insinuations. He did not know who wrote this article, but felt we ought to investigate the matter at once. After that, the Ambassador went with Macartney to look for Goodman.

[p. 288b]

[13 October 1878]

Fine weather. At four o'clock I went again to see Ambassador Wade and asked him [about the date of his departure]. He said it was not yet fixed.

During the past three days, Goodman has submitted two statements, saying that since he earned his living in London by painting, it was unthinkable that he should insult His Excellency. Now that rumours which involve his work are spreading everywhere, they have ruined his reputation and made it hard for him to find a living. He would therefore do his best to investigate the affair of the newspaper and find out what had happened. That day, he also sent in another statement of his version of the affair, saying that he had been informed of the report about his painting of Ambassador Kuo's portrait in the *Shen-pao*, but did not know from what source this report had come—from which newspaper, which month, and which day. He asked anyone who knew it to let him know.

[p. 288b]

[16 October 1878]

Fine weather. Recently, the Ambassador twice ordered Macartney to ask the *Shen-pao* by telegraph about the whole affair, but received no reply after a long lapse of time. He asked again, and even sent the money for the reply, before receiving the answer that the report was translated from the newspaper, the *Ou-wo-lun-mei* [*Overland Mail*],[1] of a certain date in April. Macartney went to that newspaper's office to inquire, and was told that although they published weekly, there was no paper on that specific day. When he asked the people working at the office, they all said they could no longer remember. Macartney feared that there was a mistake in the date and so bought the papers of that whole month. He read them through but found nothing about this affair. That night, Li Hsiang-p'u and Chang T'ing-fan returned from Paris.

[p. 289a]

[17 October 1878]

Fine weather. In the morning, the Ambassador decided to order Macartney and Goodman each to write a letter to the *Shen-pao*

---

[1] The *Overland Mail* was a weekly report on Chinese affairs which appeared from January 1877 to December 1878.

stating that the news it had published was untrue. He also ordered both of them to publish an item in the *Chai-ni-ssu-t'ai-li-ko-la-mu* [*London and China Telegraph*] and the *Lun-tun Chai-na ai-k'o ssu-p'u-lei-ssu* [*London and China Express*]. At 10 a.m. he asked me to get Goodman to come over, in order to write up a statement. When it was translated and submitted to him, the Ambassador found it too short and incomplete and so changed it to read:

I have been informed of the item reported by the Shanghai *Shen-pao*, about the recent actions of the Ambassador to England. Some have said, to my great astonishment, that this report emanated from me. I consider my reputation very important, and cannot accept the blame for this. Therefore, I now submit a few words to attest to its falsehood. The report in the *Shen-pao* about the Chinese Ambassador in London ordering me to paint his portrait, and how, on its completion, the portrait was hung in several Galleries, contained many false statements, including many designed to ridicule His Excellency; I have tried hard to find out the source of such a report but, unfortunately, have found nothing up to now. The portrait I made was done from a photograph which I used as a blueprint, having obtained it when I went to see the Ambassador with Sir Halliday Macartney, who had recommended me beforehand. After the painting was finished, I twice asked the Ambassador to come to look at it. The Ambassador praised it highly, and I was very grateful for his approbation. What possible reason would I have for inventing stories to ridicule His Excellency? Besides, the Ambassador and I cannot understand each other's languages, so that everything was interpreted by Sir Halliday Macartney. When Sir Halliday came to question me, I was very puzzled and could say nothing in return. Words which I never uttered have been put into my mouth. Even if Sir Halliday were to let the matter rest, I cannot keep silent. So I earnestly ask you to publish this statement of mine, in the hope that anyone reading the paper who might know from whom this news item in the *Shen-pao* originated would inform me at once. I would thus be most obliged. Yours faithfully, W. Goodman.

As to the statement of Sir Halliday Macartney, it was drafted in Chinese by the Ambassador himself, but was translated into English by Sir Halliday Macartney. It ran as follows:

I the undersigned, saw yesterday in the French capital the *Shen-pao* of the twentieth day of the sixth month [20 July 1878], and was very surprised to read a certain item, for I had introduced Mr. Goodman to the Ambassador to paint his portrait. On its completion the

Ambassador was not very pleased, and only after many corrections on the part of Mr. Goodman did the Ambassador say that it bore a resemblance to him. When it was hung in the Galleries, everyone who saw it praised it, and so the reputation of Mr. Goodman even spread abroad. In England, Mr. Goodman's reputation was enhanced by his having painted the portrait of the First Chinese Ambassador to England, for this was a rare occurrence. When Mr. Goodman painted the portrait, he and the Ambassador could not understand each other, and so I had to act as interpreter. If the *Shen-pao* reported these stories accurately, then I must say that I have never seen anything like this occur during my almost two years of attendance on the Ambassador. I consider these stories as insulting fabrications which put me in a very difficult position. When I returned to London from Paris to question the painter about this, he pointed to heaven and swore that he had nothing to do with it. Furthermore, I have come across no such report in other than the London papers. I feel that these words of ridicule might have come from people who wanted expressly to insult the Ambassador and so used the portrait as an excuse, or else they might have come from the pen of Mr. Goodman. But in either case it was not important, for Mr. Goodman is but a painter, and if he dared to ridicule the Ambassador there would naturally be people who would reprove him. Now the *Shen-pao* has said that the English papers often contain reports on the Chinese Ambassador which border on the humorous, but I, who have followed the Ambassador here, have read only praises in the newspapers, and never have come across anything ridiculing him. I think that the Western countries are all careful of truth and of law, and our journalists are all responsible people; that is why they never ridicule the ambassadors sent from various countries. The report in the *Shen-pao* was very much contrary to what the English people would be happy to hear. Since Mr. Goodman has already given his statement, I hope that my statement will also be published in your paper, in order to correct the false report given earlier. For although the harm done to Mr. Goodman is not so important, I consider that, since I had introduced him to the Ambassador and since I had interpreted their conversation, such insulting stories would make it very hard for me to face His Excellency again. Because of these reasons, I have to clarify the situation and give details. Yours truly, Halliday Macartney.

[p. 289a–b]

[16 December 1878]

Fine weather. In the afternoon, Goodman sent over a newspaper, the *K'o-li-ssu* Journal[1] of 17 May (Chinese calendar, fourth month, sixteenth day). It said that the paintings hung in the Gallery that day were all very beautifully painted, as though the people portrayed were really alive. Goodman's portrait of the Chinese Ambassador was of special interest. He showed both his ears, because there was a law in China stipulating that criminals should have an ear cut off as punishment for criminals, while the red button indicated his rank as a Chinese mandarin, and so the Ambassador wanted this shown also. Thus the hat was added after the portrait was finished. When the Ambassador saw this report he was very angry, saying that Goodman's brother must be an employee of that newspaper. He asked me to investigate the matter the next day.

[p. 292b]

[17 December 1878]

Cloudy and rainy. In the early afternoon I went by carriage to see Goodman. He was adamant that the newspaper report really did not emanate from him. His brother Ku Tan, [Dan Goodman] now works for the *Tai-li-t'ai-li-ko-la-fu* [*Daily Telegraph*], and has nothing to do with the *K'o-li-ssu* Journal nor is there any communication between the two papers. Now that we have found the paper, we must of course trace the person responsible.[2] At 2 p.m. I returned home. The rain stopped at night.

[p. 292b]

[Undated]

There is nothing here that is not the opposite of China. In politics, the people discuss and the ruler obeys; in family regulations, the wife proposes and the husband follows; in writing, they write from right to left [*sic*]; in books, they begin from the back and move to the front; in eating and drinking, they take soup first and then rice; the cooked dishes first and then fruit; in seating, the right is honoured and the left considered lower, the host is honoured and the guest placed in a

---

[1] Unidentifiable. Perhaps, *The Graphic*.

[2] Boulger, *Life of Macartney*, p. 291, says that Kuo threatened the *Shen-pao* with prosecution but was eventually content with an abject apology on the part of the paper. He goes on to remark that the *Shen-pao* 'never divulged the name of its informant but there was hardly any doubt that it was Kwoh's own colleague Lieu who had sought to injure him'.

lower place. For it is their invariable custom that at a party the host should sit in the centre, while the guests sit on either side. The reasons for this may be their nature, or it may be on account of their land being situated just on the opposite side of the world to China, so that the customs and systems are just reversed. All of this remains a mystery to us. As to the hours of day and night, London is eight hours behind Peking, so that when it is noon in Peking, it is 4 a.m. in London; when it is midnight in Peking, it is 4 p.m. in London.

[p. 319a]

7
Sir Halliday Macartney's Diary of the Voyage

This fragment is taken from Boulger's *Life of Macartney*, pp. 266–76; it breaks off in the middle of the account of the visit to Singapore, and no account by Macartney of the rest of the voyage has survived.

Shanghai, 1876.

1 Dec., Saturday.[1]—To-day was very wet. Fearing that the Ambassadors might be unable to get on board to-night, I called on Mr. Lind and got him to consent to their going on board to-morrow morning, the P. & O. steam-tender taking them down to Woosung. On seeing the ministers I spoke to them of the necessity of going on board to-night, and did not tell them that I could manage to put them on board by the tender to-morrow morning.

The first of the baggage began being sent down at about 3 p.m., and at 8 p.m. I was surprised and rejoiced to hear that the two ministers were on the wharf and ready to embark. I went down and accompanied them on board. The captain of the ship, not expecting them before morning, was much surprised to hear that they were alongside. I afterwards went ashore, made up my things, and called at Schmidt's to bid Chung E good-bye.

At 11.10 p.m. I left the hotel, and found them all on board most anxious about my return. The ship had not yet swung, but did so soon after I came on board. Exactly as the hour struck twelve, eight bells, the engines turned over, and the embassy was off. Stiff breezes, but fair wind.

2 Sunday.—The breeze continued to freshen, and most of us became more or less out of sorts. The two Ambassadors, having resolved on trying foreign food, as far as Hong-Kong at least, came to table. The passengers and the whole ship, indeed, were

---

[1] Saturday was in fact 2 Dec.; Macartney's entries are consequently all one day out.

much impressed with the bearing and manners of the first Ambassador, but were much less so with Lieu tajen, who on several occasions committed many grave breaches of good manners. During dinner he choked and spat, and on one occasion, after an unusually successful attempt at expectoration, called his servant and ordered him to bring the spittoon, into which he spued rather than spat. This was exceedingly disagreeable to the gentlemen sitting on the opposite side of the table, who turned away their faces and manifested the most decided signs of disgust.

3 Monday.—At breakfast he called for an egg, and proceeded to open it in such awkward manner that his fingers went into it, his long nails, or rather claws, meeting from opposite sides. With the yolk of the egg dripping from the points of his fingers and streaming over his hands he presented a curious specimen of the *corps diplomatique*.

4 Tuesday.—Having finished his dinner before the rest of us, he retired from the table and entered his cabin. We were still at our wine when his servant was seen to snatch up a lamp and go into his state-room. The captain instantly sent one of the stewards to see what he was doing with it, and in a minute he returned stating that H. E. was enjoying his smoke. The captain sent back the steward for the lamp, and with instructions to put out the Ambassador's pipe. This being carried out H. E., accompanied by his servant, went upstairs apparently in anything but the best of humours.

5 Wednesday.—To-day was a very pleasant one. The sea was nearly calm, and the weather clear and agreeably warm. A steamer which had been seen during the whole morning turned out to be the *Audacious* ironclad, the flagship of Admiral Ryder. She bore down on us on our showing the Ambassador's flag, and came quite near. For some time we thought she was going to send some one on board. We at one time thought she was going to man her yards, but it turned out that she was only going to set sail. In doing this last she made some mistake and came right in front of us, and but for our having stopped our engines we should have run into her. Many speculations were ventured as to the cause of her making this strange movement, but none seemed so likely as that it was the result of mismanagement.

6 *Thursday*.—Arrived at Hong-Kong at about 4.30 a.m. A naval officer came off immediately after our anchoring and told Hillier that he was to go ashore and receive the orders left for him by Sir Thomas Wade. Hillier on his return showed me the dispatch he had received. It directed him to place his services at the disposal of the Governor, but to be careful not to encroach on the susceptibilities of the interpreter of the Mission, native or foreign, and specially mentioned my name. The Governor's aide-de-camp came off, when it was arranged that the envoys should go and see him at two o'clock, when a guard of honour would receive them on landing and a salute of fifteen guns be fired. We went and were received by the Governor, Sir Arthur Kennedy, an old man of noble figure and mien. Hillier introduced the Ambassadors and their staff, self included, and then Sir Arthur introduced to them the Admiral (Ryder), chief judge, etc.

Sir Arthur, placing the Ambassadors one on each hand, commenced a very pompous series of short speeches, during which he told them that the Hong-Kong school had done much for China, and that we English always taught the people wherever we go. The chief Ambassador had scarcely a chance of getting in a word, and the second never did get one.

Sir Arthur told the Ambassadors that England had done a great deal in the way of enlightening their countrymen, because the English never went anywhere without taking the schoolmaster with them and founding schools. Pointing to a gentleman amongst the audience, Sir Arthur said, 'This is Mr. Stewart, the headmaster of the Government School at Hong-Kong. He has more friends amongst your countrymen than any other foreigner, and in his school has over 400 Chinese children.' Sir Arthur said had time permitted he would have been glad to show the school to the Ambassadors, and Mr. Fung E., interrupting Mr. Hillier, who up to this time had been interpreting, turned to H. E., the Ambassador, and said the Governor wished them to go and see the school. H. E. at once said he would be most happy to see it, so Mr. Fung E. let us in for a programme we had not thought of. Sir Arthur next informed the Ambassadors that they had much to see, and told them of the seven places they would touch on their way to England; no less than six of them were English possessions. Amongst the gentlemen who had been invited to attend the reception were the chief judge, Sir John Smale, and Dr. Eitel, the author of the work on Fung Shang,[1] a kind of Chinese natural philosophy. Going up to the first I reminded him of our visiting Macao together many years ago, before I left Her Majesty's service. Sir John at once recollected the occasion, and recalled to my memory a piece of advice he had then offered me. I was at the time debating with myself whether I would not send in my papers with a view to entering the Chinese service. Sir John was against the thing, and advised me very strongly to think well before doing such a thing. Now he admitted that my opinion had been juster than his, the fact of my now being on the staff of the embassy proving this.

No doubt this was quite true; still, I could not but admit that Sir John's advice when tendered was judicious. Looking back on the last fifteen years, I cannot but feel I did a risky thing in resigning my commission. All's well that ends well, so thus far, at least, I could say 'twas well I did what I did. On leaving Government House we went to the school-houses, whither Mr. Stewart had preceded us. Mr. S. received us at the door and introduced us to his assistant, Mr. Falconer. The schoolroom into which we first entered was that for the Chinese pupils. It was densely crowded with pupils, many of them adults. In the centre of them sat a Chinese master, a very mean-looking fellow, whose linen gave one the idea that there was no necessary connection between learning and cleanliness. There was a marked difference between his appearance and that of his pupils, who, if he could teach them *hsia wun*,[2] they were quite as able to teach him cleanliness. After visiting this room we went to another, in which were a considerable number of well-dressed children from ten to nineteen years of age, all of them in the European costume, and most of them Eurasians or half-castes. Amongst the latter I was surprised to see not one who had fair hair or features in the least degree European. From the school we next went to the ship. On landing we had been received by a guard of honour stationed on Pedder's Wharf, and a salute of fifteen guns; and when going off again to the ship, a similar number of guns was fired from one of the men-of-war in harbour. Chairs had been sent down from Government House for the party, but owing to the chair-coolies being all dressed in white, the procession must have appeared to the Ambassadors

---

[1] Read *feng-shui*, 'geomancy'.
[2] Read *hsia-lun*, a reference to the second half of the Confucian Analects.

more like a funeral party than one of an Ambassador and his train. On our return from the shore, Mr. Hillier told me that some mistake had occurred about the cards which had been left at Government House, two cards, one for the Governor and the other for the Admiral, having been sent in, but only one, that for the former, had reached its destined hand. The Admiral, Mr. Hillier seemed to think, felt somewhat annoyed at what appeared an oversight.

7 Dec.—The next day the Governor notified his intention of returning the Ambassador's visit, and 2 p.m. was therefore appointed for his reception. This prevented us from going ashore in the forenoon. At noon, whilst in the midst of luncheon, I was called away from the table owing to a visit from the Revd. Mr. Edge. On going on deck I found a thin, gentlemanly, clerical-looking man awaiting me, who soon introduced himself as the president or agent of some kind of the Anti-Opium Society. He had come off to see whether I would arrange with the Ambassadors for their receiving a deputation from the said society. I told him that though fully sympathizing with the aims of the society, I was afraid that the arrangements of their Excellencies would not admit of the deputation being received, and recommended him to cause the address to be presented by the society which he told me he represented in England. I promised Mr. Edge that I would do what I could to obtain for the deputation a favourable reception in England, and then bade him good-bye.

The Governor came off at two o'clock, and all the attempts I could make to move their Excellencies scarcely sufficed to get them to go up the companion stairs and meet him as he came on board. Before he arrived Kwoh, Hillier, and myself had arranged the seats where every one was to sit, but when our decision was told to Lieu tajen, and his seat pointed out to him, he grumbled something about its being based on foreign custom, and suggested that their own *Wang fu*[1] should be adopted instead. Kwoh tajen did not give any opinion as to the amendment, so when the Governor came Lieu tajen took the seat he thought he ought to occupy. The Governor sat in the middle between the two Ambassadors, Kwoh on his left, and Lieu on his right.[2] The Governor, as on the preceding day, did the talking, conducting

---
[1] Read *Wang-fa* 王法 (royal customs)?
[2] The left was the place of honour in China.

himself in the same highly dignified and pompous manner. During the interview he never said a single word to Lieu tajen, though Hillier once or twice endeavoured to direct his attention to him. Champagne and biscuits, and the indispensable tea having been produced, something was said about the jail, when their Excellencies at once, or rather Kwoh tajen for them, expressed their anxiety to see it. It was therefore arranged that so soon as the Governor had gone ashore his state barge should return for the Ambassadors, the aide-de-camp, Captain Paton, having in the meantime brought down chairs for the party to the same wharf at which we had landed the day before. As soon as the Governor had gone over the side of the ship I told Kwoh tajen of the mistake which had occurred with regard to the Admiral's card, and proposed that in order to leave no ground of offence we should call at the flagship and leave a card on the Admiral as we went ashore. We accordingly did this, leaving a card on Captain Colomb, the captain of the flagship (*Audacious*) as well. Neither of them were on board, so we were not put to the trouble of going up the ladder. I, accompanied by Fung E., delivered the two cards, and explained to the officer on duty that one of the cards which had been left the day before at the Government House was intended for the Admiral. It was just as well that we had not been detained at the *Audacious*, for when we arrived at the wharf we found Sir Brooke Roberts (*sic*) and the aide-de-camp there waiting. I had not thought of the possibility of Sir Brooke's being down, or I would not have recommended the visit to the flagship. Sir B. seemed annoyed at having been kept so long waiting, but how was I to know that he was there?

Sir Brooke throughout the whole affair must have thought himself overlooked, for the day before, when we landed, he was passed by the Ambassador, and it was only when I came out of the boat and saluted him that the omission was corrected by Sir Brooke saying to me, 'But you must introduce me to the Ambassadors,' Kwoh tajen and his colleague having got out of the boat before me in accordance with Chinese custom. I was not at hand when they arrived at the head of the flight of steps leading into the wharf, so the Ambassadors passed him without taking any notice of Sir Brooke. I ran after Kwoh tajen and informed him of the omission, and got him to go back and salute Sir Brooke. Sir Brooke is an old man who has been so long in China that he cares not now to return to England, and so stays on in the same Consulate, that of Canton, in which he was when I first came to the country. He is a poor, dried-up specimen of humanity, with prominent and well marked features from which age has taken away any rotundity of contour which he ever may have had. He was dressed in black, wore a tall hat and black silk gloves, and looked for all the world as if he were going to or coming from a funeral. At the outer gate of the jail the guard presented arms, and the assistant-governor came forward and received us. The day was fast closing in, so we had to hurry over the building. The first place to which we were conducted was the room in which the handcuffs and other means of restraining prisoners were kept. These, all of them as bright as silver, were fully explained to the Ambassadors, who were then conducted along a gallery with cloisters or cells closed by iron doors on each side. The cells each contained a prisoner undergoing solitary confinement, who at the clank of the keys stood up and approached the grating in order that they might be inspected by their unwonted visitors. Gallery after gallery of this kind, then the church and the hospital were in succession visited, in the latter carbolic acid having been plentifully applied. Lieu tajen held his nose and refused to enter; Kwoh tajen, however, did not testify any sign of having perceived anything unusual in the way of smell. As we were going from the male to the female department of the establishment, we passed through a courtyard in which were a great number, about 700 Chinese and about 50 European prisoners. At the sight of the former the Ambassadors seemed to be quite awe-stricken, but did not say anything. The prisoners were all in prison dress, and looked clean and well fed; one of them came forward and, dropping on one knee, made the accustomed salute in such a manner that I concluded he had once been a soldier. Their Excellencies moved on, and did not take any notice of him. Some of the Europeans were set about going through shot drill in quick and slow time, but though the nature of the punishment was explained to their Excellencies they either did not seem to comprehend it or approve of it. Passing the kitchens just as the food for the afternoon meal was being served out, the Ambassadors had an opportunity of seeing of what it consisted. Two or three two-wheeled hand-carts were being loaded with tin pannikins filled with rice, on the top of each of which lay three small boiled fish. The rice was good and the fish fresh, both of them presenting a strange contrast to what their Excellencies must have known would have been the ration in a Chinese prison. Li-tajen, the secretary, stooped down, and taking a little from one of the dishes pronounced it excellent.

We now entered the female wards, where in a long gallery like that seen on first entering the prison, we saw the whole of the female prisoners, one of them with a baby in her arms, all standing in a row. This sight also seemed to make a deep impression on the Ambassadors, though they did not make any remark. We had now gone over the whole establishment, when in returning by the way we came we encountered the prisoners all hurrying out into a courtyard in order to replace in the hand-carts the empty dishes in which had been served up their food. When the hand-cuffs and other instruments of correction were being exhibited to their Excellencies, thinking of the bamboo used by the Chinese perhaps, they seemed to think lightly of the effect of the cat-and-nine-tails. The Governor of the prison, seemingly unwilling that they should go away with this impression, shouted out 'No. 149!' and instantly a ferocious-looking fellow, who seemed as if he might have been a pirate, instantly presented himself, and was directed to lift his smock and show his back. If their Excellencies had underestimated the effect of the 'cat,' the mistake was soon corrected, for the back of No. 149, all raw and crossed and cut with hundreds of welts, showed how effectively it had done its work. The Ambassador asked what had been the man's offence, and without a moment's hesitation the jailor answered, 'Plucking the earrings from the ears of a woman in the street.' The jailor now shouted out another number, and in a moment its representative stepped forth. Seizing him by the ear the jailor thrust the prisoner's head on one side and showed on his neck a small red ring, the vain attempt which the prisoner had made in order to get rid of a course of indian ink inflicted on him as 'incorrigible,' destined to be banished from the colony. Thinking that the mark might not be observed, or mistaken for something else, he had returned to his old lair, but the lynx-eyed police had been too sharp for him, so he had again fallen into their hands. We were now shown some cells in which were several prisoners, some destined to several years, and others imprisonment for life. In one of these was another of those foolish engines of unproductive labour and misplaced ingenuity, consisting of a wheel and axle by which a train of machinery recording the number of turns the prisoner had made—twelve thousand—and the unmerciful index pointing at that he had still (three thousand) to make before his daily task was done. Good heavens! why could not the same ingenuity have made the poor devil to produce some useful effect? Why not have made him to grind the corn for his own bread, or raise the water for his own and his brother prisoners' consumption? The only productive effect which was shown as the result of the prisoner's labour was a web of matting. We were informed that the former Governor, Sir Richard MacDonald, had made the prisoners work on the roads and do other things tending to compensate the community for the expense to which the prisoners had put them, and we wished that Sir Arthur had done the same. Fung E. having been sent to leave farewell cards on the Governor, we left the prison and returned to the ship, Sir Brooke Roberts (*sic*) accompanying us to the shore, and the Governor's barge again taking us off.

On our way to the ship the two Ambassadors spoke in the highest terms of the order, cleanliness, and general arrangements of the prison. They made no comparison between the foreign and the Chinese manner of treating prisoners, but there cannot be a doubt as to which they would award the palm. They praised the European ability for organizing and carrying out their plans, and exclaimed, 'Who would have thought that such a great and beautiful place as that of Hong-Kong could have been created in the short space of twenty years!' The European skill shown in the selecting of such a fine harbour and such 'fung shway' were also not lost sight of. The steamer was to have gone at noon the next day, but in consequence of a steamer running into our stern during the night we were compelled to remain over until five o'clock in the morning of the following day. The Admiral did not return the Ambassadors' call, but sent an officer to say good-bye to them in his stead.

Mr. McLeavy Brown came on board and called on the Ambassadors, and left a card on me. I was not on board when he called, so did not see him. At Hong-Kong I called on Dr. Denny and received a copy of his *Chinese Folk Lore*, and two copies of a pamphlet which he had just published entitled 'China and her Apologist', being a reply to an article by Sir Charles Dilke, published, I think, in *Macmillan's Magazine*. He wished me to take a number of them and distribute them amongst my friends in

England, but under the impression that it contained strictures on Sir Thomas Wade, I excused myself from receiving them. We left Hong-Kong at 5 a.m. on the 8th, and after a run of four days arrived at Singapore.

12 Dec. —The first official who made his appearance after our getting alongside the wharf was Mr. Pickering, the official Chinese interpreter. He was a common-looking person, and seemed to feel his inferiority too much, for, despite his appearance and indifferent manner, he seemed a good fellow and to have some sterling qualities. He came to say that owing to the steamer having arrived a little before she was expected, the Colonial Secretary, Mr. Douglas, had been unable to come down and meet the Ambassadors on their arrival, but would be down in a short time. While we were thus speaking, Mr. Douglas, a tall, fine-looking man, came up and spoke to me. I at once invited him down, and introduced him to the Ambassadors as the Fu Tsung Luh.[1] Mr. Douglas presented to their Excellencies the Governor, Sir William Jervois', compliments, and desired to know what was their pleasure, adding that if they were going to land a salute of fifteen guns and a guard of honour would be in readiness to receive them. It was already one o'clock, and the Governor's palace being three miles distant, and the fort from which the salute would be fired equally distant, some time had to be allowed for preparations to be made. Four p.m. was accordingly arranged for the hour when they were to be at Government House.

I invited Mr. Douglas to tiffin, and whilst we were at table the Governor's aide-de-camp arrived, and was by Mr. Hillier introduced to the Ambassadors. Old Mr. Whampo and some other Chinese merchants belonging to Singapore also arrived, and were received by the Ambassadors when we were at tiffin. Having seen Mr. Douglas to the gangway, I observed with much regret that poor Mr. Pickering had been waiting, and no one entertaining him all the while we were below at tiffin. I was much annoyed at this oversight, and apologized to him for what must have appeared to him an unpardonable neglect.

Repairing to the Ambassadors in order to explain to them the necessity of being at the palace punctually at the hour appointed, in order not to keep the Governor and the guard of honour

[1] Read *Tu* for *Luh*.

waiting, I was surprised to hear that between that time, 2 p.m., and 4 o'clock they intended visiting the house and gardens of Whampo. I informed them that it would not be in accordance with foreign politeness or proper to call anywhere until they had paid their respects to the Governor. To this they replied that Mr. Hillier and the aide-de-camp had been parties to the arrangement, so, though still thinking it a mistake, I said no more to them on the subject. Four carriages having arrived soon after 2 p.m., we, midst a heavy rain, left the shore and entered them. The rain did not long continue, and the sun coming out in a few minutes the roads had dried, and no traces remained of it, excepting the refreshing green which it had conferred on the trees and flowers of the jungle which hemmed in the road on each side. We now drove along a road, sometimes passing amongst a few Indian then a few Chinese houses, most of them of a very inferior description. Their E.'s read the Chinese signboards as they passed, remarking that the Singapore Chinese seemed for the most part to be very poor. I informed them that we had not yet arrived at the town, and that these houses could not be taken as fair specimens of the shops of their countrymen. The stupid coachman, instead of taking us to Whampo's country house and gardens, drove us to his shop. I at once got out of the carriage and asked one of the shop-assistants to give the necessary directions for our being taken with all possible haste to Mr. W.'s house, so we were soon on the way again. The road seemed to me very long, and I began to be afraid that we were on the wrong path, and would be too late for keeping our appointment at Government House at four o'clock. I ordered the driver to make haste, and soon after a gateway, leading into a garden in the middle of which was a Chinese-looking house, made its appearance. This was the famous house and garden of the much-respected Mr. Whampo.

APPENDIX

1. Extract from the North China Herald: 'Kuo Sung-t'ao on the Christian Propaganda'

Jan. 3, 1878.

The *Daily Press* mentioned last week, that prior to the departure of His Excellency Kuo Sung-t'ao, the Chinese Ambassador to London, he received instructions from the Emperor to keep a diary in which he was to note everything that he saw during his voyage from China to Europe, the manner in which he was received at the various ports at which he would touch *en route*, and his reception at his destination by the English people and authorities. He was further instructed to record his impression of the places he visited, and to report on the manners and customs of the people, together with the commerce of the country; and the journal, when completed, was to be sent to Peking for perusal. These commands, it was stated, were faithfully obeyed, and in due course Kuo transmitted for the Imperial glance, a manuscript book filled with the result of his observations. It was perused, and orders were given by the Tsung-li Yamên to have several thousand copies of it printed in pamphlet form for distribution among the high mandarins. Hardly half of these pamphlets had been distributed, however, when one of the Censors presented a strongly-worded memorial to the Throne, praying for the withdrawal of the diary from circulation, as the memorialist considered the statements made in it reflected disgracefully upon China, the Ambassador having described everything in England as greatly superior to China; having, in fact, told the whole truth, which was unacceptable to Chinese pride. And the *Daily Press* regretted to have to add that the prayer of the Censor was granted!

Whether our contemporary is right in saying the journal has been withdrawn from circulation, on the remonstrance of a Censor who was horrified at the truths told, we are not aware. But we do know that the first section of it, describing the voyage to Europe, was printed in the Spring by the Tsung-li Yamên,

Appendix

presumably for distribution to the provinces; and we are able to give, in another column, a translation of an extract which may interest our readers. The journal, which begins with the embarkation of the mission at Shanghai on the 1st December, 1876, chronicles all the events of the voyage, its sights, scenes, and occasional discomforts, in a style which is frequently amusing; and interspersed throughout are reflections on political subjects, of which the extract we publish this morning is a specimen. Kuo's sketch of the rise, progress and divisions of Christianity is amusing in its terseness; but when he comes to speak of the course and probable effect of the religious propaganda in China, his words deserve weighty consideration, for they may probably be taken as fairly representing the view of every educated Chinese, whilst the apprehension of danger from this cause is eminently characteristic of the official sentiment throughout the country. There is no doubt that Kuo is justified, in the abstract, in claiming for China a spirit of religious tolerance, 'no restrictions being laid upon any form of worship or belief'. The opposition which is shown to Christianity arises from a political, much more than from a religious motive. Irritation there is, of the latter kind, at the condemnation of ancestral worship which has been described as the only creed deep-rooted in the Chinese mind, and at the dissension and trouble which are now and then caused by the conversion of one member of a family. But it is the quasi-political bond in which the Roman Missionaries seek to unite their converts, the political protectorate which they claim to exercise over them, and the persuasion, right or wrong, that this protectorate is sometimes exercised over criminals who are thus shielded from punishment—that chiefly cause the enmity which undoubtedly exists to the Christian propaganda. That the Ambassador's language, affirming 'how the different missions give encouragement and protection to their converts', and how, 'in Szechuen and Kweichow, the most acute sufferings have been entailed in consequence upon the people, and the mere mention of the word missionary excites a feeling of indignation in the breast, and calls forth a torrent of invective',—greatly exaggerates the case, there can be scarcely room for doubt. But it is none the less true that he expresses a feeling which is widely spread, if less intense than he describes. The suggestion of a partial remedy, contained in his closing sentences, is so exactly in accord with the Imperial decree enjoining respect for the equal rights of Christian and non-Christian Chinese, which was published on the 1st February last, that there can be little doubt of the subject having been under discussion in this sense before the departure of the mission from China. That decree was approved at the time as a spontaneous expression of tolerance, and as indicating that the 'security for the future' which Sir Thomas Wade declared to have been a guiding impulse in his recent negotiations, had been to some extent impressed as an active principle on the Chinese mind. It is interesting to discover, in Kuo's memorial, how seriously the whole subject has exercised the mind of Peking statesmen. As we said before, we do not believe that the Chinese are inclined at heart to be intolerant; and foreigners will be as pleased as the Chinese themselves, if a way can be found to obviate the irritation which the Christian propaganda does undoubtedly excite.

2. Official Apology from the Emperor of China to Queen Victoria (F.O. 17/768)

Translation of a Letter from the Emperor of China to the Queen of England, the text of which was communicated to Her Majesty's Minister at Peking by the Prince of Kung.

His majesty the Emperor of the Ta Tsing Empire greets Her Majesty the Queen of England and Empress of India.

Having succeeded to Our vast estate by the Decree of Heaven, Our desire is ever the maintenance unbroken of peaceful relations with friendly states.

In the first moon of the first year of the Reign Kuang Sü (February 1875), Margary, an interpreter of Your Majesty's Government, while proceeding with a passport from Burma to Yün Nan, was murdered upon the frontier; Colonel Browne who was accompanying him being attacked and his farther advance obstructed. Li Han-chang, Governor-General of Hu Kuang, was specially commissioned by Us to proceed to Yün Nan to make enquiry and take action in a spirit of equity, and a Decree was issued by Us commanding the Governors-General and Governors of the central and all other provinces to circulate instructions to all the authorities respectively subject to them that whenever persons bearing passports should enter their jurisdictions, they were duly to act as the treaties require.

Appendix

Li Han-chang having completed his enquiry, and having presented a report requesting that the *tu ssŭ* (major), Li Chen-kuo, and others should be severally punished, in the sixth moon of the second year (August 1876), We specially commissioned Li Hung-chang, Grand Secretary of the Wen Hia Tien, Governor-General of the Province of Chih Li, and Po (Earl) of the First Class, to proceed with full powers to Yên-t'ai (Chefoo) in the Province of Shan Tung, to consider with Wei T'o-ma (Thomas Wade), Your Majesty's Minister, by what means the case above referred to might be closed.

Li Hung-chang reporting that in the opinion of Your Majesty's Minister, Thomas Wade, it is better to secure the future than to inflict punishment for the past, We have signified Our pleasure that in accordance with what has been requested, Li Chen-kuo and the rest be graciously excused the penalties to which they were liable. We have further by decree repeated Our commands to the provincial governments to pay the most careful attention to the decree issued last year, whereby they were enjoined to afford protection required by the treaties. We have at the same time instructed the Yamên of Foreign Affairs to draft a proclamation and to forward it to the provincial governments, who are obediently to give effect thereto: to the end that there may be peace between native and foreigner.

The death of Margary however, as he was crossing the borders of Yün Nan under passport, is not only of melancholy interest in that a life was lost. Peaceful relations were jeopardized by it. Our regret is profound, and in proof of Our sincere desire for peace, We have specially selected Kuo Sung-tao, an Acting Vice-President of the Board of Ceremonies, and one of the Ministers of the Yamên of Foreign Affairs, to proceed as Our Envoy to Your Majesty's country to make known in Our stead Our friendly sentiments.

Kuo Sung-tao is known to Us for his experience and devotedness, his amiability and intelligence. He is well versed in the conduct of foreign affairs. We earnestly hope that full confidence will be reposed in him: that so the friendly relations [of our states] may continue for evermore to improve, and the increasing advantages of peace be shared by both; a result which We assume will not fail to be profoundly gratifying.

Kuang-Sü 2nd year, 9th moon, 17th day [2 November 1876].

3. Kuo Sung-t'ao's Letter *re* Appointment of Consuls (F.O. 17/794)

Chinese Legation
January 2nd, 1878.

The Right Honourable,
The Earl of Derby,
Principal Secretary of State for Foreign Affairs.

My Lord,

I had the honour, on the 23rd July last, to receive a despatch from your Lordship relative to the proposed appointment of a Chinese Consul at Singapore, and stating that [whilst there was no objection to the present appointment] the maintenance of the post of Chinese Consul, should a vacancy occur at any time must be regarded as an open matter.

Upon the receipt of this communication I reported its contents to the Chinese Tsungli Yamên.

To my report a reply has now been received. The Yamên observes that China now seeks for the first time to establish Consulates in England, and that according to your Lordship's despatch it would seem that China has not the independent power permanently to establish these Consulates. In China when any Foreign Country wishes to establish a Consulate, the Yamên, upon the receipt of a representation to that effect from the Resident Minister, immediately issues all the necessary notifications. If then when China wishes, on her part, likewise to establish Consulates in Foreign Countries, she can only do so temporarily and not permanently, it would seem as if she were unfairly treated. I am therefore instructed to make to your Lordship a representation on the subject.

According to international law each country is permitted to appoint consuls to protect the interests of its nationals residing in other countries, and to assist in the settlement of disputes between them and the natives of those countries. China up to the present had not established consulates, but as she has now appointed a Resident Minister in England, she must in all matters be guided by international law. In the treaties which China has exchanged there is no mention made of the establishment of consulates, nor is there any either made of the appointment of Resident Ministers. The appointment of Ministers and the establishment of Consuls therefore should not be regarded in different light, but should be governed by the same conditions. I would also add that, although China hitherto in the administration of commercial affairs has not been so forward as other countries, yet it is her duty to overlook her subjects in Foreign countries and to prevent as far as possible disputes and disturbances from arising. Last year whilst on my way to England I passed through Singapore and during an interview which I had with Mr. Ho-ah-kay, I discussed with him local matters. As a result of this conversation I asked your Lordship to consent to his appointment as Consul.

I have also learned from the newspapers that within the last few months the Chinese residing in Australia have had frequent disputes, but I have refrained from troubling your Lordship about this matter, because I am not familiar with all the circumstances. It would seem, however, that a Resident consul is also required there, in order that it may be discovered what is advantageous to the Chinese and what is against their interests, and disturbances prevented. This appointment would promise to be a favourable measure. As the accredited Minister of China I cannot but draw your Lordship's attention to these matters which, in my judgment, ought to be attended to.

I beg your Lordship to favour me with a reply at your earliest convenience.

I have the honour to be,
My Lord,
Your Lordship's most obedient
humble Servant,
(Signed) Kuo Sung-tao

4. Kuo Sung-t'ao's Leniency Request for John Donovan (F.O 17/768)

Chinese Legation
45 Portland Place.
3rd February 1877

The Chinese Minister presents his compliments to the Earl of Derby, and begs to inform His Lordship that on the 1st inst. a man named Donovan, was brought up before the Magistrate of the Marlborough Street Police Court and sentenced to two months imprisonment with hard labour for assaulting whilst in a drunken fit, one of the servants of the Chinese Legation. The Chinese Minister, seeing that the servant was in no way injured, and being perfectly convinced that the assault was entirely the result of the state in which Donovan was at the time, cannot but consider the sentence awarded a very heavy one. The Chinese Minister would therefore be much pleased if it were possible to mitigate or remit it, and would be extremely obliged if the Earl of Derby would move the proper authorities in this sense.

5. Kuo Sung-t'ao's Letter *re* Destruction of Mission Property at Wu-shih-shan (F.O 17/794)

Chinese Legation
November 19, 1878.

The most Noble,
The Marquis of Salisbury, K.G.,
Principal Secretary of State for Foreign Affairs,

My Lord Marquis,

I have the honor to lay before Your Lordship the substance of a despatch which has been addressed to me by Their Excellencies Ching, the Tartar General of Foochow, Ho, the Governor General of Chekiang and Fukien, and Woo, the Governor of the latter province, informing me of the mission premises at Woo Shih Shan having been destroyed. The circumstances which led to this, seem to be as follows. In the year 1850 the Revd. Mr. Welton rented a house consisting of two suites of apartments and situated on the left of the temple of Taou Shan Kwan, afterwards another house was rented on the right of the same building. A small piece of land adjacent and in the rear of the latter was rented by another missionary named Mr. Mahood. For each of these a yearly rent was to be paid by the mission.

In the year 1866 the Revd. Mr. Wolfe received over from a man named Hwang Hsiang-shêng a piece of land which the latter had illegally sold to him, the land not belonging to the man Hwang, but being public ground, the property of the Wên Ch'ang Kung Temple. In defence of public rights and to annul the purchase, one of the local gentry named Chao Fêng-yüan commenced a suit in the court of the How Kwan District Magistrate who, having heard the case, decided that the sale was illegal, but that a lease of the land should be granted to the Mission for a period of twenty years, during which rent should be annually paid to the Temple and after which the land should again be yielded up to it. At different times Mr. Wolfe made alterations in the buildings which had been leased to the mission, and without permission, and in spite of the people substituted for them Chapels and other structures of a foreign nature. Subsequent to 1871, Mr. Wolfe commenced encroaching on the mountain land, gradually and illegally enclosing it by the erection of wattle fences, which he afterwards supplemented by walls. In the summer of 1877 one of the local gentry named Lin Ying-lin and others brought this matter to the notice of Governor Ting who represented to Consul Sinclair that as the erection of storied buildings on the Woo Shih Shan was considered by the gentry and people as being injurious to the 'Fung Shway' of the city of Foochow, the provincial capital, he would propose that the Mission site should be removed to the place where a telegraphic office had recently been built and which he would give in exchange, together with a small sum of money to assist in defraying the expenses consequent on making the removal, Mr. Sinclair and Mr. Wolfe both expressed their approval of this proposal, but stated that the matter would have to be referred to the head of the Mission.

Sometime afterwards on being urged for a reply, Consul Sinclair stated that the Mission Authorities had refused to give their consent to the change, and that having referred the matter to his superiors, he would have to await their reply before doing anything further in the matter. In summer of the present year, and whilst the case was still under deliberation, Mr. Wolfe commenced building houses on the land on which he had encroached, and Lin Ying-lin and others having brought the matter before the authorities, the Prefect was ordered by the Governor General and Governor, to take his assistants the 'Ting' and the 'Chi Hsian', and go and measure the land but when they went to do so, Mr. Wolfe quarrelling with the gentry and people, brought things to such a pass that the chapel was burned down.

Their Excellencies have requested me to bring these circumstances to the notice of your Lordship, and to beg that in judging the case you will take them into your consideration and thus obviate the possibility of being misled by the onesided statements of Mr. Wolfe.

I was exceedingly grieved when I saw by the newspapers that another instance of the destruction of mission property had occurred at Woo Shih Shan, but it was not until I received the above mentioned despatch that I became aware that the suit in which it originated had been impending for many years. Mr. Wolfe was undoubtedly much to blame for building more new houses this year. According to the law and usage of nations the land and houses having been rented and not sold to him, he was not entitled to erect buildings or make changes without having first consulted and obtained the permission of the owner. Mr. Wolfe still further transgressed the Law by encroaching and in building houses on land which he had not rented. Furthermore the question of exchange of site having been discussed by the Governor and the Consul, he ought not to have gone on building houses and enraging the people but to have waited until the reply which Mr. Sinclair was expecting should have enabled a settlement to be arrived at. The Chinese Foochow people are excitable, and Mr. Wolfe unnecessarily raised difficulties and made trouble with them. In dealing with mixed cases, when Europeans and Chinese are concerned, I always endeavour to allay their mutual prejudious [prejudices], and to do what is just.

As the land which Governor Ting proposed to give in exchange for the premises now occupied by the mission, instead of being less, exceeds it; the offer, may, I think, be considered as very fair, and even Consul Sinclair admitted this. The matter ought therefore to be settled on this basis. With regard to the people who originated the disturbances and burned the mission houses, the Authorities have already ordered the Prefect and the District Magistrate to arrest them and bring them to punishment within a given time, which will on no account be extended, meanwhile as indicating the determination with which the Authorities intend to act, I may state, that the Prefect and the District Magistrate have already been deprived of their insignia of rank. Mr. Wolfe has on more than one occasion been the cause of trouble at Foochow, but of Mr. Sinclair, the gentry and the people have but one opinion as to his being considerate and conciliating. The conduct of Mr. Wolfe having often been the subject of complaints, I think it would be well if the Authorities of the Church Mission Society were consulted with a view to his being removed, for in this way only we might hope to allay the hostility which he has unfortunately excited in the breasts of the people of Foochow. I enclose a plan of the ground which I have received from Foochow, and which may assist your Lordship in understanding the matter, and trust that with a view to a just settlement being arrived at, your Lordship will take into your consideration the circumstances which I have brought before you in this despatch.

I have the honor to be,
My Lord Marquis,
Your Lordship's most obedient
humble Servant,
(Signed) Kuo Sung-tao

6. Kuo Sung-t'ao's Letter *re* Attack upon Missionaries at Wu-ch'ang (F.O 17/794)

Chinese Legation,
March 12, 1878.

The Right Honourable,
The Earl of Derby,
Principal Secretary of State for Foreign Affairs.

My Lord,
 I have the honour to acknowledge the receipt of your despatch of the 5th instant, enclosing copy of a summary of the correspondence which has passed between Mr. Fraser, Her Majesty's Chargé d'Affaires and the Imperial Yamên of Foreign Affairs with reference to an attack upon British Missionaries at Wu-ch'ang, which I have perused with deep regret.
 The Yamên of Foreign Affairs have addressed me a despatch embodying a report upon the circumstances of the case, received, in reply to orders issued by themselves, from the Governor General of Hukwang stating that Ch'êng Mao-low and seven other persons, all military candidates, had been arrested upon a charge of fomenting disorder; that they were all in turn successively inspected by Her Majesty's Acting Consul in company with the Wesleyan Missionaries, and that two of them Chêng Mao-low and Ch'êng Hêng-siang having been identified by them as having been amongst the perpetrators of the assault, and other two Chang Hung-kia and Wang Shêng-ta having confessed to having incited the crowd to the attack by shouts, had been

sentenced by the local authorities to punishments of different degrees of severity. Subsequently the despatch goes on to state, upon receipt of a despatch from Mr. Fraser, Her Majesty's Chargé d'Affaires, to the effect that up to that time neither the ringleaders nor the perpetrators of the assault had been brought to trial, the Yamên memorialised the Throne upon the subject and received an Imperial Rescript ordering the Governor General of Hukwang to effect without delay a satisfactory settlement of the case.

Her Majesty's Chargé d'Affaires, I find, lays chief stress upon the infliction of exemplary punishment upon the ringleaders of the attack. The attack, however, was made on a sudden at a time when the military candidates were assembled in considerable numbers for examination and it is quite possible therefore that there may not have been any actual ringleaders. But as Ch'êng Mao-low and Ch'êng Hêng-siang have been identified as some of the perpetrators of the assault, there can of course be no difficulty in effecting a searching investigation. In view of the large assemblage of military candidates and consequent liability of disorder, the local authorities probably did experience some difficulty in dealing with the case at the time of its occurrence. At the present time, however, a thorough examination can be made under more favourable conditions and without fear of evasion being practised; I am therefore addressing the Yamên of Foreign Affairs upon the subject to request that orders be sent by them with utmost speed to the Governor General of Hukwang that, in accordance with the terms of the Imperial Rescript already received, he lose no time in inquiring into and effecting a settlement of this case.

I have the honour to be,
with the highest consideration,
My Lord,
Your Lordship's most obedient
humble Servant
(Signed) Kuo Sung-tao

BIBLIOGRAPHY

BALDWIN, FRANCIS GEORGE C., *The History of the Telephone in the United Kingdom*. London, 1938.

BANNO, MASATAKA, *China and the West 1858–1861: The Origins of the Tsungli Yamen*. Cambridge, Mass., 1964.

BEAL, JR., EDWIN GEORGE, *The Origin of Likin (1853–1864)*. (Issued by Chinese Economic and Political Studies, Harvard Univ.) Cambridge, Mass., 1958.

BIGGERSTAFF, KNIGHT, 'The Establishment of Permanent Chinese Diplomatic Missions Abroad', *Chinese Social and Political Science Review*, xx.1 (Apr. 1936), 1–41.

——, 'The First Chinese Mission of Investigation Sent to Europe', *The Pacific Historical Review*, vi.4 (Dec. 1937), 307–20.

BIRD, ISABELLA LUCY (MRS. BISHOP), *The Golden Chersonese and the Way Thither*. London, 1883.

BLAKE, R., 'Note supplémentaire sur Fou-lin', *Journal Asiatique*, 2nd series, 202 (1923), 83–8.

BOULGER, DEMETRIUS C., *The Life of Sir Haliday Macartney K.C.M.G. Commander of Li Hung Chang's Trained Force in the Taeping Rebellion, Founder of the First Chinese Arsenal, for Thirty Years Councillor and Secretary to the Chinese Legation in London*. London and New York, 1908.

BOURNE, SIR FREDERICK SAMUEL AUGUSTUS, 'Diary of Liu Ta-jen's Mission to England', *The Nineteeth Century* (Oct. 1880), 612–21.

BUCKLEY, CHARLES BURTON, *An Anecdotal History of Old Times in Singapore, from the Foundation of the Settlement under the East India Company of February 6th, 1819 to the Transfer to the Colonial Office as part of the Colonial Possessions of the Crown on April 1st, 1867*. 2 vols., Singapore, 1902.

CAMERON, JOHN, *Our Tropical Possessions in Malayan India*. London, 1865; O.U.P. reprint, Kuala Lumpur, 1965.

CHANG CHUNG-LI; and SPECTOR, STANLEY, eds., *Guide to the Memorials of Seven Leading Officials of Nineteenth-century China*. Seattle, 1955.

CHANG HAO, 'The Anti-Foreignist Role of Wo-jen (1804–71)', *Papers on China* (Harvard University Committee on Regional Studies), 14 (1960), 1–29.

CHANG HSIEH, *Tung-hsi-yang k'ao* (1618); Kuo-hsüeh chi-pen ts'ung shu, ed., Shanghai, 1937.

CHANG HSIN-PAO, *Commissioner Lin and the Opium War* (Harvard East Asian Studies, 18). Cambridge, Mass., 1964.

CHANG I-TUNG, 'The Earliest Contacts between China and England. Li-shih-yen-chiu, 1958, No. 5', *Chinese Studies in History and Philosophy*, i.3 (Spring, 1968), 53–88.
CHANG P'EI-LUN, *Chien-yü chi*. 1918.
CHANG TE-YI, *Hang-hai shu-chi*, in *Hsiao-fang hu chai yü-ti ts'ung-ch'ao*, comp. Wang Hsi-ch'i., xi. Shanghai, 1891–7.
———, *Sui-shih jih-chi*, in ibid.
CH'EN, GIDEON (CH'EN CH'I-T'IEN), *Tso Tsung-t'ang: Pioneer Promoter of the Modern Dockyard and the Woollen Mill in China*. Peiping, 1938.
CH'EN, KENNETH, 'Hai-lu. Fore-runner of Chinese Travel Accounts of Western Countries', *Monumenta Serica*, vii (1942), 208–26.
CHIANG YEE, *Chinese Calligraphy: an Introduction to Its Aesthetic and Technique*. 2nd ed., London, 1954.
Ch'ien Han-shu. Po-na, ed.,
CHIH, ANDRÉ, *L'Occident 'Chrétien' vu par les Chinois vers la fin du XIXe siècle (1870–1900)*. Travaux de l'Institut d'histoire des relations internationales; Publications de la Faculté des lettres et sciences humaines de Paris; Série 'Texts et Documentes', Tome II. Paris, 1962.
'A Chinaman in London', *Blackwood's Magazine*, Oct. 1901, 492–8.
CHIN-LIANG, *Chin-shih jen-wu chih*. Taipei, 1955.
Chin-shu. Po-na, ed.
Ch'ing-chi wai-chiao shih-liao. Peking, 1932–5.
Ch'ing-shih lieh-chuan. Shanghai, 1928.
CHIROL, VALENTINE, *The Far Eastern Question*. London, 1896.
Chou Li. Ch'un-kuan tsung-po Shih-san ching ching-wen, ed.
Ch'ou-pan yi-wu shih-mo. Peking, 1929–31.
CH'U CHIN, 'Kuo Yün-hsien shou-cha ping pa', *Chung-ho yüeh-k'an*, i.12 (1940), 68–76.
COHEN, PAUL A., *China and Christianity: The Missionary Movement and the Growth of Chinese Antiforeignism 1860–70*. Cambridge, Mass., 1963.
Colonial Office List. London, 1876–7.
CORDIER, HENRI, *Histoire des relations de la Chine avec les puissances occidentales, 1860–1900*. 3 vols., Paris, 1902.
COWAN, CHARLES DONALD, *Nineteenth Century Malaya: The Origins of British Political Control*. London, 1961.
COWAN, CHARLES DONALD, ed., *The Economic Development of China and Japan*. London, 1964.
CRABITÈS, PIERRE, *The Spoliation of Suez*. London, 1940.
DAWSON, RAYMOND, ed., *The Legacy of China*. Oxford, 1964.
DUNSHEATH, PERCY, *A History of Electrical Engineering*. London, 1962.
DUYVENDAK, JAN JULIUS LODEWIJK, *China's Discovery of Africa*. London, 1949.

Bibliography

———, 'The True Dates of the Chinese Maritime Expeditions in the Early Fifteenth Century', *T'oung Pao*, xxxiv (1938), 341–412.
EBERHARD, WOLFRAM, *A History of China*. Rev. ed., Berkeley, 1960.
ENDACOTT, GEORGE B., *A History of Hong-Kong*. London, 1958.
———, and HINTON, A., *Fragrant Harbour, a Short History of Hong Kong*. Hong Kong, 1962.
Erh Ch'eng ch'üan-shu, Ssu-pu pei-yao ed.
Erh-ya yin-te, Harvard-Yenching Institute Sinological Index Series, Supplement, No. 18. Taipei reprint, 1966.
FAIRBANK, JOHN K., ed., *The Chinese World Order: Traditional China's Foreign Relations*. Cambridge, Mass., 1968.
FAIRBANK, JOHN K., REISCHAUER, EDWIN O., and CRAIG, ALBERT M., *East Asia: The Modern Transformation*. London, 1965.
FANG HAO, *Chung-hsi chiao-t'ung shih*. 5 vols., Taipei, 1954–5.
FEUERWERKER, ALBERT, *China's Early Industrialization: Sheng Hsuan-huai (1844–1916) and Mandarin Enterprise*. Cambridge, Mass., 1958.
FITZGERALD, CHARLES PATRICK, *China: A Short Cultural History*. 3rd ed., London, 1965.
———, *The Third China: The Chinese Communities in South-East Asia*. Melbourne, 1965.
FITZGERALD, PERCY HETHERINGTON, *The Great Canal at Suez: Its Political, Engineering and Financial History. With an Account of the Struggles of Its Projector, Ferdinand de Lesseps*. 2 vols., London, 1876.
Foreign Office List. London, 1876–8.
Foreign Office Records, China, General Correspondence. F.O.17. London, 1877–8.
Friend of China (Journal of the Anglo-Oriental Society for the Suppression of the Opium Trade). London, April 1877, August 1880.
GABAIN, ANNEMARIE VON, 'Ein Beitrag zur Fu-lin-Frage', *Sinica*, 8 (1933), 195–7.
GALLAGHER, LOUIS JOSEPH, trans., *China in the Sixteenth Century: the Journals of Matthew Ricci: 1583–1610*. New York, 1953.
GARRATT, GEOFFREY THEODORE, *Gibraltar and the Mediterranean*. London, 1939.
HAECKEL, ERNST HEINRICH PHILIPP, *A Visit to Ceylon*. London, 1883.
HAMILTON, DAVID, 'Kuo Sung-tao: A Maverick Confucian', *Papers on China* (East Asian Research Center of Harvard University), 15 (Dec. 1961), 1–29.
Han-shu, Po-na ed.
HO CH'UI-T'AO, comp., *Shuo-fang pei-sheng*. 1881; Taipei reprint, 1966.
HOLCOME, CHESTER, *The Real Chinaman*. New York, 1895.
———, *The Real Chinese Question*. New York, 1901.
Hou Han-shu. Po-na, ed.
Hong Kong Directory. Hong Kong, 1877.

Hsü Chi-yü, *Ying-huan chih-lüeh*. Tsung-li Yamen, ed., 1866.
Hsü, IMMANUEL C. Y. (Hsü Chung-yüeh), *China's Entrance into the Family of Nations: The Diplomatic Phase, 1858–1880*. Cambridge, Mass., 1960.
——, *The Ili Crisis: A Study of Sino-Russian Diplomacy, 1871–1881*. Oxford, 1965.
Hu SHENG, *Ti-kuo chu-yi yü Chung-kuo cheng-chih*. Peking, 1952.
HULUGALLE, H. A. J., *British Governors of Ceylon*. Colombo, 1963.
HUMMEL, ARTHUR WILLIAM, ed., *Eminent Chinese of the Ch'ing Period (1644–1912)*. 2 vols., Washington, 1943.
Illustrated London News. London, April 1869, February 1877.
JACKSON, ROBERT NICHOLAS, *Pickering: Protector of Chinese*. Kuala Lumpur and London, 1965.
JORDAN, J. N., trans., 'Extracts from the Diary of Tseng Hou-yeh, Chinese Minister to England and France', *The China Review*, xi (July 1882 to June 1883), 135–46.
KIERNAN, E. V. G., *British Diplomacy in China, 1880 to 1885*. Cambridge, 1939.
KING, FRANK HENRY HAVILAND, and CLARKE, PRESCOTT, eds., *A Research Guide to China-Coast Newspapers, 1822–1911*. Cambridge, Mass., 1965.
KIPLING, RUDYARD, *From Sea to Sea and Other Sketches, Letters of Travel*. 2 vols., London, 1911.
KROEBER, ALFRED LOUIS, *The Nature of Culture*. Chicago, 1952.
KU HUNG-MING (Ku T'ang-sheng), *Chang Wen-hsiang mu-fu chi-wen*. 1910; Taipei reprint, 1956.
KUO SUNG-T'AO, *Yang chih shu-wu yi chi*. 1892; Taipei reprint, 1964.
——, *Yü-ch'ih lao-jen tzu-hsü*. 1893; Taipei reprint, 1970.
——, *Shih-hsi chi-ch'eng* in *Hsia-fang-hu chai yü-ti ts'ung-ch'ao*, comp. Wang Hsi-ch'i. xi, Shanghai, 1891–7.
LACH, DONALD FREDERICK, *Asia in the Making of Europe*. Vol. i, Parts 1 and 2, Chicago and London, 1965.
LEGGE, JAMES, trans., *The Chinese Classics*. 5 vols. (i: *Confucian Analects, The Great Learning*, and *The Doctrine of the Mean;* ii: *The Works of Mencius;* iii: *The Shoo-king;* iv: *The She-king;* v: *The Ch'un ts'ew* with the *Tso chuen*), Hong Kong and London, 1861–72.
LESSEPS, FERDINAND MARIE, Vicomte de, *Recollections of Forty Years*. Translated by C. B. Pitman. 2 vols., London, 1887.
LEVENSON, JOSEPH RICHMOND, *Confucian China and Its Modern Fate*. 3 vols., London 1958–65.
LEWIS, CHARLTON M., 'The Reform Movement in Hunan (1896–1898)', *Papers on China* (East Asian Research Center of Harvard University), 15 (Dec. 1961), 62–90.
LI HUNG-CHANG, *Lih Wen-chung-kung ch'üan-chi*. Shanghai, 1921.

LIU HSI-HUNG, *Ying-yao jih-chi*, in *Hsiao-fang hu-chai yü-ti ts'ung-ch'ao*, comp. Wang Hsi-ch'i. xi, Shangai, 1891–97.
LIU TS'UN-YAN, 'Ku Hung-ming and His Interpretation of Chinese Civilisation', in *Proceedings of the Symposium on Historical, Archaeological and Linguistic Studies on Southern China, S.E. Asia and the Hong Kong Region*. Hong Kong, 1967, pp. 269–81.
London Gazette. London December 1878.
MACMILLAN, ALLISTER, comp. and ed., *Malta and Gibraltar, Illustrated: historical and descriptive, commercial and industrial facts, figures, and resources*. London, 1915.
MAKEPEACE, WALTER, BROOKE, GILBERT E., and BRADDELL, ROLAND ST. J., *One Hundred Years of Singapore: being some account of the capital of the Straits Settlements from its foundation by Sir Stamford Raffles on the 6th February 1819 to the 6th February 1919*. 2 vols., London, 1921.
MANCALL, MARK, 'China's First Missions to Russia, 1729–31', *Papers on China* (Harvard University Committee on Regional Studies), ix (1955), 75–110.
MARTIN, W. A. P., *A Cycle of Cathay*. 2nd ed., New York, 1897.
MIN ERH-CH'ANG, *Pei-chuan-chi pu*. Peking, 1931.
MORSE, HOSEA BALLOU, *The International Relations of the Chinese Empire*. 3 vols., New York, 1910–18.
MOULE, ARTHUR CHRISTOPHER, *Christians in China Before the Year 1550*. London, 1930.
NEEDHAM, JOSEPH, *Science and Civilisation in China*. 4 vols., Cambridge, 1954–
——, 'Science and China's Influence on the World', in *The Legacy of China*, ed. Raymond Dawson. Oxford, 1964, pp. 234–308.
North China Herald. Shanghai, December 1876, January, June 1877.
ONOGAWA HIDEMI, *Shinmatsu seiji shisō kenkyū* (Studies in Late Ch'ing Political Thought, Oriental Research Series No. 8, Kyoto University). Kyoto, 1960.
OWEN, DAVID EDWARD, *British Opium Policy in China and India* (Yale Historical Publications Studies VIII). New Haven, Conn., 1934.
PARKER, the REVD. A. P., 'The Diary of Marquis Tseng', *The Chinese Recorder and Missionary Journal*, xxii.7 (July 1891), 297–304; xxii.8 (Aug. 1891), 345–53.
PELCOVITS, NATHAN ALBERT, *Old China Hands and the Foreign Office*. New York, 1948.
PELLIOT, PAUL, 'Les Grandes voyages maritimes chinois au début du XVe siècle', *T'oung Pao*, xxx (1933), 237–452.
——, 'Notes additionelles sur Tcheng Houo et sur ses voyages', *T'oung Pao*, xxxi (1935), 274–314.
——, 'Encore à propos des voyages de Tcheng Houo', *T'oung Pao*, xxxii (1936), 210–22.

P'ENG TSE-YI, *Kuo Sung-t'ao chih ch'u-shih Ou-hsi chi ch'i kung-hsien* in *Chung-kuo chin-tai shih lun ts'ung*. Series I, vol. 7, Taipei, 1956.
PIASSETSKII, PAVEL IAKOVLEVICH, *Voyage à travers la Mongolie et la Chine*. Paris, 1883.
PRITCHARD, EARL HAMPTON, 'Confusion about the Portuguese and Other Europeans in Early Ch'ing China: A Case of Cultural Blindness', in *International Symposium on [the] History of Eastern and Western Cultural Contracts*. Japanese National Commission for Unesco, Tokyo, 1959, pp. 117–20.
Punch. London, February 1877.
PURCELL, VICTOR, *The Chinese in Southeast Asia*. 2nd ed., London, 1965.
RAWLINSON, JOHN L., *China's Struggle for Naval Development 1839–1895*. Cambridge, Mass., 1967.
ROWE, DAVID NELSON, ed., Index to *Ch'ing tai ch'ou pan i wu shih mo*. Hamden, Conn., 1960.
SAEKI, P. YOSHIO, *The Nestorian Documents and Relics in China*. 2nd ed., Tokyo, 1951.
San hsing-shih shu tu. 1910.
SCHAFER, EDWARD H., *The Golden Peaches of Samarkand: A Study of T'ang Exotics*. Berkeley and Los Angeles, 1963.
SCHWARTZ, BENJAMIN, *In Search of Wealth and Power. Yen Fu and the West*. Cambridge, Mass., 1964.
——, 'The Chinese Perception of World Order, Past and Present', in *The Chinese World Order: Traditional China's Foreign Relations*, ed. J. K. Fairbank. Cambridge, Mass., 1968, 276–88.
SEIICHI IWAO, ed., *List of Foreign Office Records preserved in the Public Record Office in London relating to China and Japan*. Tokyo, 1959.
SELBY, JOHN, *The Paper Dragon: An Account of the China Wars, 1840–1900*. New York, 1968.
SENDA, MASAO, *Kan'yaku Kammei Seiyō jimmei jiten*. Tenri Daigaku, Tenri, 1964.
SIMONIYA, NODARI ALEKSANDROVICH, *Overseas Chinese in Southeast Asia—A Russian Study*. Ithaca, N.Y., 1961.
The Singapore Directory of the Straits Settlements. Singapore, 1877.
SONG ONG SIANG, *One Hundred Years' History of the Chinese in Singapore*. London, 1923.
STOKES, GWENNETH, *Queen's College, 1862–1962*. Hong Kong, 1962.
Straits Times. December 1876.
TAKIGAWA KANITARO, *Shih-chi hui-chu k'ao-cheng* (Shīkī Kaichū Kosho). Taipei reprint, 1961.
T'ANG, LEANG-LI (T'ang Liang-li), *China in Revolt. How a Civilization Became a Nation*. London, 1927.
TENG SSU-YÜ, and FAIRBANK, JOHN K., *China's Response to the West: A Documentary Survey 1839–1923*. Cambridge, Mass., 1954.

The Times, London, November 1869, November, December 1876, January, February, March, September, November, December 1877, February 1878, December 1907.
TSENG CHI-TSE, *Ch'u-shih Ying-Fa jih-chi*, in *Hsiao-fang-hu chai yü-ti ts'ung-ch'ao*, comp. Wang Hsi-ch'i. xi, Shanghai, 1891–7.
——, *Tseng Hui-min-kung shih-hsi jih-chi* in ibid.
TURNER, FREDERICK STORES, *British Opium Policy and Its Results to India and China*. London, 1876.
VLEKKE, BERNARD HUBERTUS MARIA, *Nusantara: A History of the East Indian Archipelago*. Cambridge, Mass., 1944.
WANG CH'Ü-CH'ANG, *Yen Chi-tao nien-p'u*. Shanghai, 1936.
WANG HSI-CH'I, *Hsiao-fang-hu chai yü-ti ts'ung-ch-ao*. Shanghai, 1891–7.
WANG K'AI-YÜN, *Hsiang-yi-lou jih-chi*. Shanghai, 1927.
WANG, SHÊN-TSU, *The Margary Affair and the Chefoo Agreement*. London, 1940.
WANG, YI CHU, *Chinese Intellectuals and the West, 1872–1949*. Chapel Hill, N.C., 1966.
WEI YÜAN, *Hai-kuo t'u-chih*. 1844.
WENG T'UNG-HO, *Weng Wen-kung kung jih-chi*. Shanghai, 1925.
Whitaker's Almanack. London, 1877–8, 1880.
WIENS, HEROLD JACOB, *China's March Toward the Tropics: a Discussion of the Southward Penetration of China's Culture, Peoples, and Political Control in Relation to the non-Han-Chinese Peoples of South China and in the Perspective of Historical and Cultural Geography*. Hamden, Conn., 1954.
WILSON, SIR ARNOLD TALBOT, *The Suez Canal: Its Past, Present, and Future*. London, 1933.
WITTFOGEL, KARL AUGUST, and FENG CHIA-SHENG, *History of Chinese Society: Liao (907–1125)* (Transactions of the American Philosophical Society, New Series, vol. 36, 1946). Philadelphia, 1949.
WRIGHT, MARY CLABAUGH, *The Last Stand of Chinese Conservatism: The T'ung-chih Restoration, 1862–1874*. Stanford, 1957.
WRIGHT, STANLEY FOWLER, *Hart and the Chinese Customs*. Belfast, 1950.
YANG HUNG-LIEH, 'Chi Kuo Sung-tao ch'u-shih Ying-fa', *Ku-chin*, xi (16 Nov. 1942), 11–15; xii (1 Dec. 1942), 23–32.
YANG LIEN-SHENG, 'Historical Notes on the Chinese World Order', in *The Chinese World Order: Traditional China's Foreign Relations*, ed. John K. Fairbank. Cambridge, Mass., 1968, pp. 20–33.
YEN FU, *Yen yi ming-chu ts'ung-k'an*. Shanghai, 1931.
YÜ CH'ANG-HO, 'Kuo Sung-t'ao yü Chung-kuo wai-chiao', *Yi-ching*, xxxi (1937), 21–4.
YÜAN TSU-CHIH, *Hsi-yang kuan-chien*, in *Hsiao-fang-hu chai yü-ti ts'ung-ch'ao*, comp. Wang Hsi-ch'i. xi, Shanghai, 1891–97.
Yüeh-chang ch'eng-an hui-lan. Pei-yang yang-wu chü, ed.
YUNG, WING, *My Life in China and America*. New York, 1909.

INDEX

Abeel, The Revd. David: American missionary, xxii
Abyssinia (A-po-hsi-ni-ya), 39, 67, 76
Academy of Natural Sciences, Shanghai (School of Investigation and Application), 98, 110
Achilles, viii
Act of Donation, 64
Adam (Ching-ching): a Persian monk, 32
Aden (A-tan: Ya-ting), xix, xxxix, lvi, 36, 37, 38, 39, 41, 62, 70, 76
A-erh-a-t'a: Naval Officer commanding German expedition to the South Seas, 29
A-erh-chi-erh see Algeria
A-erh-pen see Albert
A-fei-li-chia see Africa
A-fei-ssu (Offices), 23
Africa (A-fei-li-chia), 36, 50, 58, 70, 76, 79, 103, 139
Ai-chi, viii
A-k'a-pa see Aqaba
A-k'e-na-heng see Capt. Cornelius O'Callaghan
Aladoni? (A-la-to-ni): an Italian passenger, 12
A-la-to-ni see Aladoni
Albert? (A-erh-pen): Naval commander of 'Borderer', 39, 120
Alcock, Sir Rutherford, xxvii, 83, 153, 154
A-le-fu Sea see Persian Gulf
S.S. 'Alert', 60
Alexandria (Ye-le-san-te), 53, 55, 57, 58
Algeria (A-erh-chi-erh), 65, 76
Allen, The Revd. Young John (Lin Lo-chih): Methodist and American Writer, *A Brief Account of China's Relations with Foreign Countries (Chung-kuo kuan-hsi lüeh-lun); Chiao-hui hsin-pao* (Weekly Review); *Memorandum on the Missionary Question*; 30, 31, 82
A-lo-pen: Nestorian missionary, 32
A-lu-wei-te see Isle of Wight
A-mao, 155
American, xxi, xliii, 12, 39, 72.

American Revolution, 111
Amherst, Lord (1816), xvii
Amoy, 1, 3, 29
A-mu-no-erh see S.S. 'Galley of Lorne'
Amur, 107
Amur River (Hei-lung River), 72
Andijan, 106
Anglo-Chinese War, 67, 68
Anglo-French, 33
Anglo-French forces, xxx
Anglo-French invaders, xxix
Anglo-French War (1857-60), 82, 89
Anglo-Oriental Society for the Suppression of the Opium Trade, 122, 129
An-hsi see Parthia
A-ni-ch'ün Islands see Ionian Islands
An Lu-shan, rebellion of, 43
Annam, xvi, 11, 76, 92
An-sheng see Anson, Sir Archibald
An-sheng, Capt. see Anson, Capt. C. V.
Anson, Sir Archibald Edward Harbord (An-sheng): English Resident Penang, 20
Anson, Capt. C. V. (An-sheng): probably son of Admiral Talavera Anson 1809-95, 19
Ao-ta-hsi-a-ssu see 'Audacious'
Ape's Head Rock (Erh-pu-ssu Ho-te), 67
A-po-hsi-ni-ya see Abyssinia
Aqaba (A-k'a-pa), 49
Arabia, 31, 34, 36, 38, 39, 41, 44, 49, 76
Arctic expedition, 20
A-sa-mi see Assam
Ashbury, J. L., 158
Asia, 50, 58, 61
Asia, Central, xxv, 72
Assam (A-sa-mi), 40, 99
A-ssu-pan see Osborne
A-tan see Aden
Atjeh War, The, 22
Atlantic Ocean, 65, 70, 71, 76
'Audacious' (Ao-ta-hsi-a-ssu): flagship of the China Squadron, xlii, 4, 5, 7, 178
Australia, lii, lvi, 11, 12, 28, 29, 83
Austria, xxi, 55, 139

Avery, Benjamin P.: American Minister in Peking, xxvii
Bāb el-Mandeb Strait, 36
Baldwin, F. G. C.: *A History of the Telephone in the United Kingdom*, 160, 161
Ballāh (Lake Pa-la), 55
Baltic, 69
Baluchistan (Pei-lu-chih), xxi, 30, 76
Barratt, Capt. W. (Pa-la-te): Master of S.S. 'Travancore', xxxix, xlii, 1, 2, 4
Barrington, Viscount, 127
Basingstoke (Po-hsing-ssu-to-k'o), 78, 151
Bayley, Capt. (Pu-lai): P. & O. Agent, 25
Baynes, Maj.-Gen. R. S. (Pei Le-ssu), 67
Beaconsfield, Lord *see* Disraeli, 80
Beal, Edwin G.: *The Origin of Likin*, xxxii
Beatrice, Princess, 119, 156
Bêche-de-mer: delicacy in demand among Chinese gourmets, 11
Belgium, 51
Bengal, 26, 40, 76
Berkshire, 151
Berlin, xli, 1
Bernhard, Helmuth Carl, 30
Beust, Count (Fu-ssu-ta): German Austro-Hungarian, 79
Bhutan (Pu-ta-la), 40
Biggerstaff, Knight: *Chinese Social & Political Science Review; Pacific Historical Review*, xxviii, xxxviii, xl
Biorn: the new opera, xlix
Birch, 20
Bird, Isabella L.: *The Golden Chersonese*, 81
Bismarck, Otto, Prince von (Pi-shih-ma): Chancellor of Germany, 30, 82
Black Sea, 65
Blake, R.: *Note supplémentaire sur Fou-lin*, Journal Asiatique, 50
Board of Punishments, 94
Board of Revenue & Population, 166
Board of Trade, 34, 35
Boat Quay, 81
Bodhisattva of Mt. O-mei, Szechwan (Samantabhadra), 26
Bombay, 38, 53, 75, 76, 77

Bond Street, 152
Bonham Street, 81
'Borderer?' (Po-erh-te): fighting ship, 39
Borel: French engineer, 52
Borneo (Wen-lai Island), 76, 77
Botanic Gardens, 16
Boulger: *Life of Macartney; The Life o, Sir Halliday Macartney*; xxxix, xlvii, xlix, xxxviii, 173
Bourne, F. S. A., *The 19th Century*, xlvii, 134, 141, 143, 144
Braddell, Roland St. J.: *Law and the Lawyers*, 18
Bradford, Earl of, 127
Brazil, Emperor of: Don Pedro II, 139, 141
Brindisi (Po-lin-ti-hsi), 53
Brisbane, 5
Britain, 21, 30, 51, 76
British Empire, The, xlviii
British Superintendency of Trade, 1
Brooke, Gilbert E.: *Botanic Gardens & Economic Notes*, 16
Brown, McLeary, 181
Browne, Col. Horace, 156, 186
Brulos, 58
Brunei, xvi, 77
Brunei, Sultan of, 76
Brussels, xli
Buckingham Palace (Po-chin-ko-en Pa-lei-ssu), xlvii, lvii, 79, 118, 119, 124, 126, 138, 139, 155
Buckley, C. B.: *An Anecdotal History of Old Times in Singapore*, 13
Buddhism, 32, 77
Buddhist Temple, 24, 25, 26
Bukit Barisan, 21
Bull of Pope Paschal II, 64
Bullock, T. L. (T'u Mai-lun), 78, 151, 152, 162
Bureau of National History, lxii
Burlingame, Anson: *Roving Ambassador to the West*, xxvii, xxxvii
Burma, xvi, xxi, 85, 99, 156
Buruts, 90
Byzantium (Fu-lin), xv, 32, 50

Caenarvon, Earl of (Henry Herbert), 155, 156
Caesar (K'ai-sa: Chia-fe sa-erh), viii, 69

Index

Caesarum, 57
Cairo (Chia-yi-lo: K'ai-lo), viii, 52, 53, 58, 117
Calcutta, li, 13, 77
Calicut (Ku-li), xix
Cambodia, xvi, xxi
Cameron, C. D.: Consul in Abyssinia, 40
Cameron, John: *Our Tropical Possessions in Malayan India*, 81, 82
Campbell, J. D.: (Chin Teng-han): Chinese Customs Service, vii, 53, 54, 78, 150, 151, 152, 154
Canning Fort, 81
Canton, xxxl, 10, 62, 98, 129
Cape Finisterre (K'ai-p'o Fei-ni-shih-t'e), 71
Cape Guardafui (Mt. Ya-te-fei), 36
Cape Otranto, Southern Italy, 1
Cape Vincent (Hsing-tzu-wen-sheng): mountain, 70
Cape Varella (Mt. Wa-lei-la): on South-East border of Annam, 11
Celestials, The, 13
Ceylon (Hsi-lan-shan), xviii, xix, xxxix, lvi, 1, 23, 24, 26, 27, 30, 36, 41, 62, 75, 76
Ceylon, Government of, 25
Chai-ni-ssu-t'ai-li-ko-la-mu (*London & China Telegraph*), 169
Champa (Chan-ch'eng), xvi, xix
Chan-ch'eng *see* Champa
Ch'ang-an, 32
Chang Hsieh: *Tung-hsi-yang k'ao*, 77
Chang Hsin-pao: *Commissioner Liu & the Opium War*, 122
Ch'ang-lo, Fukien, xviii
Chang Nan Shu Yuan, The, liv
Chang P'ei-lun, *Chien-yü chi; Ch'ing-chi wai-chiao shih-liao*; lx
Ch'ang-sha, xxxvi, lix, lxi, 129
Chang Ssu-hsiin, 125, 131, 141
Chang Te-yi (*see* also Ts'ai-ch'u; Te-ming; Te Ts'ai-ch'u): *Hang-hai shu chi (Record of my Voyage)*; xli, xlix, xl, lx. *Sui-shi jih-chi (Journal of an Embassy Official)*, xi
Chang T'ing-fan, 42, 45, 51, 168
Chang Tsai-ch'u *see* Chang Te-yi
Chao Feng-yüan, 190
Chao-hui, 90
Chao-wa *see* Java

Chapdelaine, August: French missionary murdered in China 29.2.1856, 33
Charing Cross Station, 151
Charles V, Emperor, 64
S.S. 'Charlotte Dundas', 97
Chefoo Convention (Yen-t'ai), xxviii, xxxvii, li, 30
Chekiang, lix, 2, 100, 108
Chen-chiang, 89, 129
Ch'en Chih-ho: President of the Board of War, xxix, xxx
Ch'en, Gordon: *Tso Tsung-t'ang*, xxii, 13, 106
Ch'eng Hao *style* Ming-tao: great Confucian scholar: *Erh Ch'eng chüan-shu*, 42
Cheng-Ho: Grand Eunuch, xviii
Cheng Hsüan, *style* K'ang-ch'eng: *Hou Han-shu*, 49
Cheng K'ang-ch'eng, 48
Ch'eng, King, 44
Cheng-nan Academy, lxi
Cheng Ts'ao-ju, *style* Yü-hsien: official of Kiangnan Arsenal, Shanghai, 2
Ch'eng Yi, 95
Cheng Yü-hsien, 2
Ch'en, Kenneth, lxiv
Chen-la, 12
Ch'en Lan-pin: Envoy to U.S., Spain & Peru 1875, 1, 154
Ch'en Lun-chiung: *Han-kuo wen chien lu (1744)*, xviii
Ch'en P'ing, 42
Ch'en Ping-hsiang: ship's tea-and-water boy, 24
Ch'en Ta-tuan: *Chinese World Order*, xxv
Ch'en Tu-hsiu (1879–1942): founder-member of the Chinese Communist Party, xlii
Che Wei-li *see* Jervois, Sir William Francis Drummond
Chia-fei-sa-erh *see* Caesar
Chia-la-na-ta *see* Granada
Chiang Yee: *Chinese Calligraphy*, 58
Chia-sa-lei-ko-lai-hsi-ya *see* Marquis de Casa Laiglesia: Spanish Ambassador to London, 79
Chia-ting: Annamese prefecture, 12, 77
Chia-yi-lo *see* Cairo, viii, 38
Chia-ying, xxxi
Ch'ien-lung: Atlas of China, xviii

Index

Ch'ien-lung, Emperor (1736–95), xvii
Chieh-shih, 3
Chih, Andre: *L'Occident 'Chretien' vu par les Chinois sers la fin du XIXe siècle (1870–1900)*, lxiii
Chih-kang, xxxvii, 118
Chih Li, Province of, 187
Chih-pa-lo-to, 69
Chi-lo-mu *see* Guillaume, Herbert
Chi-mi: loose rein, xxxiv
China, xviii, xxii, xxxviii, xliv, xlv, xlviii, l–liv, lvi–lx, lxii, lxiii, 11, 12, 14, 16, 29, 31–35, 39–41, 43, 45, 49–51, 54, 58, 62, 72, 73, 77, 78
China, Emperor of, xi
Ch'i-na-hsi *see* China Sea
China Navigation Steamer, li
China Sea (Ch'i-na-hsi): the Sea of the Middle Kingdom, 11, 77
Chin-chung Yüeh-chuan, 166
Ch'in Dynasty (221–206 B.C.), xxxii, xxxvi, 74
Chin Dynasty (1122–1234), xliii, 43
Chinese in Australia, 189
Chinese Communist regime, lxii
Chinese Folk Lore, 181
Chinese Foreign Office (Tsungli Yamen), xxi, xxvi, xxvii, xxxvi, xxxix, xlvi, 1, 2, 31, 41, 53, 83, 91, 92, 156, 157, 184
Chinese immigrants, 94
Chinese imperium, xvii
Chinese Legation, xlviii
Ching-ching *see* Adam
Ching-chou, 129
Ch'ing Dynasty, xviii
Ching, Sr. Julia, x
Ching-ling, 89
Ching liu party: Purification, 87
Ch'ing-liu faction: Kuo's enemies, xlv
Ch'ing monastery, 32
Ch'ing-pu, 3
Ch'in Kuan (1049–1101): poet, x
Chin-liang, *Chin-shih jen-wu chih*, xxxvi
Chin-shih: doctoral degree, xxix
Chin Teng-han *see* Campbell, J. D.
Ch'in Universal State, xvii
Chi-pa-ta-ta *see* Gibraltar
Chirol, V.: *The Far Eastern Question*, xxi, xxii
Ch'iung *see* Hainan
Ch'i-Ying, 33

Choa Ah Sia: member of Ghee Hok Society, 16
Chōshū forts, 132
Chou Ch'ang-ching, 155
Chou Dynasty, xxiv, xxxii, lxv, 48, 74
Chou Li (The Book of Chou Kuan), 85, 86
Chou philosophers, xvii
Chou Ying-shih, 2
Christ, 32
Christian of Schleswig-Holstein, Prince, 124
Christianity, xlv
Christmas 1877, 164
Chu Hsi (1130–1200), liii
Chü-jen degree, xxix
Chung E, 173
Ch'ung-hou, The Manchu: in charge of Ili negotiations, 1, 72
Ch'ung-hou, style Ti-shan *see* Mukden
Chung-kuo (The Central Kingdom), xvi
Ch'un-kuan tsung-po Shih-san ching ching-wen, ed. of *Chou Li; Ssu-ch'ang*, 48
Chün-shih-tan-ting *see* Constantinople
Church Mission Society, 192
Chusan, 1
Clarke, Col. ? (Ko-la-erh-k'o), 24, 25, 27, 51
Cleopatra, 57
Cleopatra's Needle (K'e-li-a-pei-Ni-te-erh), 57
Coal-mines, 104, 110
Cochin (K'o-chih), xix
Cochin China, 12
Cohen, P. A.: *China & Christianity*, 33, 34, 82
Colomb, Capt. Phillip Howard (Flag Capt. K'uo-lun-pu): *Manual of Fleet Evolutions*, 5, 178
Colombo, 24
Colonial Office List, 1877, 18, 24
Colorado, 45
Collingwood, R.: *The Idea of History*, lxiii
Compton, C. S.: Editor of *North China Herald*, 78
Confucius, xliv, 131
Confucius and Sons, xlii
Constantinople (Chün-shih-tan-ting), 65
Constantinople Conference, 59, 130

Index

Consul-General, Chinese, 154
Consul, Peruvian, 150
Consulates, Chinese, 188
Convention of Peking (24.10.1860), xxv
Cordier, Henri: *Relations de la Chine; Histoire des relations de la Chine avec les puissances occidentales, 1860–1900*, xxxvi, xlvi, xlvii, lvi, lxi, 137
Cornwall (K'o-erh-nu-wa-li-ssu), 74
Corps diplomatique, xlvii
Council Chamber, 64
Court of St. James, xxviii
Cowan, C. D.: Ed. *The Economic Development of China & Japan*, 2, 16, 22, 81. *Nineteenth Century Malaya*, 81
Crabitès, Pierre: *The Spoliation of Suez*, 51
Credentials, 163
Crimea (T'iao-chih): now Arabia, 50
Crimean War, 67
Crown Colony, 72
Crown Prince, 138, 141, 148
Cuba, 94
Cullen, Tom: *The Empress Brown*, 148
Customs Office, Chinese, 145, 146, 150

Daily Press, 184
Daily Telegraph (Tai-li-t'ai-li-ko-la-fu), 171
Damietta (Ta-mi-yeh-te), 58
Dancing, Western, 138, 139, 140
Dardanelles, 65
Darfour, 117
Da Silva (T'i-hsi-la-wa): officer of Ceylon, 26, 27
Dawson? (To-sun): military Attaché, 62
de Casa Laiglesia, Marquis: Spanish Ambassador to London, 79
de Lagrène, Theodore: French envoy, 33
de Lesseps, Ferdinand (Lai Sai-p'u): *Recollections of Forty Years*, translated by C. B. Pitman, 50, 51, 53
Delhi (Te-li-eh), 29, 40
Democracy, Mr., xlii
Denmark, 51
Denny, Dr., 181
Department of Rites, 94
de Penedo, Baron (P'ei-no-tu): Brazilian Ambassador to London, 79

de Rachewiltz, Dr. Boris, 58
Derby, Earl of (Te-erh-pi), l, lii, 78, 79, 150, 155, 156, 163, 164, 188, 189, 193
Derby, Lord, xlix, 59, 119, 120, 126
H.M.S. 'Devastation' (Te-fa-ssu-te-shen): ironclad, 62
Dhyāni-bodhisattvas, 26
Diary of the Hsiang-i Chamber, xxxvi
Dilke, Sir Charles Wentworth, 148
Dillon, Col. (Ti-lung, Col.), 68
Disraeli, xlviii, 78, 80
Don Pedro II: Emperor of Brazil, 139
Donovan, John, xi, 189
Douglas, Mr., 182
Douro (Tou-lo River), 71
Dredges, 83, 84
Dunsheath, P.: *A History of Electrical Engineering*, 161
Dutch, xx
Dutch Government, 22
Dutch Resident, 21
Dutch Treasury, 28
Duyvendak, J. J. L.: *China's Discovery of Africa*, xviii, xix
Dyson, J. W.: South-Western Railway Company's Superintendent at Southampton, 78
Dzungars, 90

East Africa, xviii, 66
Eastern Red Sea (A-le-fu Sea), 34
Eberhard, W.: *A History of China*, 43
Edge, Revd., 177
Edward of Saxe-Weimar, Prince, 124
Egypt (Mai-hsi: Ai-chi), viii, xv, xliii, 45, 49, 50, 51, 57, 58, 72, 76, 103, 117, 139, 153
Eitel, Dr., 175
Electric light, 160
Ellul, Jacques: modern Western thinker, lviii
Ely River, 151
Embroidery Office: Ladies' Work Society, 140
Emil, Albrecht Theodor, 30
Emmanuel, Victor (Fei-tuo-erh-jih-man-nu-erh), 7
Empress Dowager, The, xlvi, lx, lxi
Endacott, G. B.: *A History of Hong Kong*, 5, 6
Endacott, G. B. & Hinton, A.: *Fragrant Harbour*, 6, 10

Index

England, xxi, xliii, xlvii, l, liii, lxi, 3, 11, 23, 29, 36, 39, 41, 51, 59, 61, 64, 65, 67, 70, 72, 74, 80, 93, 94, 139
Erh-pu-ssu Ho-te see Ape's Head Rock
Erh-sheng see Ushant
Erh-ya, 48
Euphrates, 34
Europe, xliii, xliv, xlvi, lvii, lxi, lxiv, 3, 12, 22, 28, 35, 37, 43, 49, 51, 58, 61, 72, 73, 76, 77, 139

Fa-hsien: monk; *Fo-kuo chi* (*Record of Buddhist Countries*), xl
Fairbank, J. K.: *Chinese World Order*, xx, xxxii, 31
Fairbank et al.: *The Modern Transformation*, xviii, xx, 31, 72
Fa-lan-hsi see France
Falconer, Alexander (Fa-na-chien-erh): Assistant Inspector of Schools, 6, 176
Fa Lin-ssu see Vallings? The Revd.
Fa-na-chien-erh see Falconer, Alexander
Fang Hao: *Chung-hsi chiao-t'ung shih*, 5 vols., lxiv
Fa-p'ai-erh: German naval officer, 29
Fe-erh-ting see Fielding?
Fei Li-pu see Ford, Sir Theodore
Fei-tuo-erh-jih-man-nu-erh see Emmanuel, Victor
Fenchurch Street Station, 161
Feng K'uei-chiu, 19, 41, 51, 159, 162, 164
Feng-shui, xxxv
Feng-t'ien, 92
Feng-yi, 125
Feuerwerker, Albert: *China's Early Industrialization*, 2
Fielding? (Fe-erh-ting): Artillery Commander, 69
Fitch, John, 97
Fitzgerald, Percy: *The Great Canal at Suez: Its Political, Engineering and Financial History; The Third China: The Chinese Communities in South East Aia; Stokes Report;* 51, 52, 53, 54, 55, 56, 57, 58
'Fleurs Castle', 8
Flexner, J. T.: *Steamboats Come True*, 97
Fo-lang-chi see Franks

Foochow (Wu-shih-shan), xi, li, lii, 13, 190, 191, 192, 193
Foochow Arsenal, 91
Ford, Sir Theodore (Fei Li-pu): Chief Justice 1886, 18
Foreign Office List, 78, 79
Foreign Office Records, l, lii
Former Han, 12
France (Fa-lan-hsi), xxi, xliii, 1, 3, 23, 30, 33, 41, 51, 61, 64, 65, 72, 74, 76, 92, 139, 167
France, Emperor of, 55
France, Empress of, 55
Franco-Chinese War, 1884–5, 53
Franco-Vietnamese Treaty (1874), 92
Franks (Fo-lang-chi): a term applied to the Portuguese and Spaniards, xxi
Frazer, Mr., 193, 194
French Government, 33
Friend of China, The, 130
Frodsham, Tan Beng-choo, x
Fukien, 3, 102, 108
Fu-lin? see Byzantium?
Fulton, Robert, 97
Fung, E., 175, 178, 181
Fu-ssu-ta see Count Beust

Gallagher, L. J.: *China in the Sixteenth Century*, 33
Galle, 24, 27
S.S. 'Galley of Lorne' (A-mu-no-erh), 55
Ganges River, referred to in Buddhist writings as Heng, 26
Galves, Don Pedro: Peruvian Ambassador to London, 79
Garratt, G. T.: *Gibraltar & the Mediterranean; Gibraltar;* 69
George III, xvii
German Government, 29
Germany, xliii, 1, 3, 23, 30, 65, 72, 139, 162, 165
Ghee Hok Society, 16
Gibraltar (Chi-pa-ta-ta: Jih-pa-la-erh-ta), xxxix, 40, 67, 69, 70, 76, 151
Gibraltar, Rock of, 67, 68
Gideon Ch'en: *Tso Tsung-t'ang*, 13
Gladstone, Mr., xlvii
Gnaeus Pompeius Magnus, 69
Gök Turks (T'u-chüeh), 42
Golden Marmoset (Leontideus rosalia), 16

Index

Goodman, Dan, 171
Goodman, Walter (Ku Man): painter, 165, 166, 167, 168, 169, 170
Gordon, Gen. C. G., 117, 153, 154
Goudberg (Mt. Wan-ku-lu): peak of Bukit Barisan, 21
Government Central School: renamed Victoria College in 1889 and Queen's College in 1894, 6
Government House, Hong Kong, 5, 62, 63, 64, 69, 176, 178
Government School, 175
Gozo, 64
Granada (Chia-la-na-ta), 66
Grant, John T. (Lt.-Gen. Ko-lan-te), 62
'Graphic, The' (K'o-li-ssu), 171
Great Bitter Lake (Salt Lake), 55
Great Britain, lxi
Great Spirit, 29
Greece, xv, 31, 60, 61, 62, 76, 140
Greek Orthodox Church, 32
Greenwich, 45
Gregory, Lady (née Augusta Perse, celebrated by Yeats and Shaw), 24
Gregory, Sir W. H. (Governor K'o-lei-ka-li of Ceylon), 24, 27
Grosvenor, T. G., 134
Grubbe, Commander W. J. Hunt, 63
Guadalquivir Valley (Kuei-mei-a-fei-ssu-pei-yin), 67
Guadarranque River (Kua-ta-erh-chi), 67, 68
Gualgiya clan, 82
Guillaume, Herbert (Chi-lo-mu): Peruvian Consul, 78
Gulf of La-pi-li-ya see Gulf of Nauplia
Gulf of Nauplia (La-pi-li-ya), 62
Gulf of Siam, 12

Haeckel, Ernst: *A Visit to Ceylon*, 25
Hague, The, xli
Hai-lu (Record of the Seas): Accurate Chinese account of Europe, xx, xl
Hainan (Ch'iung), 10, 11, 77
Hall of St. Michael & St. George, 64
Hamburg, xli
Ha-mi-chih: Juchen envoy, 166
Hamilton, D: *Kuo Sung-t'ao: A Maverick Confucian*, xxix, xxxvi, xxxviii, lxii, lxiv
S.S.'Hampton' (Na-mu-tan): a Commercial Steamship Company vessel, 55
Han Dynasty, xxxii, xxxiv, xxxvi, liv, 11, 50, 80, 91, 93, 109
Han Kao-tsu, Emperor, 42
Hankow, 129
Han-lin Academy, xxix
Han-shu, 73
Hart, James H., 137, 153
Hart, Sir Robert (Ho): Inspector General of Customs, xxvii 53, 152, 153, 154
Hawaii, Minister for, 163
Hedley, William, 97
Hei-lung River see Amur River
Helena, Princess, 124
Heng-chou, 104
Heng-te see Hunter?
Herbert, Henry: Earl of Caernarvon, 119
Hertford, Marquis of, 124
Hewlett, A. R. (Yu Ya-mei by Chang: Yu Ya-chih by Liu), 119, 156
S.S. 'Hibernia', 62
Hillier, W. A. (Hsi Tsai-ming): Foreign Secretary, Peking Legation, xxxviii, 1, 10, 19, 28, 30, 41, 53, 54, 78, 115, 119, 147, 150, 152, 156, 175, 177, 178, 183
History of the T'ang Dynasty, 50
Ho, Emperor, 83
Ho see Hart, Sir Robert
Ho Ah Kay (Hu Hsüan-tse: Hu Ch'ing-hsien): Chinese Consul in Singapore, lii, liii, 81, 89
Ho Chin-shou: a Hanlin editor, xxxix, lx
Ho Ch'iu-t'ao, style Yüan-ch'uan, 74
Hochschild, Baron: Swedish Ambassador to London (Ho-shih-ch'ih-la-ta), 79
Ho Ju-chang: first Chinese Ambassador to Japan, 1
Holcombe, C: *The Real Chinese Question*, xxii
Holland, xxi, 21, 28, 51, 77
Hollywood Road Government School, 6
Ho-lo-mo-ssu see Hormuz
Honan, 93
Hong Kong, xxxix, lii, lvi, 1, 4, 5, 6, 7, 8, 10, 12, 13, 18, 25, 29, 72, 76, 121, 151, 173, 175, 182

Hormuz (Ho-lo-mo-ssu), xix
Horsburgh Island, 13
Horsburgh, John: Hydrographer: *India Directory or directions for sailing to and from the East Indies, China, New Holland, Cape of Good Hope, Brazil and the interjacent ports*, 2 vols., 13
Ho-shih-ch'ih-la-ta see Hochschild, Baron
Hospital of St. John of Jerusalem, 64
Ho-te-ssu-po-erh see H.M.S. 'Hotspur'
H.M.S. 'Hotspur' (Ho-te-ssu-po-erh), 62
Hotz, C. D. E. J.: *Beknopt geschiedkundig overzicht van den Atjeh-oorlog*, 22
Ho Yüan-ch'uan, style Ch'iu-t'ao: scholar & historian: *Shuo-fang pei-sheng*, 74
Huai-an, 129
Huai-te, see White, Capt. C. A.
Huang Hui-ho, Major, 2
Huang-p'u, 13
Huang Yü-p'ing, 42, 57, 162
Hu Ch'ing-hsien, style Hsüan-tse (Whampoa) see Ho Ah Kay
Hu Hsüan-tse (Ho Ah Kay), 13, 16, 19, 20
'Hui-yi' (Logical Combinations), 58
Hu-kuang, 120
Hulugalle, H. A. J.: *British Governors of Ceylon*, 24, 27
Hu-men forts, 89
Hummel: *Eminent Chinese*, 3, 33, 83
Hunan, xxxii, xxxvii, lxi, 108
Hung Gardens: public park for Hokkiens & Cantonese, 16
Hung-k'ou, 1, 2
Hung-mao kuei: red-haired devils, xxvi
Hunter? (Heng-te): military officer, 38, 39
Hurgronje, C. Snouck: *De Atjehers*, 2 vols. pub. in English as *The Achinese*, 22
Hu Sheng: Marxist historian, *Ti-kuo chu-yi yü Chung-kuo cheng-chih*, 72
Hsi-ai-la-ni-wa-ta see Sierra Nevada
Hsiang-t'an, 104
'Hsiang-hsing' ('Images'), 58
Hsi-chih-li see Sicily
Hsieh Ch'ing-kao: an illiterate sailor, xx, xxi, lxiv
Hsien-feng period (1851–62), 7, 33

Hsien-lo see Siam
'Hsien-shen' (God of Heaven), 32
Hsien-shen chiao see Zoroastrianism
Hsi-lan-shan see Ceylon
Hsi-li see We Island
Hsing-an mountains (Great Kingdom), 72
Hsing-tzu-wen-sheng see Cape Vincent
Hsing-yao chih-ch'ang (*Handbook of Diplomatic Procedure*), 118
Hsi Tsai-ming see Hillier, W. C.
Hsiung-nu, 42, 73
Hsüan, Duke, 59
Hsüan-tsang: celebrated pilgrim: *Ta T'ang Hsi-yü chi* (*Record of the Western Countries at the time of the Great T'ang Dynasty*), xl
Hsüan-tsung, Emperor, 92
Hsü Ch'ien-shen: Kuo's assistant envoy, xxxviii
Hsü Chi-yu (1795–1873): Governor of Fukien Province: *Ying-huan chih-lüeh* (*Brief Survey of the Maritime Circuit*), first accurate Geography of the World, viii, xxii, 34, 38, 40, 41, 69, 74, 77
Hsüeh Fu-ch'eng: Chinese Ambassador to London, xxii, 72
Hsü Immanuel: *The Ili Crisis: A Study of Sino-Russian Diplomacy; China's Entrance; China's Entrance into the Family of Nations*; xxiv, xxvii, xxviii, xxx, l, lii, lxii, lxiii, 72, 106, 119
Hsü Kuang-ch'i (1562–1633) (Paul Hsü), 32, 33

Ignazi? (Ying-na-chi-ko): an Italian passenger, 12
Ili, 90, 106, 107
Illustrated London News, The, xlviii
'Images' ('*Hsiang-hsing*'), 58
H.M.S. 'Immortalité', 4
India, xv, li, lvi, 11, 12, 15, 28, 40, 53, 72, 76, 77, 99
Indian Ocean (Little Western Ocean), 19, 22, 34
Indies, 28
Indo-China, 77
Indus River, 30
Ionian Islands (A-ni-ch'ün Islands), 61

Index

Ireland, 149
Iron mines, 104, 110
Irrawaddy River, 99
Islam, xv, xliii, 32, 39, 72
Isle of Wight (A-lu-wei-te), 77, 150
Ismailia (Jih-ssu-ma-li-ya), 55
Italy, xxi, 50, 53, 55, 61, 76, 79
I-tu-men, 89

Jackson, R. N.: *Pickering: Protector of Chinese*, 16
Jaffna, 24
Japan, xvi, 1, 12, 72, 101, 107, 116
Java (Chao-wa), xvi, xix, 55
Jervois, Lady (née Lucy Noreworthy), 14
Jervois, Maj.-Gen. Sir William Francis Drummond (Che Wei-li), English Governor, 13, 14, 15, 18, 19, 81, 182
Jesus, 30, 32
Jesus Christ, 31
Jih-ssu-ma-li-ya *see* Ismailia
John IV (Kassa): Chief of Tigre, 40
Johore, xxi
Juan Yüan (1764–1849), xxi
Judea (Yü-t'ai), Turkish, 49, 50
Ju-na *see* H.M.S. 'Juno'
Jung Hung (Yung Wing), 116
H.M.S. 'Juno' (Ju-na), English warship, Commander: J. A. Poland, 19

Kaffir War, 67
Kagashima, 132
Kagenori, Ueno (Wu-yeh-na-ou-chia-chen-no-li): Japanese Ambassador to London, 79, 99
K'ai-lo *see* Cairo
K'ai-p'o Fei-ni-shih-t'e *see* Cape Finisterre
K'ai-sa *see* Caesar
Ka-la-wei-ssu *see* Galves, Don Pedro
K'ang, Prince (Wang Hai-yang), xxxi
K'ang-hsi, Emperor, lxiv
Kansu, 93
Kan Ying, 50, 83
Kaoru, Inoue, 101, 131, 134
Kashgaria, 106
Kashmir (K'o-shih-mi-erh), 40
Kassa *see* John IV
Kazaks, 90
K'e-li-a-pei-Ni-te-erh *see* Cleopatra's Needle

Kennedy, Sir Arthur Edward (H.E. K'eng-erh-ti): Governor of Hong Kong, 5, 8, 10, 14, 175
Key, John of Kircaldy, 1
Khedive: Ismail Pasha, 51, 55
Khitan, 43
Khokand, 106
Kiangsu, lix, 100
King, Frank H. H. & Clarke, Prescott: *A Research Guide to China-Coast Newspapers*, 78
Kipling, Rudyard: *From Sea to Sea and other Sketches*, lvi
Knights of St. John, 61
Ko, 42
Ko, Earl of, 42
K'o-chih *see* Cochin
K'o-erh-li-mo: German naval officer, 29
K'o-erh-nu-wa-li-ssu *see* Cornwall
K'o-la-erh-k'o *see* Clarke? Col. of Ceylon
Ko-lan-te, General *see* Grant, John, T.
K'o-lei-ka-li *see* Gregory, Sir W. H.
K'o-li-ssu *see* '*The Graphic*'
Korea, xvi, xxxviii
Kosala, District of Oudh, 27
K'o-shih-mi-erh *see* Kashmir
Ko-wu: 'Investigating things', liii
Kreemer, J.: *Atjeh*, 2 vols., 22
Kroeber, Alfred L.: *The Nature of Culture*, xiv
S.S. 'Kronprinz', 69
Kuan Ts'ai-shu, 2
Kuang-hsu period (1875–1908), lxii, 1
Kuang-nan, Bay of, 77
Kuantung, 3, 62, 98
Kua-ta-erh-chi *see* Guadarranque River
Kuei-hai (1863–4), 7
Kuei Hao-t'ing, 121
Kuei-mei-a-fei-ssu-pei-yin *see* Guadalquivir Valley
Ku Hung-ming (1857–1928): *Chang Wen-hsiang mu-fu chi-wen*, xliv
Ku-li *see* Calicut
Ku Man *see* Goodman, Walter
Kung, Prince of Manchu House, xvii, 92
Kung-pao, short term for T'ai-tzu Shao-pao, 41
Kuo hsi *see also* lüeh-ching
Kuo-hsiang *see also* Ts'ai Jui-an
K'uo-lun-pu *see* Colomb, Capt. P. M.

Index

Kuo Sung-t'ao, Chinese Ambassador to France: *Shih-hsi chi-ch'eng* (*The Record of an Envoy's Journey to the West*); *Yang-chih shu-wu yi-chi*; *Yü-ch'ih lao-jen tzu-hsü* (*Memoirs of the Old Man of the Jade Pool*); vii, viii, xi, xxvi, xxviii to liv, lvi, lviii to lxii lxiv, 1, 2, 6, 12, 14, 16, 18, 19, 21, 30, 32, 40–43, 51, 52, 55, 58, 61, 64, 66, 67, 69, 72, 73, 76, 77, 81, 120, 157–160, 162, 163, 166–169, 171, 177, 179, 184, 187, 198
Kuo-t'i, the dignity of the State, xliv
Kuril Islands, 107
Ku Yen-wu (1613–82): Scholar, *T"ien-hsia chün-kuo li ping shu*, xviii, xxii
Kwangsi, 92
Kwantung, 89, 90, 108
Kwantung (Yüeh): provincial gazeteer of, xxi, xxxi, xxxii, 19
Kweichow, 31, 33, 34, 85, 93

Labuan, 76
Lach, Donald F.: *Asia in the Making of Europe*, xiv
Lai-hua (come to be transformed), xvi
Lai Sai-p'u *see* de Lesseps, Ferdinand
Lai-te, Admiral *see* Vice Admiral A. P. Ryder
Lake A-mei-ta *see* Tussum
Lake Manzala (Man-sa-lei), 56
Lake Pa-la *see* Ballah
Lake Sai-la-pin *see* Serapeum
Lake T'i-mu-sa *see* Timsah
La-k'o-ssu-mo *see* Luxmore, Capt.
Lambert, Rear-Admiral Rowley (Lan-po-erh-te): Capt. of flagship H.M.S. 'Narcissus', 4
Landport (Lun-tun), 77
Lan-po-erh-te *see* Lambert, Rear-Admiral Rowley
Lan-ts'ang River *see* Saigon River
Laos, xvii
Lao-tzu, lxiv
Lavalley: French Engineer, 52
Law, Chinese, 95
Law, Western, 94
Le Erh-ssu *see* Nares, Sir George Strong
Legge, James: (Lun-yü): *The Analects*; *Doctrine of the Mean*; *Four Books*; *Great Learning* (*Ta-hsüeh*); *The Book of Poetry*; *The Chinese Classics*; *The Works of Mencius*; 42, 112, 113, 122, 131
Le Pi-erh *see* Lord Napier
Letter of State, 117, 119, 120, 156, 163
Levenson, Joseph R.: *Confucian China & the Modern Fate*, lxiii
Lewis, Charlton M.: *Papers on China*, lxii
Li (protocol), xxxii
Li (profit), xliv
Li (one-third of a mile), 2, 3, 10, 11, 12, 13, 19, 20–24, 27–30
Liang Hui Wang, 42
Liao Dynasty (947–1125), xliii, 43
Liberia, Minister for, 163
Li Chao-min, 13
Li Chen-kuo, 85, 86, 121, 156, 157, 187
Li Ch'un-chai, 154
Li Han-chang, 120, 156, 186, 187
Li Hsiang-p'u, 162, 168
Li Hsing-jui, style Mien-lin: official of Kiangnan Arsenal, Shanghai, 2
Li Hung-chang (1823–1901): *Li Wen-chung-kung ch'üan-chi*; *P'eng-liao han-koa*; xxiii, xxviii, xxix, xxx, xxxi, xxxvi, xlv, xlvi, lix, lx, lxii, 2, 30, 72, 91, 96, 97, 121, 131, 156, 157, 187
Li Hung-tsao (1820–97): a conservative, xlvi
Likin (tax on merchants) xxxi, xxxii, li, 107, 108, 137, 145
Li-Ma-tou *see* Ricci, Matteo
Li Mien-lin *see* Li Hsing-jui
Lin-chih *see* Lynch, Lt.-Col. W. W.
Lin-ch'ing, 129
Lin Lo-chih *see* Allen, the Revd. Young John
Lin, Tse-hsü, 122, 123
Lin Wen-chung, Lord *see* Lin Tse-hsü
Lisbon, Port (Li-ssu-po-ya), 70
Li Shu-ch'ang, style Ch'un-chai (1837–1897): Counsellor of the Embassy: *Feng-shih Ying-lun chi* (*1894*); 2, 3, 14, 51, 117, 125
Li-ssu-po-ya *see* Port Lisbon
Li-ssu-te *see* Lister, T. V.
Lister, Patrick (P'ai-de-ssu-li-hsi-te), 11
Lister, T. V. (Li-ssu-te), 79
Li-tajen, 180
Li Tan-ya, 102
Literati, xix, xx, xxx, xxxix, 72
Little Bitter Lake, 54
Liu, Fou-yi, 125, 141, 144

Index

Liu Ho-po, 3, 30, 42, 44, 51, 154
Liu Hsi, 171, 174, 177, 179
Liu Hsi-hung: Diary: *Ying-yao jih-chi (Journal of a Voyage to England)*; xi, xxxviii, xxxix, xlvi, xlvii, l, liv, lvi, lvii, lviii, lx, lxiv, 2, 5, 13, 14, 41, 64, 73, 96, 120, 162, 165, 166
Liu Kwang-ching: *British-Chinese Steamship Rivalry in China 1873–85*, 2
Liu Shu-jen: ship's cook, 23, 24
Liu Ting-shen, lxiv
Liu, Ts'un-yan, Professor: Dean of the Faculty of Asian Studies, A.N.U. *Proceedings of the Symposium on Historical, Archaeological and Linguistic Studies on Southern China, South-East Asia and the Hong Kong Region*, x, xliv
Liu Yün-sheng, 2, 5, 18, 51, 57, 73
Liverpool, 166
Livonius, Captain (Lo-pi), 69
Li Ying-lin, 191
Lo Ch'i-ch'en, 162
Lohan Pine: *Podocarpus Chinensis, Wall*, 17
Loire Province, 74
Loire River (Lo-ya-erh), 71
London, xli, xliv, li, liii, liv, lv, lix, lxi, lxii, 11, 12, 24, 45, 53, 57, 59, 65, 71, 74, 78, 79, 98, 149, 151, 168, 172
Lo-pi *see* Livonius, Capt.
Lo Po-sun *see* Robertson, Sir D. B.
Lord of Heaven *see* Roman Catholicism
Lo-se-te *see* Rosetta
Louis XIV, 64
Louise, Princess, 126, 127, 140
Lo-ya-erh *see* Loire River
Lo Yün-han, 155
Luan, a mythical bird, 14, 17
Luan-t'o *see* Monda
Luard, Rear-Admiral W. E. (Lu-a-te), 62
Lu-a-te *see* Luard, Rear-Admiral W. E.
Lubbock, Sir John, 159
Ludwig II of Bavaria, 82
Lun-ch'uan chao-shang chü (China Merchants' Steam Navigation Company), 2
Lun-tun *see* Landport
Lun-tun chai-na ai-k'o ssu-p'u-lei-ssu (London & China Express), 169
Lun-yü see Legge, J.
Lu-p'ai-erh-te *see* H.M.S. 'Rupert'

Lu-ssu-ma-li-k'uo *see* Roosmalecocq, A.H.
Lü-sung *see* Luzon
Lu-te *see* Luther, Martin
Lu-te *see* von Roon, Count
Luther, Martin (Lu-te), 31
Luxmoore, Capt. (La-k'o-ssu-mo): Naval Instructor, Captain of 'Yang-wu', 16
Luzon (Lü-sung), 77
Lynch, Lt.-Col. William Wiltshire (Lin-chih): Infantry Commandant, 15

Ma *see* Marmora
Macao, xxi, 32, 53, 176
Macartney, Dr. Halliday (Ma Ko-li): Foreign Secretary, Peking Legation: xi, xxxviii, xxxix, xlvi, xlvii, xlviii, xlix, liii, lvi, lx, lxiv, 1, 2, 4, 6, 7, 8, 11, 12, 13, 22, 34, 36, 37, 52, 54, 57, 59, 66, 116, 118, 119, 130, 135, 141, 153, 154, 157, 159, 160, 162, 163, 167, 169, 170
Macartney, Lord (1793), xvii
MacDonald, Sir Richard, 181
Machalia, Signor (Mo-k'o-li-a): Portuguese fellow passenger, 66
Macmillan, Allister: *Malta & Gibraltar—Illustrated*, 64, 68
Madame Tussaud's, 158
'Madonna in Prayer', 165
Madras (Ma-ta-sa-la), 76
Ma-erh-ta *see* Malta
Magdala (Man-ku-te-lin): capital of Abyssinia, 39, 40, 67
H.M.S. 'Magpie' (Ma-ku-pai): English warship, 19
Mahāyāna, 26
Mahood, Mr., 190
Mai-chia *see* Mecca
Mai-hsi *see* Egypt
Mai Hua-t'o *see* Medhurst, W. H.
Mail, The: tri-weekly summary of *The Times*, 19
Makepeace et al.: *One Hundred Years of Singapore*, 16, 18
Ma Ko-li *see* Macartney, Dr. Halliday
Ma-ku-pai *see* H.M.S. 'Magpie'
Malacca (Ma-la-chia), xvi, xxi, 19, 20, 76
Ma-la-chia *see* Malacca
Malaga Port (Ma-li-ya), 66

214 Index

Malay, 20, 21
Malaya, 20, 76
Malayan Archipelago, xviii
Ma-li-ya *see* Malaga Port
Malta (Ma-erh-ta), xxxix, lvi, 61, 62, 63, 64, 69, 76
Malta, Governor of, xlvii
Mancall, M: *Papers on China*, xxv
Manchuria, 83
Manchus, 82, 90
Mandate of Heaven, xxiv, 44
Mañjuśrī: a Bodhisattva, guardian of wisdom, 26
Man-ku-te-lin *see* Magdala
Man-sa-lei *see* Lake Manzala
Man-yün, 99
Mao Hung-pin: Governor General of Kwantung & Kwangsi, xxxi
Mao Li-sun *see* Morrison, C.
Margary, R.: British Consular Officer in China, xxviii, xxxvi, 19, 30, 85, 86, 96, 120, 136, 156, 157, 186
Markham, A. H.: Commander of S.S. 'Alert', 60
Marmora (Ma): sea off Eastern Turkey, 60, 61, 65
Marquis of Salisbury, l, lii
Marseilles (Ma-sai), xli, 41, 65
Martin, W. A. R.: *A Cycle of Cathay*, xxi, xxxvii, xlvii, 64
Ma-sai *see* Marseilles
Masataka, Banno: *China & the West 1858–61*, lxiii, 92
Massawa (Ma-su-a): in Eritrea, 41
Ma-su-a *see* Massawa
Ma-ta-sa-la *see* Madras
Ma-t'i-na-ou *see* Montenegro
May 4th Movement of 1919, xlii
McLeod, Col. W. K. (Mo-li-ya-ssu), 15
Mecca (Mai-chia), 39, 44
Medhurst, Dr. Walter Henry: China missionary, 1
Medhurst, Sir Walter Henry (Mai Hua-t'o): Consul at Shanghai, vii, 1
Mediterranean Sea, 50, 58, 60, 61, 64, 67, 70, 72, 76
Meng-mai (Bombay), Governor of, 36
Meng-tzu, 42
Mencius, xliv, 42, 104
Mencius, Book of, 42
Mesopotamia, xv
Middle Kingdom, xxv, xlv, lxv

Mi-hsü River *see* Minho River
Mi-ko-erh-ssu *see* Nicolls, Brevet-Col. O. H.
Mill, James: *Elements of Political Economy*, 133
Min Erh-ch'ang: *Pei-chuan-chi pu*, xxvi
Ming Dynasty, xvii, xl, 32, 43, 63, 74, 101
Minho River (Mi-hsü River), 71
Min-ssu-ta-erh *see* Münster, Count George
Mirza Malcolm Khan (Nazim-ul-Moulk), 79
Mission of Apology, 1
Missionaries, Christian, xlv
Missionaries, French Catholic, 83
Missionaries, Protestant, 82
Missionaries, Wesleyan, 194
Missionaries, Western, 83
Mi-ti-a-lo-chi-ko a-fei-ssu: meteorological offices, 22
Mocha (Mu-chia): seaport, 39
Mo-erh-kan *see* Morgan ?
Mo-erh-k'o *see* von Moltke, General of Germany
Mogadishu (Mu-ku-tu-shu), xix
Mo-hsi *see* Moses
Mo-k'o-li-a *see* Machalia ? Signor
Mo-la-she-ssu *see* Musurus Pasha
Mo-li-ya-ssu *see* McLeod, Col. W. K.
Mo-lo-ko *see* Morocco
Monda (Luan-t'o), 69
Mondego River, 71
Montenegro (Ma-t'i-na-ou): Italian chargé d'affaires, 79
Montesquieu: *L'Esprit des lois*, translated by Yen Fu, lxi
Morgan ? (Mo-erh-kan): Garrison Commander, 69
Morocco (Mo-lo-ko), 70, 76
Morrison, C. (Mao Li-sun), 27
Morse, H. B.: *The International Relations of the Chinese Empire*, 88
Mo-san-pi-kei *see* Mozambique
Moses (Mo-hsi), 31, 32, 49, 50
Moslems, 106
Mossman, Samuel (Mu Ssu-man): former editor of *North China Daily News*, 78, 150
Mo-tzu, 145
Moule, A. C.: *Christians in China Before the Year 1550*, 32
Mt. Hsi-nai *see* Sinai

Index

Mt. Wa-lei-la *see* Cape Varella
Mt. Wan-ku-lu *see* Goudberg?
Mt. W'tai *see* Shansi
Mt. Ya-te-fei *see* Cape Guardafui
Mozambique (Mo-san-pi-kei), 66
Mu-chia *see* Mocha
Mudaliyar, 24
Mukden (Ch'ung-hou, style Ti-shan): member of Wanyen Clan & Manchu Bordered Yellow Banner; Junior Guardian of Heir Apparent; Military Governor, 41, 82, 118, 119
Mu-ku-tu-shu *see* Mogadishu
Munda, battle of, 69
Münster, Count George (Min-ssu-ta-erh), 79, 153
Murton, Henry James: Superintendent of Botanic Gardens, 16
Mu Ssu-man *see* Mossman, Samuel
Musurus Pasha (Mo-la-she-ssu): Turkish Ambassador to London, 79

Na-mu-tan *see* S.S. 'Hampton'
Nanking, lix, 98, 100
Nan-tien, 86
Napier, Gen. Sir Robert (Le Pi-erh): present Governor of Gibraltar, later Lord of Magdala, 40, 67, 68, 69
Naples, 51
Napoleon, Louis (Na-po-lun), 33, 64
Napoleon III, 70
Napoleonic Wars, 61
Na-po-lun *see* Napoleon, Louis
H.M.S. 'Narcissus': flagship commanded by Rear-Admiral Rowley Lambert, 4
Na-erh-ssu *see* Nares?
Nares? (N-erh-ssu), 62
Nares, Sir George Strong (Le Erh-ssu): English Captain, led the Arctic expedition: *Narrative of a voyage to the Polar Sea during 1875–76*, 2 vols., 19, 20, 60
Na-sai-mu-ma-la-k'e-mu Khan *see* Mirza Malcolm Khan: Persian Prince
Nassau, Prince of, 64
National Gallery, 165
Needham, Joseph: *Science & Civilization in China; The Legacy of China* ed. by R. Dawson, xiv, xviii, xix, liv, 52
Needles, The (Ni-lo-ssu), 77, 150
Neo-Confucianism, xxviii, lvii, lviii

Nepal, 27
Nestorianism, 32
Netherlands, xxi, 28
New Cambridge Modern History, The, 69
H.M.S. 'Newcastle': part of squadron under command of Rear-Admiral Rowley Lambert, 4
New Gold Mountain: English name for Australia, 12
Nicolls, Brevet-Col. O. H. (Mi-ko-erh-ssu), Artillery Commander, 15
Nile River (Ni-lo), 56, 58
Ni-lo *see* Nile River
Ni-lo-ssu *see* Needles, The
Ningpo, 89, 98
North China Daily News, 150
Northcote, Sir Stafford: Leader of the House of Commons, 80
North Pole, 60
Northern & Southern Foreigners' Board, 2
Northern Sung Dynasty (1127), xxxii, 42, 91
Nubia (Nu-po-ya), 45, 76
Nu-po-ya *see* Nubia

O'Callaghan, Capt. Cornelius (A-k'e-na-heng): Aide-de-Camp to Governor of Hong Kong, vii, 5, 6, 7, 8
Oikoumene: Asian land-mass, xv
Old Scholar's Society, 140
O-li-sa *see* Orissa
Opium smoking, 100, 105
Opium War, 1, 33, 98, 111
Opporto *see* Portugal
Ord, Sir Harry (1819–95), Governor, 16
Oriental Hotel, 24
Orissa (O-li-sa), 76, 77
Orthodox Church, 76
Osborne (A-ssu-pan), xlviii, 77, 79, 118, 119, 150, 154
Ottoman Empire, 51
Ou-wo-lun-mei see Overland Mail
'Overland Mail' (Ou-wo-lun-mei), 168
Owen, D. E.: *British Opium Policy in China and India*, li, liii
Oxford, 59
Oxford Street, xlix, 152

216 Index

Paddington, 163
Pahang, xxi
P'ai-de-ssu-li-hsi-te *see* Lister, Patrick
P'ai-la-su Islands *see* Paracel Islands
P'ai-sen: German naval officer, 29
Pa-la-erh-ta, 69
Pa-lan-ta *see* von Brandt, Max
Pa-la-te *see* Barratt, Capt. W.
Palembang (San-fo-chi), xix
Pali: *Namo* (Sanskrit: *Namah*), 26
Pamir, 106
Pan Ch'ao: *History of the Eastern Han (A.D. 25-220)*, 50
Pan Ch'ao: Military Governor of Central Asia, 83
Pangkor Treaty, 16
P'ang-p'ei *see* Pompey
Pang-ssu-fo-te *see* Pauncefote, Sir Julian
Pan Ku: *Ch'ien Han-shu Tsan (Appreciation)*, 73
Panskaya, Miss Ludmilla: research assistant, x
Pao-ch'ing, 104
Pao-chün, 109
Paracel Islands (P'ai-la-su Islands), 11
Paris, xli, l, 168
Parliament, lv
Parthia (An-hsi), 50
Pasha of Egypt, 55
Pauncefote, Sir Julian (Pang-ssu-fo-te), liii, 79, 164
Pedder's Wharf, 176
Pei-ho forts, 67
Pei-hsia-wa-erh (S.S. 'Peshawur'): vessel double the size of 'Travancore'
Pei Le-ssu *see* Baynes, Major-General R. S.
Pei-lu-chih *see* Baluchistan
P'ei-no-tou *see* de Penedo, Baron: Brazilian Ambassador to London
P'ei Yin: *Shih-chi*, 42
Peking, xli, xlvii, l, li, lxi, 19, 45, 53, 67, 88, 92, 172
Peking Legation, xxxviii
Pelcovits, Nathan: *Old China Hands & the Foreign Office*, xxvii, 30
Penang (Pi-lan): Betelnut Island, lvi, 1, 19, 20, 21, 76
Penang *babas*: Chinese settled in Penang for several generations and married to Malay women, 21
Peng Tse-yi, xxix, xliv, lxii, lxiv

Pen-p'iao (modern P'ang-p'ei) *see* Pompey
Perellos, Grand Master, 64
Perim (Pi-erh-lin), 36, 40, 76
Persia (Po-ssu), 34, 76, 77
Persian Gulf (A-le-fu Sea), xviii, 34
Peru, xxi, 1, 94
S.S. 'Peshawur' (Pei-hsia-wa-erh), 25, 36, 75, 77
Phillips: British Customs Commissioner, 78, 150
Piassetskii, P.: *Voyage à travers la Mongolie et la Chine*, xxii
Pi Ch'i-lin *see* Pickering, W. A.
Pickering, William Alexander (Pi Ch'i-lin): Chinese Interpreter/Police Magistrate/Protector of Chinese Immigration, 15, 16, 182
Piedmont, 51
Pi-erh-lin *see* Perim
Pierrepont, Hon. Edwards (Pi-lo-erh): American Ambassador to London, 79
Pi-ken-shih-fei-erh-te *see* Beaconsfield, Lord
P'i-lan *see* Penang
Pi-lo-erh *see* Pierrepont, Hon. Edwards
Pin Ch'un, xli, 155
Pin Ch'un Mission, xl
P'ing-ch'eng, 42
Pi-shih-ma *see* von Bismarck, Prince Otto
Plain Red Banner, 82
Po, 42
Po-chin-ko-en Pa-lei-ssu *see* Buckingham Palace
Po-erh-te *see* 'Borderer?'
Po-hsing-ssu-to-k'o *see* Basingstoke
Po-lai *see* Port Said
P'o-lan, Capt. *see* Poland, Capt. James A.
Poland, Capt. James A. (Capt. P'o-lan), 19
Po-lin-ti-hsi *see* Brindisi
Pompey (P'ang-p'ei: transcribed as Pen-p'iao), viii, 69
Ponsonby-Fane, 127
Port Almeira (Ya-erh-mei-li-ya), 66
Port Malaga, 66
Port Said (Po-lai), 55, 56, 59
Portland Place (Po-k'o-lun-po-li-ssu), cellars of, xlix, 45, 54, 78, 152
Portsea (P'o-tzu), 77

Index

Portugal (Opporto), xxi, 51, 65, 70, 71, 76
Po-ssu *see* Persia
Pottinger, Sir Henry, 1
P'o-tzu *see* Portsea
Po-wu-chih: *Record of Natural Sciences*, 153
Pritchard, Earl H.: *International Symposium on the History of Eastern & Western Cultural Contacts*, xxi
Privy Council, 86, 87
Protestantism, 32
Prussia, 51
Public Relations Office, P. & O., 1, 25
'Puffing Billy', 97
Pu-lai *see* Bayley, Capt.
Pu-lu-k'o-pa *see* Punjab?
Punch, xlviii
Punjab? (Pu-lu-k'o-pa), 40
Purcell, V.: *The Chinese in South-East Asia*, xix
Pu-ta-la *see* Bhutan

Qadir Khan, 43
Quarterly Review: 'Geographic & Scientific Results of the Arctic Expedition', 60
Queen's House: residence used by Governors of Ceylon visiting Galle, 27
Queensland, 5
Queen's Theatre, xlix

Railways, lxv, 97, 98, 103, 110, 111, 114, 115, 117, 118, 129, 131, 132
Reclining Buddha, 26
Red Sea, xlvi, 36-39, 41, 45, 50, 53, 70, 71, 75, 76, 117
Reform Movement, 31
Regent's Park, 152
Regiment, H.M's 28th, 7
Regulations for the Navigation of the Suez Canal, 54
Reuter Political Telegram, 24
Ricci, Matteo (Li Ma-tou): Jesuit: Journals, xx, xli, liii, 32, 33
Richard, Timothy, 31
Richards, Capt. Frederick, 51, 63
Richardson, Gen. John Luther of the East India Company, 62
Richardson, Charlotte Louisa: youngest daughter of above and wife of Governor Van Straubenzee, 62
Richardson, Mrs. Thelma, x
Robertson, Sir Daniel Brooke (Lo Po-sun): Canton Consul, 5, 8, 178, 181
Roman Catholicism (Lord of Heaven), 31, 32, 33
Roman Pope, 32
Rome, xv, xliii, 51, 72
Roosmalecocq, A. H. (Lu-ssu-ma-li-k'uo): Judge of Ceylon, 24, 25
Rosetta (Lo-se-te), 58
Rowe, David Nelson: edited *Index to Ch'ing tai ch'ou pan i wu shih mo*, 54
Royal Literary Fund, liii
H.M.S. 'Rupert' (Lu-p'ai-erh-te), 62
Russia, xxv, xliii, lxi, 23, 30, 59, 61, 62, 65, 72, 92, 106, 107, 130
Russo-Japanese War, 107
Ryder, Vice Admiral Alfred Phillips (Admiral Lai-te): *Methods of ascertaining the distance from ships at sea* (3rd edition), 3, 5, 174, 175
Ryuku Islands, xvii, xl

Sabah, 77
Sacred Edict, 33
Saeki, P. Y.: *Nestorian Documents & Relics in China*, 32
Sages, 32
Saigon, 12, 77
Saigon River (Lan-ts'ang River), 12
Sai-ko-luan (cyclone), 22
St. Andrew, 45
St. James's Palace, 123, 125, 155
St. Paul's, 142
St. Petersburg, xli, l
Sakhalin, 107
Śākyamuni, 26
Salt Lake *see* Great Bitter Lake
Salvador, Minister for: 163
Samantabhadra (Viśva-bhadra): another Bodhisattva, Right hand Assistant of Buddha, 26
Sa-ma-ssu-te, General *see* Major-General Somerset
San-fo-chi *see* Palembang
San Francisco, 93
San-yüan-li, 111
Sarawak, 77
Sassoferrato *see* 'Madonna in Prayer'
Satsuma, 132

218 Index

Schafer, Edward H.: *The Golden Peaches of Samarkand: A study of T'ang Exotics*, 11
Schall (1591-1666): a Jesuit, liii
School of Investigation & Application *see* Academy of Natural Sciences
Schwartz, Benjamin: *In Search of Wealth & Power; The Chinese World Order* ed. by J. K. Fairbank, xiv, lxi, lxiii, 13
'Science, Mr.', xlii
Scotland, 1, 25, 118
Scottish Association, 139
Selby, J.: *The Paper Dragon*, 90
Self-Strengthening Movement (tzu-ch'iang), xxiii, xxiv, xxxv
Seng-ko-lin-ch'in, Prince: famous Mongolian General, xxix
Serangoon Road, 81
Serapeum (Lake Sai-la-pin), 55
Serbia, 59
Seton-Watson, R. W.: *Disraeli, Gladstone & the Eastern Question*, 59
Seven Island Sea, 11
Seymour, Sir Francis, 118, 155, 156, 163
Shanghai, xli, xlvi, lxi, 1, 2, 4, 12, 41, 59, 65, 71, 78, 80, 88, 89, 96, 110, 145, 146, 147, 150, 162
Shanghai Customs Commissioner, 2
Shan-hai ching (*Classic of Mountains & Seas*): xl
Shan-mai: veins of the earth, xxxv
Shansi (Mt. W'tai), 26, 93
Shan-t'ou *see* Swatow
Shantung, 187
Shan-yü, 42
Shao, Duke: 44
Shaw, 24
Shen-pao: a Shanghai paper, 166, 167, 168, 169, 170, 171
Shen Pao-chen, style Yu-tan: 91, 96, 109
Shensi, 32, 93
Shen Yu-tan *see* Shen Pao-chen
Shih-t'an, 104
Shun, xxxvii
Siam (Hsien-lo), xvi, xix, 76
Siam, king of, 40
Sian, 32
Sicily (Hsi-chih-li): Italian Island, 61
Sierra Nevada (Hsi-ai-la-ni-wa-ta), 66, 69

Silvertown, 161
Silvertown India Rubber Works, 160
Simoniya, N. A.: *Overseas Chinese in South East Asia—A Russian Study*, xix
Sinai (Mt. Hsi-nai), 49
Sinclair, Consul: 191, 192
Singapore, lvi, 1, 4, 12, 13, 15, 16, 18, 19, 41, 45, 76, 182, 188, 189
Singapore Directory of the Straits Settlements, 15
Sinkiang, 106
Sino-French Convention, 1860: 33
Sino-French Treaty of Tientsin, 33
Sino-French War, 87
Smale, Sir John (Szu-mei-erh-ssu): Chief Justice, vii, 5, 175, 176
Smith, Adam: *The Wealth of Nations*, 133
Socotra (Su-k'o-te-la), 36, 76
Somerset, Maj.-Gen. (Sa-ma-ssu-te, Gen.), 67
Son of Heaven (T'ien-tzu), xvi, xvii, 141
Song Ong Siang: *One Hundred Years' History of the Chinese in Singapore*, 81
Southampton (Su-shih-a-mu-tun), 55, 75, 77, 78, 98, 151
South Australia, Governor of, 81
Southern Sung Dynasty (1127-1279), xxxiii, 42, 43, 91, 109
Southern Seas (Straits Settlements), 72, 76
South Kensington, 141
South Sea Islands (S.E. Asia), 77
South Seas, 28, 29, 40
Spain, xxi, 1, 3, 30, 51, 65, 66, 67, 69, 70, 71, 76, 77
Ssu-chüeh-erh-te *see* Stewart, Frederick
Ssu-li-wen-sheng *see* Stevenson?
Ssu-te-lo-pan-hsi *see* Van Straubenzee, General Sir Charles T.
Steamships, lxv, 97, 98
Stephenson, Sir Rowland: Railway Engineer, 102, 129
Stevenson? (Ssu-li-wen-sheng), 40
Stewart, Frederick (Ssu-chüeh-erh-te): Inspector of Schools, 6, 175, 176
Stokes, Gwenneth: *Queen's College*, 6
Stonecutter's Island, Hong Kong: convict hulk, 8
Straits *see* Dardanelles
Straits of Malacca, 22

Index

Straits Settlements, 12, 15, 22, 72, 76
Straits Settlements, Government of, 81
Straits Times: Editorial, lxiv, 13, 16
Sudan, 117
Su-erh-shih *see* Suez
Suez (Su-erh-shih: Su-sai), xl, 49, 50, 51, 52, 53, 54, 70
Suez Canal, 22, 36, 51, 55, 77
Sui Dynasty, 99
Sui-pien Cheng-shih: *Investigation into the Realities of the History of Frontier Pacification*, xxxiv, xl
Su-k'o-te-la *see* Socotra
Sultan of Kedah, 21
Sultan of Turkey, 59
Sulu, xvii
Sumatra, 21, 28, 77
Sun Chia-ku, xxxvii, 118
Sungari River (Sung-hua River), 72
Sung Dynasty, lix, 41, 43, 74, 101
Sung-hua *see* Sungari River
Sung Sheng, lxiv
Su-shih-a-mu-tun *see* Southampton
Su-tsung, Emperor, 43
Swatow (Shan-t'ou), 3, 129
Sweden, xxi
Switzerland, xxi, 51
Szechwan, 31, 33, 34, 93
Szu-mei-erh-ssu *see* Smale, Sir John

Ta Ch'in: present day Rome, 50
Ta-ch'in monastery, 32
Ta-fan-k'ou-erh *see* S.S. 'Travancore'
Tagus River, 70
Tai-li-t'ai-li-ko-la-fu see 'Daily Telegraph'
Taiping rebellion, xxix, xxxi, xxxii
Taipings, 82, 105, 117
Tai Sheng, 147
Tai-shu: pouch rat: kangaroo, 14
T'ai-tsung, 43
T'ai-tzu Shao-pao *see* Kung-pao
Taiwan, 3
Takigawa Kamitarō: *Shih-chi hui-chu k'ao-cheng*, 42
Taku, xxix, 89
Ta-mi-yeh-te *see* Damietta
Ta-mo-sen *see* Tomlin, G. L.
T'ang the Completer: legendary founder of the Shang State, 42
T'ang Dynasty, xxxii, 32, 43, 50, 91, 99, 109

Tangalla, 24
T'ang Liang-li: *Chinese in Revolt*, 83
T'ang Te-chün, 121
Tan-pu-lai *see* Templer, F. B.
Tao, lvii, 72
Tao-kuang, Emperor, 105
Tao-kuang period 1821–51, 33
Tathāgata: Śākyamuni Buddha, the 'Once Released', 27
Taylor, A. J. P.: *The Struggle for Mastery in Europe 1848–1918*, 51, 59
Te: moral influence: virtue, xxxii, 23
Tea-parties, 136, 138, 139
Technology, Chinese, lxv
Technology, Western, 112, 113
Teck, Duke of, 124
T'e-erh-le *see* Taylor?
Te-erh-pi *see* Derby, Earl of
Te-fa-ssu-te-shen *see* H.M.S. 'Devastation'
Tejen River *see* Tagus
Te-la-fa-erh-gan *see* Trafalgar Bay
Telephone, 161
Te-li-eh *see* Delhi
Te-ming *see* also Chang Te-yi, 118, 119, 125
Templer, F. B. (Tan-pu-lai): Military Secretary, 24, 25
Ten Commandments, 49
Teng & Fairbank: *China's Response to the West*, lxi, lxiii
T'eng Wen-kung (B), 42
T'eng-yüeh, 86, 87
Tenterden, 164
Test River, 151
Te Tsai-ch'u *see* also Chang Te-yi, 2, 3, 19, 41, 45, 51
Thames, 57
Theodore II, 40
Three Dynasties, 103, 109
H.M.S. 'Thunderer' commanded by Capt. Colomb, 5
Ti: barbarians, xxxiii, 42, 43
T'iao-chih *see* Crimea
Tibet, Northern; 43
Tibetan lamas, 26
T'ien-hsia (All Under Heaven), xvi
Tientsin, 31, 82, 90, 98, 129, 147
Tientsin affair, 31, 33, 41
Tientsin Massacre, 31
T'ien-tzu see Son of Heaven
Tigre (T'i-ko), 55
Tigris, 34

T'i-hsi-la-wa *see* Da Silva
T'i-ko *see* Tigre
Ti-li-po-li *see* Tripoli
Ti-lung, Col. *see* Dillon?
'Times, The', xlix, l, li, 19, 41, 53, 55, 57, 62, 63, 69, 70, 77, 78, 166
Timsah (Lake T'i-mu-sa), 55
Ting Jih-ch'ang, 91
Toi-fung: typhoon, 22
Tomlin, G. L. (Ta-mo-sen): Assistant Jailer of Victoria Gaol, 8, 9
Tongking, 92
H.M.S. 'Topaze': part of Squadron under command of Rear-Admiral Rowley Lambert, 4
To-sun *see* Dawson?
'Tottering Lily of Fascination' (Madame Kuo): Kuo's concubine, xlviii, lx
Tou-lo River *see* Douro
Tower of London, 132, 149, 159
Trafalgar Bay (Te-la-fa-erh-gan), 70
S.S. 'Travancore' (Ta-fan-k'ou-erh): P. & O. mail steamer, xxxix, xlii, lxiv, 1, 7, 25
Treaty Ports, xxvii
Treaty of Aigun, 72
Treaty of Campo Formio, 61
Treaty of Kiakhta, 72
Treaty of Livadia (1879), 72, 119
Treaty of Nerchinsk, 72
Treaty of Paris, 61
Treaty of Peking, 72
Treaty of Saigon, 12
Treaty of St. Petersburg, lx
Treaty of Tilsit, 61
Trincomalee, 24
Tripoli (Ti-li-po-li), 59, 61, 76
Ts'ai Jui-an, styled Kuo-hsiang: aide to Tseng Kuo-fan, 13, 116
Ts'ai Kuo-hsi: Ts'ai Kuo-hsiang's younger brother, 13
Ts'en Yu-ying, Governor of Yunnan & Kweichow, xi, xxxvi, 85, 86
Tseng Chi-kang, lix, 100
Tseng Chi-tse, Marquis: *Tseng Hui-min-kung shih-hsi jih-chi*, xxx, li, lvii, lx, lxi, lxii, 81
Tseng Kuo-fan: most powerful statesman of the T'ung-chih period, xxiii, xxiv, xxviii, 13
Tso-chuan, 59
Tso Ping-lung, 81

Tsungli Yamen: Chinese Foreign Office, xxi, xxvi, xxvii, xxxvi, xxxix, xlvi, 1, 2, 31, 41, 53, 83, 91, 92, 156, 157, 184
Tuan Hsi-yi (Tuan Sheehey?), 21
T'u-fan, 43
Tu Lien-che: *Biography of Ho in Hummel; Eminent Chinese*; 74
Tulisen: *Yi-yü lu*, lxiv
T'u Mai-lun *see* Bullock, T. L.
T'ung-chih period, xxviii, 13, 50, 51, 55
T'ung-chih Restoration, lxiii
Tungusic Jurchen: ancestors of the Manchus, 43
Tunis, 51, 65, 76
Tunisia (T'u-ni-ssu), 64
T'u-ni-ssu *see* Tunisia
Turkey, 58, 59, 61, 64, 65, 76, 130, 143
Turner, F. S., 122, 130
Turyūd, lxiv
Tuscany, 51
Tussum (Lake A-mei-ta), 55
Tyndal, liii
Tzu: styles, vii
Tzu: watch, 1
Tzu-Ch'iang *see* Self Strengthening Movement
Tz'u Hsi, Empress Dowager, xxxix

Uighurs: Turkish, 43
Underground Railway, London, 133
United States, 1, 30, 154
United States of America, 51
Urumchi, 106
Ushant (Erh-sheng), 74

Valleta, 62
Vallings?, The Revd. (Fa Lin-ssu), 36 37
Van Straubenzee, General C. T. (Ssu-te-lo-pan-hsi): Governor and Commander-in-Chief, Malta, 62, 64
S.S. 'Venetia' (Wei-ni-ha), 53, 75
Venice, 61
Verbiest (1623–88): Jesuit, liii
H.M.S. 'Victor Emmanuel' (Fei-tuo-erh-jih-man-nu-erh): wooden sailing vessel named after the ruler of Italy, Capt. George W. Watson, 7
Victoria Gaol, 8

Index

Victoria, Queen: raised to Empress of India; xi, xlviii, lvii, 20, 40, 117, 120, 128, 131, 138, 141, 148, 150, 156, 161, 163, 186
Victoria Station, 162
Vidal-Dubray, 53
Vlekke, Bernard H. M.: *Nusantara*, 22, 28
Von Bismarck, Prince Otto (Pi-shih-ma): Chancellor, 30
Von Brandt, Max (Pa-lan-ta): German Ambassador, 137
Von Gabbin, A.: '*Ein Beitrag zur Fu-lin*' (Sinica), 50
Von Moltke, Count (Mo-erh-k'o): General, 30
Von Roon (Lu-te): Military Councillor, 30, 31, 82

Wa-ch'en-han *see* Waghorn, Thomas
Wade, Sir Thomas, xxvii, xxviii, xxxvi, xxxvii, xxxviii, 1, 30, 88, 96, 106, 107, 110, 115, 116, 118, 119, 120, 121, 153, 156, 157, 163, 168, 175, 182, 186, 187
Waghorn, Thomas (Wa-ch'en-han): English naval lieutenant, 53
Wai-fan: external vassals, xvii
Wales, Prince of: 123, 124, 125, 126
Walker Art Gallery, 166
Wa-lu-k'a-la-ma temple (Vālukārāma: means 'Sand Hermitage'), 27
Wan-chou: south of Ch'iung (Hainan), 10
Wang Chü-ch'ang: *Yen Chi-tao nien-p'u*, xli
Wang Fu-chih (1619–92): Ch'ing materialist philosopher, xxix, liii
Wang Hai-yang *see* Prince K'ang
Wang K'ai-yün: *Hsiang-yi-lou jih-chi*, xxx, xxxvi, xxxvii, xxxix
Wang Po-ch'iu, xix
Wang, S. T.: *The Margary Affair & the Chefoo Agreement*, xxviii, 30, 121, 156, 157
Wang Wen-ch'ing: Hokkien businessman in Penang, 20
Wang Yang-ming (1472–1528), liv
Wan-kuo kung-pao (*The Globe Magazine*, later called *Review of the Times*): originally a weekly review *Chiao-hui hsin-pao*, 31

Wan-li period, 32
War of Spanish Succession, 67
Washington, George, 111
Watson, George W.: captain of H.M.S. 'Victor Emmanuel', 7
Wei-erh-ssu-li *see* Wellesley Province
Wei-li-le: a European lady, 29
Wei-li-ya-mo I, *see* Wilhelm I, Emperor
Wei-ni-ha *see* S.S. 'Venetia'
We Island (Hsi-li), 21
Wei-te-lin *see* Wellington
Wei Yüan: *Hai-kuo t'u-chih* (*1844*), xxii
Wellesley Province (Wei-erh-ssu-li), 19, 21, 76
Wellington (Wei-te-lin), 70
Wells of Moses: an oasis 3 miles from Suez, 52
Welton, The Revd., 190
Weng T'ung-ho (1830–1904): tutor to the Emperor: *Weng-kung kung jih-chi* (*ting-mao*) *Weng wen-kung kung jih-chi* (*yi-wei*); *Ch'ing-shih lieh-chuan*, xxvi
Wen-hsiang, 82
Wen, King: Father of King Wu, 42
Wen-lai Island *see* Borneo
Wen-tse *see* Windsor
Wen Wen-chung-kung, 31
West, The; xl, xli, xlii, xliv, xlv, liv, lvi, lix, lxiii
Western Han Dynasty, 50, 69
Western Mongols, 90
Western (Protestant) religion, 31
Westminster Abbey, 143, 144
Whampo, Mr., 182, 183
Whampoa House, 81
Whampoa *see* Hu Ch'ing-hsien
Wheatley, P.: *The Golden Chersonese: Studies in the Historical Geography of the Malay Penninsula before A.D. 1500*, xix
White, Capt. C. A. (Huai-te) of S.S. 'Peshawur', 25, 36, 60, 77
Wiens, H. J.: *China's March toward the Tropics*, xix
Wilhelm I, Emperor (Wei-li-ya-mo I), 29, 30
William IV, 120
Wilson, A. T.: *The Suez Canal*, 52, 53
Windsor (Wen-tse), 79, 163
Windsor, Queen of, xli

Wittfogel, K. A. & Feng chia-sheng: *History of Chinese Society: Liao*, 43
Wo-jen (1804–72): a leading conservative, xxvi
Woking (Wo-to), 78, 151
Wolfe, John Revd.: Church of England missionary, lii, 190, 191, 192
Woosung, 173
Wo-to *see* Woking
Wright, Mary C.: *Chinese Conservatism; The Last Stand of Chinese Conservatism*, lxiii, 51
Wright, S. F.: *Hart & the Chinese Customs*, 54
Wu, King: founder of Chou Dynasty: *see also* King Wen, 42
Wu, Madame: wife of J. D. Campbell, 151, 152
Wu-ch'ang, 193
Wu-ch'ang, siege of, xi, xxix, lii
Wu Lan-hsiu, lxiv
Wu-shih-shan *see* Foochow
Wu-shih-shan Mission, 190, 191, 192
Wu-sung railway, 136
Wu T'ing-fang, 154
Wu-yeh-na-ou-chia-chen-no-li *see* Ueno Kagenori: Japanese Ambassador

Ya-erh-mei-li-ya *see* Port Almeira
Yakub Beg: Khokandian soldier, 106
Yang-chou, 129
Yang Hung-lieh, lxiv
Yang Ping-nan, lxiv
Yangtse River, 99, 129
Yang-wu: Foreign affairs group, xxx
'Yang-wu': naval paddle steamer, 13, 16, 116

Yang Yü-k'e, Brigadier General, 85, 86
Yao, xxxvii
Yao Yen-chia, xxvi, 30, 74, 159, 162, 167
Yao Yüeh-wang, 131
Yeats, 24
Ye-le-san-te *see* Alexandria
Yen Ching-ming (1817–92): Yamen minister, xxvi
Yen Fu (1853–1921): future political scientist; translator of Western writers; lxi, lxii, 13, 133
Yen-hsi, 155
Yen-t'ai, 96, 157, 187
Yen-t'ai *see* Chefoo Convention
Yen Yüan (1635–1704): philosopher, liii
Yi, 42, 43
Yi-ch'ang, 87
Yi-jen-ta-ta, 69
Ying-na-chi-ko *see* Ignazi?
Yüan cartography, xviii
Yu Ch'ang-ho, lxiv
Yu-chi (Chinese Major), 15
Yüeh *see* Kwantung
Yueh-chang ch'eng-an hui-lan, 2
Yueh-ching, styled Kuo-hsi, 13
Yüeh-chou, 129
Yüeh Fei, 166
Yüeh-lu Academy, xxviii
Yung-chen period (1723–36), 33
Yung-cheng, Emperor (1724), 33, 105
Yung-lo period (1405), xviii
Yunnan, 19, 85, 88, 99, 108, 120, 136
Yü-t'ai *see* Judea
Yu Ya-chih *see* Hewlett, A. R.
Yu Ya-mei *see* also Yu Ya-chih

Zoroastrianism (*Hsien-shen chiao*), 32
Zoulah Bay, 40